COMPUTING TOMORROW
FUTURE RESEARCH DIRECTIONS IN COMPUTER SCIENCE

Edited by
Ian Wand and Robin Milner

Published by the Press Syndicate of the University of Cambridge
The Pitt Building, Trumpington Street, Cambridge CB2 1RP
40 West 20th Street, New York, NY 10011-4211, USA
10 Stamford Road, Oakleigh, Melbourne 3166, Australia

First published 1996

Printed in Great Britain at the University Press, Cambridge

A catalogue record for this book is available from the British Library

Library of Congress cataloguing in publication data available

ISBN 0 521 46085 9 hardback

Contents

Contents

Preface

Computing has developed at an extraordinary pace since Alan Turing's crucial discovery in 1936. Then we had log tables, slide rules, filing cabinets, the postal service and human clerks. Now we have computers which will calculate at unimagined rates, vast data bases and global electronic communication. We are swamped with information which can be used in countless ways. The resulting impact of computing technology on society, both at work and at play, has been profound - some say it has transformed the nature of society itself. The revolution shows no sign of abating. But are there technical obstacles in our way which must be cleared in order to enhance our progress? And what conceptual advances are needed if we are to place the revolution on a firm scientific footing? Indeed, what are the major research issues confronting computing today?

The United Kingdom has been a major innovator in computing. The first stored-program digital computer ran in the UK. Many of the crucial ideas in computer architecture and programming came subsequently from researchers in this country. Over the last fifteen years, partly spurred on by publically-funded programmes such as Alvey, and partly driven by the promise of commercial exploitation, the volume of computing research has risen dramatically. Results have poured out into books, journals and conference proceedings. The atmosphere surrounding computing research has reflected the excitement of making crucial, formative discoveries. The subject has raced ahead.

This book brings together of the views of a distinguished group of Computer Scientists from the United Kingdom. The editors asked each contributor to set out the research position in his chosen subject and then to outline the important research problems that his subject now faced. Atkinson, Hoare and Milner look at different aspects of the theoretical basis of computing - what are the appropriate models for describing computing and how can they be detailed in simple mathematics? Bundy and Gazdar show how computers can be used to carry out tasks, such as the analysis of natural language, previously the exclusive domain of human beings. They show, despite the heady enthusiasm for Artificial

Intelligence some years ago, and despite much technical progress, that many of the ambitious goals remain. Littlewood and McDermid report on the current drive to use computers in demanding applications, such as those requiring high levels of safety or reliability. Can we, for example, use computers in systems which must only fail, at most, once in a thousand centuries? Brown and Peyton Jones describe the lessons to be learned from moving research prototypes into the marketplace. Darlington, Gray, Gurd & Jones, Joseph, and Needham report on a wide range of new applications and architectures, including parallel functional programming, large data bases, global personalised systems, real-time systems and communications - witness to the wide scope of computing today. Davenport plots the relationship between mathematics and computing, particularly the use of computers for symbolic manipulation and their role in mathematical discoveries. Will computers become the essential assistant for all mathematicians as they have become for other scientists? Finally Newman questions whether we have been addressing the right issues in computing research. Have we, for example, given sufficient attention to the relationship between the human user and the system?

The reader may be struck by the enormous range of knowledge and skills that our subject demands; from product design and customer requirements at one end, through engineering research on large-scale system (hard and soft), to growing mathematical foundations at the other end. Several authors point out the blurred boundary between research and development, and the chance spark necessary to move the research idea to the market place. Some mention the connection between funding and research, a keenly felt issue given the swing away from computing as a fashionable area for research funding and given the decline of funding from military sources following the end of the Cold War.

Our aim here is both to demonstrate the vitality of computing research and to show that there is a wide range of scientific and engineering problems that require solution if our subject is to progress. Above all, the contributors bear witness to a development which is rare enough in human history: the birth of a new discipline rich both in intellectual endeavour and in the possibilities for improving the human condition. We hope our collection will serve both as a useful reference point for new researchers and as a celebration of an exciting period of research.

Ian Wand and Robin Milner
25 October 1995

Contributors

M.D. Atkinson, School of Mathematical and Computational Sciences, North Haugh, St Andrews, Fife KY16 9SS, Scotland
mda@cs.st-and.ac.uk

P.J. Brown, Computing Laboratory, University of Kent at Canterbury, Canterbury, Kent CT2 7NF, England
P.J.Brown@ukc.ac.uk

Alan Bundy, Department of Artificial Intelligence, University of Edinburgh, 80 South Bridge, Edinburgh EH1 1HN, Scotland
a.bundy@ed.ac.uk

John Darlington, Department of Computing, Imperial College, 180 Queen's Gate, London SW7 2BZ, England
jd@doc.ic.ac.uk

J.H. Davenport, School of Mathematical Sciences, University of Bath, Bath BA2 7AY, England
jhd@maths.bath.ac.uk

Gerald Gazdar, School of Cognitive and Computing Sciences, University of Sussex, Brighton BN1 9QH, England
Gerald.Gazdar@cogs.susx.ac.uk

P.M.D. Gray, Department of Computing Science, University of Aberdeen, King's College, Aberdeen AB9 2UE, Scotland
pgray@csd.abdn.ac.uk

Yi-ke Guo, Department of Computing, Imperial College, 180 Queen's Gate, London SW7 2BZ, England
yg@doc.ic.ac.uk

J.R. Gurd, Department of Computer Science, Oxford Road, University of Manchester, Manchester M13 9PL, England
john@cs.man.ac.uk

C.A.R. Hoare, Computing Laboratory, University of Oxford, Wolfson Building, Parks Road, Oxford OX1 3QD, England
carh@comlab.ox.ac.uk

C.B. Jones, Department of Computer Science, Oxford Road, University of Manchester, Manchester M13 9PL, England
cliff@cs.man.ac.uk

Mathai Joseph, University of Warwick, Department of Computer Science, Coventry CV4 7AL, England
mathai@dcs.warwick.ac.uk

Bev Littlewood, Centre for Software Reliability, City University, Northampton Square, London EC1V 0HB, England
b.littlewood@cs.city.ac.uk

John A. McDermid, High Integrity Systems Engineering Group, Department of Computer Science, University of York, Heslington, York YO1 5DD, England
jam@cs.york.ac.uk

Robin Milner, Computer Laboratory, University of Cambridge, Cambridge CB2 3QG, England
Robin.Milner@cl.cam.ac.uk

R.M. Needham, Computer Laboratory, University of Cambridge, Cambridge CB2 3QG, England
Roger.Needham@cl.cam.ac.uk

William Newman, Rank Xerox Research Centre, 61 Regent Street, Cambridge CB2 1AB, England
newman@europarc.xerox.com

Simon Peyton Jones, Department of Computing Science, University of Glasgow, 8-17 Lilybank Gardens, Glasgow G12 8RZ, Scotland
simonpj@dcs.glasgow.ac.uk

Hing Wing To, Department of Computing, Imperial College, 180 Queen's Gate, London SW7 2BZ, England
hwt@doc.ic.ac.uk

Ian Wand, Department of Computer Science, University of York, Heslington, York YO1 5DD, England
imw@cs.york.ac.uk

1

The Complexity of Algorithms

M.D. Atkinson

Abstract

The modern theory of algorithms dates from the late 1960s when the method of asymptotic execution time measurement began to be used. It is argued that the subject has both an engineering and a scientific wing. The engineering wing consists of well understood design methodologies while the scientific one is concerned with theoretical underpinnings. The key issues of both wings are surveyed. Finally some personal opinions on where the subject will go next are offered.

1.1 Introduction

The concept of 'algorithm' is the oldest one in computer science. It is of such antiquity in fact that it may appear presumptuous for computer scientists to claim it as part of their subject. However, although algorithms have been part of scientific tradition for millennia it was not until the computer era that they assumed the major role they now play in these traditions. Indeed, until a few decades ago most scientists would have been hard-pressed to give significant examples of any algorithms at all. Yet algorithms have been routinely used for centuries. Generations of school children learnt the algorithms for addition, subtraction, multiplication, and division and could use them with all the blinkered competence of a mechanical computer. Few of them would ever have stopped to wonder how it was that they allowed the computation, in a matter of moments, of quantities far beyond what could be counted or imagined. These elementary algorithms are amazingly efficient but it was not until the computer era that questions of efficiency were seriously addressed. Had they been so addressed the mathematical curriculum might have been different. For example, I can remember, as a schoolboy in the 1950s, being told how to find the greatest common divisor of two integers by finding their prime decompositions and taking the intersection of these decompositions; it was only years later that I was able to understand that this method was exponentially worse than Euclid's algorithm which, for all its antiquity, I did not meet until graduate student days.

Nowadays this ignorance of efficiency issues has largely disappeared. For while computer scientists were not present at the birth they have, in the last 25 years, witnessed the childhood, adolescence, and early maturity of a subject that is now a central, some would say *the* central, part of computer science – the complexity of algorithms. This subject embraces the foundational questions of what efficiency means and how to measure it, the technical apparatus for designing efficient algorithms, and the classification of problems according to how efficiently they can be solved.

This chapter is about the scientific theory of algorithms but it is worth mentioning that algorithms have also had a cultural impact. The ubiquity of computational techniques has brought an awareness of the idea of algorithm to many disciplines and it is now recognised that the notion of a process scripted by a set of rules is useful beyond those processes that are scripted by computer programs. At a trivial level it embraces the idea of a boss giving instructions to a subordinate. More seriously it encompasses the causing of mechanical devices to perform their due functions through appropriate button presses and lever movements. For example, driving a car (once a few basic mechanical skills have been learnt) is essentially the diligent pursuing of the Highway Code prescriptions – and, generally, the more diligent the pursuit the more effective the outcome (*pace*, all teenage male firebrands!). Of course there are also many examples of machines in manufacturing and design which one programs to make various industrial components. Although these machines may not have the power of a universal Turing machine they are, nevertheless, carrying out algorithms. It is now common to hear terminology such as 'This recipe is a good algorithm for making cakes' or 'This machine is carrying out its wash, rinse, and spin dry algorithm.' The notion of algorithm has become part of our culture and for this the development of algorithms in computer science is largely responsible.

The key idea that supports most of the theory of algorithms is the method of quantifying the execution time of an algorithm. Execution time depends on many parameters which are independent of the particular algorithm: machine clock rate, quality of code produced by compiler, whether or not the computer is multi-programmed etc. Changing these parameters changes the execution time by a factor which will be common to every algorithm. Clearly, when we are trying to quantify the efficiency of an algorithm we should ignore these factors and measure what remains. Not surprisingly the execution time of an algorithm is a function of the values of its input parameters. If we know this function (at least, to within a scalar multiple determined by the machine parameters) then we can predict the time the algorithm will require *without running it*. (We might not wish to run it until we knew that it would complete in a reasonable time.) Unfortunately this execution time function measure is generally very complicated, too complicated to know exactly. But now a number of observations come to the rescue. The first is that it is very often possible to get meaningful predictive results by concentrating on one parameter alone: the total size of the input (rather than the precise values of each input parameter). The second is that execution time functions are often the sum of a large number of terms and many of these terms make an insignificant contribution to function values: in mathematical terms, it is the asymptotic form of the function that matters rather than the precise form. The final observation is that, in practice, we wish only to know either an upper bound on the execution time (to be assured that it will perform acceptably) or a lower bound (possibly to encourage us to develop a better algorithm).

To sum up these observations: we measure the execution time of an algorithm as a function $T(n)$ of a single quantity n (the size of the entire input), we are interested only in the asymptotic form of $T(n)$, and, if necessary, we shall be content with upper and lower bounds only on the asymptotic form. To express these ideas we use O, Ω, θ notation for upper bounds, lower bounds, exact bounds on $T(n)$. Thus $T(n) = O(f(n))$ means that, apart from a multiplying constant, $T(n)$ is bounded above by $f(n)$ as $n \to \infty$. The Ω notation is for lower bounds, and the θ notation is for those happy situations where lower and upper bounds coincide.

The O notation was borrowed from mathematics rather than invented for the expression of upper bounds on algorithm execution times. It was adopted by algorithm designers, principally Knuth (see Knuth, 1973a), during the 1960s as the asymptotic approach to upper bounds gained acceptability. By the time Aho, Hopcroft and Ullman published their celebrated book (Aho *et al.*, 1974) the notation was well established.

The theory of algorithms has a number of goals. The practical goals are those of any engineering discipline: to provide ready-made tools (algorithms for solving frequently occurring problems) and successful

methodologies (algorithm design strategies) for constructing further tools
and end products. In addition the subject has a purely scientific side
whose goals are to create the mathematics required to produce the engineering tools and to answer foundational questions about whether algorithms of various types exist; like any pure science this is also studied
for its own interest. The two wings of the subject interact with each
other in many ways and it is important that researchers in the subject appreciate both of them. The next two sections survey some of
the key features of the subject. Greater detail can be found in modern
texts such as Cormen *et al.* (1992), Brassard & Bratley (1988), Manber
(1989); Knuth's classic volumes (Knuth 1973a,b, 1981) still repay study;
some state-of-the-art surveys are to be found in van Leeuwen (1992).

1.2 Algorithms Engineering
1.2.1 The blast furnace: design methodologies

To illustrate the standard design methodologies and their effectiveness
we shall give a number of case studies – example problems which are
solved by applying off-the-shelf techniques. It will be seen that most of
the techniques are variations on a single theme: structured decomposition of a problem into subproblems. The most appropriate variation in
any single case can often only be chosen by an experienced algorithms
engineer.

The first problem is a numerical one of a sort that often occurs in
scientific programming. For simplicity we have chosen a fairly particular
version but it should be clear how to extend the solution to more general
cases. Let x_0, x_1, a, b be given integers and suppose that $x_2, x_3, \ldots$ are
defined by the recurrence equation

$$x_n = ax_{n-1} + bx_{n-2}.$$

(In the special case $x_0 = 1, x_1 = 1, a = b = 1$ the sequence $x_0, x_1, x_2, \ldots$
is the sequence of Fibonacci numbers.) The problem is to compute, for
some given non-negative n which might be quite large, the value x_n.
Since x_n is defined recursively a natural algorithm would be

```
function X(n)
    if n=0 then x0 else
    if n=1 then x1 else
        aX(n-1) + bX(n-2)
```

This algorithm is grossly inefficient. A very standard piece of algorithmic analysis shows that its execution time $T(n)$ grows in proportion to the nth Fibonacci number, i.e. as $((1 + \sqrt{5})/2)^n$.

There is an obvious improvement one can make (obvious in this case, but deriving nevertheless from a standard design technique called dynamic programming). One computes and stores all of $x_0, x_1, x_2, \ldots, x_{n-1}$ before computing x_n. This algorithm is

```
function X(n)
    array Y[0..n]
    Y[0]:=x₀; Y[1]:=x₁
    for i=2 to n do Y[i]:=aY[i-1] + bY[i-2]
    Y[n]
```

Clearly, the execution time of this algorithm grows in proportion to n rather than exponentially. Stark differences like this used to be cited as evidence that recursion was inherently less efficient than iteration. Of course, it is not the overheads of recursion which make the first algorithm less efficient than the second – it is a different algorithm, causing a different computation, which just happens to be wildly inefficient.

Usually, an improvement from an exponential to a linear running time is cause to be content but, in this case, we can do substantially better still. There is a well-known mathematical technique for solving linear recurrence equations. In this particular case it tells us that the solution has the form $K_1\lambda_1^n + K_2\lambda_2^n$ where K_1 and K_2 are constants and λ_1 and λ_2 are the roots of $\lambda^2 - a\lambda - b = 0$ (unless $\lambda_1 = \lambda_2$ when the solution has the form $(K_1 n + K_2)\lambda^n$). Unfortunately λ_1, λ_2 need not be rational (indeed, they may not even be real), and it seems dubious to introduce irrational numbers into a problem whose statement and answer involve only integers, so we seek some other idea. The original recurrence may be re-written as

$$(x_{n-1}, x_n) = (x_{n-2}, x_{n-1}) \begin{pmatrix} 0 & b \\ 1 & a \end{pmatrix}.$$

Put $v_n = (x_{n-1}, x_n)$, $A = \begin{pmatrix} 0 & b \\ 1 & a \end{pmatrix}$ so that $v_1 = (x_0, x_1)$ and, for $n > 1$, $v_n = v_{n-1}A$. Then, of course, $v_n = v_1 A^{n-1}$ so, once A^{n-1} is known, v_n (and so x_n) can be obtained in a small number of further operations (four multiplications and two additions though algorithm designers don't like to be precise about such details!). The computation of nth powers is another piece of off-the-shelf technology:

```
function power(A,n)
   if n=0 then identity_matrix else
   begin
      Y:= power(A,n div 2)
      if even(n) then Y² else Y²A
   end
```

The powering algorithm has been obtained by the standard design technique called Divide and Conquer. Its execution time $T(n)$ satisfies

$$T(n) \leq T(n/2) + L, \quad \text{where } L \text{ is constant,}$$

and so $T(n)$ grows at worst logarithmically in n.

A doubly exponential improvement from the algorithm initially suggested by the form of the problem is very impressive but the important point is that this gain in efficiency has been achieved by calling on entirely standard machinery in algorithm design. Before leaving this example, a more pragmatic remark should be made. The possibility of integer overflow in the above problem has been ignored for simplicity. In fact, overflow may easily occur because it is possible that x_n may be very large. To overcome the overflow problem some method for representing and handling large integers must be used. Such methods have been extensively investigated and many efficient techniques are known.

We saw in this example two basic design paradigms: Divide and Conquer, and dynamic programming. It is useful to compare the two. Both achieve their ends by defining and solving smaller subproblems which, in the most interesting cases, are smaller versions of the original problem. The Divide and Conquer strategy is goal-directed: each subproblem further decomposes into smaller subproblems and the entire computation is often visualised as a top-down process with recursion as the most natural implementation technique. Dynamic programming on the other hand is more commonly regarded as a bottom-up process: a number of small subproblems are first solved, these are combined to solve larger subproblems which are in turn combined to solve even larger subproblems. This view of the technique more often suggests an iterative solution. However, the difference between the two techniques does not lie in the top-down/bottom-up dichotomy. What distinguishes dynamic programming from Divide and Conquer is the explicit tabulation of subproblem solutions. This implies that dynamic programming comes into its own for those problems where there are many duplicates in the collection of subproblems that is defined.

It might be thought from this account that dynamic programming is a more powerful design technique than Divide and Conquer since, with care, any algorithm discovered by Divide and Conquer may be re-implemented to look like the result of a dynamic programming design. But that misses the point. Divide and Conquer is a conceptual tool which encourages a certain way of thinking, and this way of thinking has proved to be highly successful in a large number of designs. It is more profitable to regard the two techniques as partners in any problem which can be solved by decomposition into subproblems. The Divide and Conquer technique will usually be tried first. If it does lead to an algorithm to solve the problem the next step is to examine the efficiency of the algorithm. If the efficiency is unacceptable because many dupli-cate subproblems are being solved then the algorithm can profitably be re-engineered by dynamic programming. It is not always easy to identify precisely which subproblem solutions should be tabulated and it would be interesting to have automatic tools to aid in this analysis.

There are a number of other design paradigms that have proved use-ful. The first that we discuss, inductive design, could be described as a special case of both Divide and Conquer and dynamic programming although that does not do justice to its utility. The idea is very simple: we try to construct a solution to a problem of size n from the solution to an $(n-1)$-sized problem. Although this is just another way of solving a problem by focusing on smaller, similar subproblems it has two ad-vantages. The first is that we tap in to our mathematical experience of proving theorems by simple induction and this often suggests a suitable technique. Second, when the technique is successful, it tends to produce rather simpler designs than Divide and Conquer. The reason for this is that Divide and Conquer generally produces its most efficient results when the subproblems into which the original problem is partitioned are of roughly equal sizes – and this expectation is usually incorporated into any design attempt. Divide and Conquer corresponds to complete rather than simple induction and so is naturally more complex. To il-lustrate inductive design I have chosen a problem which has been much studied as an example of the automatic derivation of algorithmic so-lutions from problem specifications (Gries, 1990; Bates & Constable, 1985).

The problem is called the Maximum Segment Sum problem. One is given a sequence $x_1, x_2, \ldots, x_n$ of n numbers and is required to find two indices i, j to maximise

$$S_{ij} = x_{j+1} + \ldots + x_i.$$

Since there are many dependencies among the S_{ij} one would expect that brute force calculation of all of them will not be the best method. Instead we can define $s_i = x_1 + \ldots + x_i$ so that $S_{ij} = s_i - s_j$. The problem is therefore to compute m_n where

$$m_r = \max_{0 \le j \le i \le r}(s_i - s_j).$$

The inductive design method tries to compute m_r from m_{r-1} so we need to express m_r in terms of m_{r-1}. Clearly,

$$
\begin{aligned}
m_r &= \max_{0 \le i \le r} \max_{0 \le j \le i}(s_i - s_j) \\
&= \max_{0 \le i \le r}(s_i - \min_{0 \le j \le i} s_j) \\
&= \max(m_{r-1}, s_r - \min_{0 \le j \le r} s_j).
\end{aligned}
$$

This equation gives hope that inductive design will be successful and it also indicates that $t_r = \min_{0 \le j \le r} s_j$ will enter the calculation. The quantity t_r can also be computed by inductive design for, obviously, $t_r = \min(t_{r-1}, s_r)$. Finally, s_r itself has an inductive definition as $s_{r-1} + x_r$. Putting these observations together, with proper initialisations, the algorithm emerges as

```
m0:=0
s0:=0
t0:=0
for r=1 to n do
sr:=sr-1 + xr
tr:=min(tr-1, sr)
mr:=max(mr-1, sr - tr)
end
```

In practice the algorithm would use single variables for each of s_r, t_r, m_r.

In addition to these decomposition techniques for algorithm design there are some heuristic techniques which are particularly useful for optimisation problems. We mention three: the greedy heuristic, simulated annealing, and genetic algorithms. The greedy heuristic is the most widely applicable of the three and is the simplest. It is characterised by the strategy of always choosing what appears to be the best action at every stage with no forward planning to see whether this might be inadvisable. The algorithms so produced are called *greedy* algorithms. This strategy sounds so naive that it scarcely deserves to be honoured by a title. Yet the greedy heuristic can often produce optimal algorithms or algorithms whose departure from optimal can be quantified. Because many algorithms have been devised by this method there is a large body of experience for assessing new greedy algorithms. There is, moreover, a fairly general matroid framework due to Korte and Lovasz (Korte & Lovasz, 1981) which can sometimes demonstrate that a greedy algorithm is optimal.

Simulated annealing is a method based on randomisation techniques. The method originates from the annealing of solids as described by the theory of statistical physics and was introduced into combinatorial optimisation in Kirkpatrick *et al.* (1983). The basic idea is to model an optimisation problem as a search through a space of configurations. In searching for an optimal configuration one passes from one configuration to another according to certain probabilities. In this respect the method appears similar to a random walk through configuration space as described by a Markov chain. In a 'pure' Markov chain the next configuration might be worse (according to some optimisation measure) than the current one. However, in simulated annealing, there is a 'temperature' parameter c which is gradually decreased and which controls the probabilities of the Markov chain. Initially, transitions to worse configurations might be quite common but, as c decreases to zero, they become rarer.

There have been many applications of simulated annealing (see Collins *et al.* (1988) for a survey). The general experience is that, while near-optimal solutions can be found in many cases, the technique tends to be rather slow. This is unsurprising since the method is so general. Indeed, all simulated annealing applications can be regarded as parametrised versions of a single algorithm.

Genetic algorithms (Holland, 1975; Goldberg, 1989) have much in common with simulated annealing. They are also parametrised versions of a single algorithm and they proceed iteratively with each stage being determined probabilistically from the previous one. However, rather than keeping just one candidate configuration at each stage, the genetic algorithm keeps a whole population of candidates which it updates from one generation to the next by rules called fitness selection, mutation, and cross-over (biological terminology is ubiquitous in the subject). In the basic genetic algorithm the configurations are represented by fixed length character strings. The next generation consists of configurations

from the previous generation that have passed a fitness test (their optimisation measure was high), configurations which are mutations (small
variations in the configurations of the previous generation) and, most
importantly, pairs of configurations 'born' of two parent configurations
by cross-over. In cross-over two parent configuration strings $\alpha\beta, \gamma\delta$ give
rise to offspring $\alpha\delta, \beta\gamma$. When the genetic algorithm achieves some termination criterion the best configuration in all generations is taken as
the result.

Simulated annealing and genetic algorithms have many attractions.
Both offer a packaged framework that 'only' requires the problem at
hand to be encoded in a suitable form, both can point to a stream of
successful results (of course, researchers tend to report their successes,
not their failures), and both have a fashionable language of discourse.
The greedy technique, simulated annealing, and genetic algorithms are
increasingly sophisticated methods of heuristic search for a solution in a
large pool of possibilities and that fact remains even when the colourful
language has been stripped away. Nevertheless, it is likely that even
better heuristics exist, although they may well prove harder to analyse.

1.2.2 The tools of the trade: standard algorithms

An early realisation in computing was that certain tasks occur over and
over again in program construction. The early libraries of machine-
coded subroutines were a first attempt to categorise those tasks. Nowadays those libraries have become vastly larger collections of machine-
independent software maintained by international organisations such as
NAG (Numerical Algorithms Group). The result is that a modern-day
software designer has a huge toolbox of standard components from which
to build new algorithms. It is impossible to survey with any adequacy
the full range of this toolbox; creating it has probably been the major
activity of algorithm designers for forty years. To give some idea of
where the main efforts have been concentrated I shall give my own view
of how to categorise these algorithms, with some examples from each
category. I would classify the standard algorithms under three broad
headings: searching, numerical, and combinatorial.

Searching Algorithms

In this category might be placed all the algorithms for accessing the
many data structures that have been devised for representing large collections of information (search trees, heaps, hash tables, external files,
etc.), graph searching techniques such as are used in Artificial Intelli-

gence, and garbage collection algorithms. The category would include also string-processing techniques such as fast pattern matching and the algorithms required for solving the special problems in molecular biology thrown up by the human genome project.

The development of algorithms of this type, more so than in any other area, has gone hand in hand with devising subtle methods of structuring data. Indeed, sometimes it is only through the invention of a new data structure that improvements in performance are obtained. Currently however, data structuring is at a crossroads. Some designers have been reluctant to sacrifice the final ounce of efficiency and have not adopted a disciplined approach to building complex structures. The result has been a mushrooming of very specialised structures and it is difficult to discern underlying methodologies. Data structuring now needs a period of consolidation to allow the best results to come to the fore and to allow the subject to be re-engineered with fewer basic components.

Data type abstraction has not hitherto figured much as an algorithm design tool because, unlike procedural abstraction, many existing languages have few or no mechanisms to support it. Yet data type abstraction has a well developed theory that ought to be contributing more to the design of algorithms. A re-examination of data structuring tools would also permit us to make some judgements on which abstract data types were truly fundamental just as we judge some algorithms to be more fundamental than others.

Numerical Algorithms

Algorithms for numerical problems (matrix calculations, ordinary and partial differential equations, curve fitting, etc.) appeared the earliest in computer science. Handling the mismatch between the continuous problems of numerical analysis and the discrete nature of physical computers has always presented great challenges in error analysis. These challenges are being met in two ways. Systems for performing multi-precise arithmetic have long been used to reduce propagated rounding error and the asymptotic complexity of the best algorithms for the operations of arithmetic has steadily improved. Multi-precise arithmetic is the first line of defence in the control of error propagation but, ultimately, it only delays the problem as more ambitious calculations are mounted and a more fundamental solution must be found. The *forte* of numerical analysis is the construction of numerically stable algorithms and, in this, it has been very successful; most common numerical problems (see Press *et al.* (1992), for example) now admit solutions where the truncation error is small and the rounding error can be controlled.

But error analysis is only a sufficient tool when *numerical* solutions to numerical problems are sought. Increasingly, nowadays, there is a demand for *symbolic* solutions. Research activity in symbolic algebra has been very intense in the last two decades and the tendency has been to produce integrated systems rather than stand-alone modules. Mathematica and Maple both offer very large libraries of routines for classical algebraic operations and an integrated programming language. For 'higher' algebra, particularly group theory, CAYLEY (Cannon, 1984) and its successor MAGMA are the most powerful systems. From a systems design perspective AXIOM (Jenks & Sutor, 1992) appears most attractive since it presents a common view of the classical and algebraic data types. It is important to have such a common view; it brings together the two communities of researchers in computer science and algebra who have been involved in algebraic computation and makes it more likely (as has not always been the case) that they will each be aware of the other's field.

Combinatorial Algorithms

In this context combinatorial algorithms are those that manipulate objects which require some computer representation not automatically provided by the basic hardware. Examples are permutations, graphs, geometric objects such as polygons, finite state automata, and languages. Research under this heading is very fragmented because the various combinatorial areas are very different. Nevertheless there are some common strands.

One such strand is the generation of combinatorial objects uniformly at random. There are two approaches to this problem. One approach is through encoding each object as an integer in a certain range, or as a sequence of such integers; this reduces the problem to generating one or more integers uniformly at random. For example, free labelled trees can be handled in this way using the Prüfer encoding, and binary trees can be handled by encoding them as a normalised bit sequence (Atkinson & Sack, 1992). The other approach is more indirect but has led to results in other areas. It models the population from which the random object is to be chosen as a graph. Each node is an object in the population and two nodes are adjacent if they are 'closely related in structure'. Then, starting from some initial node, a random walk on the graph is defined. The theory of Markov chains can be used to compute the probability that a walk has reached a given node after t steps. When the probability distribution has settled down to a uniform distribution (which happens under quite mild conditions) the walk is terminated and the current node is selected. In practice the entire graph (which may be very large) is not stored, only the current node; the next node on the walk is constructed by randomly varying the previous one and it overwrites the previous node. Of course, the most important issue is how fast is the convergence to the stationary distribution and this has long been known to depend on the second largest eigenvalue of the matrix that specifies the probability transitions. During the 1980s a large number of results on 'rapidly mixing' Markov chains were found which allowed the method to be applied in many situations. Examples, further details, and references are given in Jerrum & Sinclair (1989).

Another common strand is 'combinatorial explosion'. Combinatorial algorithms are frequently very time-consuming because they need to investigate a large space of possibilities and face the issue of NP-completeness (subsection 1.3.2).

The fastest growing area in combinatorial algorithms is undoubtedly computational geometry which has numerous applications (graphics, robotics, geographic information systems, etc.). The subject addresses both classical geometric problems (such as congruence (Atkinson, 1987) and convex hulls (Preparata & Shamos, 1985)) and significant new problems (such as Voronoi diagram computation and visibility; the survey by Yao (van Leeuwen, 1992, Chapter 7) has a large bibliography of results on all these new problems). After a frenetic first 15 years of theoretical activity software systems (e.g. Sack *et al.*, 1994) which allow geometric algorithms to be built from standard components are now being developed.

I conclude this section with an example of a problem which, when it was first posed, seemed so hard that it was proposed (Cade, 1985) as the basic ingredient of a cryptographic protocol (the security of such protocols depend on the supposed difficulty of carrying out particular computations). Yet, in the end, the problem proved very easy to solve merely by using standard algorithms. Unfortunately, there are now so many standard algorithms that it is virtually impossible to know of them all; a dictionary of algorithms would be very useful.

One is given a polynomial $f(x)$ of degree $n = rs$ (monic with no significant loss in generality) and is required to find monic polynomials $g(x), h(x)$ (if they exist) of degrees r, s such that $f(x) = g(h(x))$. Let $F(x) = x^n f(x^{-1})$ and $H(x) = x^s h(x^{-1})$ be the reverse coefficient polynomials corresponding to $f(x)$ and $h(x)$. Then it follows from $f(x) = g(h(x))$ with a little elementary algebra that

$$F(x) = H(x)^r \mod x^s.$$

This type of congruence can easily be solved for $H(x)$ by the lifting algorithm called Hensel's lemma (see subsection 1.3.1). Once $h(x)$ is known, $g(x)$ can be determined by interpolation; one chooses $r+1$ values $\alpha_0, \alpha_1, \ldots, \alpha_r$ such that $h(\alpha_0), h(\alpha_1), \ldots, h(\alpha_r)$ are distinct and obtains $g(x)$ by interpolation from the values $g(h(\alpha_i)) = f(\alpha_i)$. Not only do algorithms for all these steps exist, they are, courtesy of the fast Fourier transform (see subsection 1.3.1), very efficient indeed (execution time $O(n \log^2 n \log \log n)$). More details are given in von zur Gathen (1990).

1.3 Algorithms Science

The line between algorithms engineering and algorithms science is very blurred. The distinction I would like to make is between the development of algorithms following trusted design techniques incorporating trusted components (engineering) and the invention of techniques and novel algorithms whose existence, *a priori*, was not even clear (science). Of course, the latter has fewer achievements but it is crucial for the former. In this section I shall outline some discoveries that are more properly classified under algorithms science even though hindsight sometimes reveals that they might have been discovered by using a general technique.

1.3.1 Pinnacle algorithms

From time to time a new algorithm is discovered which changes the way a part of the subject develops. I have chosen (with great difficulty from a large pool of candidates) four such algorithms as examples of first class science. The examples show that the idea of isolated boffins working in back rooms is misleading. All these algorithms (and families of algorithms) have depended on previous researchers preparing the ground.

Newton–Raphson Iteration

The famous iterative formula $x_{n+1} = x_n - (f(x_n)/f'(x_n))$ for generating a series of numbers which, under certain widely applicable conditions, converges rapidly to a root of $f(x) = 0$ goes back, in certain forms at least, to Sir Isaac Newton. It is a simple idea but a great one. Its importance came initially from its multitude of uses in numerical analysis where, of course, there is also a multi-variable numerical generalisation. Since then it has been recognised as the basic procedure in 'Hensel's

Lemma', an important technique first arising in p-adic number theory and now important in computational number theory. More recently it has been used in symbolic power series manipulation systems where one works to a polynomial modulus rather than a numeric one.

The Fast Fourier Transform

Fourier transforms have long been an important tool in data analysis. To calculate with them numerically the original *continuous* function has to be replaced by its values at n *discrete* points and certain sums involving complex roots of 1 then have to be computed. For many years these computations were thought to be somewhat impractical since the number of operations depended on n^2. In 1965 the famous $O(n \log n)$ algorithm was announced (Cooley & Tukey, 1965) and immediately revolutionised many applications (optics, acoustics, signal processing, etc.). Interestingly, the algorithm can be described in a classic Divide and Conquer framework; indeed it is now a popular example of this principle in many algorithms textbooks although it does not seem to have been discovered in this way. The fast algorithm has also had an impact within the theory of algorithms since it gives rise to an asymptotically fast method for polynomial multiplication and, thereby, many other algorithms in symbolic algebra have been improved.

Karmarkar's Linear Programming Algorithm

The simplex method has been the workhorse of linear programming from its very early days. Although the method usually performs well it has a rare exponential worst case. In 1979 Khachian published his ellipsoid method which showed that linear programming was, in principle, solvable in polynomial time; unfortunately the method has, in practice, a disappointing performance. When Karmarkar introduced his method based on projective transformations in 1984 (Karmarkar, 1984) there was general acceptance that it was a significant theoretical breakthrough but some initial scepticism about its practicality. However, it quickly became apparent that the method was very competitive with the simplex algorithm, sometimes outperforming it substantially. AT&T soon released a commercial software product based on the algorithm (trademark KORBX (Cheng *et al.*, 1989)) and there have been many papers exploring its performance and studying the theory.

The Elliptic Curve Factoring Algorithm

The apparently esoteric activity of factoring very large integers became of much wider interest when the RSA encryption scheme was proposed in Rivest *et al.* (1978). Its security seems to rest on the difficulty of factoring integers, as do many of the later encryption schemes. At that time the best algorithms for factoring integers were developments of an old method dating back to Fermat. In 1985 H.W. Lenstra (Lenstra, 1987) introduced a method which was remarkable for its novelty, simplicity, and efficiency. The method is based on the fact that the set of points on an elliptic curve over a field form a group under an appropriate composition rule. Despite this theoretical basis the method can be implemented in just a few lines of code. It is comparatively efficient, especially in the case where the integer to be factored has a relatively small divisor while not performing as well as the quadratic sieve method (Pomerance, 1984) for 'hard' integers (products of two primes of similar value). Nevertheless, the method was a revolution for the factoring problem and showed that new algorithms are not necessarily complex to program.

1.3.2 Unifying theories

To lay claim to being scientific any subject has to have theories which place their components in uniform contexts. We have already seen the method of stipulating execution time which is a unifying theme throughout the theory of algorithms. It is also possible to carry out the actual analysis of execution times by appealing to a theory based largely on the theory of recurrence relations. A very simple example is the execution time of a loop:

```
for i=1 to n do P(i)
```

If $P(i)$ has execution time $S(i)$ then, clearly, the execution time of the loop satisfies

$$T(n) = T(n-1) + S(n).$$

In this particular case the recurrence is easily unwound as a summation but things are not always so easy. Consider two procedures P, Q with a single parameter $n \geq 0$ defined as

```
function P(n)
if n>0 then Q(n-1); C; P(n-1); C; Q(n-1)


function Q(n)
if n>0 then P(n-1); C; Q(n-1); C; P(n-1); C; Q(n-1)
```

where C denotes any statements taking time independent of n. The execution times $S(n)$ and $T(n)$ of $P(n)$ and $Q(n)$ satisfy, at least approximately,

$$S(n) = S(n-1) + 2T(n-1) + K_1,$$
$$T(n) = 2S(n-1) + 2T(n-1) + K_2,$$

where K_1 and K_2 are constants. The theory of recurrences shows that $S(n)$ and $T(n)$ both grow in proportion to λ^n where $\lambda = (3 + \sqrt{17})/2$ is the largest eigenvalue of the matrix $\begin{pmatrix} 1 & 2 \\ 2 & 2 \end{pmatrix}$.

Recurrence equations also arise commonly in analysing Divide and Conquer algorithms. Here, recurrences like

$$T(n) = aT\left(\frac{n}{b}\right) + f(n)$$

are typical and, when the form of $f(n)$ is known, can usually be solved. Further examples appear in Greene & Knuth (1982).

However, the most significant unifying ideas in the theory of algorithms come from structural complexity theory which addresses efficiency issues on a much larger scale. It attempts to make statements about execution time efficiency which are valid for all algorithms which solve a particular problem and which hold no matter what computational device is used. For example, the device may not have a random access memory; the memory might be in linear form and the price of accessing the nth location might be proportional to n (or worse). Given this degree of generality it is hardly surprising that lower and upper bounds on the complexity of optimal algorithms cannot be stated with much precision. A significant realisation, due initially to Edmonds (1965), is that the class P of problems which admit solutions that can be computed in polynomial time (i.e. whose execution time is bounded by a polynomial function of the input size) is an 'absolute' class – it does not depend on any particular computational model. Structural complexity theory is concerned with such absolute classes and the relationships between them.

After P, the next most important complexity class is called NP. The formal definition of NP is a little technical but essentially NP is the class of problems for which the validity of a solution can be checked in polynomial time. The most famous example is the Travelling Salesman Problem – does a given graph have a Hamiltonian circuit? This problem does lie in NP since the validity of a putative Hamiltonian circuit can be confirmed in a polynomial number of steps.

The central question in the complexity of algorithms and certainly one of the most important problems in the whole of science is whether P = NP. Although P = NP appears extremely unlikely, no proof is known despite intensive efforts over two decades. One of the reasons that the question is so important is that NP contains, as was first proved by Cook (1971), certain 'complete' problems which are provably as hard as any in NP. If any one of these NP-complete problems could be solved in polynomial time then it would follow that P = NP. Hundreds of NP-complete problems have been found in an astonishing diversity of areas (Garey & Johnson, 1979). The general belief is that P ≠ NP and so proving that a problem is NP-complete is usually taken as an indicator that it has no efficient solution. When faced with solving an NP-complete problem in a feasible amount of time one may therefore need to resort to heuristic techniques (which is why the heuristic techniques of subsection 1.2.1 are used so extensively) or be reconciled to finding a sub-optimal solution.

Progress on proving that P ≠ NP has been slow and it is unlikely to be settled in the next few years. The most striking contribution was made by Razborov (1985) for which, in 1990, he was awarded the Nevanlinna medal. One can represent a computable function by a Boolean circuit – an acyclic network of gates representing simple Boolean operators such as OR and NOT. Since AND, OR, NOT are a basis of Boolean functions it follows that functions which are computable in polynomial time can be represented by circuits with a polynomial number of gates of these types. Thus if we could show that a certain function necessarily required a superpolynomial number of gates we would know that it was not computable in polynomial time. Razborov, using a method of approximation, managed to prove that some functions associated with NP-complete problems could not be computed in a polynomial number of gates of a *monotone* circuit (where only AND, OR are allowed). His method has subsequently been refined by other researchers to show that some NP-complete problems require an exponential number of gates of a monotone circuit (Andreev, 1985).

1.4 The Crystal Ball

There are thousands of researchers developing new algorithms in numerous specialised areas. The algorithms they invent will depend much more on their specialised areas than on the discovery of new central tenets in the theory of algorithms. It may therefore seem that the direction of general algorithmic theory will be driven by applications rather than from within the subject; that is, the engineering side will dominate the scientific side. Nevertheless, it is important that the scientific side flourishes for past experience reveals that it has nourished the engineering aspects in an essential way. Unquestionably, work on the P = NP question will continue but it is impossible to be so categorical about other strands of the subject. Despite this I would like to offer a personal view on questions the general theory should next address.

I have hinted already that abstract data typing should become a more serious tool in algorithm design. Of course it has long been promoted as an important *program* development tool. In addition there is also an elaborate theory of algebraic specification (Ehrig *et al.*, 1992) which, at the very least, demonstrates that abstract data types (ADTs) are worthy objects of mathematical study. But I think there is more to abstract data types than this.

There is a strong analogy between ADTs and abstract algebra. ADTs are defined in terms of a permitted set of operations on the instances of the data type in question. Already this recalls abstract algebra. Indeed any category of algebraic objects can lay just claim to being an ADT. Thus, groups are sets which 'support' a 0-ary, 1-ary, and 2-ary operation (with certain important additional properties). This analogy is clearly visible in modern symbolic algebra systems; for example, the AXIOM system reference book (Jenks & Sutor, 1992) treats both ADTs and algebraic objects on an equal footing as 'domains'. There is also an interesting parallel having to do with representation. ADTs might be concretely represented in a number of ways (a priority queue as a heap or as a binomial queue, for example) just as the objects of abstract algebra might have one or more concrete representations (a group as a set of permutations or a set of matrices, for example). One might argue that the realisation that data types should be defined independently of their representation was as profound as the nineteenth century realisation that algebraic objects did not have to be studied in any fixed representation. Abstract definition in algebra was the first step in an impressive development throughout this century which led to fundamental applications in quantum theory, crystallography, and relativity (Loebl, 1968; Schwarzenberger, 1981). The long-term benefits of a study of properties of ADTs are, of course, impossible to foresee but the historical parallel with algebra is very encouraging.

Despite there being an infinite number of data types there is only a small number of them that recur frequently in software and algorithm design (stacks, queues, arrays, dictionaries, etc.) suggesting that some data types are more fundamental than others. Exactly the same phenomenon occurs in algebra and, significantly, the natural algebraic systems (groups, rings, modules etc.) have very rich theories. It is at least plausible that the commonly occurring data types will also have very rich theories. Hitherto, ADTs have been primarily used as a software design tool but now that a cohort of fundamental ADTs has emerged the time is ripe for these to be studied for themselves. Even before the idea of abstract data type emerged Knuth, Tarjan and Pratt were considering the functional behaviour of stacks and queues (Knuth, 1973a; Tarjan, 1972; Pratt, 1973) viewing them as restricted computers and investigating their power. More recently Beals and I (Atkinson & Beals, 1994) have begun a similar study of priority queues and have obtained some very promising results. This work is currently being extended at St Andrews to other data types and has already suggested a new approach to studying non-determinism in computer networks (Atkinson et al., to appear). Our hope is that, ultimately, through a taxonomy of properties of fundamental data types the software designer will know which are most likely to be of use in specific applications just as a taxonomy of algorithm design techniques (Divide and Conquer, greedy heuristics, dynamic programming, etc.) is a guide to inventing appropriate algorithms.

2

Building Novel Software: the Researcher and the Marketplace

P.J. Brown

Abstract

Much of the software we use today arose from new ideas that emanated from researchers at universities or at industrial research laboratories such as Xerox PARC. Researchers who are concerned with building novel software are usually keen to get their creations out into the field as soon as possible. This is partly because they may get extra brownie points from their research sponsors, but, perhaps more importantly, because usage in the field often leads to new insights, which in turn result in the next step forward for the research.

Nevertheless, building something that people will use means making big sacrifices in the research aims. In particular the prime quality of any research, novelty, must be kept in check.

My work for the past decade has been in on-line documents, a topic that is fairly close to the market-place. I will relate some experiences of the trade-offs between research aims and the market-place, and put this in the context of the future lines of development of the subject.

2.1 Introduction

The aim of this chapter is different from most of the others. I wish to consider researchers at the applied end of the spectrum: people engaged in creating novel software tools. I will analyse my experience over the past ten years in trying, reasonably successfully, to create novel software tools in the electronic publishing area – specifically in hypertext – and will try to draw some general lessons which may help future research.

A typical aim of the software tools researcher is to pioneer a novel interface style, such as a successor to the desk-top metaphor, or to pioneer a new approach to an application area – the Walter Mitty dream that most of us have is a breakthrough equivalent to the discovery of the spreadsheet.

21

There is a lot of this kind of research going on, and the eventual outcome should be a flow of successful new software products in the market-place. Unfortunately, in the UK especially, this has failed to happen. Although many novel software products on the market have indeed originated at Universities or industrial research laboratories, few of the inspirations have in recent years come from the UK and even fewer are the products of UK companies. For example in an article in *Computing* in August 1993 entitled 'UK firms founder in software league', the results of the Ovum *1992 Software Product Markets Europe* report are analysed: there are only 15 Europe-based firms in the top 50 of software suppliers in Europe, and of these only three are UK-based. (Indeed this total of three only arises from taking a generous view of what UK-based means.) The problem, a much-quoted one, is that the researchers are not getting products to the market-place, and that the UK is worse than most in this aspect.

Part of the problem is doubtless the attitudes of those of us involved in this research; many of us are far too introspective. We develop tools aimed only at computer scientists exactly like ourselves. All too often – certainly in over half the cases – the words 'exactly like ourselves' are just right: the tool is only usable by its creator. The introspection, sadly, carries over to student projects. Frequently, when one sees a list of projects, it is dominated by tasks related to the compiling of programs rather to using the computer for real-world tasks.

It is, nevertheless, far too simplistic to say that the problem can be solved by changing people's attitudes. Indeed even if the researcher does manage to make the mental leap and see the world as a typical computer user would, rather than a highly atypical one like the researcher herself, there remains the phenomenon that brings a mixture of joy and exasperation to all creators of software: users never behave as you expect them to. As, for example, Needham & Hopper (1993) point out, the only thing you can expect is that novel software will be used in an unexpected way.

Thus it is vital, if the creations of researchers are to reach the market-place, to have a feedback loop involving real usage. A main theme of this article is to highlight some of the sacrifices that researchers must make in order to make this feed-back possible, and to show some of the benefits.

2.2 The Feedback Loop

The ideal sequence proceeds as follows.

(1) The researcher has a brilliant idea – the killer application that

will make spreadsheets obsolete, if you want to pursue the Walter Mitty example.

(2) The researcher's team builds a prototype.

(3) Real users use the prototype. Some difficulties are thrown up, but, on the positive side, a few users use the prototype in an entirely unexpected yet extremely effective way. The original brilliant idea can be generalized – it is even more brilliant than it first appeared to be. It may be that the unexpected usage is so different that it lies right outside the field of usage imagined by the researcher – indeed the researcher's imagined use may be shunned. Then the original idea is still a brilliant one, but not for the reasons the researcher thought.

(4) A new prototype is built, and step (3) is repeated.

It is vital that the user feedback is not based on toy examples. As another article in this volume (Peyton Jones) argues in depth, unrealistically small examples lead to wrong conclusions.

2.3 An Illustration

In order to illuminate this feedback loop and the general goal of getting research to the market-place, I will now introduce a piece of my past research, whose success is probably due to good feedback from users. I will try to draw general lessons about the costs and benefits.

The research began in 1982. At that time graphics workstations, following the pioneering work at Xerox PARC, were just beginning to appear. My research was concerned with presenting documents to be read from a computer screen rather than from paper. In 1982 – and it is still partly true today – documents displayed on screens were just reproductions of paper documents. Not surprisingly, given all the advantages of paper, users preferred paper. It would be a huge coincidence if the best way of presenting material on screen turned out to be the same as on paper, especially as displaying a document on the computer opens up new facilities such as searching, adapting material to the user's needs, and multimedia. The advent of the workstation, and the new interface style that came with it, opened the way to novel approaches for presenting on-line material.

Note that the aim of the research was based on an application: reading documents from a computer screen. This is perhaps a reason for success. All too often my research has been driven by the technology, and the fascination with the technology has become so great that real-world applications of the technology have faded into the background.

As an aside, a great aid at the beginning of the research was the SERC's bold initiative of making graphics workstations available to researchers in the UK at an early stage. The initiative got a bad name because of problems of management and problems with the chosen PERQ system, but such problems are almost inevitable in any initiative that aims to move before the market does. Now, perhaps because memories fade, my many unhappy experiences with the PERQ can be recalled with a smile rather than a tear. I now feel that my research benefited greatly from the initiative.

2.4 Industrial Involvement

By 1984 the research had produced a prototype, which had seen a limited amount of real usage. The system was called *Guide*. Guide can be classed as a hypertext system, though – perhaps because of its application-oriented aims – it differed from other hypertext systems in that it was not based on screen-sized 'cards' and not based on links. (Indeed the difference remains today, though inevitably, as products have copied the good features from each other, differences have become blurred.)

Probably the most significant event in the whole research programme happened in 1984 when a start-up company, OWL (Office Workstations Ltd), became involved. By 1986 OWL had produced an implementation of Guide for the Macintosh, billed as the world's first personal computer hypertext system. Soon after this a PC product was created, and this has sold tens of thousands of copies – not a blockbuster but a steady earner. Most importantly, the retail product led to much profitable corporate business. For example the Ford Motor Company in the USA has all its workshop manuals in Guide form, and General Motors is treading a similar path.

A huge number of government programmes in the UK have been involved with technology transfer between academia and industry, and it is interesting to recall how the collaboration with OWL came about: *it happened by chance*. OWL, who were – and still are – based in Edinburgh, were visiting a colleague at the University of Kent Computing Laboratory, and were shown Guide as they passed through a room. Everything else developed from the chance meeting. It is significant, however, that, unlike the majority of UK companies, OWL were going round universities in order to find out what new things were happening. On the university side, we were receptive to such visits.

My own experience of working with industry is that collaboration is much easier *outside* the government schemes that supposedly foster industry/university collaboration. The reason is simple: these schemes inevitably have artificial rules and, given any set of artificial rules, academics and industrialists are past masters at cooking up artificial programmes that fit these rules. If you really want to get something done, however, you do better to keep out of the schemes: as a managing director of a small company (who had better be nameless) said to me about a scheme that gave 25% extra government funding: 'I would need more than 25% to put up with all the hassles and delays caused by working within the scheme.'

2.5 Feedback from the Marketplace

The OWL products obviously involved considerably change to the University's Guide prototype. The interface was made to fit accepted styles, some esoteric features were dropped, and the general design was adapted to fit a small computer – personal computers really were small in 1986. Nevertheless the principles of Guide remained intact. What OWL did, therefore, was to surround a radical product with a friendly and familiar casing.

The University's prototype itself evolved into a product which has sold in pleasing numbers on Unix workstations. This product involves many more research-oriented and speculative features than OWL's Guide does. I will use the term *UNIX Guide* when talking about the University's product.

The OWL involvement led to huge benefits to the research programme. OWL's staff, being closer to the market-place and to technical developments that were about to affect the market-place, gave insights into new application areas, particularly multimedia and CD-ROM. Indeed as a result of OWL, I was a participant in the first CD-ROM conference (Lambert & Ropiequet, 1986), held in Seattle in 1986. Without OWL I would not have had the opportunity to anticipate the impact of CD-ROM in the electronic publishing field.

Perhaps an even bigger impact than OWL's staff arose from OWL's customers. Inevitably most of the feedback from customers is, in research terms, mundane: they want features like more flexibility in the use of fonts, or compatibility with the XYZ graphics format. Nevertheless once in a while a real gem comes along: the customer who has

exploited a feature in an unexpected but highly effective way. I describe
an instance of that later, when I am discussing some technical matters.
It is, however, worth quoting at this stage an extreme example of a user
gem, since it illustrates so well the difference between the customer's
view of the world and the designer's. One customer, Paul Frew, has
become a hypertext poet – perhaps the first such. His creation, 'Hy-
perwalt', has achieved some critical acclaim. He says that he was really
excited when he came across Guide's button mechanisms because to him
they were a *new literary form*. This was not a concept that figured in
the original requirements specification for Guide!

2.6 Success?

OWL's involvement led to a number of successes. Guide won the BCS
technical award in 1988, and, in North America, was nominated for, but
did not win, the *Byte* magazine award for the year. OWL was taken
over at a price per share that was an immense multiple of the original
cost.

Ironically, in terms of research funding, these successes were setbacks.
It became much harder to obtain research funding, presumably because
Guide was too close to the market. I felt this was unfair because Guide
had helped create this very market – but then I would. Nevertheless, I
sometimes feel that the best approach for continuing research funding is
to get close to the goals of the research but never quite to achieve them.

The OWL takeover, though a financial triumph for the original in-
vestors, was arguably a setback for the Guide product. It did not seem
to sit very comfortably in a large diverse corporation. Interestingly, the
world has now turned full circle, and, as a result of a management buy-
out, Guide is now marketed by a small company again: InfoAccess in
Seattle.

2.7 Conservative or Radical?

I would now like to move on to discuss specific issues in running a research programme with the aim of producing prototype products that
can be used to get real user feedback. (For more details of these issues,
explored from a hypertext viewpoint, see Brown (1992).) Obviously sacrifices need to be made, and the nearer a research programme is to the
theoretical end of the spectrum the less acceptable these sacrifices are.
Thus I would like to re-emphasise that I am talking about research at
the practical end of the spectrum; at the theoretical end it is often much

better to take an idea to its limit and *not* to dilute it with pragmatic compromises.

The first issue for the practically oriented is this: if you are designing a new approach to software, how radical can you afford to be? As I have said, we all dream of being able to change the world completely, but few, of course, achieve it. Some isolated *dramatic* successes are the early work in the Cambridge University Mathematical Laboratory, the work at Xerox PARC already mentioned, the work at Bell Laboratories, and the first spreadsheet. (It is interesting to note that Xerox PARC and Bell Laboratories were research institutions with a largely free rein – a freer run than UK universities now have.)

To be realistic, particularly if you are a small team, it is safer to be radical in only a few ways. Let me give some examples relating to the Guide work. Users who view a document expect to find a scroll-bar and a searching mechanism. As it happens, the conventional scroll-bar and searching mechanisms, based as they are on static linear documents, are completely wrong for Guide, which has a model where documents appear to grow and shrink, and where documents may be distributed or even created on the fly by running a program and piping its output into Guide. Various radical attempts have been made to design new scrolling and searching mechanisms for this new environment, but none has found any user acceptance. It would have been better in retrospect if the research effort had been confined to Guide's basic document model, which is both novel and acceptable to users, and the accoutrements had been left in their boring conventional forms. Indeed the conventional packaging was surely a factor in the success of OWL's Guide product.

UNIX Guide has maintained a radical approach in its treatment of menus. Any UNIX Guide document can act as the Guide menu: this has the merit of great flexibility and internal consistency, and has indeed been greatly exploited in real applications. It does, however, mean that Guide is not compatible with, say, Motif's menu style, and thus a large number of conservative users are driven away. OWL forsook this approach to menus – neat and elegant as it may be – and stuck to what the conservatives wanted.

The issue of radicalism/conservatism carries down to lower-level issues such as file formats. We researchers always see our own creations as the centre of the world, with the rest of the world's software as a minor adjunct. To combat this, I try to remember the wise words of an OWL salesman 'Users do not want hypertext: they want solutions. Hypertext is only ever part of the solution.' The statement is equally true if you substitute any other technology for hypertext. Thus if you design a hypertext system it is going to be a loser unless it fits with other software tools such as spelling checkers, databases, version control systems, ... After some early disastrous design decisions had been corrected, UNIX Guide adopted a manner of working that allowed it to be integrated with all the other available UNIX tools. This has been a continuing strength.

It is interesting to contrast this approach with that of another hypertext system, *Intermedia* (Yankelovich *et al.*, 1985). In research terms Intermedia has probably contributed more than any other system. However, because it worked in its own special world it is now, sadly, largely dead.

2.8 Straitjacket

In spite of the accepted truth that novel software is always used in ways that the designers never imagined, designers often inadvertently impose a straitjacket on the way it is used. Many examples of this occur in the field of CSCW, a field where real usage is now only beginning. A lot of CSCW systems impose roles on the participants, roles that are based on existing practices that are not computer-supported. Inevitably the new environment leads to a change of practices, and the roles that the software imposes make it unusable.

It is, of course, easy to see the mistakes of others. However, in my own current research field, hypertext, or more generally, electronic publishing, the mistakes have been as great. Ideally every electronic publishing system should be *policy-free*: the author should not be constrained to a particular style. Certainly an author or organisation should be able to design their own policy, or house style, and impose this, but the system should not impose one all-embracing style. It is a sad monument to our failure, therefore, that if you look at any electronically produced document – whether a hypermedia presentation or a modest piece of paper produced by a word-processor – you can guess what system has produced it. Thus the system has either imposed a policy or made it hard for the user to escape from some default policy.

This imposition of a policy is particularly tragic in hypertext systems: we do not yet know how best to present material on computer screens – even textual material, let alone multimedia material – and thus it is particularly unfortunate that all hypertext systems impose an authorship policy.

There are instances in UNIX Guide where, instead of supplying a set of primitive features that can be freely combined, a large number of policies have been dumped into a bucket and the bucket has then been presented to the author. (For those who know Guide the mechanism for glossaries is a particularly bad example of this.) Worse still, a price of having a community of users is that there is a demand for compatibility between one version and the next, thus perpetuating mistakes.

In spite of a lot of bad, author-constraining, features, however, Guide has one shining success, and this relates strongly to the user-feedback cycle. From the very start, Guide has had a mechanism for grouping buttons (hot-spots) together; when a button within a group is selected, the entire group, which may include ordinary text and pictures as well as buttons, is replaced by the selected button's replacement. The original motivation was targeted at the case where the reader replies to a question posed by the author, e.g. the author might ask the reader to pick a geographical area by selecting one of a group of mutually exclusive buttons labelled *North*, *Central* and *South*. The grouping mechanism was therefore called an *enquiry*.

When OWL's Guide product went out into the field, some imaginative users showed that the enquiry mechanism generalised what were previously thought to be two different approaches to hypertext:

- the approach where a document is a continuous scroll, with buttons within it that can fold/unfold text;
- the approach where a document is split up into separate cards, often corresponding to the size of a screen.

Thus Guide authors had the ability to take either approach and, most interestingly, to take a hybrid approach involving a split screen. Such an approach, which in the initial design of Guide was not even considered – indeed it still seems ridiculous at first sight – was the basis of one of the most successful UNIX Guide applications. This is ICL's *Locator* system (Rouse, 1991), used to diagnose fault reports.

2.9 Customizing

The next, and penultimate, issue I would like to discuss is a siren that is always trying to lure software researchers to their doom. The siren is called customizing. The illusion that the siren uses to entice us on to the rocks is the generalized system, which, by setting a few parameters, can be customized to serve a wide variety of roles.

When I was a research student in the late sixties the siren was extolling the merits of extensible languages. A basic core language could be customized, by adding a few tables and procedures, to look like COBOL; a few twiddles of knobs gave it the capabilities of APL instead, whereas for LISP ... . The siren organized extensible languages conferences, to which we flocked. She also showed us UNCOL, the universal intermediate language that could be tailored to meet the needs of every programming language and every machine architecture. Indeed the siren has managed to make use of UNCOL many times over the years.

More recently, in HCI, the siren has introduced the general interface that can be customized to cover everyone from beginner to expert. The interface may even customize itself automatically by adapting its behaviour as the user progresses.

The siren's success in HCI has caused her to use a similar strategy in hypertext. Thus SS *Guide* set out towards the rocks which are labelled 'the single hypertext document that can be tailored to any type of user and to any type of usage from tutorial to reference'. UNIX Guide contains a host of customization facilities, but I have never seen them successfully used except in a most simplistic way.

In any area there is, of course, a degree of customization that is entirely feasible. Hypertext has, for example, its guided tours, whereby a user may, for example, visit a limited number of pages within a more general document. The moral is, however, that such customization has severe practical limits – often because stepping beyond certain limits leads to a combinational explosion – and researchers grossly underestimate what the limits are.

To reinforce the theme of this article, these gross misconceptions by the researchers are only possible if there is no user feedback or if the researchers fail to notice that there is a slew of customization facilities that no real user ever seems to master.

2.10 Wrong Emphasis

Researchers may, on the one hand, adopt the maxim that the user is always right. On the other hand the researchers may take the somewhat arrogant view that their role is to educate the users. So far this article has committed itself to the former approach. To add some balance I will end with an issue where the best approach is, I believe, the arrogant one of ignoring the clamour of users saying what they want, and instead providing what the researcher thinks they really need. The issue relates to maintenance.

The whole focus of electronic publishing, including hypertext, has been on one-off or short-lived documents. In spite of all the lessons of software engineering, there is no attention to the problems of maintaining documents. Instead the emphasis, which is driven by user demands, is on ever more complex facilities for *creating* documents, and these are likely to make maintenance problems even greater. If I had to guess which research direction in electronic publishing will be most important in the future it will be attention to maintenance, especially, of course, when it relates to really large documents. Some, but not all, of the work in software engineering will have parallels in document maintenance.

Thus I hope that researchers will educate users to switch their emphasis from fancy features for creating documents to such issues as discipline, higher-level abstractions, checking and verification.

Perhaps we researchers also have to educate ourselves. It is human nature that researchers will be more drawn to producing gee-whizz effects than by 'boring' areas such as checking and discipline. Nevertheless as an application area matures the gee-whizz effects become ever more of an irrelevance.

Another way that we computing researchers need to educate ourselves, incidentally, is to spend more time looking outside the computing field. Although I have claimed that maintenance of large documents might be the most important research area in electronic publishing, the issues that will really dominate are ones of intellectual property and copyright, where technical work of computer scientists can only play a small part.

2.11 The Future

I will end by summarizing first my hopes for the future of electronic publishing, and then the particular message of the paper.

Like everyone else I would like to see a world of electronic publishing where:

- Authors can give free reign to their creative talents, helped rather than constrained by their software tools.
- Creation of documents, especially multimedia ones, is economically viable even in cases where the potential readership does not run into four figures. This is not an issue I have discussed explicitly here, but it relates to discipline and high-level abstractions.
- Mmaintenance of documents is feasible over long periods, thus allowing documents with a high initial cost to recoup this over time.
- The world that the user sees is an integrated one, with tools slotting together, either visibly or invisibly, to perform the task in hand, and to give the illusion of a single uniform document covering all available information.

- Following on from the above, authors and readers do not waste huge amounts of time on the minutiae of finding/obtaining documents, getting them to print out, overcoming incompatibilities, etc.
- Finally – and this is the biggest and probably vainest hope of all – a world where new approaches can find their place, rather than a world where twenty-year-old practices lumber on, continually proliferating the twenty-year-old mistakes. My belief is, however, that the best way of achieving this is an incremental one of introducing an advance on one front at a time, rather than aiming to destroy the user's previous world in one go.

Finally, a good way of encapsulating the main theme of this paper is to take a recent quote from Brian Kernighan, referring to one of the many successful and (reasonably) novel products that have emanated from Bell Labs.: '... the reason for its success is that the design is pragmatic, a set of engineering compromises instead of a set of religious beliefs.' There is room for researchers to produce elegant failures or pragmatic successes, but perhaps we have too much admired the former rather than the latter.

3

Prospects for Artificial Intelligence

Alan Bundy

Abstract

Artificial Intelligence (AI) has had a turbulent history. It has alter-
nated between periods of optimism and periods of pessimism. Why
does this field of computer science evoke such strong feelings? What has
it achieved in the past and what can we expect of it in the future?

I will present my personal view of the nature of AI research and use
this to try to answer some of the questions above.

3.1 A Potted History of Artificial Intelligence

In artificial intelligence we attempt to emulate human (and other animal)
mental abilities using computer programs and associated hardware.

The goal of building an intelligent artificial entity is a potent one
and has excited enthusiasts throughout history. The advent of the electronic computer reinvigorated this enthusiasm and initiated the field of
artificial intelligence. The first call to arms came from Alan Turing's
classic 1950 paper in *Mind*, (reprinted in Turing (1963)), but the birth
of the field can be dated from the 1956 Dartmouth conference, which AI
pioneers like McCarthy, Minsky, Newell and Simon attended.

These were heady days. The pioneers were young and conscious of
the power of the new computing machinery. They quickly discovered
some new computational techniques which appeared to be the key to
general-purpose intelligence. The prospects for artificial intelligence
looked good. Large-scale projects sprang up to take advantage of the new
technology. Unfortunately, these pioneers drastically underestimated the
difficulties of AI and made optimistic predictions that have proved to be
an embarrassment to the field.

By the end of the 60s it was clear that AI had not made the predicted
progress. Many promising new computational techniques had not scaled

33

up to real problems. For instance, resolution theorem proving had initially looked promising as a general-purpose reasoning procedure. It built a train of argument from a set of rules by searching through all possible combinations. It could be used to solve simple problems, but on problems of moderate hardness it became bogged down in the search; exhausting the storage capacity and exceeding the time limits on the available computers. Funding agencies became more circumspect. In 1973 the Lighthill report recommended the cessation of SERC support for AI in the UK. Some people were disillusioned and left the field. Those remaining developed a new realism about the difficulty of the AI problem and the likely timescale for its solution.

This pessimism changed with the invention of expert systems. Although AI systems were still limited to solving 'toy' problems, it was discovered that this description fitted many problems of industrial interest. By strictly circumscribing the domain of interest to a narrow area of knowledge and a small number of problem types, AI techniques were able to cope with the search problems and provide automated solutions. Expert systems were particularly good at diagnosis or classification tasks, and such applications were found in abundance. As long as the domain was not too broad and dealt with an area of specialist knowledge, expert systems could provide commercially viable solutions. Unfortunately, general-purpose or 'common-sense' reasoning was still unattainable.

AI was reinvigorated. By the early 80s new IT support schemes were set up which included a strong AI element. The Japanese Fifth Generation Project (1982–92) started this trend. It was followed, in the UK, by the Alvey Programme (1983–88), in which the AI component was known, for political reasons†, as 'Intelligent Knowledge-Based Systems'. The European Esprit Programme (1985–) has a strong AI component and in the USA DARPA support for AI increased.

Most experienced AI researchers were wary. They had seen this before and were careful not to make any unwarranted promises (see, for instance, SERC (1983)). It was made clear that the hard problems posed by AI could not be solved by a short period of accelerated funding. Not everyone was so careful. In particular, the field was growing rapidly in size. AI groups were springing up in multinational and computing companies. New AI start-up companies were being founded, especially in the areas of expert system software houses, AI programming languages

† That is, to avoid upsetting the critics of AI.

and specialist hardware. The academic community was recruiting new researchers. Some of the new converts (and a few old hands) let their zeal for the new technology suppress their judgement.

By the end of the 80s the increased funding for IT in general and AI in particular was ebbing. The Alvey Programme finished in 1988. The Japanese Fifth Generation Project was winding down and DARPA support was decreased by the end of the Cold War. There was a shake-out of many of the AI start-up companies. Some critics pronounced the failure of AI (see, for instance, Wilson (1990)). They claimed that the strong expectations of AI researchers had not been realised despite the heavy funding; that these expectations never would be realised because they were ill-founded; and that investing further money in AI would be to throw good money after bad.

This renewed pessimism from some critics of AI is not felt by the practitioners in either academia or industry. Most feel that AI has some sound achievements behind it, has established itself as a discipline and has expectations of continued solid progress. AI techniques have now become pervasive in industry, investment in AI has been maintained and there is a continuing demand for further use of AI in strategically important areas of business and government. For instance, a recent report by the US Department of Commerce (Anon, 1994), described AI as 'of increasing importance to the international competitiveness of U.S. corporations'. It claimed that 'about 70–80% of the Fortune 500 firms now use AI to varying degrees' in areas such as design and engineering, process control, scheduling and planning, part making, factory automation, inspection, monitoring and computer integrated manufacturing. Among many major AI success stories, it singled out:

- a program that automatically processes and indexes newswires for Reuters at an estimated saving of $1.25 million in a recent year; and
- the DART program used for logistical planning during the Gulf War, which it claimed had alone 'more than offset all the money the Advanced Research Projects Agency had funneled into AI research in the last 30 years'.

3.2 Why Does AI Envoke Such Strong Emotions?

From the above turbulent history you can see that AI envokes strong emotions both positive and negative. Why is this?

I believe that both reactions stem from a misconception about the field shared by both some advocates and some critics. It is important to identify and correct this, because only then can one develop realistic expectations about AI and hence make useful predictions about where it might go in the future.

The misconception I call *mental vitalism*. It is that intelligence requires some special ingredient. Some AI critics call this special ingredient a 'soul', 'spirit', 'intentionality' or 'consciousness'. They see it as having a mystical or magical quality that will resist scientific investigation. AI is, therefore, incapable of building anything that will be 'really' intelligent and is restricted to pale simulations of the 'real thing'. So attempts to build 'real intelligence' are doomed to failure and money spent in such attempts is wasted.

Advocates of strong AI believe that no natural phenomenon can for ever resist scientific investigation. They predict that we will eventually understand natural intelligence and will then be able to use this understanding to build an artificial intelligence that *is* the 'real thing'.

However, even some AI enthusiasts suffer from a version of mental vitalism. But for them the special ingredient is not magical and will eventually be discovered. This discovery will be a key breakthrough which will lead to a huge leap in the abilities of AI programs. The key ingredient has been variously thought, for instance, to be 'common sense', 'learning' or 'reflection'. AI enthusiasts rarely suffer from mental vitalism in a pure form, but it can be detected as a hidden thread, for instance, in discussions about whether a particular program is 'really AI' or about the key role of some particular facility, e.g. learning.

If AI requires only the understanding of some key ingredient which is amenable to scientific study then concentrated effort on that ingredient should bring a breakthrough, possibly in a short timescale. Such reasoning has caused AI to be the victim of fashion. New paradigms promise the long-awaited key ingredient. Optimistic predictions of a breakthrough are made. Funding agencies become enthused by the predicted applications. A bandwagon effect starts, but then peters out when the predictions fail to materialise. Some AI advocates are disappointed, disillusioned and made angry by the apparent failure; the AI critics feel vindicated. In fact, the new paradigm has usually added something to our understanding, if not as much as some had hoped.

3.3 The Nature of AI

Although AI has failed to meet the optimistic predictions of an imminent breakthrough, there has been gradual progress in our understanding of the mechanisms of intelligent behaviour. Looking back over the last four decades of AI research we can form a more considered account of the nature of the field that can give a more accurate prediction of its future development.

AI is best seen as the exploration of a space of computational mechanisms whose behaviour is more or less intelligent. Progress in AI consists of: the invention of new mechanisms; the discovery of their theoretical and empirical properties; the understanding of their interrelations and tradeoffs; and their application to new problems. Sometimes these computational mechanisms appear to work in a similar way to the mechanisms underlying natural intelligence. They may then serve as a model to help us understand intelligence in humans or animals. This activity is called *cognitive science*. More often, they work in ways that are quite different from those that arise in nature, but they may still be useful as a component in an application.

If AI is merely the study of new computational techniques one may wonder whether anything distinguishes it from the rest of computer science. The relationship is rather like that between pure and applied mathematics. AI is like the latter. It draws on the computational techniques of computer science but it also develops its own. Just as applied mathematics focusses on mathematical techniques with the potential to model physical phenomena, AI focusses on computational techniques with the potential to emulate intelligence.

A useful methodology to discover new mechanisms is *exploratory programming*. This starts with a scenario of intelligent behaviour, e.g. a dialogue in English, the learning of some skill, the recognition of a scene. From a vague initial idea a program is built to generate this scenario. This program is tested on new examples and gradually refined by a run, debug, edit cycle until the programmer is satisfied with its performance†.

This exploratory programming methodology has been the target of much criticism of AI, especially from the theoretical computer science community. There are elements of both justice and unfairness in this criticism. Such an *ad hoc* methodology is no way to develop a robust program. It is the antithesis of the structured programming and formal methods techniques advocated by software engineers. However, as a 'brainstorming-like' technique for generating and developing new ideas it can be valuable – provided matters do not stop there. The exploratory programming should be followed by a 'rational reconstruction', a theoretical analysis and extensive and systematic testing. The ideas embed-

---

† Or runs out of time.

ded in the exploratory program must be crystallised into a form where their properties and relationships can be studied and where they can be readily transported into new applications. Unfortunately, this later analysis was often omitted in the early history of AI. Whereas the 'neat' school of AI advocated theoretical analysis, the 'scruffy' school rejected it as inappropriate for AI mechanisms. Some 'scruffies' went so far as to adopt the slogan that 'the theory was in the program'.

The neat school is now in the ascendant in academic AI research†. Theoretical and empirical analysis is now standard. Mathematics is in widespread use as a theoretical tool. As a result we are now developing a good understanding of the range of mechanisms that have been developed in AI. Methodological issues are by no means resolved (Cohen, 1991), but they are much discussed and a consensus is emerging on the importance of combining theoretical and empirical investigations.

3.4 The Fragmentation of the Field

AI can be viewed as a forcing ground for new computational techniques. The emulation of intelligence provides a very challenging goal. As they strive to attain it, AI researchers are forced to go beyond the existing range of techniques and develop new ones. Sometimes these new techniques prove successful and open up new areas of application.

As the techniques become better understood a new field may crystallise around them. Some researchers may prefer to concentrate their activity on this new field. It is often more concrete and targeted than the AI which gave birth to it. In this case the new field breaks away from AI. In the past this has happened in the areas of functional and logic programming, game playing, algebraic manipulation, automated program development and expert systems, to name only a few. The birth can be traumatic – the breakaway group rejecting their birthplace, e.g. as too vague and woolly compared to the certainties of their new home. Thus AI loses credit for its successes. This is often characterised as AI being the study of things we do not yet understand. One could draw an analogy with the way in which philosophy has spun off new fields like physics, psychology and linguistics.

More recently, the whole field of AI is threatened with fragmentation. This is partly a result of its improved maturity and growth. Most sub-areas of AI have become more technical, e.g. more mathematical. More

---

† This is not yet true of commercial applications but, given the normal timescale from invention to profitable application, we should not expect an immediate 'trickle down'.

mental investment is now needed to study these areas. It is no longer possible to be a 'Renaissance Man'. Since the increased investment in AI in the 80s, far more people are in the field. The major international AI conferences are attended by thousands of people. They have many parallel sessions, each specialising in a different area. Few AI researchers now stray far outside their own speciality.

Each major sub-area of AI now has its own international conference series. There are conferences in vision, computational linguistics, automated reasoning, knowledge representation, learning, etc. Around these conferences distinct research communities have crystallised. They have their own agenda. Few AI researchers now actively pursue the goal of building a general-purpose intelligent entity†. Most are engaged on the detailed study of a narrow range of mechanisms for a particular kind of task, e.g. visual perception, common-sense reasoning, natural language understanding. Like expert systems, their applications are narrowly focussed.

Despite their narrow daily focus, many AI researchers retain the dream of understanding general intelligence and see their particular research topic as contributing to this in some distant future. Support for a general AI community remains high, as witnessed by the only slightly diminished support for general AI conferences, e.g. IJCAI, AAAI, ECAI, despite the recent reductions in financial support.

3.5 The Invisibility of AI Applications

Many applications of AI have found their way into the market place. However, this commercial success is not always visible for two reasons: the timescale and the nature of the applications.

In every science, the timescale from the first research idea for a new application and its appearance as a commercial product is usually much longer than the original researchers anticipate. As Milner has pointed out‡, ideas in computer science often take 20 years to be realised in products. On that timescale the AI techniques involved in an application have usually become unfashionable. The particular area of AI may itself have broken away and ceased to be regarded as AI at all. An obvious example of this is automated chess. Mini-max based chess programs are a common high street product. This was the application singled out by Turing for an initial assault in AI. The mini-max algorithm was one of

---

† Although there are a few exceptions, e.g. the SOAR project at Carnegie–Mellon University.

‡ For example, in his unpublished invited talk to JFIT-93.

the† first AI techniques to be invented. But game playing hardly features in current AI conference programmes; it is essentially an independent area. Other examples can be found in algebraic manipulation systems and the use of fuzzy logic in domestic appliances. Thus, by the time they appear, AI gets no credit for these products because the techniques on which they are based are no longer regarded as part of the field, either by the product developers‡, who have left AI, or by current AI researchers, who regard these techniques as 'old hat' and (a touch of mental vitalism here) 'not really AI'.

The other cause of invisibility is that AI techniques are often integrated with more conventional computational techniques in an application. To the casual user the final product may show no outward sign of containing AI techniques. In the early days of expert systems most applications consisted solely of AI techniques, e.g. rule-based programming. Many start-up companies specialised in the supply of expert system shells and/or custom-built expert systems, often on specialised AI hardware, e.g. the Lisp machines. As the market matured it was found necessary to integrate AI with conventional programming techniques and to implement systems on general-purpose hardware in general-purpose programming languages. The specialist AI companies evolved to occupy vertical market niches, e.g. decision-support systems, computer-aided manufacture, with AI techniques as just one weapon in their armoury. They stopped exhibiting at general AI conferences in favour of conferences in their specialist application area. To the outside observer it might seem that the application of AI had faltered, but in fact this invisibility was a symptom of success. AI techniques had become an accepted part of computing technology and were integrated into the mainstream. They were no longer remarkable and, hence, not remarked on.

There are now numerous examples of systems which have produced dramatic gains in productivity, quality or cost savings by embedding AI technology. The AI components in such a system may be quite small in size, but are often vital to the success of the overall system.

3.6 The Role of Mathematics

Whenever scientists want to strengthen the theory of their subject they turn to mathematics. AI is no exception. Mathematics has always

---

† If not just 'the'.

‡ A rare exception here is the use of 'AI' and 'Fuzzy Logic' labels by some Japanese manufacturers of domestic appliances.

played some role in AI – more in some areas than in others. But as AI has matured, mathematics has played a stronger role in all areas.

- New kinds of mathematics have been used in those areas of AI that were already mathematical.
- Areas of AI that were not previously very mathematically oriented have started to experiment more with mathematical techniques.
- New kinds of mathematics are being developed in AI.
- Exploratory programming is no longer the dominant methodology of AI.

I will discuss examples of this phenomenon in three AI areas.

3.6.1 Vision widens its mathematical net

Vision is the area of AI concerned with the emulation of visual perception. It has always been one of the more mathematical AI areas, making strong use of geometry to design image-processing algorithms. This use of mathematics has gradually become more sophisticated. Here are some examples.

Originally objects were modelled as smooth shapes, whereas, in reality, many objects are rough. To model this roughness, vision researchers have recently turned to fractal geometry. The basic shape of the object is modelled as before, but a fractal envelope is superposed on this to represent the surface texture. The index of this fractal can be varied to give different degrees of roughness. The idea comes from computer graphics, where it is used to produce images. In AI vision it is used to analyse visual data to build a model of the underlying shape and the surface texture, e.g. for recognition or as a representation for robot planning.

Visual processing is uncertain. Uncertainty may arise, for instance, from noise in the data, doubts about the positions of instruments or variations in their performance. To cope with this uncertainty, vision researchers have recently turned to stochastic geometry, which combines geometry with statistical inference. This enables the integration of information from several sources, e.g. measurements from different instruments or the same instruments at different times. It also facilitates the combination of information which is known with different degrees of certainty, e.g. you may be more certain of the direction of a particular input than of its distance, or of the data from one instrument than another. All this information can be fused using a maximal-likelihood estimate on a messy space of data to give the best fit.

3.6.2 Learning becomes more mathematical

In contrast to vision, machine learning was traditionally one of the least mathematical areas of AI. Early work was characterised by the exploratory programming methodology. However, in recent years this situation has radically changed.

Many early learning algorithms consisted of building decision trees from positive and negative examples of a concept. The decision tree generalised the data and provided a program for recognising the concept from future data. The problem was essentially the same as the data classification problem already studied in statistics, but this similarity was not immediately recognised, causing many wheels to be reinvented. Fortunately, the relationship to statistics is now well understood and the best work, in what in AI is called similarity based learning, now builds on prior work in statistics.

But AI is concerned with more than just automatic learning of decision trees and the ability to classify. In inductive logic programming, for instance, recursive programs are built from examples of input/output data. Learning more complex structures calls for more sophisticated algorithms and different kinds of mathematics. As its name suggests, inductive logic programming makes a strong call on mathematical logic for the basic algorithms for generalising complex structure from simple examples. More surprisingly it also calls on information theory to decide whether the generalisation has been successful in condensing the information present in the original data into a more succinct form.

The recent revival of interest in neural nets was caused by the invention of a learning rule which could train some neural nets containing hidden nodes. In 1969 neural net research was effectively killed off as a result of a critical analysis by Minsky and Papert. This showed that, without such hidden nodes, their representational range was very limited. The new learning rule, and its successors, are derived from ideas in dynamic programming and optimisation. The theoretical analysis and prediction of the behaviour of such learning rules draws on quite sophisticated ideas from statistical mechanics, chaos theory and other areas of mathematics.

3.6.3 Knowledge representation invents new mathematics

Knowledge representation is the area of AI concerned with how both factual information and skills can be represented in a computer so that they can be extracted from the environment, reasoned about and used to direct action. This area has been a battleground for disputes between neats and scruffies. The neats have taken mathematical and philosophical logic as a firm foundation on which to build knowledge representation formalisms. The scruffies argued that logical formalisms failed to capture many of the properties of knowledge, e.g. its uncertainty and the possibility of revision in the light of new evidence. They argued for more *ad hoc* representations that more accurately captured these fallible characteristics.

This battle now seems to have been won by the neats. Their winning weapon was to invent new kinds of logic with the desired properties of uncertainty and fallibility. These are called *non-monotonic* logics. The term 'non-monotonic' is a reference to their common feature: an old inference may cease to be valid when new information is made available. This feature enables them to deal with default information. In the absence of information to the contrary a default may be assumed and used in reasoning. Later information may contradict this and the tentative inference must then be withdrawn. Non-monotonic logics represent a new kind of mathematical formalism. They have received a mixed reception from logicians. Some are excited by the new possibilities such logics present; others regard them as an aberration. But they have made a major difference in AI, causing an explosion of work into the theoretical foundations of knowledge representation.

3.6.4 Other Uses of Mathematics in AI

The above three sections give an illustration of the increasing important role of mathematics in AI. These are not isolated examples. Other examples include the following.

- Approaches based on probability theory have largely replaced more *ad hoc* approaches to the representation of uncertain reasoning.
- Operations research and plan formation are becoming more closely integrated.
- Non-well-founded sets from mathematical logic are being used to represent knowledge and belief.
- New kinds of logic are playing a key role in the parsing of natural languages.
- The natural language and speech areas have started to use statistics on large corpora of examples.

3.7 The Role of Experiment

Theory is only one half of a science; the other is experiment. In AI, experimentation is especially important because it has proved impossible to assess the potential of a technique without it. Many AI techniques have looked promising in theory but application has exposed serious practical difficulties. Resolution theorem proving is a good example. In theory, it seemed capable of emulating reasoning in many areas of AI. In practice, the explosion of the search possibilities restricted it to only simple problems. This practical discovery was one of the early disappointments of AI.

On the other hand, some AI techniques look unpromising in theory, but prove to be more successful in practice. Consider, for instance, the restriction of resolution to Horn clauses. This restriction makes available lots of ways of curtailing search, so that resolution is made more practical. Unfortunately, Horn clauses are a very special case of logical formulae, so one might expect that we would rarely be able to take advantage of this restriction. The empirical surprise is that Horn clauses are ubiquitous; many problems of practical interest fall within this class. This could not have been predicted from theory alone. The logic programming language, Prolog, was designed to take advantage of this empirical observation. Prolog programs are collections of Horn clauses, which enables its search to be restricted.

In the early days of AI a rather casual attitude was often taken to experimentation. Many early AI programs only simulated intelligence on the worked examples described in the paper. In the words of Bobrow *et al.* (1977, p. 172),

If their users depart from the behaviour expected of them in the minutest detail ... [the programs] turn to simulating gross aphasia or death.

As AI has matured, systematic experimentation has become more commonplace.

- In similarity based learning and neural nets, programs are typically trained on large corpora of examples and then tested on even larger corpora. Standard corpora are used for comparison of learning programs.
- Automatic theorem proving has developed a large corpus of 'challenge problems' on which provers are routinely tested and compared.
- Computational linguistics has developed large corpora of natural language utterances on which to test parsers, etc.

These examples are typical and similar examples can now be found in most areas of AI. As a result today's AI programs are a lot more robust than their predecessors.

Of course, there is still lots of room for improvement. A recent survey of AAAI-90 conference papers (Cohen, 1991) contains a good discussion of the issues and an investigation of the current situation. Among several methodological criticisms of the AAAI-90 papers was the observation:

Not only were average-case hypotheses and predictions rare, so too were follow-up experiments.

However, the very existence of this article and its positive reception by the AI community show a new AI awareness of the importance of experimental methodology. The article also contains some evidence that AI methodology is moving in the right direction.

The commercial application of AI techniques has also served to tighten up AI methodology. A number of software engineering techniques for expert system development have evolved. For instance, the KADS methodology combines insights from AI, software engineering and psychology. It suggests a modular construction of expert systems in which factual and control knowledge are separated. This simplifies development, validation and subsequent maintenance and, hence, leads to more robust systems.

3.8 What of the Future?

In a field as broad and diverse as AI it is difficult to make detailed predictions. However, from the nature and history of the field discussed above, we can draw some general observations.

- AI will continue to serve as a forcing ground for new computational techniques. As the space of AI mechanisms is further explored, new ones will be invented and refined.
- Some of these new techniques will find useful applications – but the timetable from invention to profitable application may be decades.
- Some of these new developments will lead to the formation and break-away of new fields of computing.
- The formalisation of AI techniques is now a well established part of AI methodology and will continue. Both existing and new techniques will be theoretically analysed and empirically tested. The deeper understanding of the techniques that this engenders will provide assurances of the robustness and reliability of products built with AI techniques.

On the other hand there will be a need to present mathematically oriented techniques in a way that is accessible to mathematically unsophisticated users.

- AI techniques will continue to be integrated with more conventional computational techniques in final products. This will force the reimplementation of AI techniques using standard software and hardware in order to simplify integration.

- The ready availability of cheaper and more powerful computers and the increased use of computers by non-specialists will increase the demand for AI techniques in computer products. We turn to this prediction in the next section.

3.9 An Increased Demand for AI Techniques?

The cost of computer hardware has plunged over the last few decades. As a result more and more computer power is available to more and more people. This has changed information technology in ways that will favour the use of AI techniques in computer products.

Cheaper hardware is changing the economics of computer use. The bottleneck is shifting from hardware costs to software costs. Techniques that used to be considered uneconomically inefficient are making a comeback. Examples that spring to mind include genetic algorithms, neural nets, case based reasoning, inductive learning, hill-climbing. All of these originated in AI. What they have in common is that it is easy for a user to program using them, but that they are computationally expensive to run. This tradeoff suits the current economic situation. Thinking Machines Inc. have pioneered this kind of application using their SIMD Connection Machine, to which it is ideally suited. The use of such AI techniques is likely to develop in tandem with the growth of parallel computers.

As computers have become cheaper, more people are using them – and using them directly, not via a data-processing department. Indeed, many of these computers can be found embedded in everyday household objects: washing machines, hi-fi systems, cars, etc. Necessarily, most of these new users are not computer professionals. For them, ease of use is at a premium. Better human–computer interfaces offer a partial solution to this problem. The computer must also do more of the work. In particular, users want to describe their problems in their own terms and have the computer make the connection to the available solutions, i.e. computers have to be smarter. Many AI areas can contribute to this goal. As examples I will consider four such areas of AI.

Speech Processing Speech processing covers both the generation and recognition of speech. Both can be useful in making computers easier to use. Speech input can be useful as an alternative to keyboard/mouse input for novices, the disabled or those whose hands are occupied with other tasks. Similarly speech output can be a useful supplement to other forms of information presentation.

Isolated word or limited vocabulary speech recognition systems have been commercially available for some time. The main research area is in the recognition of continuous speech for reasonable vocabularies. This has proved to be a very difficult topic, but real progress now seems to be being made, and we can expect steady and incremental improvements over the next decade.

Machine Vision The processing of visual images might have a greater impact than speech processing. Images can be used to define a task, e.g. pointing to an object to be moved by a robot. Information in graphic form can be transformed by visual processing.

Machine Learning Machine learning techniques hold the promise of instructing computers by example. This has already been pioneered in the use of similarity-based learning techniques to construct expert system rules from positive and negative examples of the required behaviour. Using inductive logic programming it is possible to construct simple recursive programs from input/output pairs.

Automated Reasoning Automated reasoning consists of the construction of arguments by linking together chains of inference rules. It can be used to bridge the gap between the information held in a computer system and the information required by a user. For instance, databases can be extended by the use of inference rules which combine individual facts together to infer information not explicitly recorded. Human expertise can be captured in rule form and used to draw conclusions from a situation described by a user. Specifications of a processing task can be transformed into an efficient program for doing that task.

3.10 Science *vs.* Technology in AI

Despite the promise held by current and future AI applications, it would be a mistake to assess AI purely as a branch of information technology.

For instance, research geared to the application of known techniques and the development of existing applications would be self-limiting. The law of diminishing returns would eventually set in and the supply of new products would slowly dwindle. The main potential of AI is as a forcing ground for new techniques, and this arises from viewing AI as a science.

Most AI researchers are ultimately driven by the quest to understand the nature of intelligence. Although their daily concern will be the development of a new technique, their long-term goal is the understanding of the space of such techniques and the ways in which they interact to produce intelligent behaviour. One does not have to be a believer in strong AI to find this activity worth while. The quest for artificial intelligence gives a strong intellectual stimulus to invent and explore new computational techniques – which advances informatics whether or not it succeeds in its final aim.

As AI matures, it not only produces a wider circle of such techniques, but it also deepens its understanding of these techniques so that they are more easily and robustly applied. This is particularly so in the wider use of mathematics in AI, which leads to better predictions about the performance of AI mechanisms and, hence, more reliable applications. It is also true of the more systematic use of experiments to explore the feasibility of applying AI techniques to particular problems.

There are unlikely to be any sudden breakthroughs in AI. Success in AI is not waiting on the discovery of some *key to intelligence*. It is slow and steady as the space of AI mechanisms becomes better understood. Accelerated funding of AI in the hope of achieving such a breakthrough is sure to lead to disappointment. But reduced funding based on a misconceived notion of failure would be even more mistaken. In any science success is gradual and occurs over a long timescale. This is especially so when the goal is as hard as the understanding of intelligence.

Acknowledgements

My thanks for comments on earlier drafts of this paper go to David Basin, Frank van Harmelen, Pat Hayes, Jim Howe, Andrew Ireland, Sean Matthews, Robin Milner, Brad Richards, Dave Robertson, Peter Ross, Alan Smaill, Austin Tate and Ian Wand.

4

Structured Parallel Programming: Theory meets Practice

John Darlington, Yi-ke Guo, Hing Wing To

Abstract

We address the issue of what should be the proper relationship between theoretical computer science and practical computing. Starting from an analysis of what we perceive as the failure of formally based research to have as much impact on practical computing as is merited we propose a diagnosis based on the way formally based research is conducted and the way it is envisaged that results from these areas will be translated into practice. We suggest that it is the responsibility of practitioners of theoretical computer science to work more closely with the practical areas in order to identify ways in which their ideas can be used to augment current practice rather than seeking to replace it. As a case in point we examine functional programming and its relationship to programming parallel machines. We introduce a development, structured parallel programming, that seeks to combine the theoretical advantages of functional programming with established practice in these areas. We show how the full power of functional programming, for example high-level abstraction and program transformation, can be made compatible with conventional imperative programming languages, providing practical solutions to many long standing problems in parallel computing.

4.1 Introduction

We characterise formally based computer science as the attempt to apply fundamental ideas in the logic and mathematics of computation to practical computing problems. Developments here include, for example, functional and logic programming, program transformation, studies of concurrency and formal program specification and verification. The hope underlying much of the research in these areas is that the mathematical foundation of these approaches will make possible radical so-

49

lutions to many deep seated and long lasting problems in computing. However, despite many highly distinguished and innovative contributions at the academic level, the observation must be that much of this work has so far had little direct impact on practical computing.

We identify three phases of formally based research. There is, of course, pure theory, fundamental investigations into the mathematics of computation. Then moving closer to practice there is applied theory, often called formal methods, the conscious attempt to adapt ideas from pure theory to practical purposes. Finally there is development, the final stages of producing a workable technology from ideas generated in the previous two areas. There is much activity in the middle area but this is where things seem to go wrong. Although many ideas start out looking very promising very few get translated fully into practice. Work in this area has become a field in its own right rather than an active link between theory and practice.

The reasons for this partial failure are many. The very dynamism and radical development of what we will call conventional computing paradoxically make it hard for radical solutions to be adopted and the astonishing progress in many areas helps disguise the failure of the more *ad hoc* methods to solve several deep-seated problems, particularly in the areas of software development and maintenance.

However, it is our belief that some of this failure must be ascribed to the way practitioners in the more formally based areas have sought to develop and to apply their work. In several such areas, for example functional or logic programming, there has been a hope or belief that these technologies could totally replace conventional approaches and provide comprehensive, radical, solutions at both the software and hardware levels.

Often the agenda for the formally based work is set by some superficial observation of the origin of the problems that require solution. For example it is easy to ascribe all the problems of software developments to the properties of the imperative languages currently used or to observe that more reliable software products could be produced if systems were formally verified. These observations often lead to the belief that the main requirement is the construction of some alternative, formally based vehicle, for example a new-style programming language or a theorem proving system. Having established these long term goals the formal activity often decouples from the practical arena and sets up long term, self-contained, research programmes. These programmes often become inward-looking, generating their own problems and hence their own solutions. Only after these vehicles have been constructed does attention revert to how they are to be applied and often the harsh truth is that much of what is produced is inappropriate and inapplicable.

This tendency leads to formally based working becoming de-coupled from practice. Thus technologies are developed that often ignore many important aspects of the problems they are meant to address, concentrating on what the technology can do rather than what are the problems it should solve. Furthermore the low level of interaction with either conventional computing or the application domains means that when novel solutions are developed they are packaged and presented in ways that are incompatible with existing practice, in which very large investments have been made, and seem very alien to both application developers and conventional computer science practitioners. Often it is envisaged that much of common practice will be abandoned, which is economically and socially unlikely. The result is that many very useful, perhaps partial, results from the formal areas never get applied.

However, it is still our belief that long term solutions to many fundamental problems, particularly in the areas of software development and re-use, cannot be solved without adoption of some of the ideas underlying the formally based approaches. The responsibility, therefore, clearly lies with workers in the formally based areas to alter their practices and develop closer working relationships with practical computing in order to focus on translating the advantages of their approaches into a practical context. We are not proposing the abandonment of the formal agenda, rather that an extra activity should be included, that of working in a more closely coupled way with conventional computing, identifying those aspects of the formal approaches that are capable of having an impact and then working to package these results in a manner that makes them compatible with current practice, augmenting the current technology rather than seeking to supplant it.

We will attempt to illustrate our thesis by examining what we believe to be a successful application of this agenda where the formally based area is that of functional programming and the practical one that of programming parallel machines. It has long been observed that the properties of functional languages endow them with many fundamental advantages making possible, for example, software development via rigorous program derivation or transformation and parallel execution without any explicit programmer control. Indeed this approach has proven very successful in guiding the design of parallel architectures that have now resulted in a commercial product (Darlington & Reeve,

1981). However, the wider agenda of building a complete functional language software and hardware solution has not succeeded generally. The reasons for this are certainly the resistance of the software industry to adopting radical solutions but also the failure of the functional language community to confront and solve certain practical problems concerned with the predictability and efficiency of the execution of such languages on parallel architectures.

Nevertheless the functional languages do possess properties that could make a significant contribution in these areas. We identify these as

- The availability of powerful data and control abstraction mechanisms
- The separation of meaning and behaviour conveyed by the Church–Rosser property
- The availability of meaning-preserving program transformation rules

The question, as discussed above, is how to package these properties in a way that makes them available and compatible with conventional approaches to programming parallel machines, which we identify as the use of standard imperative languages such as Fortran or C augmented in an *ad hoc* manner with constructs such as message passing.

In the following we present an approach that, we believe, combines the important aspects of functional languages with conventional parallel programming. This methodology, which we call *structured parallel programming*, amounts to using functional programming techniques to provide a high-level, uniform abstraction of all essential aspects of a program's parallel behaviour. Thus a functional specification of the configuration of a parallel computation can be defined which coordinates the parallel execution of programs which can themselves be expressed in any conventional, imperative, language such as C or Fortran. As all the essential features of parallelism are abstracted into a functional language this level inherits all the desirable properties of functional programming and we can, for example, apply transformations to optimise parallel programs to target architectures safe in the knowledge that such optimisations are mathematically rigorous (Burstall & Darlington, 1977; Backus, 1978; Bird, 1986; Meertens, 1989).

This article is organised into the following sections. In section 4.2, we discuss the problems of parallel programming and propose an approach based on the use of a functional coordination language as a new uniform model for general purpose parallel programming. In section 4.3, we introduce the structured parallel programming framework, SPP(X), and a particular SPP instance, Fortran-S taking Fortran as the base language. Finally, we summarise our work in the conclusion section.

4.2 Practical Issues of Parallel Programming

The von Neumann model of sequential computation succeeds because there is a direct mapping from constructs in programming languages to execution behaviours of machines. Issues of resource allocation, such as memory allocation, are resolved by the compilers or run-time systems, with generally no major performance implications. The universality of the von Neumann model guarantees portability of sequential programs both at the language level, and most importantly, at the performance level. Usually there is no unexpected degradation of performance when moving programs to alternative platforms.

This convenient picture does not carry over to the parallel case. Here the complexity of concurrency, the diversity of the machine type and the effect resource allocation can have on performance mean not only that parallel program development is a complex affair but, critically, that effective portability is lost. Even if portability is maintained at the language level there is no guarantee that performance will not change dramatically when moving programs to alternative platforms and require radical re-writing of the program.

The two extreme solutions to this problem have been labelled *explicit* and *implicit* parallel programming. Explicit parallel programming involves controlling all a program's parallel behaviour, such as process creation and placement and communication, using low-level constructs typically embedded in conventional imperative languages. This route leads to great complexity and loss of portability. The alternative implicit route available with functional languages relies on relegating control of parallel behaviour to intelligent compilers and run-time systems. Unfortunately this promise has not been fulfilled and implicit systems generally lead to highly inefficient executions. Attempts to remedy the situation with annotations lead to explicit programming through the "back door".

Gelernter and Carriero (1992) proposed the notion of coordination languages as the vehicle of expressing parallel behaviour. They wrote:

We can build a complete programming model out of two separate pieces – the *computation model* and the *coordination model*. The computation model allows programmers to build a single computational activity: a single-threaded, step-at-a-time computation. The coordination model is the glue that binds separate activities into an ensemble. An ordinary computation language (e.g.

Fortran) embodies some computation model. A coordination language embodies a coordination model; it provides operations to *create* computational activities and to support *communication* among them.

Applications written in this way have a two-tier structure in general. The coordination level abstracts all the relevant aspects of a program's parallel behaviour, including partitioning, data placement, data movement and control flow, whilst the computation level expresses sequential computation through procedures written in an imperative base language. Such a separation enables the problems of parallel optimisation to be addressed separately and at a suitable level of abstraction. This is in contrast to the use of low-level parallel extensions where both tasks must be programmed simultaneously in an unstructured way. This coordination approach of separating meaning and behaviour provides a promising way to achieve the following important goals:

- **Re-usability of Sequential Code**: Parallel programs can be developed by using the coordination language to compose existing modules written in conventional languages.
- **Generality and Heterogeneity**: Coordination languages are independent of any base computational language. Thus they can be used to compose sequential programs written in any language and can, in principle, coordinate programs written in several different languages.
- **Portability**: Parallel programs can be efficiently implemented on a wide range of parallel machines by specialised implementations of the compositional operators for target architectures.

Although developing coordination languages has become a significant research topic for parallel programming (Gelernter & Carriero, 1992) there is still no general purpose coordination language designed to meet the requirements of constructing verifiable, portable and structured parallel programs. Developing a higher-level, generic and extensible coordination system for the structured organisation of parallel behaviour is one of the major practical problems of parallel programming.

In this paper, we propose an approach for parallel coordination that allows all essential aspects of parallelism, e.g. data partitioning and distribution, communication and multi-thread control, to be expressed uniformly as functional primitives or skeletons within a single *Structured Coordination Language* (SCL). In SCL, skeletons have a precise declarative meaning, formalised as higher-order functions, are amenable to analysis and optimisation and have well defined parallel behaviours.

The details of the parallel behaviour of a given skeleton can be tailored to guarantee efficient execution on a target machine.

4.3 SPP(X): A Structured Parallel Programming Scheme

In this section we present a structured parallel programming scheme, SPP(X), where parallel programs are constructed by composing programs written in a conventional base language using a set of high-level functional coordination forms known as *skeletons*. Applications written in this way have a two-tier structure. The upper layer, known as the structured coordination language (SCL) abstracts all the important aspects of a program's parallel behaviour and expresses it as compositions of appropriate skeletons. The SCL is thus used to coordinate the parallel computation of sequential threads which are written in a conventional base language, BL, providing the lower layer.

4.3.1 SCL: A Structured Coordination Language

SCL is a general purpose coordination language where all aspects of parallel coordination are specified as the composition of the following three classes of skeletons:

Configuration Skeletons: Coordinating Data Distribution

The basic parallel computation model underlying SCL is the data parallel model. In SCL, data parallel computation is abstracted as a set of parallel operators over a distributed data structure, for example, distributed arrays. A **configuration** models the logical division and distribution of data objects. Such a distribution has several components: the division of the original data structure into distributable components, the location of these components relative to each other and finally the allocation of these co-located components to processors. In SCL this process is specified by a `partition` function to divide the initial structure into nested components and an `align` function to form a collection of tuples representing co-located objects. This model, illustrated in Figure 4.1, clearly follows and generalises the data distribution directives of HPF. Applying this general idea to arrays, the following configuration skeleton `distribution` defines the configuration of two arrays A and B:

```
distribution (f,p) (g,q) A B =
      align (p ∘ partition f A) (q ∘ partition g B)
```

Throughout this paper we will use 'curried' notation to define functions, thus `distribution` is a function defined with four arguments, the first two of which are pairs explicitly formed using the tupling notation,

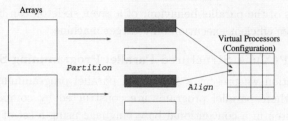

Fig. 4.1. Data Distribution Model

'(,)'. The distribution skeleton therefore takes two function pairs, f and g specify the required partitioning (or distribution) strategies of A and B respectively and p and q are bulk data movement functions specifying any initial data re-arrangement that may be required. The distribution skeleton is defined by composing the functions align and partition.

A more general configuration skeleton can be defined as

```
distribution [(f,p)] [d] = p ∘ partition f d
distribution (f,p):fl d:dl =
          align (p ∘ partition f d) (distribution fl dl)
```

where fl is a list of distribution strategies for the corresponding data objects in the list dl and ':' denotes the infix operator, known as 'cons', that builds a list by adding an item to the front of the list.

Applying the distribution skeleton to an array forms a configuration which is an array of tuples. Each element i of the configuration is a tuple of the form $(DA_1^i, \ldots, DA_n^i)$ where n is the number of arrays that have been distributed and DA_j^i represents the sub-array of the jth array allocated to the ith processor. For brevity, rather than writing a configuration as an array of tuples we can also regard it as a tuple of (distributed) arrays and write it as $<DA_1, \ldots, DA_n>$ where the DA_j stands for the distribution of the array A_j. In particular we can pattern match to this notation to extract a particular distributed array from the configuration.

Configuration skeletons are capable of abstracting not only the initial distribution of data structures but also their dynamic redistribution. Data redistribution can be uniformly defined by applying bulk data movement operators to configurations. Given a configuration C: $<DA_1, \ldots, DA_n>$, a new configuration C': $<DA_1', \ldots, DA_n'>$ can be formed by applying f_j to the distributed structure DA_j where f_j is some bulk data movement operator defined by specifying collective communication. This behaviour can be abstracted by the skeleton `redistribution` as defined in Darlington *et al.* (1995). SCL also supports nested parallelism by allowing distributed structures as elements of a distributed structure and by permitting a parallel operation to be applied to each of the elements in parallel. An element of a nested array corresponds to the concept of *group* in MPI (1993). The leaves of a nested array contain any valid sequential data structure of the base computing language. Skeletons supporting nested parallelism are specified in Darlington *et al.* (1995).

Elementary Skeletons: Parallel Arrays Operators

In SCL, we use a set of second-order functions as `elementary skeletons` to abstract essential data parallel computation and communication patterns. The basic functions specifying data parallelism include

- `map` which abstracts the behaviour of broadcasting a parallel task to all the elements of an array,
- a variant of `map`, the function `imap` which takes into account the index of an element when mapping a function across an array,
- the reduction operator `fold` which abstracts tree-structured parallel reduction computation over arrays.

Data communication among parallel processors is expressed as the movement of elements in distributed data structures. In SCL a set of *bulk data movement functions* are introduced as the data parallel counterpart of sequential loops and element assignments at the structure level. These elementary skeletons for communication can be generally divided into two classes: *regular* and *irregular*. The following `rotate` function is a typical example of regular data movement.

```
rotate ::  Int → ParArray Int α → ParArray Int α
rotate k A = <<i := A((i+k) mod SIZE(A)) | i ← [1..SIZE(A)]>>
```

Here the expression '`<< i := f i | i ← [1..k] >>`' is an 'array comprehension' that denotes the array indexed from 1 to `k` whose `i`th element is `f i`.

For irregular data movement the destination is a function of the current index. This definition introduces various communication modes. Multiple array elements may arrive at one index (i.e. many-to-one communication). This is modelled by accumulating a sequential vector of elements at each index in the new array. Since the underlying implementation is non-deterministic no ordering of the elements in the vector may be assumed. The index calculating function can specify either the destination of an element or the source of an element. Two functions, `send` and `fetch`, are provided to reflect this. Elementary skeletons can be used to define more complex and powerful communication skeletons required for realistic problems.

Computational Skeletons: Abstracting Control Flow

In SCL the flexibility of organising multi-threaded control flow is provided by abstracting the commonly used parallel computational patterns as **computational skeletons**. The control structures of parallel processes can then be organised as the composition of computational skeletons. For example, in SCL, the SPMD skeleton, defined as follows, is used to abstract the features of SPMD (Single Program Multiple Data) computation:

```
SPMD []              = id
SPMD (gf, lf) : fs   = (SPMD fs) ∘ (gf ∘ (imap lf ))
```

The skeleton takes a list of global–local operation pairs, which are applied over configurations of distributed data objects. The *local operations* are farmed to each processor and computed in parallel. Flat local operations, which contain no skeleton applications, can be regarded as *sequential*. The *global operations* over the whole configuration are parallel operations that require synchronisation and communication. Thus the composition of `gf` and `imap lf` abstracts a single stage of SPMD computation where the composition operator models the behaviour of *barrier synchronisation*. In SCL conventional control flow is also abstracted as computation skeletons. For example, the `iterUntil` skeleton, defined as follows, captures a common form of iteration. The condition `con` is checked before each iteration. The function `iterSolve` is applied at each iteration, while the function `finalSolve` is applied when the condition is satisfied.

```
iterUntil iterSolve finalSolve con x
    = if con x
      then finalSolve x
      else iterUntil iterSolve finalSolve con (iterSolve x)
```

Variants of `iterUntil` can be used. For example, when an iteration counter is used, an iteration can be captured by the skeleton `iterFor` using the counter to control the iteration.

By abstracting data distribution, communication and multi-thread control flow uniformly as basic skeletons, the SCL system supports the

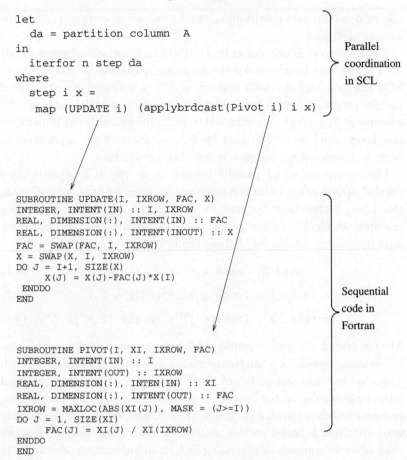

```
let
  da = partition column  A
in
  iterfor n step da
where
  step i x =
    map (UPDATE i) (applybrdcast(Pivot i) i x)
```

Parallel
coordination
in SCL

```
SUBROUTINE UPDATE(I, IXROW, FAC, X)
INTEGER, INTENT(IN) :: I, IXROW
REAL, DIMENSION(:), INTENT(IN) :: FAC
REAL, DIMENSION(:), INTENT(INOUT) :: X
FAC = SWAP(FAC, I, IXROW)
X = SWAP(X, I, IXROW)
DO J = I+1, SIZE(X)
    X(J) = X(J)-FAC(J)*X(I)
 ENDDO
END
```

```
SUBROUTINE PIVOT(I, XI, IXROW, FAC)
INTEGER, INTENT(IN) :: I
INTEGER, INTENT(OUT) :: IXROW
REAL, DIMENSION(:), INTEN(IN) :: XI
REAL, DIMENSION(:), INTENT(OUT) :: FAC
IXROW = MAXLOC(ABS(XI(J)), MASK = (J>=I))
DO J = 1, SIZE(XI)
    FAC(J) = XI(J) / XI(IXROW)
ENDDO
END
```

Sequential
code in
Fortran

Fig. 4.2. Parallel Gaussian Elimination Program

structured construction of parallel program by composing coordination skeletons using a set of well defined parallel data types. For example, a parallel Gaussian elimination program is presented in Figure 4.2 where SCL is used to define the parallel structure coordinating sequential program components written in Fortran 90.

4.3.2 Benefits of structured coordination

The ability to compose functional skeletons determines that the framework is inherently **extensible**. Other, higher-level, possibly application specific, parallel coordination mechanisms, such as ones specifying irregular or dynamic data partitioning, can be defined as compositions of the simpler skeletons.

The framework is also **generic**. Different imperative languages can be used as the base languages for the sequential components. For example, SCL can be combined with Fortran and C to produce two structured parallel programming systems. In principle, any sequential language, for example SQL, could be coordinated by SCL. Indeed, different imperative languages could be coordinated by SCL within a single application in order to provide a heterogeneous software architecture.

The expression of all parallel behaviour by the SCL layer enables parallel optimisation to be accomplished by program transformation on this layer, rather than by analysis of complex, imperative code. For example, an algebra of communication can be developed to optimising data movement. Examples of these algebraic laws are

$$\text{send f} \circ \text{send g} = \text{send (f} \circ \text{g)} \tag{4.1}$$

$$\text{fetch f} \circ \text{fetch g} = \text{fetch (g} \circ \text{f)} \tag{4.2}$$

$$(\text{rotate k}) \circ (\text{rotate j}) = \text{rotate (k + j)} \tag{4.3}$$

The use of such can lead to considerable improvements in the cost of communication, especially when communication can be completely removed. The algebraic axiomatisation of communication optimisation has been intensively studied in the context of developing an optimal compiler for conventional data parallel languages (Li & Chen, 1991). The commonly used approach is based on the analysis of index relations between two sides of an assignment. Since, using SCL, communications are explicitly specified in terms of a set of well defined communication operators, the index based analysis can be systematically replaced by transformation rules abstracting the optimisation of communication behaviour.

Moreover, as all parallel behaviour arises from the behaviour of known skeletons, they can be implemented by pre-defined libraries or code templates in the desired imperative language together with standard message passing libraries providing both efficiency and program portability.

As an exercise in developing a concrete SPP language we are designing a language, Fortran-S, to act as a front end for Fortran-based parallel programming. Conceptually, the language is designed by instantiating the base language in the SPP scheme with Fortran.

Fortran-S can be implemented by transforming Fortran-S programs into conventional parallel Fortran programs, that is sequential Fortran augmented with message passing libraries. Currently, we are building a

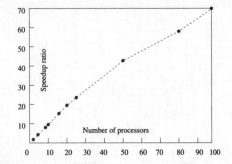

nprocs	time(sec)	speedup
1	521.41	1.0
4	133.22	3.9
8	66.11	7.9
10	52.73	9.9
16	32.88	15.9
20	26.55	19.6
25	21.46	24.3
50	12.31	42.3
80	8.95	58.2
100	7.44	70.1

Fig. 4.3. Parallel matrix multiplication: speedup

prototype system based on Fortran 77 plus MPI (MPI, 1993) targeted at a Fujitsu AP1000 machine (Ishihata *et al.*, 1991). The matrix multiplication example has been translated to Fortran 77 plus MPI on an AP1000. Due to the richness of information provided by the Fortran-S code, the performance data is very encouraging, as shown in Figure 4.3 for an array size of 400×400.

4.3.3 Parallel matrix multiplication: a case study

To investigate the expressive power of SCL, in this subsection we define the coordination structure of two parallel matrix multiplication algorithms using SCL. The two following matrix multiplication algorithms are adapted from Quinn (1994).

Row-Column-Oriented Parallel Matrix Multiplication

Consider the problem of multiplying matrices $A_{l \times m}$ and $B_{m \times n}$ and placing the result in $C_{l \times n}$ on p processors. Initially, A is divided into p groups of contiguous rows and B is divided into p groups of contiguous columns. Each processor starts with one segment of A and one segment of B. The overall algorithm structure is an SPMD computation iterated p times. At each step the local phase of the SPMD computation multiplies the segments of the two arrays located locally using a sequential matrix multiplication and then the global phase rotates the distribution B so that each processor passes its portion of B to its predecessor in the ring of processors. When the algorithm is complete each processor has computed a portion of the result array C corresponding to the rows of A that it holds. The computation is shown in the Figure 4.4.

The parallel structure of the algorithm is expressed in the following SCL program:

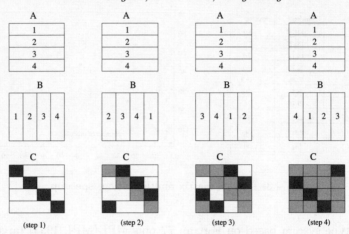

Fig. 4.4. Parallel matrix multiplication: row-column-oriented algorithm

```
ParMM ::  Int → SeqArray index Float →
          SeqArray index Float → SeqArray index Float
ParMM p A B = gather DC
  where
    <DA, DB, DC> = iterFor p step dist
    dist = distribution fl dl
    fl = [(row_block p, id), (col_block p, id), (row_block p, id)]
    dl = [A, B, C]
    C = SeqArray ((1,SIZE(A,1)), (1, SIZE(B,2)))
        [ (i,j) := 0 | i ← [1..SIZE(A,1)], j ← [1..SIZE(B,2)] ]

step i <DA, DB, DC> =
    SPMD [(gf, SEQ_MM i)] <DA, DB, DC>
    where
        newDist = [id, (rotate 1), id]
        gf X = redistribution newDist <DA, DB, X>
```

where SEQ_MM is a sequential procedure for matrix multiplication. Data distribution is specified by the distribution skeleton with the partition strategies of [((row_block p), id), ((col_block p),id), ((row_block p),id)] for A, B and C respectively. The data redistribution of B is performed by using the rotate operator which is encapsulated in the redistribution skeleton. The example shows that, by applying SCL skeletons, parallel coordination structure of the algorithm is precisely specified at a higher level.

Block-Oriented Parallel Matrix Multiplication

This time we wish to multiply an l × m matrix A by an m × n matrix B on

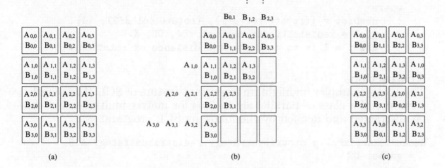

Fig. 4.5. Block-oriented algorithm

a $p \times p$ processor mesh with wraparound connections. Assume that l, m and n are integer multiples of p and p is an even power of 2. Initially both A and B are partitioned into mesh of blocks and each processor takes a $(l/p) \times (m/p)$ subsection of A and an $(m/p) \times (n/p)$ subsection of B (Figure 4.5(a)). The parallel algorithm staggers each block at row i of A to the left by i block column positions, and each block column i of B upwards by i block row positions (Figure 4.5(b)) and the data is wrapped around (Figure 4.5(c)). The overall algorithm structure is also an SPMD computation iterated p times. At each step the local phase of the SPMD computation multiplies the pair of blocks located locally using a sequential matrix multiplication program and then the global phase moves the data: each processor passes its portion of A to its left neighbour and passes its portion of B to its upper neighbour. The SCL code for this algorithm is shown below:

```
matrixMul :: Int → SeqArray index Float →
             SeqArray index Float → SeqArray index Float
matrixMul p A B = gather DC
  where
    <DA, DB, DC> = iterFor p step dist
    dist = distribution fl dl
    fl =[((row_col_block p p), (rotate_row df1)),
        ((row_col_block p p), (rotate_col df1)),
        ((row_col_block p p), id)]
    dl = [A, B, C]
    C = SeqArray ((1,SIZE(A,1)), (1, SIZE(B,2))
       [ (i,j) := 0 | i ← [1..SIZE(A,1)], j ← [1..SIZE(B,2)] ]
    df1 i = i (* to indicate the distance of rotation *)

step i <DA, DB, DC> =
    SPMD [(gf, SEQ_MM 0)] <DA, DB, DC>
```

```
where
    newDist = [(rotate_row df2), (rotate_col df2), id]
    gf X = redistribution newDist <DA, DB, X>
    df2 i = 1 (* to indicate the distance of rotation *)
```

Abstraction

The above examples highlight an important feature of SCL. The parallel structure of a class of parallel algorithms for matrix multiplication can be abstracted and defined by the following SCL program:

```
Generic_matrixMul p distribustrategy redistribustrategy A B
  = gather DC
  where
    <DA, DB, DC> = iterFor p step dist
    dist = distribution distribustrategy [A, B, C]
    C = SeqArray ((1,SIZE(A,1)), (1, SIZE(B,2)))
        [ (i,j) := 0 | i ← [1..SIZE(A,1)], j ← [1..SIZE(B,2)] ]

step i <DA, DB, DC> =
    SPMD [(gf, SEQ_MM i)] <DA, DB, DC>
    where
        gf X = redistribution redistribustrategy <DA, DB, X>
```

Thus, the row-column-oriented and the block-oriented parallel matrix multiplication programs become instances of the generic parallel matrix multiplication code by instantiating the corresponding distribution and redistribution strategies. That is, the SCL code for generic parallel matrix multiplication defines an *algorithmic skeleton* for parallel matrix multiplication. This example shows how an application-oriented parallel computation structure could be systematically defined.

4.4 Conclusion

20 years of research devoted to parallel programming have greatly enriched the state of the art on the research on parallel programming systems. However, there is still no single model which abstracts all parallel architectures uniformly, resulting in a loss of control over certain important aspects of the behaviour of parallel programs. We contend that the necessary breakthrough will rely on the development of a uniform mechanism for specifying, reasoning and optimising parallel control. In this article we have introduced a structured parallel programming framework, SPP(X), by adopting the use of high-level functional abstractions of all relevant aspects of parallel behaviour. The techniques embodied is our approach can be seen as a synthesis and extension of the ideas embodied in several alternative approaches to parallel programming, data

parallel languages (Sipelstein & Blelloch, 1991), the coordination notation (Gelernter & Carriero, 1992) and skeletons (Darlington & To, 1993). Again we contend that it is the power of functional languages that enables these approaches to be generalised and unified. With this functional abstraction of parallel behaviour, transformations can be applied to optimise all parts of a program's behaviour, data distribution and movement as well as computation, safe in the knowledge that such optimisations are mathematically rigorous.

Moreover, SCL provides a complete interface between the application specialist and the conventional platforms provided by the imperative languages and run-time support systems. This interface inherits all the desirable properties of the functional languages and can be as wide as desired as long as sufficiently powerful transformations are available to map the higher-level constructs down to the lower-level, kernel, computational patterns. It thus satisfies our criteria of being compatible with conventional approaches and since it is incrementable, we can build more and more functionality into this layer as desired.

The approach is explicitly designed to be applied to existing conventional languages and to generate code in standard imperative languages and run-time libraries that are implemented on a wide range of platforms. The work therefore satisfies our twin requirements of being compatible with conventional approaches while greatly enhancing the capabilities that could be made available to application developers in the area of parallel programming. We believe that all the advantages of the functional approach have been retained but packaged in a way that is totally compatible with general practice. We put this forward as a successful example of what can be achieved if a conscious effort is made to translate the, undoubted, advantages of the formally based approaches into realistic contexts.

5

Computer Science and Mathematics

J.H. Davenport

Abstract

Computer science and mathematics are closely related subjects, and over the last fifty years, each has fed off the other. Mathematicians have used computers to prove (or disprove) traditional results of mathematics, computer scientists have used more and more advanced mathematics in their work, and new areas of mathematics have been inspired by questions thrown up by computing.

5.1 Introduction

The academic subjects of mathematics and computer science, the oldest science and one of the newest, are closely related. This article considers the various ways in which they interact, and each influences the development of the other.

It is worth noting that we do *not* consider here the influence of computer technology (and the associated communications revolution) on the infrastructure and sociology of mathematics. Developments such as

- CD-ROM publication (particularly of *Mathematical Reviews*),
- electronic databases (again one thinks of *Mathematical Reviews*, but also of the *Science Citation Index*, which, even in its paper form, could not be compiled without computers),
- electronic manuscripts and camera-ready copy,
- ftp preprint systems and
- electronic mail

have changed, and will continue to change, the way in which mathematicians consider, and add to, their literature, but this is not *specific* to mathematics, even though mathematicians have often been in the vanguard of such movements, presumably because of their general use of computers.

5.2 The Influence of Computers on Mathematics

Mathematicians have always numbered prodigious calculators among their kind, be they numerical calculators or symbolic ones (Delaunay's lunar theory (1860) contained a 120-page formula). Hence it is not surprising that the digital computer soon interested some pure mathematicians. With its help, they could perform far larger calculations than before, and investigate phenomena that were inaccessible to human computation. Computations in group theory were among the first examples of pure mathematics to be done on computers (Haselgrove, 1953)†. Today the computer can be a valuable help to many mathematicians, particularly those working in algebra or number theory, to produce well-tested conjectures. An excellent set of examples is given by Churchhouse (1988).

One of the first areas of pure mathematics to be revolutionized by computer-produced calculations was algebraic geometry: more particularly the theory of elliptic curves, where Birch & Swinnerton-Dyer (1963) used EDSAC 2 to compute the group of rational points on many elliptic curves. This evidence led them to formulate the 'Birch–Swinnerton-Dyer conjectures', relating the group of rational points on an elliptic curve E with the behaviour of the corresponding ζ-function near 1.

Since then many other areas of mathematics have benefited from the ability of the computer to perform larger and larger, but always finite, computations. Most of these areas could be loosely described as 'algebra', but there has also been large-scale use of computing in the theory of dynamical systems, for example. In general, this use of computers leads to the observation of patterns of behaviour, and hence, as in the Birch & Swinnerton-Dyer case, to a conjecture about a pattern applying to an infinite number of cases.

Occasionally, the computation may complete a proof. The most prominent example of this is the proof of the Four-Colour Theorem by Appel & Haken (1977a)‡, where 1200 hours of CPU time were used to show that every map contains at least one of 1482 configurations (i.e. that this set of configurations is unavoidable), and that every one of these is

---

† Leech (1963) comments, 'pressure on space was severe, and it was possible to do no more than exhibit that the method was feasible for automatic computations', but shortly thereafter genuinely new computations were being performed on computers.

‡ Appel & Haken (1977b) provides a readable introduction to this proof.

in fact a reducible configuration, i.e. if it exists in a map that cannot be four-coloured, then there is a smaller map that cannot be four-coloured. This implies that the configuration cannot exist in a minimal map which is not four-colourable, and, since these configurations are unavoidable, that a minimal counter-example cannot exist, i.e. all maps are four-colourable. Since much of the book-keeping was done by hand†, there were several mistakes, mostly minor. A more serious one was found by Schmidt (1982), but this was comparatively easily repaired. The robustness of the entire proof is discussed by Appel & Haken (1986).

There are also several examples where an analytic method solves the theorem for 'sufficiently large' cases, and a finite number of smaller cases remain to be checked. For example, Erdös' (1932) proof of Bertrand's postulate, that there is always a prime number between N and $2N$, works for all $N > 468$, leaving the smaller values to be checked by hand. Fortunately, a computer is not needed in this case.

Very often, computer calculations may disprove a conjecture. This happens very often, and without comment in the literature, in the early days of an investigation: an idea is formed, the mathematician thinks 'I'll try a few more computations', and the idea is demonstrated to be false, or to require sufficient amendment to become a new idea, which may itself be further tested, and so on. A more serious example of this is provided by Haselgrove (1958) who disproved a conjecture of Pólya (that for all $x \geq 2$, the number of natural numbers less than x with an odd number of prime factors is not less than the number of such numbers with an even number of prime factors), indirectly‡ showing that the conjecture is false, and a counter-example is likely around $1.845 \cdot 10^{361}$.

---

† A consequence of the 'batch' method of working employed at the time.

‡ Computation can often be used for indirect proofs of this nature. For example, the number

$$R = 2270104812954373633342599609474936688958753364660847800381732582470091626757797353897911515174049166747880487470296548479$$

is 'obviously' not prime, since in 0.37 seconds we can compute that $3^{R-1} \not\equiv 1 \bmod R$, which contradicts Fermat's Little Theorem that $x^{p-1} \equiv 1 \bmod p$ for all primes p if $x \not\equiv 0$. Actually finding the factors of R, i.e. a direct proof that R is not prime, took approximately 830 mips-years, and set a new record in June 1993 for general-purpose factoring (Lenstra, 1993). R was proposed as an example of the RSA public-key cryptographic scheme – see page 79.

These factorizations are amongst the most impressive achievements of parallel computation to date, uniting thousands of machines of different kinds to perform the 'sieving' stage of the computation, then using massively parallel SIMD machines, often with 16 384 processors, to perform the data reduction.

The most spectacular instance of a computer-assisted disproof of a conjecture is the Odlyzko & te Riele (1985) disproof of the Mertens (1897)† conjecture, that if $\mu(n)$ is $(-1)^k$ if n is the product of k distinct primes, and 0 otherwise, then $|M(N)| = |\sum_{n=1}^{N} \mu(n)| \leq \sqrt{N}$ for $N > 1$. A stronger version of the conjecture, that $|M(N)| < \sqrt{N}/2$ for $N > 200$, had been made by von Sternack (1897, 1913), but this had been disproved indirectly by Jurkat (1961, 1973), and directly by Neubauer (1963), who showed that $N = 7.76 \cdot 10^9$ was a counter-example. Experimental work by Good & Churchhouse (1968) had suggested that the Möbius function $\mu(n)$ was behaving like a pseudo-random variable, taking values of ± 1 with probability $3/\pi^2$ each, and 0 the rest of the time. If $\mu(n)$ were truly random, we could apply the central limit theorem, which would imply that

$$\limsup_{N \to \infty} \frac{M(N)}{\sqrt{N \log \log N}} = \frac{\sqrt{12}}{\pi},$$

which would in turn imply the ultimate (after $\sqrt{\log \log N}$ became large enough) falsity of the Mertens conjecture, and the truth of the Riemann hypothesis. The truth of the Mertens conjecture implies the existence of integer relationships among the various γ_i‡. Odlyzko & te Riele therefore computed the first 2000 γ_i to 100 decimal places, using 40 hours of CDC Cyber 750 time. They then looked for integer relationships among the γ_i, using the recently discovered algorithm for finding short vectors in integer lattices (Lenstra *et al.*, 1982): a process which consumed 10 Cray-1 hours. Odlyzko & te Riele remark

Our disproof of the Mertens conjecture is not due to advances in computer technology (since we used much less computer time than was used by te Riele in the earlier work), but to a major breakthrough in diophantine approximation methods ...

It should be noted that the Odlyzko & te Riele method is also indirect, in that it shows that the Mertens conjecture is false, without exhibiting any particular N for which it is false. Indeed, their calculations show that there is an N with $M(N) > 1.06\sqrt{N}$, and an N with $M(N) < -1.009\sqrt{N}$, even though all N for which $M(N)$ has been computed

---

† However this conjecture really goes back to Steltjes (1885), who also claimed to have a proof.

‡ As is traditional, we let $\zeta(s) = \sum_{i=1}^{\infty} 1/i^s$ or its analytic continuation, and let $\rho_j = \sigma_j + i\gamma_j$ denote the j-th complex zero of ζ. The Riemann hypothesis is then that all $\sigma_j = 1/2$.

satisfy $|M(N)| < 0.6\sqrt{N}$. It seems plausible that the first counter-examples to the Mertens conjecture are around 10^{30}.

None of these examples has changed the nature of mathematics. The computer has been used to increase the power of the mathematician, but that power has been deployed in the same way as before. Despite a sensational[†] article claiming the contrary (Horgan, 1993), this has been the major impact of computers on mathematics, as an aid to the mathematician, whose job has not fundamentally changed, merely been made easier (for a given example: more realistically, the mathematician can now tackle larger problems for a given effort).

5.3 Effectivity in Mathematics

Mathematicians traditionally asked questions of the form 'does x exist?' Of course, one way to prove that x exists is to construct it, but there are other ways, notably a proof by contradiction or the indirect methods discussed above for the existence of factors of R, or of counter-examples to the Pólya and Mertens conjectures. Having shown that x exists, one can then ask whether the existence is *effective*: that is, is there a method for constructing x?

A classic example is that the greatest common divisor of two numbers exists (since $\mathbf{Z}$ is a unique factorization domain), and Euclid's algorithm can be used to construct it, so the existence is effective. The same is true for the greatest common divisor of two univariate polynomials over an effective field, since the ring of polynomials is a unique factorization domain, and Euclid's algorithm can be applied. Conversely, whilst it is not too difficult to prove that such polynomials are the product of irreducibles, it is much harder to find this decomposition effectively, since the naïve technique used for the integers, start at 2 and work up, does not work since there are potentially infinitely many polynomials of a fixed degree (greater than 1) which might divide a given one, and the programmer needs some bounds on the coefficient size as well as the degree. We make some observations on the complexity of this problem on page 81 *et seq.*

The explicit recognition of effectivity as a question can be traced back[‡] to the start of this century or even earlier, when Russell's destruction of Frege's theory forced mathematicians to look at the foundations of their subject. Brouwer (1907) was led to formulate intuitionism, and other

---

† The article asks 'was the proof of Fermat's last theorem the last gasp of a dying culture?' and describes Wiles under the heading 'A Splendid Anachronism?'

‡ A more detailed history can be found in Curry (1963, pp. 8–16).

workers, notably of the German school, tried to determine whether their theorems and methods were *constructive*, or *effective*, in the sense that the answer could be obtained in a finite number of steps. The following example (Heyting, 1956, pp. 1–2) illustrates the point. Consider the following two definitions.

(i) p is the greatest prime such that $p - 1$ is also prime, or $p = 1$ if such a number does not exist.

(ii) q is the greatest prime such that $q - 2$ is also prime, or $q = 1$ if such a number does not exist.

It is clear that (i) defines a unique number, viz. $p = 3$. On the other hand, there is no known way to compute q. The key intellectual debate then breaks out over statements like the following:

(iii) If $q = 1$ then A is true else A is true.

The intuitionist would say that the truth of A has not been determined, whereas the conventional mathematician would say that A was true, but its truth was not effective. The problem becomes more relevant to the computer scientist when we consider the statement

(iv) If $q = 1$ then A is $f(\ldots)$ else A is $g(\ldots)$.

One has to agree that A cannot be effectively computed until we can determine the value of q, i.e. solve the 'twin primes' conjecture. Using the theory of recursively enumerable but non-recursive sets, we can replace dependence on a conjecture by formal uncomputability in this setting. Many mathematicians, be they intuitionists or not, have therefore tried to decide what items can be effectively computed: Hermann (1926) was one of the early pioneers, early results were codified by van der Waerden (1930a), and Mines *et al.* (1988) describe the recent state of the art. It is worth noting that the same movement gave rise to much work that is now regarded as fundamental computer science, but was created as mathematical logic: the names of Church, Gödel, Post and Turing spring to mind.

The existence of computers has given a new lease of life to studies of effectivity: particularly as we move from classical algebra 'x exists' to computer algebra 'x can be computed', or, more accurately, 'x can be computed, and here is a completely explicit algorithm for doing so'. This is particularly evident in the domain of polynomial factorization†, but the same problems can occur elsewhere (Davenport & Trager, 1990) discuss the problem of unique representation of fractions). We remind the reader that a unit is an element that divides 1 (so that 1 and −1 are the only units in **Z**, whereas in **Q** every non-zero element is a unit), a prime is a non-unit that cannot be represented as the product of two non-units, and that in a unique factorization domain, every element has a unique representation as a product of primes, up to order and multiplication by units. The classical statement

(v) If K is a unique factorization domain, then so is $K[x]$

is true, but its computational equivalent

(vi) If factorizations can be computed in K, then they can be computed in $K[x]$

is false. In fact, quite a lot has to be known about K, particularly if it is of finite characteristic‡, before factorizations can be computed in $K[x]$.

The problem of effectivity in calculus, by which we mean the manipulation of formulae by differentiation, (indefinite) integration etc., is an interesting one. Differentiation is inherently an effective process: one applies the sum, product and chain rules. Integration is a very different matter: the problem 'given a formula f, find a formula g such that $\int f = g$' is essentially the problem 'find g such that $g' = f$'. While f is a given formula, there is no obvious limitation on the class of formulae in which to search for g. Indeed, until we have defined what class of formulae is acceptable, the question is meaningless, since we can always solve the traditionally insoluble $\int e^{-x^2}$ by defining the function erf via

$$\mathrm{erf}(x) = \int_0^x \sqrt{\frac{2}{\pi}} e^{-y^2} \mathrm{d}y,$$

and then writing $\int e^{-x^2} = \sqrt{\pi/2}\,\mathrm{erf}\,x$.

These questions were first addressed by Liouville (1835), who proved a

---

† The original examples are due to van der Waerden (1930b) and Fröhlich & Shepherdson (1956). There is a presentation from the point of view of computer algebra by Davenport *et al.* (1991)

‡ Seidenberg (1974) introduced 'Condition P', which roughly speaking amounts to the ability to compute p-th roots in a field of characteristic p. This is necessary to distinguish the irreducible polynomial $x^p + y$ from the perfect p-th power $x^p + 1$.

result now known as Liouville's Principle, that, for elementary† formulae g, roughly those generated by exponentials, logarithms and the solution of algebraic equations, it was only necessary to look for g of the form

$$g = g_0 + \sum_{i=1}^{n} c_i \log g_i,$$

where g_0 lies in the same field as f (call it L), the c_i are algebraic constants, and the g_i lie in $L(c_i \ldots, c_n)$.

Of course, there are still an infinite number of possible g in this class, but the class is much more restricted than might have been thought. Based on this theorem, various quasi-algorithmic procedures for integration were developed during the 19th century, but these were essentially too complicated for human use, and also somewhat limited in their scope. Indeed, the prevailing view was given by Hardy (1916, pp. 47–48) (in this context, 'pseudo-elliptic' means 'elementary'):

No method has been devised whereby we can always determine in a finite number of steps whether a given elliptic integral is pseudo-elliptic, and integrate it if it is, and there is reason to suppose that no such method can be given.

The impact of computer algebra systems led to a desire to integrate. The first methods were essentially heuristic, emulating human processes (Slagle, 1961), but soon the emphasis passed to algorithmic methods. The first major break-through was made by Risch (1969), who produced an algorithm for integrating purely transcendental elementary functions (i.e. those in which no root of an algebraic equation is used, either explicitly or via identities such as $\sqrt{x} = \exp\left(\frac{1}{2}\log x\right)$). Davenport (1981) solved Hardy's problem, and Bronstein (1990) solved the general problem of finding elementary integrals for arbitrary elementary functions. Modern research focuses on more efficient algorithms, possibly producing more 'natural' results (either shorter, or with fewer branch cuts), or on extensions of the idea of 'elementary' to allow error functions, exponential integrals, dilogarithms or other special functions.

† If K is a field of functions, the function θ is *an elementary generator* over K if:

  (i) θ is algebraic over K, i.e. θ satisfies a polynomial with coefficients in K; **or**
  (ii) θ is an *exponential* over K, i.e. there is an η in K such that $\theta' = \eta'\theta$, which is only an algebraic way of saying that $\theta = \exp\eta$; **or**
  (iii) θ is a *logarithm* over K, i.e. there is an η in K such that $\theta' = \eta'/\eta$, which is only an algebraic way of saying that $\theta = \log\eta$.

An overfield $K(\theta_1, \ldots, \theta_n)$ of K is called a *field of elementary functions over K* if every θ_i is an elementary generator over K. A function is *elementary over K* if it belongs to a field of elementary functions over K.

From integration it is a short step to consider the solution of ordinary differential equations. Here too there has been much algorithmic progress, especially in the case of linear differential equations. An effective algorithm exists for deciding if a second-order linear differential equation has elementary or Liouvillian† solutions. In principle the same can be done for n^{th}-order linear differential equations, though the complexity rises steeply with n‡. It is also possible to tell if a linear differential equation has solutions that can be expressed in terms of the solutions of second-order linear differential equations such as Bessel functions. However, these methods tend to be fairly slow, and do not extend to non-linear equations, so the solution of differential equations tends to be a mixture of the algorithmic and the heuristic (often involving mathematically sophisticated methods, such as Lie symmetry for non-linear equations with $n > 1$). The situation is rapidly changing: a good survey is given by Singer (1990).

5.4 The Impact of Computer Science on Mathematics

Computer science has had a significant impact on several areas of mathematics, notably in the area of algebra (including number theory, set theory, logic etc.). As described above, computer algebra has sharpened the interest in effective computation: Mines *et al.* (1988, p. vi) state

The computers created a widespread awareness of the intuitive notion of an effective procedure, and of computation in principle, in addition to stimulating the study of constructive algebra for actual implementation, and from the point of view of recursive function theory.

The requirements of writing a program to find a solution prompt investigation into *efficient*, rather than just *effective*, methods of solving many problems. The abstract question of how efficient these methods are, or can possibly be, leads to the area of complexity theory, to be discussed later.

We have already seen how the lattice reduction algorithm of Lenstra *et al.* (1982) has been used in disproving the Mertens conjecture. It has many other implications, some of great practical importance, others more theoretical. Its impact on polynomial factorization is discussed in the next section.

---

† 'Liouvillian' extends the idea of 'elementary' by allowing arbitrary integrals to be used in the construction of functions, rather than just $\log \eta$, which can be viewed as $\int \eta'/\eta$. Liouvillian functions are therefore the solution of algebraic, or first-order linear differential, equations.

‡ Singer & Ulmer (1993) have significantly improved the case $n = 3$, and there is much work in progress in this area.

The Buchberger (1970) algorithm is an interesting example of the evolution of an effective, and then an efficient, idea. From the algebraic point of view, a set of m polynomials $f_1, \ldots, f_m$ in n variables over a field k define an *ideal* $(f_1, \ldots, f_m)$: the set of all polynomials which can be obtained by multiplying the f_i by polynomials and adding the results, i.e.

$$(f_1, \ldots, f_m) = \left\{ \sum_{i=1}^{m} g_i f_i : g_i \in k[x_1, \ldots, x_n] \right\}, \tag{5.1}$$

when we say that the f_i *generate* the ideal.

Equally, one can look at the situation geometrically: the polynomials then define a *variety* over k (or its algebraic closure) defined by the points where all the f_i are zero:

$$\begin{aligned} V(f_1, \ldots, f_m) \;=\; \{(x_1, \ldots, x_n) \in k^n : \\ f_1(x_1, \ldots, x_n) = \cdots = f_m(x_1 \ldots, x_n) = 0\}. \end{aligned}$$

The variety or ideal may not be evident from the original f_i provided: in particular the ideal may be the whole polynomial ring (in which case the variety is empty, and the polynomials are inconsistent), or zero-dimensional (in which case the variety consists of a finite set of points) or have non-zero dimension (in which case the variety contains some lines, or surfaces or ...). 30 years ago, it was far from clear that questions such as 'what is the dimension of this ideal' or 'are these two ideals equal' could be effectively solved.

Buchberger's algorithm transforms the initial set of polynomials into another set, a *Gröbner base*, which generate the same ideal as the original set, but which have the property that every element of the ideal can be expressed in the form (5.1) *without cancellation of leading terms*. For example, if we take the equations

$$\left\{ g_1 = x^3 y z - x z^2, g_2 = x y^2 z - x y z, g_3 = x^2 y^2 - z \right\},$$

it is far from obvious what variety they define. The corresponding (computed with respect to the purely lexicographical order $x > y > z$) Gröbner base, though, is

$$\left\{ x^2 y^2 - z, x^2 y z - z^2, x^2 z^2 - z^3, x y^2 z - x y z, y z^2 - z^2 \right\}$$

and from the last of these polynomials it is obvious that either $z = 0$ or $y = 1$. If $z = 0$, then the Gröbner base reduces to $\left\{ x^2 y^2, z \right\}$, i.e. either $x = 0$ or $y = 0$, so this component of the variety reduces to the two lines $x = z = 0$ and $y = z = 0$. If $y = 1$, then the Gröbner base reduces to $\{x^2 - z, y - 1\}$, so this component reduces to the parabola $x^2 = z, y = 1$. If we choose a different order $(z > y > x)$, the same result is more obvious: the Gröbner base is now

$$\{z - x^2 y^2, x^3 y^4 - x^3 y^3\}.$$

The answer becomes even clearer if we ask an algebra system to factorize the polynomials for us, thus performing a partial decomposition of the variety. In Axiom (Jenks & Sutor, 1992) we could say the following:

```
(1)-> groebnerFactorize [x**3*y*z-x*z**2,_
                         x*y*y*z-x*y*z,x*x*y*y-z]
                    2
  (1)   [[1],[z,y],[z - x ,y - 1],[z,x]]
                    Type: List List Polynomial Integer
```

which shows that, apart from the 'component at infinity' $1 = 0$, there are three components: $z = y = 0$, $\begin{cases} z = x^2 \\ y = 1 \end{cases}$, $z = x = 0$. Gröbner bases can be used for solving systems of polynomial equations, proving theorems of Euclidean geometry (see page 85), and many other tasks: see the survey of Buchberger (1985).

The original version of Buchberger's algorithm can be written as follows:

Input $B = \{g_1, \ldots, g_k\}$; B is the basis of an ideal I;
Output $G = \{g_1, \ldots, g_n\}$; G is a Gröbner base of the same ideal;
$n := k$
$G := B$
$P := \{(i,j) : 1 \leq i < j \leq k\}$;
             P is a set of pairs of integers
while P is non-empty
      do Choose $(i,j) \in P$;
           $Q := S(g_i, g_j)$;
           $P := P \setminus \{(i,j)\}$;
           Reduce Q with respect to G;
           if $Q \neq 0$ **then** $(*)$
                 $P := P \cup \{(i, n+1) : 1 \leq i \leq n\}$;
                 $g_{n+1} := Q$;
                 $G := G \cup \{Q\}$;
                 $n := n + 1$;
return G;

where $S(f, g)$, the S-polynomial of f and g, is defined by letting f_l and g_l be the leading terms of f and g, letting h be the l.c.m. of f_l and g_l, and defining

$$S(f, g) = \frac{h}{f_l} f - \frac{h}{g_l} g,$$

i.e. the minimal linear combination of f and g such that the leading terms cancel; and the 'Reduce' operation subtracts multiples of polynomials in G from Q so as to remove from Q any term which is, or is a multiple of, the leading term of any element of G.

One could ask why this is an algorithm, i.e. why it terminates. When the algorithm originally appeared, termination was guaranteed by the Hilbert Basis Theorem, which guaranteed that step ($*$) could only be executed finitely often, and hence that the whole algorithm was finite. However, the Hilbert Basis Theorem did not bound the number of times the step could be executed, and hence termination, while guaranteed, was not effective. Since then, effective versions of the Hilbert Basis Theorem have appeared, stimulated by the requirements of computer algebra, so that termination is now effective, even if not always efficient.

Since this original algorithm appeared, many improvements have been, and continue to be, made. One major area of improvement is that of reducing the number of S-polynomials to calculate. This was addressed by Buchberger (1979) who showed that, if $S(f, g)$ and $S(g, h)$ have both been calculated, and if the leading term of g divides the l.c.m. of the leading terms of f and h, then it is not necessary to compute $S(f, h)$. This has been generalized into a far more powerful test by Backelin (unpublished).

Another area of improvement has concentrated on the question of how the polynomials are ordered, in particular which term in a polynomial is the 'leading term'. For example, in $x + y^2$, do we consider x to be the leading term because x comes before y (assuming that we are using alphabetical order on the variables) – a *purely lexicographical* ordering, or do we say that y^2 is the leading term because it has total degree 2 and x has total degree 1 – a *total degree* ordering? Assuming that we have chosen a total degree ordering, there may be many terms of the same total degree: which of them is the leading one? Here we have a choice between lexicographical and reverse lexicographical ordering. As we have seen above, the choice of ordering affects the Gröbner base that is produced, but the information derivable from the Gröbner base in terms of dimension etc. is the same. While results for individual problems can vary widely, it seems that total degree orderings are nearly always better than purely lexicographical orderings, and that, within total degree orderings, reverse lexicographical ones are better than lexicographical ones.

There is one piece of information that is much easier to obtain from a purely lexicographical ordering than from a total degree one, and that is the numerical expression of the variety, assuming that it is zero-dimensional, i.e. consists of a finite number of points. Faugère *et al.* (1993) have produced an algorithm that converts a total degree Gröbner base of a zero-dimensional ideal into a purely lexicographical one, so that the method of choice for finding the solutions consists of computing a total degree Gröbner base first, then converting it into a purely lexicographical one, then reading off the solutions. As an example of the progress that has been made in computing with Gröbner bases, consider the following problem: the *cyclic n-th roots problem*,

$$a_1 + a_2 + \cdots + a_n = 0$$
$$a_1a_2 + a_2a_3 + \cdots + a_{n-1}a_n + a_na_1 = 0$$
$$\vdots \qquad \vdots \quad \vdots$$
$$a_1 \ldots a_{n-1} + a_2 \ldots a_n + a_3 \ldots a_na_1 + \cdots + a_na_1 \ldots a_{n-2} = 0$$
$$a_1 \ldots a_n = 1.$$

In 1986, it had been demonstrated that, for $n = 4$, the corresponding variety was not zero-dimensional. The author succeeding in demonstrating that, for $n = 5$, the variety was zero-dimensional, and had 105 solutions. Recent progress has advanced to $n = 7$, where the variety has 924 solutions (Backelin & Fröberg, 1991). Advancing from 4 to 7 may not seem much until the reader understands that the complexity is exponential in the number of variables, but such is the case (for zero-dimensional systems). The extra computation has provided insight, and it has now been proved that the variety is zero-dimensional if, and only if, n has no repeated factors, so the next case to tackle is that of $n = 10$, which is probably a long way off.

Research into public-key cryptography has been responsible for increasing interest† in efficient methods in number theory. Indeed, whereas Hardy (1940) could claim 'very little of mathematics is useful practically,

---

† A process described by H.W. Lenstra Jr as 'The discovery of oil in the garden of number theory' (1990 MSRI lectures, unpublished).

and that little is comparatively dull' (p. 89), and state that 'the 'real' mathematics of the 'real' mathematicians, the mathematics of Fermat and Euler and Gauss and Abel and Riemann, is almost wholly 'useless'' (p. 119), this is certainly no longer the case†. Public-key cryptography concentrates on mathematical computations which are easy to compute, but difficult to invert.

The RSA scheme (Rivest *et al.*, 1978) relies on the public key being a pair (N, e), and the secret key being some number d such that $(x^e)^d \equiv x \bmod N$ for 'almost all' x. N is chosen to be the product of two large primes $N = pq$, e is relatively prime to $\phi(N)$, and d is such that $de \equiv 1 \bmod \phi(N) = (p-1)(q-1)$: 'almost all x' then means 'all x relatively prime to N'. Computation of d from e and N is equivalent to the factorization of N, which is currently a very time-consuming process for large N – see the second footnote on page 68. Modern methods of factoring rely on quite sophisticated number theory, such as:

- the distribution of numbers with factors of certain sizes, as used in the MPQS and PPMPQS methods (Caron & Silverman, 1988; Pomerance, 1985; Silverman, 1987);
- the properties of algebraic number fields (Lenstra & Lenstra, 1993);
- the properties of elliptic curves (Lenstra, 1987; McKee, 1994).

5.5 Complexity Theory

Complexity theory deals with the question 'how fast can we do this computation?' Since technology is rapidly changing, it makes no sense to record statements such as 'this takes 5 seconds' as absolute theorems, but rather to record results such as 'the time taken to sort n objects is $O(n \log n)$'. We are no longer considering one problem, but rather a family of similar problems related by a size parameter n, and ask how the time taken, generally on some abstract model of real computers, varies as a function of n. There are then two different questions:

- **upper bounds**: produce an algorithm that solves the problem in time $O(F(n))$;

---

† This is not to say that one should regard such mathematics as only, or even partially, justified by its utility. The justification for mathematical research is that stated by Hardy: its permanent aesthetic value. It may well have utility, but that may not become apparent for many years, and should not be the criterion for judging it *as mathematics*. Just as certain studies of partial differential equations are justified as being part of electrical engineering, so certain studies in combinatorics or number theory can be justified as part of information engineering, and at that point, questions of utility are very relevant.

- **lower bounds**: show that any algorithm to solve the problem must take time at least $\Theta(f(n))$.

Both are interesting problems, though the techniques required are generally different. An upper bound is generally inferred from a particular algorithm, and this algorithm may, or may not, be of use in practice, and this utility may change with changes in the underlying technology, because larger problems can now be tackled, and the ultimate superiority of a method which takes time $100n^2$, over one which takes time n^3, comes when $n = 100$, which at any given moment in the evolution of computing may or may not represent a feasible computation. Lower bounds are not of such direct practical interest, but they may well prevent futile searches for algorithms which cannot exist, such as a sorting algorithm which requires only $O(n)$ comparisons to sort n objects.

Complexity theory has made major contributions to practical computing: sorting in $O(n \log n)$ operations, the Fast Fourier Transform and its applications, such as fast multiplication of large integers, the concept of complexity classes and the $P = NP$ question, and so forth. Nevertheless, complexity theory answers questions about what to do when n is 'large enough', and not all practical problems fall into this class, though more do than some cynics think†. Like any mathematical tool, its application has to be made with common sense. D.E. Knuth is reported as saying that 'computer science is that area of mathematics where $\log \log n = 3$', presumably meaning that when $\log \log n = 2$, the problem is small enough that a non-optimal algorithm can solve it, but when $\log \log n \geq 4$, the problem is intractable, and not even the optimal algorithm can made any real headway. However, this analysis applies to low-complexity algorithms, where the difference between $n \log n$ and $n \log^2 n$ can be vital, and not to problems like Gröbner bases, where the complexity can be doubly exponential.

One area which illustrates the pitfalls of using complexity theory as a guide to the algorithms to use in practice is that of polynomial factorization. The usual method of polynomial factorization can be viewed as follows, where for simplicity we consider univariate polynomials with integer coefficients, and only worry about the dependence on n, the degree of the polynomial to be factored.

---

† For example, it is possible to multiply n-word integers in $O(n^{\log_2 3} \approx n^{1.58})$ multiplications, and this can be more effective even when $n = 2$ (Juffa, 1994), contradicting the popular view that this method is only effective for 1000 bits or more.

(i) Ensure that the polynomial f is square-free (by taking the greatest common divisor of f and df/dx).

(ii) Pick a prime p (in practice, several p will be chosen, and the one which gives the fewest factors used) such that f remains square-free modulo p.

(iii) Factorize f modulo p.

(iv) Lift this to a factorization modulo an appropriate power p^k, by use of Hensel's Lemma.

(v) Combine the factors thus found to obtain the true factors over the integers.

The first four steps all take time polynomial in n, generally $O(n^2)$ or $O(n^3)$. In the last step, the number of factors may be $O(n)$, so the number of combinations required may be $O(2^n)$ (Swinnerton-Dyer, 1970). Hence the worst-case running time of this algorithm is exponential in n, even though such cases are rare†. The algorithm for finding short vectors in integer lattices (Lenstra *et al.*, 1982) can be used to replace the last step by the following one.

(vi) For each factor g of f modulo p^k, find the corresponding, i.e. that divisible by g modulo p^k, irreducible factor of f over the integers, by looking for its coefficients as a short vector in the lattice of all multiples of g modulo p^k which divide f.

Since the number of factors is at most n, and the 'short vector' algorithm takes polynomial time, this step is polynomial-time – a clear improvement. Unfortunately there are various practical points that need to be considered.

- Step (v) of the algorithm is often unnecessary, or needed very much less often than the worst case would imply.
- The value of k for the 'short vector' variant has to be substantially larger than that for the usual algorithm, thus increasing the cost of step (iv) and ensuring that much larger integers have to be manipulated.
- This 'polynomial' step (vi) in fact has a running cost of the form $O(n^{10})$, and n has to be quite large (in fact, 59) before 2^n becomes greater than n^{10}.

---

† Though not as rare as one would like. It is a striking example of the perversity of mathematics that such cases are often found when factoring polynomials that come from problems involving algebraic extensions, and so crop up more often in practice than one would naïvely hope.

- Abbott *et al.* (1985) have shown that the cost of failed attempts in step (v) can be drastically reduced, so that the coefficient before the exponential is perhaps only 10^{-6} of what one might have thought (thus moving the notional break-even point even higher – say to $n = 84$).

For these reasons, no major computer algebra system actually uses the 'short vector' variant in practice. Presumably, the advance of hardware technology and the wish of users to tackle ever larger problems will ultimately change this situation. It should also be noted that, when it comes to the factorization of polynomials over algebraic number fields, ideas based on the 'short vector' variant are significantly more practical than the traditional ideas.

Another area of interest is the question of multiplication of matrices. Naïvely, it takes n^3 multiplications to multiply two $n \times n$ matrices, and in particular eight to multiply two 2×2 matrices:

$$\begin{pmatrix} a & b \\ c & d \end{pmatrix} \begin{pmatrix} e & f \\ g & h \end{pmatrix} = \begin{pmatrix} ae + bg & af + bh \\ ce + dg & cf + dh \end{pmatrix}.$$

However, Strassen (1969) showed that it is possible to perform such a matrix multiplication with seven scalar multiplications. A slightly more efficient variant, due to Winograd, is the following:

$$\begin{pmatrix} t_1 + bg & t_2 + t_3 + (a + b - c - d)h \\ t_2 + t_4 - d(e - f - g + h) & t_2 + t_3 + t_4 \end{pmatrix},$$

where

$$
\begin{aligned}
t_1 &= ae \\
t_2 &= t_1 - (a - c - d)(e - g + h), \\
t_3 &= (c + d)(f - e) \\
t_4 &= (a - c)(h - f).
\end{aligned}
$$

The reader will have noticed that there are substantially more (15, even if maximal re-use is done) additions involved in this scheme than in the naïve scheme, and indeed on most of today's computers, this scheme would be slower than the naïve one. However, this scheme can be used recursively, so that the multiplication of 4×4 matrices can be expressed in terms of the multiplication of 2×2 matrices:

$$\begin{pmatrix} a_{1,1} & \cdots & a_{1,4} \\ \vdots & \ddots & \vdots \\ a_{4,1} & \cdots & a_{4,4} \end{pmatrix} \begin{pmatrix} b_{1,1} & \cdots & b_{1,4} \\ \vdots & \ddots & \vdots \\ b_{4,1} & \cdots & b_{4,4} \end{pmatrix} =$$

$$\begin{pmatrix} A & B \\ C & D \end{pmatrix} \begin{pmatrix} E & F \\ G & H \end{pmatrix} = \begin{pmatrix} AE + BG & AF + BH \\ CE + DG & CF + DH \end{pmatrix},$$

where $A, \ldots, H$ are 2×2 sub-matrices. This can be performed in seven multiplications of 2×2 matrices, each of which requires seven scalar multiplications, giving a total of 49 scalar multiplications. Similarly, two 8×8 matrices can be multiplied in 343 scalar multiplications, rather than the 512 needed by the naïve method. In general two $n \times n$ matrices can be multiplied using $n^{\log_2(7)} \approx n^{2.807}$ scalar multiplications. Furthermore, each decomposition requires a certain number of additions, but the number of these can be shown to be at most five times the number of multiplications, so the total cost of the additions is also $O(n^{\log_2(7)})$, leading to the rather surprising conclusion that this method will, for large enough n, also require fewer additions than the naïve one – experiments show that this method is more advantageous when $n > 40$.

This method was followed by a variety of increasingly ingenious and asymptotically faster ones: Pan (1981) produced an $O(n^{2.522})$ one. At this point it was tempting to conjecture that the cost of multiplying two $n \times n$ matrices was $O(n^{2.5})$, but this was also soon broken, and the current record is held by Coppersmith & Winograd (1990) with an $O(n^{2.376})$ method. The only sensible conjecture now seems to be that the cost of multiplying two $n \times n$ matrices is $O(n^{2+\epsilon})$, since (what follows is a simple example of a *lower bound* proof) the n^2 entries of the product matrix are linearly independent[†], and therefore have to be produced by at least $O(n^2)$ multiplications.

None of these more recent algorithms is of any practical use, and the study of the theory of fast matrix multiplication has essentially become a branch of pure mathematics, albeit one originally inspired by a very practical problem.

5.6 Automated Theorem-Proving

In principle, mathematical proof is a formal logical process, and one amenable to computerization. After all, the formal definition of a proof in mathematical logic is 'a sequence of well-formed formulae, each of which follows from the previous ones by one of the rules of inference', so

---

[†] Suppose one of the answers, say the (k, l)th element, were linearly dependent on the rest, so that we could write $c_{k,l} = C + \sum_{(i,j) \neq (k,l)} \lambda_{i,j} c_{i,j}$, where C and the $\lambda_{i,j}$ are absolute constants independent of the input matrices. Then if the matrices to multiply have only $a_{k,1} = 1$, all other $a_{i,j} = 0$, and $b_{1,l} = 1$, all other $b_{i,j} = 0$, then in the product all $c_{i,j} = 0$ except that $c_{k,l} = 1$, thus proving that $C = 1$. If we now take $a_{k,1} = 2$, we see that $C = 2$ as well, i.e. a contradiction.

certainly checking whether a proof is correct (i.e. satisfies this definition) should be very easy, and generating proofs not much more difficult. In practice, things are not so simple, and the informal mathematical reasoning that is actually used in mathematics is not as easy to computerize as one might think. One area of mathematics often held up as an area of great rigour is that of Euclidean geometry, and indeed there have been some successes in this area. Computerized techniques are credited with the 'minimalist' proof of Euclid's proposition I.VI: *If the angles at A and B in the triangle ABC are equal, then the sides AC and BC are equal.* **Computerized proof**: the angle at A is equal to the angle at B, the angle at B is equal to the angle at A, and the side AB is equal to the side BA. Therefore the triangles ABC and BAC are congruent (I.XXVI), so the side AC of the triangle ABC is equal to the side BC of the triangle BAC, as required.

Traditional proof: bisect the angle at C (I.IX), letting the bisector meet the side AB at D. Then the triangles CDA and CDB are congruent (I.XXVI), since the angles at C are the same by construction, the angle at A is equal to the angle at B by hypothesis, and the side CD is common. Therefore the side AC is equal to the side BC, as required.

In fact, both proofs are wrong from the strictly Euclidean point of view, since they use later results than I.VI. However, it is possible to restructure Book I so that I.VI is not needed until after I.XXVI, at which point both proofs are valid.

The first proof has an elegant simplicity about it that lets one believe that computerized proof is useful. However, much research in computerisation of geometry recently has gone in a very different direction: the premises and conclusion are converted into coordinate form as polynomials, and then one can check algebraically that the conclusion follows from the premises. If the conclusion lies in the ideal generated by the premises, which can be checked by Buchberger's algorithm, then the theorem is certainly true. There are, however, various catches to be considered.

(i) It might be the case that the conclusion C does not lie in the ideal I generated by the premises, but that C^2, or some higher power, does lie in I. In this case the theorem is still true, since if $C^2 = 0$, then $C = 0$. Saying that 'some power of C is in I' is the same as saying that $C \in \sqrt{I}$, where $\sqrt{I}$, the *radical* of I, is $\{p : \exists n : p^n \in I\}$. It is possible to use Buchberger's algorithm to compute radicals (Gianni *et al.*, 1988), though in practice it may be easy to prove that $C \in \sqrt{I}$ without computing $\sqrt{I}$.

(ii) It might be the case that $C \notin \sqrt{I}$, which would mean that the theorem was not true when the coordinates were interpreted as complex numbers, but nevertheless the theorem might be true when the coordinates are restricted to being real numbers. This may happen for apparently trivial reasons, for example a complex line can be perpendicular to itself, as in the case of the line through $(0, 0)$ and $(1, i)$, but it can also happen for fundamental reasons, as in the case of the following result: *If 9 distinct points in the plane have the property that, on the line through any two of them there is a third, then the 9 points are collinear.* This is false if complex coordinates are allowed, since we can let the nine points have x and y coordinates taken from the set $\left\{ 1, \frac{1+\sqrt{3}i}{2}, \frac{1-\sqrt{3}i}{2} \right\}$. However, if only real coordinates are allowed, then the result is true†.

(iii) The theorem may not be true as stated, because some exceptional degenerate cases need to be ruled out. For example, the theorem stated above would not be correct without the word 'distinct', since allowing different points to coincide makes a mockery of the statement.

For these reasons, other methods besides a simple resort to Gröbner bases are necessary, but nevertheless coordinate-based proof techniques have become very powerful (Stifter, 1993).

In other areas of mathematics, the actual reasoning used to prove results is even further removed from the formal definition of a proof, and automated theorem-provers have had little success in demonstrating new results, or even checking non-trivial results automatically. A telling example of this is given by Russinoff (1985), who took a version of the Boyer–Moore theorem prover, one of the most powerful such theorem-provers available, which had already been used to verify the correctness (not the complexity!) of the RSA encryption scheme. This meant that the theorem-prover already had lemmas relating to modular arithmetic, modular exponentiation and Fermat's Little Theorem and Euler's The-

---

† Suppose it is false, and let P be a point of minimal non-zero distance from a line through three other points, say A, B and C. Let Q be the point on the line ABC closest to P. Then at least two points lie on one side of Q, say A and B, with A between B and Q. Then A is not on the line PB, but is closer to PB than P is to AB, thus contradicting the minimality of P. The proof only applies to real coordinates, since we are assuming that distances are ordered and positive.

orem at its disposal. Yet in order for the Boyer–Moore theorem-prover
then to prove Wilson's Theorem (that $(p-1)! \equiv -1 \bmod p$ if p is prime,
a result that the author frequently proves in one minute to undergrad-
uates who have just learnt similar results), Russinoff had first to state
44 subsidiary lemmas, whose proofs the theorem prover had to discover.
This experience, that what looks like routine mathematical reasoning is
actually quite difficult for computer programs to handle, is not unique,
and one has to be sceptical about the possibilities of computers doing
significant mathematics in the near future.

The Automath project (de Bruijn, 1980) aimed 'to develop a system
of writing entire mathematical theories in such a precise fashion that
verification of the correctness can be carried out by formal operations on
the text'. A lot of the subsequent work in this project has concentrated
on the formal language in which such theories can be expressed, and
the implications for the typed λ-calculus. Some powerful claims have
been made for Automath, notably that the 'loss factor', i.e. the extent
to which an Automath text is longer than the corresponding natural
language text, is constant, possibly of the order of 10 or 20, and does not
increase as the material becomes harder. Some significant mathematics
has been translated or written in Automath, notably Landau (1930), but
nevertheless the project has not had any major impact on mathematics.
There has, however, been very substantial impact on computer science,
notably in the areas of 'propositions as types' and algorithms for the
typed λ-calculus.

5.7 Conclusion

Computing has certainly enhanced the power of the mathematician to
explore mathematics, and to prove mathematical results. These uses of
computers have not changed the nature of mathematics, but have merely
improved what can be done.

More fundamentally, the advent of digital computing has changed
the shape of mathematics in a way that is still evolving, and one that
traditional classifications have yet to come to grips with. At the risk
of simplifying grotesquely, in the pre-computer days, 'pure' mathematics was divided between the discrete and the continuous, and 'applied'
mathematics was actually 'applied continuous mathematics'. Problems
posed in this 'applied' mathematics naturally gave rise to more abstract
– 'pure' – problems of continuous mathematics. Nowadays, a significant amount of computer science is applied discrete mathematics, and
these applications are giving rise to more abstract – 'pure' – problems

of discrete mathematics. It can easily be argued that most of the papers presented at conferences such as STOC or FOCS are pure mathematics rather than computer science, or indeed that such distinctions cannot sensibly be made.

One change that has *not* happened, despite the claims made for artificial intelligence in the past, is any significant use of artificial intelligence or automated theorem-proving inside pure mathematics. This does not mean that such research is automatically useless, merely that it has not had the effect on mathematics that some have expected. It may well have an effect on some of the applications of mathematics, especially on the routine theorems that need to be proved if one is to prove that a program is correct.

6

Paradigm Merger in Natural Language Processing

Gerald Gazdar

Abstract

This article considers the major change that has taken place in natural language processing research over the last five years. It begins by providing a brief guide to the structure of the field and then presents a caricature of two competing paradigms of 1980s NLP research and indicates the reasons why many of those involved have now seen fit to abandon them in their pure forms. Attention is then directed to the lexicon, a component of NLP systems which started out as Cinderella but which has finally arrived at the ball. This brings us to an account of what has been going on in the field most recently, namely a merging of the two 1980s paradigms in a way that is generating a host of interesting new research questions. The chapter concludes by trying to identify some of the key conceptual, empirical and formal issues that now stand in need of resolution.

6.1 Introduction

The academic discipline that studies computer processing of natural languages is known as *natural language processing* (NLP) or *computational linguistics* (the terms are interchangeable). NLP is most conveniently seen as a branch of AI, although it is a branch into which many linguists (and a few psycholinguists) have moved. In Europe, NLP is dominated by ex-linguists but this is not the case in the USA where there is a tradition of people moving into the field from a standard computer science background.

It is tempting to say that NLP is the academic discipline that studies computer processing of the written forms of natural languages. But that would be misleading. The discipline that studies computer processing of the spoken forms of natural languages is known as *speech processing* or just *speech*. Surprisingly, perhaps, speech and NLP are really rather separate disciplines: until recently, there has been little overlap in the personnel involved, the journals and conferences are largely disjoint, and the theoretical approaches and methods used have had little in common. Speech research studies the problems that are peculiar to processing the spoken form of language whereas NLP research, in principle at least, studies problems that are common to the processing of both spoken and written forms of natural languages.

Using Thompson's (1983) terminology, it makes expository sense to treat NLP as composed of three main sub-areas with respect to the goals of the researchers involved: (i) theory of linguistic computation, (ii) computational psycholinguistics, and (iii) applied NLP. In what follows, I shall largely concentrate on (i), but will pause here to comment briefly on (ii) and (iii).

Computational psycholinguistics involves the construction of psychologically motivated computational models of aspects of human natural language processing. Such computer models are used to generate hypotheses and detailed sets of predictions about human linguistic behaviour. These hypotheses and predictions are then tested experimentally using standard psycholinguistic techniques.

Applied NLP involves the construction of intelligent computational artefacts that process natural languages in ways that are useful to people other than computational linguists. The test of utility here is essentially that of the market. Examples include machine translation packages, programs that convert numerical data or sequences of error codes into coherent text or speech, systems that map text messages into symbolic or numeric data, and natural language interfaces to databases.

Theory of linguistic computation is a rather grand title for the study of the computational, mathematical and statistical properties of natural languages and systems for processing natural languages. It includes the development of algorithms for parsing, generation, and acquisition of linguistic knowledge; the investigation of the time and space complexity of such algorithms; the design of computationally useful formal languages (such as grammar and lexicon formalisms) for encoding linguistic knowledge; the investigation of appropriate software architectures for various NLP tasks; and consideration of the types of non-linguistic knowledge that impinge on NLP. It is a fairly abstract area of study and it is not one that makes particular commitments to the study of the human mind, nor indeed does it make particular commitments to producing useful artefacts. However, like some other parts of AI, the main headings on theoretical NLP's agenda continue to be set by both psychological and application-driven considerations. If it were not for the brute fact that the world contains more than five billion primates that are demonstrably able to produce and comprehend natural languages, mathematical linguists would long ago have been able to present convincing formal demonstrations that such production and comprehension were impossible. And if it were not for the fact that the employment of these primates to understand and generate natural languages is often frighteningly expensive (witness the costs of translation in the EU bureaucracy), it is unlikely that theoretically oriented computational linguists would find institutions that were willing to pay their salaries.

Cutting across the trichotomy of goals just outlined, there is a trichotomy of task: (a) language understanding, (b) language generation, and (c) language acquisition. The majority of NLP research over the last thirty years has concerned understanding, although the amount of generation work done appears to be on an upward slope. Some applications of NLP clearly require both understanding and generation: machine translation and automatic abstracting, for example. Apart from a very few computational psycholinguistic models, acquisition has been notable only for its almost total absence from the pre-1990 NLP literature. But this situation has changed, for reasons we will attend to later.

6.2 Two 1980s Paradigms

The theoretical end of NLP research is currently in the midst of a major conceptual shift caused by the merging of two paradigms that were, until about 1990, widely seen as wholly antithetical (see, e.g., Sampson, 1987). In order to give a sense of the context in which this shift has occurred, I shall present below a hypothetical NLP application and suggest how each paradigm might have set about building a system to deal with that application in, say, 1988.† In order to eliminate the many constraints and compromises required by real work on applications, my hypothetical scenario will presuppose generous access to funds, person-years, and machine cycles. My hypothetical systems builders can thus give free rein to their theoretical preferences as of 1988‡.

It is 1988. The Finnish government has funded the development of a huge relational database packed with every conceivable type of fact

---

† Readers in search of the real history, along with relevant background in information theory and statistics, should skip this section and read Church & Mercer (1993) instead.

‡ I am grateful to Yorick Wilks for unintentionally suggesting this example to me.

about Finland and its inhabitants. This database has the potential to answer almost any question one might think to ask about Finland. Access to the database is widely available: you can dial in by modem, there are terminals in most public buildings, and the database is connected to all the national networks. But there is a problem. In order to interrogate the database, you need to use SQL. As a result, only a very small proportion of the Finnish population make any direct use of the facility. What is required is a natural language interface to the database, specifically a Finnish interface to the database. Two teams, which I shall refer to as LOGIC and NGRAM, each agree to provide such an interface in return for significant fractions of Finland's GNP. The LOGIC team builds a morphological analyser to decode the syntactic information carried by Finnish inflectional affixes. They write correspondence rules for this analyser in a declarative notation that gets compiled into finite state transducers. This analyser is able to map *varatkoon* into `reserve IMPV ACT SG 3`, for example†. The next layer of their system is a syntactic one that includes a grammar written in a declarative notation which resembles that of context-free phrase structure grammar, but where the nonterminal symbols represent directed acyclic graphs (*feature structures*) and where information is copied and merged by means of graph unification. The grammar is accompanied by a lexicon written in the same language as used for the grammar, but with extensive use of macros to reduce redundancy, and by a parser that combines classical context-free parsing technology with the unification operation, data structures that record successful and partly successful rule applications, and various other refinements. The lexicon encodes semantic information in a dialect of the lambda calculus and, as a result of this and relevant unifications, the result of a parse is both a syntactic analysis and a translation of the sentence into a logical representation intended to denote the 'literal meaning' of the sentence uttered. A further, pragmatic, component provides a general AI theorem-prover together with axioms relating to principles of orderly discourse. This pragmatic component is able to infer the intended meaning from the literal meaning delivered by the parser, together with the discourse axioms, the intended meanings of preceding utterances, and information drawn from the database itself. A further, trivial, component translates the logical expression representing the intended meaning into a synonymous SQL query which is then used to interrogate the database of information about Finland. The LOGIC

† The example is taken from Koskenniemi (1983, p.60).

system is really a little more complex than my description implies because there are a number of additional black boxes, including one that is intended to identify the referents of pronouns, and there is a sophisticated flow of control that allows, for example, semantic information to help resolve uncertainties at the morphological level, *inter alia.*

The approach adopted by the NGRAM team is totally different. They begin by eliciting several million questions that members of the Finnish public tell them that they would like to be able to put to the database. They then employ every computer scientist in Finland for many months in order to get each of these questions competently translated into the equivalent SQL query. The result, a table of several million Finnish question–SQL query pairs, is handed over to a dedicated CRAY Y-MP which spends several weeks producing a large table of probabilities. Ignoring alignment issues and other complications, we can think of each entry in this new table having the form 'when Finnish word Y immediately follows Finnish words W and X then Y corresponds to SQL expression Z with probability p'. This table largely exhausts the NGRAM team's Finnish interface to the database. For any query expressed in Finnish, it can be used to construct the sentence of SQL that is most likely to express the sense of that query.

In the event, and despite having a devastating effect on Finland's national debt, neither LOGIC nor NGRAM was able to deliver a system that anyone wanted to use. It is not hard to find the reasons for these failures. The problems that beset a pure LOGIC-type system are ambiguity, brittleness and complexity. Pure LOGIC-type systems are brittle because the only eventualities they can cope with are those that they have rules for. Ambiguity is inescapable at every level of analysis. A ten-word sentence can easily contain seven or eight words which are multiply lexically ambiguous as to sense and/or syntactic category. These lexical ambiguities multiply out against each other when it comes to arriving at syntactic structures and semantic representations for the whole sentence. The problem caused by this pervasive lexical ambiguity is further compounded by purely syntactic ambiguities that arise in constructions like coordination, prepositional phrase attachment, and noun–noun compounding. Church & Patil (1982) established that the ambiguities caused by these ubiquitous constructions proliferate according to the Catalan number series (1, 1, 2, 5, 14, 42, 132, 469, 1430, 4862, ...) and thus get very large very quickly. Worse, as Hobbs *et al.* point out in one brief but damning sentence, 'the problem of syntactic ambiguity is AI-complete' (1992, p.269). Macias & Pulman make the same point in relation to the semantic indeterminacies induced by quantifiers, anaphoric expressions, and noun compounds: deciding between candidate interpretations 'requires reasoning about the context ... and presupposes a solution to many of the classical problems of Artificial Intelligence' (1993, p.73). A problem is AI-complete if its solution requires a solution to the general AI problem of representing and reasoning about arbitrary real-world knowledge. Computational complexity follows in ambiguity's wake. Even for natural language sentences that turn out ultimately only to have a single semantically coherent interpretation, there will normally be a great deal of ambiguity that is local to particular stages of analysis, ambiguity which eventually gets resolved only after many cul-de-sacs have been explored.

The problems that beset a pure NGRAM-type system are those of nonlocal context and the sparseness of the data. These problems entail that such systems are ineffective for longer sentences (ten or more words). One kind of nonlocal context problem that a pure NGRAM-type approach encounters is a consequence of the interaction of a universal formal property of natural languages and a key property of the frequency distribution of words. The formal property is the existence of discontinuous dependencies in linguistic material. Such dependencies occur in morphology (as in German **ge-*wes*-en**) to a limited extent, but become omnipresent in syntax. Examples include subject–verb agreement, determiner–noun agreement, comparative constructions, reflexive pronouns, and relative clauses. In such syntactic cases, there is normally no upper bound on the amount of linguistic material that can separate the two dependent elements. As a consequence, any approach that restricts itself to a particular finite window on the text is bound to fail to identify some proportion of these dependencies. Of course, that proportion falls as the size of the window increases. Unfortunately, attempts to increase the window size beyond two or three words (*bigrams* or *trigrams*) encounter data sparseness in the shape of a nearly vertical brick wall known as Zipf's law (1935)†. Zipf's law is a well established empirical generalization about the frequency distribution of words that says that frequency is inversely proportional to rank. Thus, for example, if the tenth most frequent word in a corpus of text occurs once in every 100 words, then we would expect the thousandth most frequent word to occur only once in every 10,000 words. Plotting frequency against rank thus gives us a doubly exponential curve. Familiar but low-ranked

---

† See Baayen (1991) for useful discussion and references to the relevant literature subsequent to 1935.

words occur with very low frequencies. The converse also holds: familiar high-ranked words occur with very high frequencies. Thus a lexicon containing just the 3,000 most highly ranked words includes 80% of the vocabulary found in a forty-million-word corpus of computer manuals (Black *et al.*, 1992, p. 186). However, a simple NGRAM-type approach is not concerned with these frequencies *per se* but rather with the frequency with which a word occurs in the context of one or more specific contiguous words. Calculating such frequencies reliably requires enormous corpora even when the number of context words is restricted to two. And increasing the size of the corpus does not itself provide a solution since, as Gale & Church point out, vocabulary increases with corpus size: 'the problem only gets worse as we look at more data' (1990, p.283 n.2). Using more than two context words is simply infeasible, and likely to remain so. Thus the NGRAM approach is restricted to a three-word window and this is simply too small to get a handle on many of the instances of discontinuous dependency that show up in natural language texts.

The context problem is not one that is restricted to syntax. In determining the senses of homonymous or polysemous words, the distal context can be all-important. Gale *et al.* note that 'it is common to use very small contexts (e.g., 5 words) based on the observation that people seem to be able to disambiguate word-senses based on very little context ... we have been able to find useful information out to 100 words (and measurable information out to 10,000 words)' (1992a, p.250 n.1). Consider, for example, the following passage:

Unsteadily, Holmes stepped out of the barge. Moriarty was walking away down the towpath and into the fog. Holmes ran after him. 'Give it back to me', he shouted. Moriarty turned and laughed. He opened his hand and the small piece of metal fell onto the path. Holmes reached to pick it up but Moriarty was too quick for him. With one slight movement of his foot, he tipped the key into the lock.

The word *lock* has (at least) two senses: one denoting devices used to secure doors, cars, and safety deposit boxes, and another denoting a gated section of water which allows vessels to move from one level to another. In the example given, the distal context set up by the words *barge* and *towpath* indicates (to a human reader) that it is the second sense which is relevant to the interpretation of the final sentence. However, that sentence also contains the word *key*, a word which is strongly associated with the first, irrelevant, sense of *lock*. Any approach to sense resolution that uses a small window will choose the wrong sense for *lock* in this kind of example.

The reader should not be misled by the rather negative tone of this section. The hypothetical Finnish scenario was deliberately designed to bring out the worst in both paradigms. Sensibly applied, each paradigm can point to notable successes. Thus, for example, a simple NGRAM-type system with a two-word window is able to assign words to their parts of speech with around 95% accuracy, which may well be as good as a human can achieve. And LOGIC-type technology has allowed us to engineer usable natural language interfaces to databases for nearly a decade. Commercial products providing such interfaces have been on the market for much of that time. But such interfaces can only currently be made to work when the database deals with a rather narrow domain (personnel records, stationery stocks, cricket results, or whatever). Finland may be a small country but a database that contained every conceivable fact about that country and its inhabitants would cover a domain that is just about as wide as one can envisage†.

6.3 A Digression on the Lexicon

One important change that took place in NLP over the 1980s was somewhat orthogonal to the division between symbolic and probabilistic work. That change was the growth in the role of the lexicon. At the beginning of the decade, the lexicon was seen as a component of little theoretical interest, a list-like repository of simple correspondences at best, and a compilation of idiosyncrasies and irreducibly exceptional behaviour at worst. Several facts conspired to change this view. One was the early 1980s work on computational morphology (much of it on Finnish) which made it obvious to English-speaking NLP researchers that words had internal structure (even English words). If the lexicon was the component that described the words of a language, as by definition it was, then it needed to embody some kind of grammar of words. The focus on morphology also highlighted another characteristic of words: they could not simply be divided into those that behaved regularly (*cat/cats*) and those that were totally irregular (*ox/oxen*). Rather, words displayed a continuum from total regularity to total idiosyncrasy, through various shades of subregularity (*caught, fought, taught, ...*). And this was an observation that applied, not just to morphology (where it is very obvious), but also to the phonological, orthographic, syntactic and semantic

† See Copestake & Sparck Jones (1990) for an overview of 1980s natural language database interface technology.

properties of words. At the very least, lexicons needed machinery to encode subregularity.

But this innocent-looking requirement is a Trojan horse. Total regularity is just a special limiting case of subregularity. If you have machinery that can describe subregular facts then you can surely describe regular facts with the same apparatus. And, if you can describe regular facts within the lexicon, then it isn't obvious that you need a separate component to describe such facts *outside* the lexicon. Grammars, in particular, were a notable victim of this logic: by the end of the 1980s most of the grammatical frameworks widely used in NLP only had two or three purely grammatical rules left, all the rest of the work being done by the information coded in the individual lexical entries. The new descriptive power of the lexicon may have made this legicide possible, but much of the enthusiasm for eliminating grammatical rules came from computational linguists working on grammars. Linguists had appreciated since the mid-1960s that almost all the phenomena once thought of in terms of Chomskyan transformational rules were subject to lexical exceptions – which is just another way of saying that they were proper subregularities. Unfortunately, linguistics has not yet developed an adequate general theory of subregularity.

In the mid-1980s, NLP researchers working on the lexicon started to import ideas relating to default inheritance from AI work on knowledge representation, especially the tradition known (somewhat misleadingly) as 'semantic nets'. Although work falling under that rubric had been going on for a quarter of a century, it was not until the mid-1980s that this work began to be put on a sound mathematical footing (as in Touretzky, 1986). And the vast majority of work that had been done up until that time related to general issues in AI knowledge representation†. A variety of lexical knowledge representation languages (LKRLs) were developed that used inheritance (normally default inheritance) to express generalizations about lexical items at all levels of description, from the phonological through to the semantic. The fruits of the activity in this area since the late 1980s can be seen in such collections as Daelemans & Gazdar (1992) and Briscoe, de Paiva & Copestake (1993). Implicit in much of this work is a kind of 'radical lexicalism' which maintains that almost everything that needs to be said declaratively about natural languages for NLP purposes is best said in the lexicon and stated in the

---

† Although Sowa points out that the very first implementation of a semantic network *eo nomine* was for the lexicon of a machine translation system at Cambridge in around 1960 (Sowa 1992, p.1495).

LKRL. On this view, the lexicon should absorb all of morphology and syntax, most of phonology and semantics, and possibly even eat away at the edges of pragmatics. Thus, for example, Schabes & Waters (1993) present a form of context-free grammar in which *every* rule is lexical.

One byproduct of the upsurge in probabilistic work has been the rediscovery that there are great differences in the patterns of lexical and syntactic statistics associated with the naturally occurring corpora that emerge from different communicative activities (Biber, 1993). Consider, for example, the various senses of the English word *tender*. Of the 358 occurrences of this word in the COBUILD corpus 95% have an adjectival sense and only 4% have the contractual nominal or verbal sense (Baayen *et al.*, 1993). By contrast, in the MUC-5 English joint venture (EJV) corpus, every single occurrence has the contractual nominal or verbal sense. The frequency profile of function words can also vary dramatically from one type of corpus to another. For example, the word *the* heads the rank list for the EJV corpus, but is way down at the 27 position in a corpus of Metropolitan Police incident reports†. And Magerman & Marcus report that prepositional phrase attachment preferences associated with particular prepositions are specific to domain of discourse (1991b, p.235).

Three consequences follow from such observations: the first is that, where lexicons are concerned, bigger does not mean better. A lexicon that contains both the contractual and the adjectival senses of *tender* is going to make processing the EJV corpus harder than will a smaller lexicon that excludes the adjectival senses. Jacobs *et al.* call this the 'I see a cow' problem: 'a large dictionary greatly increases the degree of ambiguity by introducing low-frequency possibilities' (1990, p.363) and Ayuso *et al.* draw attention to the problem caused by 'the greatly increased search space inherent in large vocabularies' (1990, p.354).

The second consequence is that lexical statistics calculated on the basis of large corpora that attempt to be representative of a wide variety of language use are very unlikely to be useful for processing any particular variety. And the third consequence is that the only way to be confident in a set of probabilities is if they have been compiled from material drawn from the intended domain. Hopes for a large generic lexicon of English which includes probabilities and which can simply be plugged into NLP applications as a ready-made component are entirely misplaced. Analogous points can be made in connection with the

† I am grateful to Lynne Cahill for drawing these facts to my attention.

generic utility of machine-readable versions of existing published general dictionaries.

6.4 Recent Research

The symbolic NLP of the 1980s potentially has the virtues of accuracy and subtlety but lacks efficiency and robustness. The probabilistic NLP of the 1980s potentially has the virtues of efficiency and robustness but lacks accuracy and subtlety. The logic of these observations is to attempt a merger of the two. And that is exactly what is now happening. The leading figures of the two 1980s paradigms caricatured above are now publishing work that builds quite explicitly on insights drawn from the other paradigm. For example, Fred Jelinek, the pioneer of trigram-based NLP, is a coauthor of Black *et al.* (1993), a paper which uses a context-free feature-based unification grammar as the basis for a new type of probabilistic parser, whilst Fernando Pereira, a key figure in the symbolic NLP of the 1980s, is a coauthor of Pereira *et al.* (1993), a paper which applies sophisticated statistical techniques to the task of isolating sense distinctions.

A representative piece of 1990s NLP research starts with a large corpus of text that has been annotated in some way under native speaker supervision. The individual words in the text may, for example, have been tagged with a judgement as to their correct part of speech or marked with a pointer to the appropriate sense in a dictionary, or each sentence in the corpus may have been assigned a partial or total parse tree under some assumed grammar. Crucially, the corpus annotations represent the best available human judgement as to what is going on in the text in the relevant respects. This annotated or parsed corpus then constitutes a source from which one can extract probabilities that can be used to guide the choices made by an automatic word-tagger, parser, sense-disambiguator, etc.

The original trigram-based approaches to NLP adopted a finite state view of their domain – the statistical model is Markovian. From the point of view of a grammarian, it is both hard and unnatural to model natural language syntax in terms of finite state grammar. It is easier and more natural to use context-free phrase structure grammar (CF-PSG)†. As a consequence, probabilistic CF-PSG‡ has become a popular model in recent work (see, e.g., Jelinek & Lafferty, 1991). Given a probabilistic

---

† See Gazdar & Pullum (1985) for discussion. One way to have your cake and eat most of it too can be found in Pereira (1990).

‡ See Wetherell (1980) for discussion and references.

CF-PSG, one can calculate the probability of any sentence that it generates and identify the most probable parse for each sentence, among other things. One option is to map the rule probabilities into probabilities for an LR parse table and then use that for parsing. An alternative approach, advocated by Briscoe & Carroll (1993), is to associate probabilities with the LR parse table directly†. This move has the advantage that the probabilities can be made sensitive to a limited structural context outside the local mother+daughters tree fragment defined by a single CF-PSG rule. Against this, there is the apparent disadvantage of having factual information about syntactic usage buried in a processing component. However, as Briscoe & Carroll (1993, p.49 n.6) point out, it should be possible to map such parse table probabilities over into conditional probabilities on CF-PSG rules that are sensitive to a certain amount of structural context, such as those found in the work of Chitrao & Grishman (1990) and Magerman & Marcus (1991a). Such moves incur a cost. Simple probabilistic CF-PSGs have the same polynomial parsing complexity as nonprobabilistic CF-PSGs. But existing algorithms pay an exponential price in grammar size once the probabilities are made sensitive to structural context (Magerman & Weir, 1992, p.44).

More radical steps can be taken in attempting to get the probabilities sensitive to the appropriate notion of context. One is to move (slightly) away from CF-PSG. For example, linear indexed grammar (LIG) is one of a family of polynomial parsable 'mildly context-sensitive' extensions to the CF-PSG formalism, and one that builds in a mechanism that allows access to the structural context of a rule (Gazdar, 1988; Vijay-Shanker & Weir, 1991). Schabes (1992) defines a stochastic lexicalized version of LIG and shows how the standard CF-PSG reestimation algorithm can be adapted so as to provide the relevant probabilities for rules written in such a formalism. Schabes is actually using LIG as a formal substitute for tree adjoining grammar (TAG), another member of the mildly context-sensitive grammar family. Resnik (1992) presents a probabilistic lexicalized version of TAG directly but leaves the issue of determining the relevant probabilities for further research. Black *et al.* go further and advocate what they call 'history-based grammars' in which the probabilities can be made sensitive to 'any element of the output structure, or the parse tree, which has already been determined, including previous words, non-terminal categories, constituent structure, and any other linguistic information which is generated as part of the

† Cf. Bobrow (1991), who advocates the use of probabilistic agendas for chart-based parsing.

parse structure' (1993, p.34). Another kind of move is to use all the subtrees found in a large corpus-based multiset of parse trees as a grammar: each subtree is construed as a rule and it has a probability derived directly from its frequency of occurrence in the corpus (and this can be calculated trivially, of course). Standard parsing algorithms lead to exponential time complexity with such a grammar, but Monte Carlo techniques allow parsing to take place in bounded polynomial time (Bod, 1992, 1993)†.

Largely orthogonal to the question of how best to associate probabilities with grammatical rules, is the question of how best to notate a grammar intended for the description of natural languages. The traditional CF-PSG notations which employ monadic nonterminals and a fully specified order of daughters in rules have two serious disadvantages in this application. The first is that such notations are unable to capture a wide variety of self-evident generalizations about the syntax of a language (e.g., generalizations about agreement phenomena and generalizations about constituent order). *A priori*, it seems reasonable to suppose that the relevant statistical generalizations will shadow the grammatical generalizations rather than cutting against them. The second, which follows from the first, is that a very large number of separate rules are required in order to achieve respectable coverage. A large rule set causes a problem for probabilistic CF-PSG since it makes it much harder to discover what the probabilities are.

These concerns were addressed in nonprobabilistic NLP work of the 1980s in a variety of ways, of which we will consider two here. The most important is the move away from monadic nonterminals to the directed acyclic graphs known as feature structures‡. These complex nonterminals allow large sets of standard CF-PSG rules to be collapsed by leaving some nonterminals partially underspecified, by using variables or unification to ensure partial identity across nonterminals, and so forth (see Gazdar (1983) for discussion and references). The use of such complex nonterminals and their associated schematic rules has begun to figure in the most recent probabilistic work (e.g., Black *et al.*, 1993; Briscoe & Carroll, 1993).

The descriptive problem caused by the fixed order of daughters in

---

† Bod's work represents a kind of memory-based approach to parsing. Daelemans (1994) advocates the pervasive application of memory-based 'lazy learning' techniques to NLP tasks and reports promising results.

‡ Mathematically, this move can take one out of CF-PSG altogether if the set of nonterminals used is allowed to be nonfinite.

a standardly notated CF-PSG rule was addressed by the introduction of the ID/LP notation for (a proper subset of) CF-PSGs (Gazdar & Pullum, 1981). This notation separates the immediate dominance (ID) and linear precedence (LP) components of a set of CF-PSG rules into two distinct sets of rules. For typical natural language grammars, the total number of ID and LP rules is significantly less than the number of rules in an equivalent, but standardly notated, CF-PSG. Sharman *et al.* (1990) introduce probabilistic ID/LP format grammars by direct analogy with standard probabilistic CF-PSGs.

Probabilistic grammars require both grammars and probabilities. Finding out what those grammars and probabilities should be is a major problem. In an ideal world, we would have access to an algorithm that would digest a modest-sized corpus of raw text and soon afterwards provide us with a set of rules together with the relevant probabilities. The world is currently less than ideal. An algorithm is available that will digest an enormous corpus of raw text very very slowly and then offer us a set of CF-PSG rules together with relevant probabilities. Unfortunately, the set of rules that it has to offer is rather unlikely to bear any resemblance to something that a linguist would recognize as a reasonable grammar (Pereira & Schabes, 1992, p.128). This matters because only a reasonable grammar will lead to reasonable parse trees, where a reasonable parse tree is to be understood as one that will allow semantic interpretation to take place. In this less than ideal world, probabilities are now usually calculated not on the basis of raw text, but on the basis of a corpus of text that is fully or partially annotated with parse trees arrived at on the basis of a known grammar – a 'treebank' (Marcus *et al.*, 1993). This enterprise is itself not without problems. The grammar used is likely to be a general-purpose wide coverage grammar, not hand-crafted for the specific kind of text involved. And the treebank has either to be built by hand or else to be sorted by eye from the profuse output of a nonprobabilistic parser. Both processes are rather slow and require the (expensive) use of a linguistically sophisticated labour force. As a consequence, few treebanks are available and those that do exist are modest in size (a few million words). The small size makes it hard to estimate the probabilities associated with the less frequently used rules. The use of a pre-existing grammar, rather than one induced from the data, also reduces the robustness of any parser that makes use of it.

To address these problems, the automatic inference of linguistic information from raw (or lightly cooked) text has become a key area for theoretical NLP research, after many decades of neglect (see Marcus *et al.*, 1990). The light cooking that is often done involves putting the raw text through a program that assigns part-of-speech tags to each word. The output can be checked and corrected by a human quite quickly since such programs are now remarkably accurate (better than 95%). Tagging is an NLP task where probabilistic methods and rule-based methods appear to be equally effective (Brill, 1992; Kupiec, 1992)†. Probabilistic taggers can be trained, in the first instance, on surprisingly small human-tagged corpora (as few as 64,000 words) and can assign tags to unknown words with 85% accuracy (Weischedel *et al.*, 1993).

Current taggers approach a corpus with a built-in set of part-of-speech labels. It would be more satisfactory, especially for languages whose syntax has been less exhaustively studied than English, if algorithms were available that would allow one to induce a tag set from a corpus with little or no human intervention‡. This is a hard problem for several reasons: firstly because many words occur with more than one part of speech; secondly because factors unrelated to part of speech may be reflected in gross distributional differences, as with subject and nonsubject pronouns in English (Brill *et al.*, 1990, p.279 n.6); thirdly because syntactic and semantic factors are confounded in the observed distributions; and fourthly because languages manifest part of speech in very different ways. In English, the part of speech of a word is usually reflected in its linear position relative to other words. In some other languages, the part of speech of a word may have little to do with linear position, but a lot to do with the morphological markings that it exhibits.

Given a tagged corpus, Brill & Marcus (1992) present a technique for automatically inferring a kind of CF-PSG from it by considering the intersubstitutability of pairs of tags with single tags and creating scored binary expansion rules on that basis. The high-scoring rules can then be regarded as a grammar for the corpus and used in a parser that seeks to maximize the aggregate score for the parse tree. This approach achieves enough success to warrant further investigation although it is subject to some of the misgrouping problems noted by Pereira & Schabes (1992) in connection with the induction of probabilistic CF-PSGs from raw text.

Apart from its part of speech, the most important syntactic property of a word is its 'subcategorization frame' which is the list of constituents with which the word combines to form a phrase. Thus one sense of the

---

† And, arguably, complementary, as in the work by Tapanainen & Voutilainen (1994) which reports 98.5% accuracy from a system that combines probabilistic and rule-based taggers.

‡ See Brown *et al.*, (1992) and Schütze (1993) for the current state of the art.

verb *make*, for example, has the subcategorization frame [NP VP] as in *make the man burn it*. If one could somehow induce all the subcategorization frames associated with the words in a corpus then one would have gone a long way towards inducing a grammar for that corpus. The state of the art in this area depends heavily on *a priori* knowledge about the language in the corpus. Manning (1993) presents a probabilistic system that takes as input a corpus that has been fed through a stochastic tagger. The system, which is currently restricted to verbal subcategorization, makes use of a good deal of hand-coded knowledge about the syntax of English including a finite state parser and a list of 19 possible frame-types. Brent's (1993) probabilistic system is likewise restricted to verbs but does not operate on tagged text. Instead, it uses a grammar for English function words and a set of syntactic and morphological heuristics to help decide the part of speech of open class words. It seeks to establish whether a verb occurs in one of only six specified subcategorization frames.

This section has concentrated on syntax because the work resulting from the marriage of the probabilistic and symbolic traditions is heavily concentrated on syntactic matters. But there is one area of semantics where progress has been made, namely the use of statistical methods to determine the relevant sense of an ambiguous word. This is a fundamental issue for NLP since many words are ambiguous as to sense and determination of sense is a prerequisite for further semantic processing. The idea at the heart of all the recent work on this topic is a simple one: different senses of a word are likely to occur in different lexical environments. Thus one sense of the word *lock* can be expected to occur in lexical contexts which include words like *door, key, safe, pick, locksmith,* etc., whilst another sense can be expected to occur in lexical environments which include words like *canal, barge, bridge, towpath, lock-keeper,* and so forth. In order to be able to compile some useful numbers one needs to have access to a corpus in which the words have their senses identified in some way. Computational linguists have recently exhibited a great deal of ingenuity in finding, or synthesizing, such corpora without recourse to the labour and expense of *de novo* sense-tagging by hand. Three kinds of resources have been used to this end: machine-readable dictionaries, machine-readable thesauri, and bilingual corpora.

Guthrie *et al.* (1991) used the lexical content of definitions in a machine-readable dictionary as the basis for discovering the words that co-occur most commonly with each sense of a word as flagged by the dictionary's subject coding. In a development of this work, Cowie *et al.* (1992) describe the use of simulated annealing to find the optimal assignment of senses to all the words in a sentence simultaneously†.

In Yarowsky's (1992) approach, the index categories of Roget's thesaurus were taken as sense flags. The machine-readable text of an encyclopedia was divided into subcorpora corresponding to each index category based on the occurrence of words thus indexed. These subcorpora were used to identify the words that could act as the best markers of the relevant sense in virtue of being both frequent and distinctive. The extent of the occurrence of these markers in a 100-word context surrounding a word of unknown sense provides a basis for determining the most likely sense with an accuracy of better than 90%.

Homonymy is rarely preserved under translation into another language and this fact can be used for sense identification if a bilingual corpus is available and if words are aligned across the two language components of the corpus (Brown *et al.*, 1991). It is less obvious that bilingual corpora can help with polysemy since one would expect many kinds of regular or subregular polysemy to be preserved under translation‡. This preservation of polysemy is actually helpful in a machine translation application, but it limits the utility of information derived from bilingual corpora in monolingual applications. The linguist's distinction between homonymy and polysemy is not made in much of the recent NLP literature, but it probably should be since it might help to explain both the mixed results on test examples and the inconsistency across human judges in some tasks (see the discussion in Gale *et al.* (1992a)).

A limitation of all the techniques for sense determination just outlined is that they depend on the prior existence of laboriously hand-constructed resources, albeit ones that were constructed for purposes other than natural language processing. But large bilingual corpora exist for very few language pairs, and suitably coded machine-readable monolingual dictionaries and thesauri for languages other than English are also hard to find. What is needed ultimately is some way of detecting the fact that a word has alternative senses directly from corpora. A promising beginning to what is likely to prove to be a difficult task can be found in Pereira *et al.* (1993) who use a hierarchical clustering technique applied to verb–noun pairs (transitive verbs and the head nouns of their direct objects). This technique seems to be able to identify quite subtle sense distinctions in both nouns and verbs. Another promising

---

† Simulated annealing has also been advocated for stochastic parsing by Sampson (1986, 1991; Sampson *et al.*, 1989).

‡ See Kilgarriff (1993, 1995) for a theory of regular and subregular polysemy.

technique, proposed by Dagan & Itai (1994), involves the use of corpus-derived statistics connected with sense relations from one language to facilitate disambiguation in another language. One factor that should serve to make the alternative sense discovery task easier than it would otherwise be is the observation that words almost always maintain a consistent sense for the duration of a discourse (Gale *et al.*, 1992b).

6.5 The Next Few Years

Much influential work has used particular large corpora, such as IBM office correspondence or Canadian Hansard, because they exist, not because a real-world application demanded their use. For many such applications, the available corpora will be relatively small. There is thus a need for more research on statistical methods that will be able to extract useful numbers from modestly sized corpora (Dunning, 1993).

Whatever the size of corpus, Zipf's law ensures that one will always have sparse data problems and more work is needed to find the best ways of dealing with them (Dagan *et al.*, 1993).

Although existing machine-readable dictionaries and thesauri will rarely, if ever, be directly useful in an NLP system, they can be used to bootstrap the lexicons for such systems, as Yarowsky's (1992) work with *Roget's Thesaurus* makes plain. There is plenty of scope for further research in this vein.

Almost all the 1990s NLP work cited in this chapter deals exclusively with English. But English, like any other language, has a specific set of characteristics that are not typical of languages as a whole. In particular, English has rather little by way of inflectional morphology. Much recent probabilistic work pretends it has none. Such a pretence would be utterly bizarre for a language like Finnish, and it is counterproductive even for English (Ritchie *et al.*, 1992). More generally, there is a need for probabilistically oriented NLP work on languages that are typologically distinct from English (e.g., those with relatively free constituent order).

If one takes morphology seriously, then one is inevitably forced to make finer distinctions than those standardly provided by part-of-speech tags. One needs to distinguish singular and plural nouns, tensed and untensed verbs, accusative and nominative pronouns, and so on. There is a great deal of room for experimentation in associating probabilities not (just) with gross part-of-speech labels, but with the individual featural components of syntactic categories.

The implications of adopting fully lexicalized probabilistic grammars such as those proposed by Schabes (1992; Schabes & Waters, 1993) have yet to be fully absorbed. In a fully lexicalized grammar, the entire syntax of the language is holistically distributed through the lexicon and there are no grammatical rules outside the lexicon. There are thus no probabilities associated with rules, but only probabilities associated with syntactic components of lexical entries. At least two consequences follow. One is that such lexicons have to be structured in a way that recaptures whatever nonspurious generality was previously expressed in nonlexical rules. Another is that because lexical entries bring together *all* the orthographical, morphological, syntactic and semantic information that relates to a particular lexical item, there is much more scope for bringing different sources of probability to bear simultaneously, than there is in more traditional approaches where the grammar is free-standing.

As noted in section 6.3, inheritance lexicons currently appear to be the best way to encode lexicalized grammars. But the existing lexical knowledge representation languages for inheritance lexicons do not have principled ways of handling probabilities (often, indeed, no way of handling them at all). Augmenting these languages with probabilities raises all kinds of interesting issues. For example, in the symbolic case, overriding an inherited default value for a feature F on a node N typically has no consequences for the values for F at the siblings of N. But, with probabilities, changing the value for one member of a class will typically have consequences for the values of all the other members of that class.

From a radical lexicalist perspective, inducing a morphological analysis of a language from a corpus, inducing a part-of-speech set from a corpus, inducing word-to-subcategorization frame mapping from a corpus, inducing a grammar from a corpus, and inducing a set of sense classes from a corpus are all aspects of the *same* task, namely that of inducing a lexicon from a corpus. And, analogously, the various tasks of estimating the probabilities associated with these aspects of language are all tasks that relate to estimating lexical probabilities of various kinds. More than terminology is at stake here since these different aspects of lexical description are mutually constraining and thus mutually informative. Taken individually, many of these tasks look to be very hard. Taken together, they may turn out to be somewhat easier.

We know that corpora drawn from different communicative activities differ greatly one from another in respect of word frequencies, construction frequencies, and so forth. We also know that every natural corpus that has ever been examined obeys Zipf's law. But in between these two extremes we know rather little. Apart from Zipf's law, we do not know what lexical properties, if any, have some useful generality. To take a rather concrete example, does it make sense to talk of a 'core lexicon' for English? If we took the intersection of the 3,000 most frequent words from each of five very different English corpora and found that it contained 1,000 words, then we might be inclined to say 'yes'. But if we then looked more closely at the 1,000 words and discovered that in some corpora *to* was almost always used as a preposition and *get* was almost always used as a passive marker, whereas in other corpora *to* was almost always used as an infinitive marker and *get* was almost always used as a synonym of *acquire*, then we might start to wonder if 'yes' was really the right answer.

Vocabulary increases with corpus size. No matter how big one's lexicon, previously unknown words will always be encountered (Gale & Church, 1990). Robust NLP systems must have machinery for coping with them. Even if the form of the word is in the lexicon, it does not follow that the lexicon will contain the relevant sense. Green reports that, over a wide range of written discourse, between 10% and 25% of the content word tokens are used with senses that are not listed in large published dictionaries†. Doubtless this rather large percentage can be reduced in lexicons that have been induced from, or trained on, a corpus of material from the domain of application. But even if the problem can be reduced to 1% (which seems very unlikely), that still leaves a significant problem for a robust system to address (since 1% of words implies, say, 10% of sentences).

There is a flipside to the last item. Suppose, for example, that we have a 3,000 word lexicon that includes 80% of the word tokens an application meets, but that we would need to increase its size to 30,000 words in order to include 90% of the word tokens it meets. And suppose also that we have a bit of machinery that more or less copes with unknown words (what 'copes' means depends rather heavily on the application). Under these circumstances it is not self-evident whether a given sum of money is best spent on increasing the size of the lexicon by 27,000 words, or on greatly improving the performance of the unknown-word machinery. The former would reduce the number of unknown word tokens encountered by 50%. The latter might well double the quality of the performance of the unknown-word machinery. More generally, now that lexicon development (whether by person or by machine) has become a central activity for NLP, the field needs to establish and deploy notions of marginal utility and marginal cost to apply to that development process.

† Georgia Green, unpublished work, University of Illinois at Urbana Champaign. See also the type and token coverage figures reported in Krovetz (1994)

Moving from CF-PSG to probabilistic CF-PSG does not, of itself, offer any great gain in robustness. If a sentence is ungrammatical, then it will not get a parse. If a sentence involves a construction that is not covered by the probabilistic grammar, then either it will not get a parse or else it will get parsed wrongly. Of course, actual probabilistic grammars generally are much more robust than their nonprobabilistic precursors. But that has much more to do with the fact that they are tuned to particular types of text rather than attempting to be grammars for the 'language as a whole'. There is a tradition of probabilistic NLP which is totally robust at the syntactic level of description – it will always deliver a parse tree (Sampson, 1986, 1991; Sampson *et al.* 1989). This approach works, in part, by having a trivial grammar. Every rule is permitted, although most possible rules have infinitesimal probabilities. This is an appealing idea. But it has the effect of pushing the robustness problem into the semantic analysis component. Wherever it belongs, robustness has not yet achieved the status of a solved problem.

There has been a lot of NLP work on discourse, but little or none of it has been of a kind that connects with the work considered in section 6.3. However, the Gale *et al.* (1992b) 'one sense per discourse' result suggests that searching for more such connections could be a profitable line of enquiry.

None of the work discussed in this paper has dealt with language generation. The probabilistic wave does not seem to have reached the generation beach yet. But probabilities clearly have a potential role to play in language generation. For example, if a generation system maps a meaning M into a string of words S, it is not really sufficient that S has a parse tree that corresponds to M. For the generation system to have a good chance of conveying its intended meaning, it is necessary that the most probable parse tree for S correspond to M. And, if probabilities are to be useful for both generation *and* interpretation, then they had better be declaratively expressed. If the numbers are buried in the procedural code for a parser then they are not likely to be much use for generation.

Finally, Brill's (1992) paper demonstrates that a nonprobabilistic rule-based tagger that has been automatically induced from, and tuned to, a corpus, can work as well as its probabilistic competitors. Before the field gives up totally on nonprobabilistic systems, we need to know if analogues to Brill's approach can be made to work for parsing†, sense

† New work by Zelle & Mooney (1994) implies that inductive logic programming techniques can derive effective deterministic parsers from parsed corpora.

assignment, and the other NLP tasks that presently provide grist for the stochastic mills.

Acknowledgements

I am grateful to Lynne Cahill, Roger Evans, Georgia Green, Adam Kilgarriff, Steve Pulman, Henry Thompson, Max Wheeler, and Yorick Wilks for things that have found their way into this article.

7

Large Databases and Knowledge Re-use

P.M.D. Gray

Abstract

This article argues that problems of scale and complexity of data in large
scientific and engineering databases will drive the development of a new
generation of databases. Examples are the human genome project with
huge volumes of data accessed by widely distributed users, geographic
information systems using satellite data, and advanced CAD and engineering design databases. Databases will share not just facts, but also
procedures, methods and constraints. This together with the complexity
of the data will favour the object-oriented database model. Knowledge
base technology is also moving in this direction, leading to a distributed
architecture of knowledge servers interchanging information on objects
and constraints. An important theme is the re-use not just of data and
methods but of higher-level knowledge. For success, a multi-disciplinary
effort will be needed along the lines of the Knowledge Sharing Effort in
USA, which is discussed.

7.1 Introduction

The research area of databases is a very interesting testing ground for
computing science ideas. It is an area where theory meets reality in the
form of large quantities of data with very computer-intensive demands
on it. Until recently the major problems were in banking and commercial
transactions. These sound easy in principle but they are made difficult
by problems of scale, distributed access, and the ever present need to
move a working system with long-term data onto new hardware, new
operating systems, and new modes of interaction. Despite this, principles for database system architecture were established which have stood
the test of time – data independence, serialised transactions, two-phase
commit, query optimisation and conceptual schema languages. Thanks
to these advances the database industry is very large and very success-

ful. However, we are starting to meet a whole new range of challenges, and we shall need to develop new architectures and adapt and extend established principles.

In some ways there is an analogy with the way in which physicists at the start of this century faced with the phenomena of radioactive decay and the constancy of the speed of light had to develop new theories of quantum behaviour and relativity, whilst still maintaining much of classical physics. Similarly, computer science needs to respond to the challenge of a new generation of applications by developing new architectures and theories. In the database field it is the extension into the area of large scientific and geographic databases and engineering design which is driving us forward to meet the so-called killer applications. Classical relational database technology is (and will remain) very successful for commercial use, but we need new approaches elsewhere.

In this article we shall see how problems of scale and complexity of data are leading to more complex data models and an advanced database technology for storing objects and for integrating constraints and procedures with data. Thus database technology is starting to merge with knowledge base technology. Also, as the data grows we need to distribute it but we also need to share it and re-use it more effectively. We cannot have everyone keeping their own duplicate copies of rapidly growing databases or, worse still, rediscovering the knowledge. We need knowledge servers, some with problem-solving ability and some containing large nets of connected facts, probably structured as objects. But such sharing is not the only way of re-using knowledge. One theme running through this chapter is that knowledge must be transformed in order to be re-used. Thus, instead of just shipping binary executable images around, we need to combine constraint declarations and procedures from various sources and use them to generate code that is tailored to the form of data on servers. Thus, before knowledge can be re-used, it must be transformed! We start the argument, however, by looking at how problems of scale are changing our entrenched habits.

7.2 Problems of Scale

Some of the stress factors involved are problems of scale. As Dijkstra (1972) noted, we kid ourselves by a simple numerical induction into thinking that what we can do twice we can do ten times, and hence a thousand or even a million times, whereas a change of size of several orders of magnitude changes the nature of the problem (and of its solution)! Just think of the problem of building an index to a 1-terabyte table; it would take days! Likewise making a dumptape! But agencies with satellite data are already talking about needing space for 10,000 terabytes! The human genome project (Frenkel, 1991) needs to search for fragments, often with fuzzy matching, in a sequence of letters that if printed in this typeface would stretch for 5,000 miles. In fact we have only learnt how to cope with sequences about a mile in length. Furthermore, we cannot expect to keep this sequence all in one place. It will have to be maintained in segments on numerous different sites, each of which will be continuously refined and updated and will be accessed by people from all over the world. These are real problems which when solved will open up new opportunities in drug design and in genetic engineering. Likewise we have to make satellite data more easily available, so that we are not forced into more space launches to rediscover it!

In the early decades of computing there was a great emphasis on how to do a computation, and a fascination with mechanisms and with speed. Initially there was a fascination with programming languages and then with operating systems and most recently with fine-grain parallelism. All the time there was pressure for faster compilers, more efficient disc operating systems, faster networks and super-computers. We seemed always to treat the problem of speed as being more important than the problems of size which come in dealing with very large programs or very large collections of data. Now that we have very large main memories, and networks that link terabytes of data, it is time to take seriously the problems of size and sharing of information resources. Indeed the availability of very large main memories and gigabyte discs at very cheap prices is the main change in computing over the last decade. It is hard to think back to a time only ten years ago when many groups worked with a PDP-11 with 64K memory and a Winchester 100Mb disc, and no wide area network.

7.3 Coping with Complexity

In this new era we have to deal with complexity of applications and also complexity and size of stored knowledge. Thus we are used to the idea of complex program structures but we must also get used to the idea of complex stored data structures, not just arrays of integers or large relational tables. In general we have very complex directed graphs joining nodes of mixed types, and commonly containing subgraphs with a recursive tree structure. This aspect of complexity is made even worse by problems of scale, as Dijkstra points out.

One of the great triumphs of database theory has been to make all this tractable, and to allow one to deal with it without getting lost, or having multiple updates corrupt it. If one tries to draw an instance-level graph showing pointers between related instances, then one pretty quickly gets into a tangled mess of crossing lines. The secret, discovered by Bachmann (1973), is to draw the graph not at the instance level but at the type level, so that for each type of data one can see what types of data point to it and vice versa. Thus in a Bachmann diagram or an Entity–Relationship diagram (Figure 7.1) each box or node represents a different entity type, shown once only, and chains of directed arcs represent hierarchies at the instance level, whilst cycles represent recursive tree structures.

It is not a long way from database entity types in a Bachmann diagram to object classes in an object-oriented programming language. The difference is that database objects are persistent and do not disappear at the end of running the program. Also these objects are shared by a variety of users, and are allowed to be independently updated and to evolve whilst retaining links to other objects. Thus it is not sufficient just to keep a saved state or memory dump, as on a single-user database. This has led to the development of the *object-oriented database*. Furthermore, the problem of serialising concurrent transactions on such an object database is not easy, especially where deletions are involved.

The move to object-oriented databases has been driven by a variety of needs. In the first place, the tabular relational model is an inadequate representation of reality. Thus, in order to represent real world events, there was a need to develop much richer conceptual data models, with explicit identifiers for objects instead of keys for tuples. These data models map much more easily onto an object-oriented programming model, because there is such a close correspondence between object classes and a Bachmann diagram. The reverse is also true in that the construction of large object-oriented programs is greatly helped by using a good semantic data model in designing the classes (Gray *et al.*, 1992).

7.4 Knowledge Re-Use

A second reason for using object-oriented databases is the need for knowledge re-use. As applications get bigger and more complicated it becomes too hard for any one programmer to understand all the lines of code. Consequently more people are adopting the object-oriented idea of encapsulating behavioural methods with the object class, and hiding details of the implementation. Once a good class description has been built and tested it is encapsulated for re-use like an electronic compo-

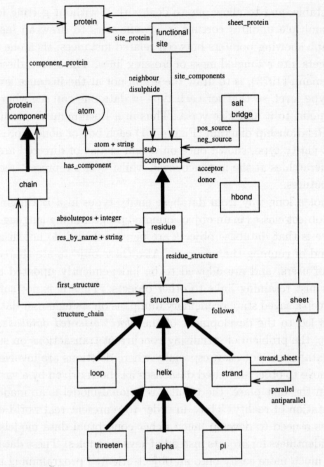

Fig. 7.1. Bachmann diagram for protein structure database (Kemp *et al.*, 1990). Each entity type (object class) is shown as a rectangle. Relationships between objects are represented by labelled arrows. Thick arrows point from specialised subclasses to their superclasses. Three-dimensional coordinates of atoms in structures are held as compound values shown by an ellipse.

nent. This is the attraction of Smalltalk (and of C^{++} when it is well written).

The Smalltalk class library, which has evolved over almost a decade, has been a major success story in encouraging code re-use. It has been much more successful than a Fortran subroutine library for two reasons. Firstly, instead of having subroutines with a large number of parameters and some global variables we have methods with a small number of object-identifiers or other parameters. In effect, the object becomes a natural bundle of parameters, whereas it is easy to make mistakes with long parameter lists and tedious to understand their description. Secondly, thanks to the use of inheritance, it is possible to specialise the description of an object by overriding some method definitions and adding others. Thus one can re-use inherited methods which saves rewriting. In fact, the first instinct of a Smalltalk programmer is to browse the class hierarchy for a suitable class definition, and then to specialise it where needed.

This theme of re-use extends naturally to object-oriented databases. Originally databases were about sharing large numbers of facts and maintaining them. With an OODB it becomes natural also to store the methods in the database, so that they too can be shared and re-used by a wide variety of users. This is important for maintaining the data in accordance with the *principle of data independence*. This principle was established in an early ANSI/SPARC report (ANSI) and it says that application programs must see data descriptions through a conceptual schema of abstract type declarations, which hides details of data storage. The reason for this is so that one could copy the data into a more suitable representation (for example with space for extra attributes or with extra indices or using a different kind of B-tree) without having to alter the application code. Clearly, this can only be done if the methods for accessing or updating the data items are simultaneously changed to correspond and thus they should be stored with the data. However, with an OODB we can extend this further to include methods that calculate with the data and derive new information, even though many of these will use more primitive methods to access the data, and so will not need to be changed following a change of storage.

There is another reason why it is valuable to store a wide variety of method definitions with an OODB, and this is to do with the growth of communications networks. With the availability of wideband networks we are less likely to bring the data to a monolithic program running on a single processor, and more likely to do parts of the computation on various remote processors. It thus makes more sense for this code to reside on remote machines. For many conventional programmers and scientists this involves quite a change of mindset. They are used to thinking of data as large Fortran arrays, and they start by sucking data from a database into these arrays. However, the client–server model is already beginning to change this. Here, part of the computation is done on the client and the part which is data-intensive is done on the server.

This saves time particularly when part of the computation is used to test and select data items. It thus makes sense to do these tests with stored methods on objects, where possible. With a distributed architecture of knowledge servers it makes sense to have them share an OODB, so that objects 'carry their methods with them'. In fact what are actually sent round the network are the object-identifiers, whilst master copies of the objects and their methods are kept for update purposes on the OODB.

7.5 Knowledge as Rule Bases

We must now try to define more clearly what is meant by 'knowledge' and what forms it comes in, especially if we envisage large knowledge servers. We have seen how modern databases have the capacity to store not only large numbers of atomic facts, but also large networks of related objects with complex structures, and significant amounts of code. But here we are describing storage at the *symbol level* instead of what Alan Newell (1982) called the *knowledge level*. At this higher level we are talking about knowledge of how to solve a certain class of problem, or processing expertise in a certain domain. This covers a large area of AI research.

Early attempts concentrated on, where code was held in production rules of the form 'if conjunction of conditions then execute state-changing action'. These needed a separate data-driven interpreter, and the idea was that the interpreter would pick out and chain together rules according to the problem, effectively composing a program to solve the problem on demand.

Furthermore, the rules were seen almost as independent units of information which could be accumulated in any order. The greater the number of rules, the more powerful was the system. Alas, in real applications it turns out that many of the rules are devised to meet a specific problem and are not really re-usable. Often this is because extra control information has been added to the rule in order to guide the interpreter. Worse still, as more rules are added it may interfere with the way in which previous rules used to chain together, and so extra control information has to be added to stop this interference, thus reducing re-usabilityeven further.

These difficulties with production rules led to a rival approach based on predicate logic, using a knowledge base of Horn clauses and a goal-driven interpreter such as Prolog (Gray, 1984; Sterling & Shapiro, 1986). This was very successful for building decision trees used in diagnostic applications. Here the mode of computation is more like recursive evaluation of deeply nested conditional expressions, which does not have the side-effects of assignment that make production rules so awkward. Thus at run-time it is possible to compose a decision tree (or that part of it that is needed) out of a large rule base accumulated in any order (Milne, 1991). However, once again there is a tendency to include control information such as the explicit ordering of rules and the notorious 'cut' operator in Prolog, which makes the information harder to re-use. Also, often the non-determinism in the rules can become very limited, for example when each rule for achieving a sub-goal starts by testing the type of an object given as argument. In this case the search for a sub-goal definition becomes very much like picking a method definition out of a large class library and the model for re-use becomes like that in an object-oriented program.

It appears that the attempt to make large rule bases by analogy with large fact bases has failed. Instead, people have followed up on the correspondence between frame-based systems and object-oriented databases. Thus frames (which were originally templates for events described in sentences) have become units of storage containing pointers to other frames. They also have attached procedures (demons) associated with some data items. In this representation, backward chaining rules become deterministic methods of the form 'if you want to achieve this goal on this object with these parameters then achieve these sub-goals on these related objects'. Forward chaining rules become attached procedures triggered by updates of the form 'if you update this value so that it moves out of range or fails some condition and the following other conditions are true on related objects then abort the update or do some compensating update or recompute some data values ... '.

Furthermore the idea of storing knowledge uniformly in units of rules has been largely abandoned. Instead, we have knowledge stored in a variety of specially compiled forms which are appropriate to the domain and the kind of questions or tasks. Where simple diagnosis is required one builds a decision tree. Where complex diagnosis based on a deeper understanding is required then it pays to build an object model of the real world and use the methods or triggers to run simulations which compute desired or expected states of the world (this is sometimes called model-based reasoning). Where partial or uncertain knowledge is concerned, then one tries to use fuzzy logic or build causal nets or attach weights to evidence. In a classic article Drew McDermott (1986) has concluded, somewhat despairingly, that, for all cases except pure deduction, we have to abandon the idea of storing knowledge declaratively, which is the goal of most logicians. We can no longer expect to hold almost all knowledge in the form of a vast collection of well formed predicate logic sentences, in the manner of Russell and Whitehead. Instead we must have a much more operational view of knowledge, concentrating on *how* it is to be used.

A consequence of this view is that people are concentrating on knowledge as stored on servers and expert problem solvers distributed over a network. The problem solvers incorporate compiled procedural knowledge which knows how to take the factual knowledge and solve certain classes of problem. Thus we take seriously the view that knowledge is compiled for a specific use, and move to a much more operational or encapsulated view of it. Each knowledge server or problem-solver must present an external interface to users or other solvers on the network, whilst hiding details of knowledge storage and knowledge compilation. Instead of offering transparent access to declarative knowledge, it offers to execute various commands or operations on pieces of knowledge.

7.6 Constraints as Knowledge

We have been exploring ways to store procedural knowledge in large knowledge bases. We have seen that the simple idea of storing rules led to knowledge at too small a level of granularity, which was too specialised to its application for it to be re-used. Hence the trend to use much larger chunks of specially compiled knowledge. There is, however, another way to get slightly larger units of knowledge, which are indeed independent and can be held in a declarative form. These units are *constraints* referring to whole classes of objects or selected subsets of them. For example consider the following integrity constraint referring to an object model of patients in the Colan language (Bassiliades & Gray, 1994):

> For each p in patient such that status $(p) = $ 'allergic'
> not exists c in components (drugs taken (p))
> such that c is in allergies (p).

This constraint is what is known in database terminology as an integrity constraint. It prohibits certain kinds of updates, and describes a kind of invariant boolean property of the state of these object classes that must be maintained true by any update. It is more flexible than a rule in that it can be used in a variety of ways.

(1) It can be used to generate a number of data-driven rules which are triggered by a proposed change to one of the attributes and

which check whether the invariant would be preserved, and if not carry out some abort or compensating action (Embury *et al.*, 1993).

(2) It can be used as part of a backchaining system, for example one that is searching for suitable drugs for a patient. In general it adds an extra sub-goal which meets the constraint and restricts the solution set further (King, 1984).

(3) The textual version of the constraint can be stored in the database and quoted by an explanation facility when a violation is detected.

Thus we see that constraints have to be transformed in some way before they can be used as part of a programming system. This is the price we pay for keeping them as independent units of knowledge. This does not contradict McDermott's dictum given earlier since the knowledge does get transformed into a special form suitable for use, but it recognises that some kinds of knowledge can conveniently be held in one form and transformed into several alternative forms on demand.

There are strong parallels here with query optimisation. Indeed, a query on an object-oriented database can be thought of as a collection of constraints on the result and its components (Gray *et al.*, 1992). The main technique of query optimisation is to transform the ordering of the constraints, usually so that some term in one of them can be used as a generator for a very restrictive set of values that is then used as the basis for generating the set of solutions. For example instead of generating all persons and testing for one whose age is 101 or name is Aristotle, one can use an index to find such people directly. One can also do semantic query optimisation, where for example (King, 1984) if one is looking for a ship over 30,000 tons, one can use a constraint that only aircraft carriers displace over 25,000 tons and thus one need only enumerate aircraft carriers in the search. Thus constraints can be used in an intelligent way to restrict a search space.

A further interesting development is in special purpose constraint satisfaction packages (van Hentenryck, 1991). We have been familiar with some of these, such as linear programming packages or equation-solvers. The point about the newer class of solver is that they are not totally deterministic, and they can do an intelligent search through a combinatorially large search space, although they may not be guaranteed to find all solutions. In consequence they can improve on the performance of simple techniques of backtrack search used in backward chaining. They can also do reasoning by elimination, which is similar to setting up a number of possible worlds and reasoning about them until all are eliminated save one. Thus it may in future be better to pass around knowledge in the form of constraints, which can then be transformed for internal use by a variety of packages and techniques, instead of passing knowledge as rules which can only be used by one kind of interpreter.

There is an important connection between this view of constraints and the principle of data independence given earlier (Gray & Kemp, 1994). That principle requires one to express queries in a set-theoretic form using only terms declared in the conceptual schema. The query then has to be evaluated against the storage schema. However, this is not just a simple macro-expansion or an interpretation. Instead, it involves re-thinking the query evaluation plan, making use of auxiliary data structures and indexes and choosing a good order of evaluation. The resultant form of the query may look very different depending on what kind of storage schema is used (relational tables, or a graph structure of objects, or Prolog clauses). When we consider constraints instead of queries, the same principle applies. The final form of the constraint may look very different when expressed in a data-driven form as against a goal-driven form, but it is still the same knowledge being re-used.

This way of viewing re-use has some consequences for programming techniques. The dominant programming language is currently C^{++}, and the dominant mode of re-use is by re-using procedures with strong static type checks. This encourages the programmer to think very precisely about the data representation, often at the level of arrays, pointers and bitmaps, and to code it very tightly for fast execution. Once such code is encapsulated it cannot be taken apart or re-ordered. Whilst it is necessary to adopt this approach in real-time systems and in low-level algorithms (e.g. for B-trees or sorting) it is not good for higher levels of software which are knowledge intensive or database applications. In fact, it may be that our approach to software engineering and formal methods is too conditioned by low-level software. Instead, at the higher levels, we need to keep our knowledge in a much more flexible form, using very high-level languages and high-level type declarations (conceptual schemas) that do not commit us to a precise storage representation. It means that more compiling, code-generation and program transformation will take place at run-time. Programmers will spend a significant part of their time writing code to transform other pieces of code or to generate pieces of C, or else invoking tools to do it.

The argument for doing this is twofold. Firstly it makes software evolution easier, and secondly it allows global optimisation. In the first case, we must take seriously the proposition that some data is so long-lived that it may well outlast the programming languages currently in fashion. Thus we must beware of the legacy problems caused by having fragments of code, compiled by elderly compilers for ageing languages, existing in large OODB or knowledge bases. There are already problems of legacy software, where people dare not replace procedures or change data formats, since they do not know what side-effects this may have. By hanging on to knowledge as high-level constraints and code-generating it for new forms of storage organisation we keep it fresh and active.

The second point concerns global optimisation. It is a well known phenomenon in operational research that one can optimise part of a system in a way that inhibits overall optimisation. Thus we must stop programmers writing tight code committed to a particular storage representation which may tie the rest of the system to an unsuitable representation. Instead, as a positive example we can cite the optimisation of queries which include calls to Daplex method code stored in an object-oriented database. In this case the method code was held not in compiled form but as a list comprehension. Thus we could allow the optimiser as a privileged program to break the encapsulation of the code and combine it with the rest of the query so as to permit global query optimisation, with a new starting point and elimination of repeated computation of sub-expressions (Jiao & Gray, 1991), and hence very significant performance improvement. By analogy, we can see the possibility of collecting a variety of stored constraints from different sources concerned with a complex engineering design problem. We can then send them to an appropriate constraint solver which thus has all the information in a flexible form and can also retrieve measurements from a database, in order to solve the problem.

7.7 Networks for Knowledge Sharing

Another important aspect of knowledge re-use concerns the distribution of knowledge. Until recently people expected to get most of the knowledge or data that they worked with from their own machine or from a local server. Thus although people routinely email other people worldwide, they are more cautious about sending queries to remote databases. Instead they prefer to browse around directories on remote sites and then transfer whole files to their own filespace for deeper investigation. Transferring files may work when one is looking at facts. It does not work well when one is working with highly structured knowledge that is regularly updated. Thus we need to change people's behaviour and perceptions in the search for knowledge.

Starting in 1991, a group in the USA (Neches *et al.*, 1991) has been looking at this under the title of the Knowledge Sharing Effort (KSE). They envisage both people and programs asking questions of remote knowledge-servers, in the same way that people currently can type SQL on a terminal to query data on a remote host, or that expert systems can formulate and send off their own SQL queries to get data as needed. However, they need a more complex control and command language than SQL, which they call KQML (Knowledge Query and Manipulation Language). It is expected that queries in KQML will return selected objects as object-identifiers, instead of returning whole files. This saves time and space on the user's machine, and it also gets over the problem of keeping multiple copies of files. The object-identifiers received may then be used as a part of further more specific queries which are sent to the remote server. In some ways this is analogous to a hypertext web, where the hypertext program either generates or contains embedded queries which are used in place of static links to objects. The embedded query retrieves from the server further hypertext which is kept up to date, and may in turn contain hypertext buttons which activate other embedded queries.

However, KQML allows for an altogether more sophisticated architecture than using a single identified remote server. Instead, it is oriented towards a world in which autonomous servers come onto a network, speaking a language or a dialect that is not necessarily known to the client. Thus requests are initially made to a *mediator* or knowledge broker. The mediator is an expert system which knows about available knowledge sources and can read the KQML header so as to decide which source is appropriate or worth trying. The body of the message or query, which contains the details of the task, is encoded in an intermediate interchange format called KIF. Further, instead of passing the message straight to the knowledge-server, the mediator may invoke a *facilitator* process to act as a knowledge transformer in the conversation between client and server.

A facilitator may be required for a number of reasons (Wiederhold, 1992). The most obvious is where the knowledge is stored in a different representation language. Another possibility is that data or results may need presenting in a different style, or using a different style of interaction. This is often the job of a database view, but people are demanding a wider range of graphic multi-media interfacing. Another possibility is that the knowledge-server might be a robot directly gathering information which needs a series of simple low-level goals in place of a high-level goal set by the mediator.

A mediator, at its most ambitious, can be used to set up a collection of co-operating processes to find and deliver the desired knowledge. This means accessing more than one knowledge-server, with results from one server being transformed and passed to another server, rather in the manner of a distributed database query. However, it is different in that it is not just to do with joining large sets or intersecting tables from different sites, instead it is a question of moving pieces of knowledge around and processing and adding value to them at each site.

A further complication also has a parallel in distributed database query answering. This is the situation where the client and the knowledge server are using slightly different database schemas, even if they are using the same knowledge representation language to describe the schema. Thus the same words may be used to represent slightly different things, and certain pieces of information may need to be derived instead of being retrieved directly. In a distributed DBS this is overcome by defining a global schema, and predefining views to map into this schema. In knowledge processing the corresponding concept is a common ontology, which is a richer concept taken from natural language research.

Neches in Neches *et al.* (1991) defines an ontology as *the basic terms and relations comprising the vocabulary of a topic area, as well as the rules for combining terms and relations to define extensions to the vocabulary.* However, it is something more than just a dictionary of terms together with grammar rules and semantic checks. Some people talk about an *ontological commitment*, meaning that before one can even write down any assertion or theorem or other form of knowledge one must first take decisions committing one to a particular representational viewpoint. Thus if I start talking about the 'salary of an employee' to another knowledge source, then we must first check that we use the same words for the same concepts (e.g. is salary net of tax?) but more significantly we must share some kind of entity–relationship model, and know about related things like 'pay-day', 'hiring' and 'salary-cheque'. This is all part of an ontology which is itself formally expressed in some meta-language or interlingua. The KSE is using Ontologinua developed by Gruber (1993) at Stanford, and Gruber is currently collecting and comparing a variety of such ontologies, which provide a basis for the exchange of both problem-solving knowledge and domain specific knowledge.

The Knowledge Sharing Effort (Patil *et al.*, 1992; Swartout *et al.*, 1993) was set up in 1991 with funding from ARPA and a coordinator paid for by NSF. Its original aims were given in Neches *et al.* (1991). It has four working groups. One deals with collection of ontologies and is headed by Gruber and Tenenbaum. Another deals with interchange of knowledge expressed in different Knowledge Representation Languages (KRL). This is tackled by developing a universal intermediate interchange format (KIF) into which each KRL can be translated (much as is done with portable compilers). Another group is working on refining KRL's by specifying a layered structure (KRSS) for them. The main issue there is how much inference should be done by the KRL interpreter, and what inferential power it is assumed to possess, compared to the problem solver. The final group on external interfaces headed by Finin and Wiederhold is developing a universal high-level knowledge manipulation language KQML. This is seen as a kind of knowledge communications protocol for use by mediators and facilitators on a network. Each piece of knowledge on the network will be encoded in KIF, but wrapped in a package with a KQML header, which will help the mediator to decide what to do with it. KQML is basically a command language with about 30 different commands. Parameters to commands describe what ontology to use and how to return the answers, independent of the implementation of the knowledge server. It thus enables new servers to come on line and extend the capability of an existing network.

This kind of architecture is very appealing. It makes use of the greatly increased communication bandwidth that is becoming available. Instead of concentrating on small grain parallelism it uses large grain division-of-labour parallelism, with mediators setting up tasks on a variety of servers. One big unknown, reported by the KQML group, is how to return answers which point into a complex semantic network. This is very similar to the problem of returning objects from a remote object-oriented database. Indeed, one of the initial goals was to use an OODB as a 'substrate under the knowledge representation system to provide a persistent object store for knowledge base objects'. Thus we need to exploit the similarities between frame-based KRL and OODB in order to make good use of database technology.

7.8 Conclusion

The combination of mediators, facilitators and a variety of ontologies on one large knowledge sharing network is an exciting vision. It brings together a number of different areas of computing science that have almost grown into separate disciplines. We need advances in object-oriented databases in order to structure the knowledge, and enhance its re-usability. We need to adapt constraint satisfiers so that they can work as semi-autonomous problem-solvers which are passed constraints and other knowledge across the network. We need advances in conceptual modelling and natural language in order to understand ontologies, and how to use knowledge based on one ontology to answer questions based on a closely related one. We need advances in AI and the theory of co-operating agents in order to have effective mediators. Finally, we need good distributed database and object request broker technology adapted to make this all work efficiently on a very large scale, so that the problems of scale are taken seriously.

It would help enormously if there were a domain with a large network that would provide a series of hard, but very necessary, applications to drive the project. It is possible that the human genome project will be suitable. The project is by nature distributed, with large numbers of centres world-wide producing sequence data. Some of the centres are also producing data in the form of complex three-dimensional structures. These can be put together in an object-oriented database, which is particularly valuable as a way of representing protein classification and for grouping sets of similarly shaped components (Kemp *et al.*, 1994). In the genome sequence data there are several different ways of classifying proteins, for example according to function or according to evolution. A protein sequence may be placed in one family based on evolution, and another category based on function. This too can be represented nicely in an object-oriented datamodel.

A powerful technique is to align a new sequence with a number of other sequences, representing mutants produced by evolution, in order to show which parts of the sequence stay unchanged. Where the three-dimensional structure of one of the sequences is known, a program on a knowledge-server can then use this alignment to suggest the structure of the new sequence by the technique of homology modelling. Already there is an autonomous ftp server at the European Molecular Biology Laboratory at Heidelberg (Rost *et al.*, 1994) which will take a message giving a new sequence and search for similar sequences in various sequence databases, then automatically do a multiple alignment, and pass the results to a program which predicts the presence of helix and sheet backbone structures. Finally the results are emailed back without human intervention.

Here we see the paradigm of sending data to distributed knowledge-servers at work, in an early form, which is clearly going to expand. However, as more knowledge servers appear there will be a greater need for mediators. Likewise, currently there is a simple shared ontology based on standards set by protein crystallographers who distribute the structural data, and by the genetic code used in sequences. However, once programs start to reason and to exchange information about geometrical shapes and causality in enzyme reaction mechanisms then there will be a need for a richer ontology.

Richer ontologies are already needed in the area of engineering design and CAD. Here there already exist very large databases of parts and components, and we are beginning to make use of object-oriented databases for specialisation of parts and storing various kinds of methods. There are various very sophisticated application programs, but each of them requests design data in a special form appropriate to itself and the ontology is not made explicit. Thus it is not easy to get them to work together and we do not achieve the knowledge re-use that is the main theme of this chapter. Likewise we need a better understanding of the role of constraints in engineering design, so that we can make use of powerful generic constraint satisfiers, instead of having simpler techniques hard-wired into applications programs. Note that we are not just saving the time required to re-code a procedure from a library, instead we are using a technique that is quite hard to think about and too hard for most programmers to code; but they can easily set up constraints to pass to a solver. That is the significance of treating problems at the knowledge level instead of the symbol level, since we are able to reorganise the solution of the problem and bring more powerful techniques to bear.

Thus I conclude that the architecture of distributed knowledge-servers and the theme of knowledge re-use will increasingly occupy computing scientists in the years to come. I also believe that it will be driven by large data intensive scientific and engineering applications.

8

The Global-yet-Personal Information System

J.R. Gurd and C.B. Jones

Abstract

The editors of this volume set out to compile a set of personal views about the long-term direction of computer science research. In responding to this goal, we have chosen to identify what we perceive as a long-term challenge to the capabilities of computing technology in serving the broader needs of people and society, and to discuss how this 'Grand Challenge' might be met by future research. We also present our personal view of the required research methodology.

8.1 Introduction

Much of present-day computer technology is concerned with the processing, storage and communication of digital *data*. The view taken in this contribution is that a far more important use of computers and computing is to manage and manipulate human-related *information*. Currently, the provision of such structured information has been tackled at the level of single organisations (company, institution, government department, etc.) by the use of *databases* which are often limited to single functions within the organisation. Databases are *closed*, in the sense that the information itself can be viewed in a limited number of ways, and the ways in which it can evolve are carefully controlled. Interaction between databases containing related data is prohibited, except through the mediation of human experts. This is an unnecessarily restricted concept of information processing, and one which fails to recognise its real social and economic potential. We foresee a huge market for *personal* information services based on *open* access to a continually evolving *global* network of stored information. Although there are significant technical difficulties associated with creating and controlling such networks and services, we predict that the economic incentives will ensure that the

127

necessary development occurs and that this information market will –
within a period of decades – dwarf the market in computing machinery
and software.

With regard to the research methodology, we speculate that computer
science is evolving into the more general discipline of *informatics* and
consider the nature of informatics as an emerging science.

8.1.1 The importance of information

Information is an extremely potent commodity whether for individual
humans or for organisations. Time and again we have seen cases where
access to the right information at the right time saves lives, creates
wealth, improves the environment, etc. etc. The contribution made
by Gutenberg to the dissemination of information is discussed in the
seminal work of Marshall McLuhan (1962). The exponential progress in
science, technology and engineering would have been impossible without
our ability to disseminate technical information. Today's computing and
communications technology can support an enormous growth in information access, inducing who knows what changes in our society. However,
two things threaten further progress: one is the worrying question of
whether we will actually drown in the amount of undigested data which
is now available to us; the other is whether, in spite of the potential
availability of information, we simply cannot gain access to it, either because we are unaware of its existence or because there is no structured
way to search for the items in which we are interested.

CD-ROMs containing enormous quantities of data are advertised in
the national press; the Internet is an international network whose capacity is growing at a phenomenal twenty per cent per month; an enormous
amount of raw data is available as strings of ASCII characters over the
Internet; use of the 'World Wide Web' is growing at a rate which beggars
the imagination. It is tempting to imagine that we live in an information-
rich age, since there is this potentially enormous wealth of information
that can now be accessed electronically. On the other hand, unnecessary
difficulties impede legitimate use of electronically controlled information
to such an extent that individuals could consider themselves at the same
time information-poor.

In order to understand this paradox, it is crucial to distinguish between information and the raw data. In this article, we use the two
terms as follows:

data – uninterpreted byte streams

Raw data is stored on magnetic media. It is a slight simplification to say that it has no structure; in fact, the byte stream can contain bytes marking some structure, but this is only given meaning by execution of specific programs (see below). An interesting example of this is the markup notation provided in SGML (Standardised Generalised Markup Language).

information – collections of named data items, linked – for example – by relations

Here, information about information structures is accessible by programs: in many database systems, the data dictionary is itself accessible†.

Such information – in the above sense – that we do have access to derives from *databases* stored in digital computer systems. Such databases act as passive 'data warehouses', containing a vast quantity of raw data that has to be carefully garnered and then painstakingly interpreted by human 'users' before it can be put to good use. Programs which actively seek information can be envisaged and, indeed, some exist, but they are currently primitive. Enquiries which require access to more than one database face almost insuperable problems of *incompatibility*, in interface protocols, data organisation, data formats, etc.

In order to amplify this criticism, let us first exemplify the positive ways in which computer systems have already managed to transform our lives. Rather than a factory filled with robots, consider the impact of 'EPoS' (Electronic Point-of-Sale) on a supermarket belonging to a large chain: it no longer needs to carry most of its stock in its storeroom; computer tracking of sales, plus planning of deliveries, enables the shelves to be restocked more or less directly from lorries. This ensures fresher produce and less wastage, and reduces the cost of holding stock. Stocking of the warehouse and dispatch of vehicles are also controlled by computer. When customers go into the supermarket, they collect goods whose identity is recognised via a barcode ('EAN', in the UK) which is used both to locate the price for the customer's itemised bill and to update the stock level; the customer has the option of paying for the purchases via a transaction, controlled by a plastic card, which ultimately ends up in a change in bank balances (one of many transactions carried out without the intervention of a human being).

---

† For the sake of brevity, we shall frequently use the term 'information' to mean, strictly speaking, 'information embodied in [the] raw data'.

8.1.2 Problems in accessing information

Limitations in the benefit of computer systems result from the difficulty of accessing and/or updating information, and this is equally easy to exemplify. There are an enormous number of examples where information which *is potentially available* somewhere in the world is either difficult or impossible to access. Even though we would be prepared to pay for access to such information, and it would increase the effectiveness and/or fulfilment of our lives, we find ourselves unable to get it; indeed, all too often it is only the notorious 'hackers' who are prepared to expend the necessary time and ingenuity to access useful information.

An example which again affects most individuals is the need to plan journeys. Let us look at what is currently available. Some information – such as flight delays – is freely available on 'Teletext'. It is possible to go into a travel agent and to discuss with a human agent the plans for, say, an airline trip. Travel agents normally use computers which enable them to see both the potential routings and the status of bookings on various flights. But there is in fact no reason why we need to go to the travel agent. Many of us have sufficient access to information processing facilities that, if we could only access the database directly (as the French can for train bookings via 'Minitel'), we could handle the booking ourselves. More importantly, many journeys are not straightforward cases of travelling by air. What we would really like to do is to look at a range of possibilities comparing (combinations of) train, car and air routes: it would be desirable to find out about available trains without having to log on to a totally separate database; one would also wish to know about the economics of renting a car and undertaking part of our journey by road (and the probable conditions of the roads); at the same time, we would like to be able to access information about the availability of hotel rooms at prices acceptable to us, and perhaps their vicinity to starred restaurants! If all of the data were in one database, this programming task would be well within the state of the art. It would not be difficult to write a computer program which also stored information about our preferences and which, on being given the starting points and finishing points and approximate times of our desired journey, would come back to us with a range of options ordered by our stated desires. But the crucial difficulty is that up-to-date information can only be obtained by accessing *a range of* relevant databases.

Of course, end-users do not always act solely in a personal capacity. There are innumerable examples where corporate users of information systems would like to have access to a range of related information at the same time. For example, a company which is planning new water treatment plants needs an enormous range of information: firstly, demographic information, especially projected changes in population; it needs information about the terrain in which potential water storage facilities could be built; weather information needs to be correlated with geographic information about rivers, including their rates of flow; perhaps information is required on the state of pollution in those rivers, in order to plan further processing facilities; and so on. Much of this information *is available* in databases and, given network access, could be obtained in seconds. The challenge faced by anybody wishing to undertake such an engineering project is to access information from a variety of sources in a range of information structures, to correlate it and present it appropriately, probably to a fixed and tight time schedule, in order to facilitate rapid planning. There is in fact a huge economic advantage to an engineering concern in being able to access and process information quickly.

One can find examples where there are even larger financial consequences, and where immediate access to a wide variety of accurate information sources can give the decision makers a huge advantage over their rivals. For example, multi-national companies about to take long-term investment decisions might benefit from access to information about investment support and taxation incentives, etc. around the world; or governments may wish to base decisions on interest rate changes on the instantaneous state of the economies of other countries.

Everyone can benefit from access to multiple sources of computer-based data, suitably interpreted as the human-related information it represents. Such information would be even more useful if it could be integrated in a reasonable way (Malone *et al.*, 1987). However, there are severe technical problems standing in the way of this ideal.

Our contribution to this volume is founded on the twin beliefs:

(i) that making *all* such stored information potentially and readily accessible, in integrated form and on an individual basis, will create a potent new driving force for the global economy; and

(ii) that reaching such a position constitutes a 'Grand Challenge' for research in computer science (or, more generally, informatics).

8.1.3 Background

As we have pointed out already, the state of the art is represented by database technology, which is closer to data management than information management. Furthermore, most of the effort in developing databases so far has been devoted to compiling the data. Even this has been done only on an *ad hoc* basis; the data is gathered by whatever means are available, and then humans are challenged to gain access to it. Increased processing power can be thrown at the human–computer interface to overcome the inconveniences resulting from the *ad hoc* gathering of data but even this is insufficient and a new breed of employee, the 'database access adviser', has had to emerge to help the real 'end-users' gain access to the information they really want. The scientific activities of chemists are now supported by hundreds of databases; in many cases, access requires support from advisers. In office management terms, while computers may have supplanted filing clerks, they have not been able to replace administrators responsible for search 'strategy'.

It might be argued that this approach at least has the merit of simplicity, thereby minimising the opportunities for human error. However, even in the simplest systems of today, numerous anecdotes serve to warn us that any strong faith in our information systems is misplaced. The growth of electronic news boards and news groups is itself a fascinating example of information dissemination routes which were unthinkable twenty years ago. One such news group (`comp.risks`) records some of the horror stories which occur when computer systems are poorly designed or used in inappropriate ways. A common cause of many of the unfortunate experiences seems to be our inability to distinguish the information in our databases from the situation in the 'real world' that it purports to represent.

Little can be done to protect a system from being given *incorrect* information (that is, information that incorrectly represents the external reality). For example, people whose death is inaccurately reported can no longer resolve the mistake as readily as Mark Twain did with his humorous cable to the Associated Press; they can find that they are no longer allowed to hold a driving licence and they become a non-person as far as the relevant computer system is concerned; they can even be prosecuted for driving in this state (although it is presumably possible that they might avoid having to pay tax!).

The problems of keeping the abstractions inside a computer in step with the reality of the world about which they are supposed to record information are enormous and often revolve around issues of uniquely identifying objects which are reviewed in Kent (1978). While we were writing this article there was a newspaper report that the UK Driver and Vehicle Licensing Agency had been investigated by the National Audit

Office and it was found that *one third* of the records about drivers and *one quarter* of the information about vehicles contained errors.

A more subtle difficulty is that stored information may be *unverifiable*. For example, when bank customers call into question so-called 'phantom withdrawals' from their accounts (via ATM bank terminals), banks often deny that this can happen and the very nature of electronic withdrawal makes resolution of the dispute impossible.

Even if we can trust the stored information, it may only be available in a form that is *incompatible* with our needs. For most databases, only certain stylised interactions retrieve information in exactly the right form for immediate and 'natural' use. Such interactions usually correspond to the circumstances specified in the original system design (although many systems do not even satisfy their design criteria). When circumstances change, and information has to be accessed in ways not foreseen in the specification, new problems can arise. For example, the retriever may make unwarranted assumptions about what the information means. A ubiquitous problem is that of properly identifying or naming an intended entity. To cite but one example: one of the authors, on publishing his first UK book (*Software Development: a Rigorous Approach*), received a letter from the British Library requesting information (e.g. date of birth) and asking whether he was the same Clifford Jones as had written *A Companion to the Sunday Service*! This kind of mistaken identity is easy to understand, but difficult to do anything about. The consequences might be less amusing if the database involved information about, for example, terrorists.

Another important consideration is that certain kinds of trustworthy information may be *inaccessible*, either because access is forbidden (e.g. by law), or because access is impossible by design, or because access simply costs too much (in terms of either money or time).

Note that these difficulties are associated with relatively simple and self-contained information systems: the warning is that even these can misfunction.

8.1.4 Summary

It must be clear by now that we see the crucial challenges for the future of computing to be in the compiling and accessing of human-related, symbolic information. This is in contrast to the view of computing, typified by the US President's High Performance Computing and Communication initiative, which believes that important advances in the past have been due to the provision of ever more computational power, and that market growth depends on more of the same. Although many (physical) scientists and research engineers seem able to absorb – in a Parkinson-like way – any amount of computing power which is made available to them, they represent a particularly narrow aspect of the economy and society at large†. We believe that the real potential of computers both for the average member of the general public and for institutional decision makers has not yet been, and will not be anything like, realised until facilities are available for 'mining' large bodies of information which are widely dispersed. This also contrasts with the way in which databases are viewed at present; they are usually designed for a single, organisation-oriented purpose, and to be 'closed' to the outside world.

Hence, wherever information may be stored, we wish to have access to it and the ability to use it for our own purposes. This implies that we want to view our information system as being at the same time

global – information stored in the totality of all physically distributed repositories should be potentially accessible, subject to provision of the physical means to access the raw data;

open – except where there are proprietary reasons for secrecy, access to all information should be both allowed and encouraged – subject to payment at the appropriate market rate, anybody should be entitled to access the information for whatever purpose they desire; and

personal – information should be structured in a way which facilitates access and individuals should be able to obtain access in a way which fits their stated preferences.

The system meeting these requirements would be known as the Global-yet-Personal Information System: **GyP∫IS**.

Because of our change of focus from computation to information access we prefer to use the term *informatics* rather than computer science. We understand by this term study of the capture, storage and retrieval of information as well as the more traditional, computational aspects of our subject.

---

† But we must not lose sight of the way in which embedded computing has grown: television sets are now being designed with 0.5 Mbyte of control software, hand-held telephones with 1 Mbyte and even the humble shaver appears to need 2 kbytes of software!

8.2 The Global-yet-Personal Information System

$$\boxed{\text{GyP}\int\text{IS}}$$

This section explores the technical, legal, social and economic issues governing the provision of global, open and personal information. We commence by defining some terms.

8.2.1 Terminology

A traditional view of a computer system is that it entails the following five activities:

- input (capture of data from human sources);
- storage (of data);
- processing (changing or rearranging data);
- communication (physical movement of data); and
- output (delivery of data to human 'users').

However, from the *user's* point of view, the *interaction*, via input and output, is the only thing that matters. The fact that storage, processing and communication are needed is a property of the internal system, and ideally should be invisible to the user. Yet, in practice, these matters are only too visible to the user. For the moment, we shall concentrate on the user's view; we shall focus on information rather than data, and pretend that decisions on storage, processing and communication are hidden. To mark this change of view, we will use the terms *compiling* and *accessing* of information, in place of input and output of data, respectively. We shall use the term *information system* rather than computer system, and we shall refer to an information *repository* rather than a database.

Two examples should suffice to show how this view can define human–computer interactions in diverse application areas.

Query Processing – In a relational database, the processes of updating internal information and making queries are well defined, and are the only actions entirely visible to end-users. Of course, for queries to be *efficient*, someone needs to know how the data dictionary is structured, but this is usually a computer specialist, rather than a 'true' end-user: we term such a specialist a *moderator*.

Numerical Simulation – It is traditional to think that other application areas, such as scientific simulation, are fundamentally different from query processing, but there are in fact many similarities. Consider, for example, numerical weather prediction: information about the current global state of the weather is gathered by a mixture of human and electronic means, and this provides the initial state for a 'time-stepping' simulation that iterates until it has computed the projected state of the weather at some required time in the future. The projected state is then post-processed into a form suitable for human assimilation (e.g. via graphical 'visualisation'). The details of the simulation (and the gathering of starting data plus the interpolation of the initial state) are of concern only to physical scientists and computing experts: the immediate end-users, i.e. the weather forecasters, wish to concern themselves only with interpretation of the simulated results of the physical model. Of course, the 'true' end-users are the people who rely on the outcome of the forecasts. Even though this example involves a considerable amount of processing (in the simulation), it is still, from the user's point of view, a matter of first compiling the necessary input information and then accessing the formatted results.

Another motivation is provided by Vannevar Bush's picture of the scientist's desk: 'Memex' (Bush, 1967), which clearly recognises the importance of connections between items of information. Using this as a model, we can begin to imagine what a 'virtual classroom' might be like as a networked learning environment: we expect such an environment to be more important than libraries to future generations of students.

8.2.2 Technical Difficulties

We have already mentioned some of the difficulties inherent in trying to manage and manipulate information in traditional, closed, database systems: these problems are exacerbated in the GyP∫IS. Although the Internet is providing access to a phenomenal collection of ASCII files (often structured by HTML), there is only limited provision for access to structured information. Some awareness of the difficulty facing one of the oldest publishing ventures is indicated by the conference organised in 1994 on *The Future of the Dictionary*.

The global system requires access to information stored in physically distributed repositories. The problem is not primarily that of compiling the information, since so much is already available. So the technical challenge for informatics lies in developing techniques that allow uniform and effective access to the immense variety of existing and yet-to-emerge repositories.

At the most trivial level, there is the problem of data formats. The authors of this article chose to work mainly on Unix systems which are linked together by a departmental Ethernet but, at some stages of the development, they wished to edit some of the text on Mac Powerbook machines. One way of transferring data between the two file systems was to write floppy discs in a third (MS-DOS) format! Although software exists to 'smooth' such transactions, it does not completely hide the multiplicity of underlying data formats. Indeed, it can sometimes cause even more confusion by failing in an obscure fashion as it tries unsuccessfully to hide one thing too many.

There are major technical problems associated with identifying in a global network exactly which piece of information is being referred to by a query. It is well known that it is inadequate to refer to people in a large organisation solely by their names; extra qualifying information, such as date and/or place of birth, is used in order to try to disambiguate references. However, the global nature of the GyP∫IS makes it essential that programs are capable of handling *dialogues* in order to ensure that the required entity has been located. An example here is that, whereas the name 'Cliff Jones' is currently unique within the department in which the authors work, it is far from unique in particular geographical areas within the UK.

Moreover, because the information contained in the global network is continually evolving in a distributed fashion, there can be no concept of an instantaneous 'snapshot' of the state of the information. Hence it is impossible to conduct any 'exhaustive' searches to determine whether a particular entity exists at a particular time. To take another example, the name 'John Gurd' could well be unique in the world at this moment, but there is no tractable way of establishing this as a fact. One of the main reasons for the present dominance of 'closed' information systems is that they can be (and are) designed so as to avoid these problems.

Another problem with multiple, distributed repositories is that they rarely yield the required information in a 'ready-to-use', uniform fashion (note that this is a different problem from the incompatibility of raw data formats). Even if correct information is stored, correlation and integration between different sources often proves impossible and, even where it is feasible, it requires the concerted assistance of a variety of highly skilled information access advisers (note that these have different skills from database access advisers, although their job descriptions are similar). Some of these are what we might call 'repository-oriented', in that they are closely associated with the repository and are knowledgeable about how to make efficient queries concerning its information: these are akin to the *moderators* (and database access advisers), introduced in subsection 8.2.1. Other advisers are predominantly 'user-oriented', in that they understand how the retrieved information is to be used, and hence how it should be presented, regardless of its raw format: we call these *presenters*. Yet other advisers fall in between these two extremes, and are capable of viewing information from both the user and the repository end: these are normally employed by the end-users to search out the required information, so we call them *seekers*. If all these advisers are to be replaced by some form of computation, significant technical developments will be necessary since performance comparable to humans would require far greater *adaptability* of 'programmed' behaviour than has been exhibited hitherto in information systems.

Moreover, it is crucial for the kind of applications we have identified that information is accessed and correlated while it is still 'current'. The moderators, seekers and presenters will have to work to hard 'deadlines', leading to further technical difficulties associated with deciding how much time and 'effort' to devote to searching for, and then processing, relevant data and information. Reliable notions of 'expedience' and 'approximation' will be needed.

A final interesting problem is the effect of the 'longevity' of information on attempts to integrate multiple information sources. Many companies have gone through generations of computer systems which have provided progressively more performance and better economics. They frequently face the problem of needing to access 'old' information which they wish to correlate with 'new' information, perhaps for legal reasons. In the aircraft industry, for example, it is necessary to be able to determine the source of materials in aircraft which were built decades ago; decades in computing represent several generations of hardware and quite probably several generations of database technology. The problems which, for example, insurance companies face in accessing old records are equally severe.

In this context, it is interesting to go back into the history of information systems *within* individual corporations. When computers were first commercially available in the 1960s, many large organisations, such as the major motor car manufacturers, designed computer systems to support different parts of their operations. A computer system might be introduced by a company to control order processing; then a different computer system would be designed to control mechanical production; a third system might be used to control painting, and another system for controlling the stocking of cars; yet one more system could be needed for the forwarding of cars to the manufacturer's dealers; etc. As each need was identified, so a new system was developed to 'satisfice' (Simon, 1969) it. It was not long before senior management realised not only that this multiplicity of different computer systems was inefficient but that it was leading to new sorts of 'clerical' problems which had not been encountered in the manual information processing age. The availability of more powerful and cost-effective hardware, together with the advent of database software, started a trend towards greater integration of information systems. However, it was by no means easy to integrate systems that had been developed separately. It quickly became apparent that even such basic concepts as 'when a car has been sold' were interpreted differently by users (and hence the designers) of the separate information systems. Whereas human beings were able to react to such inconsistent views of the company's operation, their electronic counterparts could not. In fact, more than one corporation failed in its first attempts to develop integrated information systems.

Today, one still finds (Aiken *et al.*, 1994; see also Premerlani & Blaha (1994) in the same journal) that:

The U.S. Department of Defense (DoD) currently maintains more than 1.4 billion lines of code associated with thousands of heterogeneous, noncombat information systems ... The Department is often unable to obtain correct information from the data stored in the various existing databases due to a lack of standardized data and data structures across systems. Submitting the same query to each of the more than 20 payroll systems can result in not just multiple answers, *but in multiple kinds of answers*. At times, consolidating the query responses has proved to be an impossible task.

All in all, we must recognise that the creation of suitable means for flexible access to global information poses significant scientific and engineering research challenges for the emerging discipline of informatics.

8.2.3 Economic, social and legal issues

The challenge extends outside informatics, to society at large and, in particular, to economics and the law. For example, a primary vision of the GyP∫IS is that it will form a 'driving force' for the economy. People and organisations will be prepared to pay well for information services. This kind of reasoning has been applied previously, for example, in the case of the French Minitel system for the provision of telephone-based information services. In fact, the return on sales of Minitel services has been such that the initial decision to *give away* all the necessary hardware infrastructure has been entirely vindicated. Even more than in the recent past, manufacturers will have to consider the value of the services provided, rather than the material products produced. Just as software creation now absorbs far more of a developed country's GNP than hardware purchase, we predict that within a few decades the new open information 'market' will dwarf both of these.

Society will need to consider the wider implications of an open information market. Once proprietary motivations for keeping information secret have been overcome (and we believe that the economic advantages of exploiting information may well cause this to happen), detailed consideration of the whole concept of ownership and regulation will need to be undertaken; issues of responsibility and liability will have to be resolved (and one can only hope that this is done with more understanding than was evident in the UK Data Protection Act). The dangers of 'Wire Pirates' are discussed in Wallich (1994).

On the social front, the displacement of human advisers by computational activities, plus the emergence of jobs in the new information service 'industry', will precipitate yet another round of 'reskilling' of the workforce. The effects of this need not be negative: for example, the French Government has estimated that more than 300,000 new jobs were created as a result of the introduction of the Minitel system.

There are also technical challenges which follow from obvious legal constraints. For example, it is easy to make a case that no information should ever be destroyed (simply new versions created), and this poses further complications for referring to specific items unambiguously.

As an amusing circularity, some of the most commercially exploited, machine-readable, information sources are already those used by lawyers. But, whereas these are paid for by subscription, the issue of how one will pay for (relatively diverse) sources of information is itself a problem which will have to be solved by the 'information industry'.

8.2.4 Summary

Briefly, then, we envisage the development of a global and open information system that responds quickly and that is tailored to our personal requirements. In parallel, we anticipate the evolution of society to a state in which such a system will 'fit'. Each aspect poses substantial challenges: evolving a strategy to overcome these is what we call the **GyP∫IS Challenge**.

8.3 The States of the Arts

The previous section has set the overall objective; we now consider this from several different technical perspectives. The choice of these particular viewpoints is based primarily on our perception of the structure of present-day computer science (and is reflected in the range of topics covered by the other contributions to this volume). However, they also suggest to us a rationale behind the emerging discipline of informatics that we feel motivated to investigate further in Section 8.5. The comments in this section are intended to identify research challenges rather than propose solutions.

8.3.1 Programming view

A prevalent view in computer science is that software can be developed to solve any problem: programming languages are Turing-complete, so programs can be written to solve any computable problem. Hence it might be thought that the GyP∫IS Challenge could be met by developing appropriate programs.

To see that this view is naïve, one can look back to the evolution of the interface between programs and data. Initially commercial systems were constructed which processed sequential files; these files were commonly on magnetic tapes. The interface between the program and the files was by *read* and *write* statements which brought individual *records* into the store of the computer, processed them and then moved them out again. With the advent of large direct access stores (e.g. discs), database systems began to evolve where programs could obtain direct access to records via *keys*. This led to a generation of online systems, but computer programs were still written to read, process and replace records one at a time. It is only gradually that programs and database descriptions have come to be viewed as being expressible in the same language. There are now machines which have an addressing space which goes across the whole of the memory, including the filestore (so-called 'one-level stores'). These make it much easier for a program to be viewed as manipulating data whose description is stored within the program. An interesting comparison can be made with so-called 'persistent' programming languages, such as Smalltalk, where a naming structure is used which makes all data of interest directly addressable by the program.

The GyPʃIS Challenge adds a new dimension to this problem in that it is necessary to access information from many different sources. The discussion of 'Open Systems' in Hewitt *et al.* (1984) and the recently proposed concept of 'Megaprogramming' (Wiederhold *et al.*, 1992) seem to begin to address this need. In the latter approach, integration of accesses to multiple information sources is viewed as a mega-programming task: in order to facilitate expression, the mega-programmer is provided with a richer-than-usual set of interface routines, and a careful procedure is described for installing new or modified mega-modules. The problem with this approach is that only the mega-programmer can respond to change. This contravenes our requirement for adaptability *within* the electronic part of the information system. Nor do we believe that a mega-programmer would be able to anticipate changes at design-time and program the response to these. It is always the unforeseen changes in the environment that cause the greatest problems.

8.3.2 Database view

Of all the constituent parts of traditional computer science, database research ought to be the most germane to the GyPʃIS Challenge.

One popular database design approach takes the (not unreasonable) position that information consists of *entities* and *relations*. These entities and relations are simply abstractions of the things which surround us in the physical world, so we can think of entities as people, places, geographic data, flight data, and we can think of relations as facts which link entities together, such as that a certain person is booked on a particular flight, that a certain flight is expected to arrive at a certain time, etc. Indeed, this simple entity–relation view is one way of designing closed information systems (see, for example, Rumbaugh *et al.* (1991) or Coleman *et al.* (1994) for a description of its use in 'OMT' or 'Fusion', respectively). Relational databases cement this view as a way of storing and accessing information. In spite of its success, as measured by the use of relational database systems, it should be regarded as no more than one example of a way of structuring information.

Even within closed information systems, there is a challenge of ensuring that the expected connection is preserved between the 'artificial' entities and relations inside the information systems and the 'real' entities and relations in the world about us. This is exactly what goes wrong when it is falsely recorded that somebody has died: the relation in the information system no longer corresponds to the perceived reality.

Michael Jackson (1983) proposes an approach to designing information systems where the physical world is first understood and then appropriate methods are designed to link changes to its abstract representation in our computer system to events in the physical world.

It is important to realise that the design of such a system changes the world in which we live: future generations of system have to reflect the fact that the transactions in one system have become part of the physical environment for future information systems. As has been observed by Manny Lehman (Lehman & Belady, 1985), the presence of an information system changes the environment and effectively guarantees that the users' requirements will change. For example, consider the way the world has changed now that we can use our 'Switch' (Electronic Funds Transfer) card in the supermarket. In this context, even the old abstraction of bank notes has disappeared: the customer's bank balance is reduced, the supermarket's bank balance is increased, and no 'paper' ever moves between the relevant banking institutions.

Where current database technology lets us down is in coping with open information access. The notions of a pre-defined data dictionary and fixed ways of locating entities are so ingrained and central to accessing the information contained that they dominate all description. Any access that fails to conform with this in-built structure is destined to fail (usually in an obscure fashion). It is revealing that the 'Human Genome' project has had to make a major investment in development of novel database technology†.

The companion article in this volume by Peter Gray, on 'Large Databases and Knowledge Re-use', illuminates the way in which 'the database view' may evolve towards the GyP∫IS goal. In particular, it foresees wider re-use of knowledge achieved via object-oriented database technology and further development of 'mediator' and 'facilitator' objects that fulfil some of the functions of our seekers, moderators and presenters.

However, the development of 'better' database technologies is not of itself going to solve all the GyP∫IS problems. As articulated so clearly by William Kent (1978), it is always going to be necessary to view data from some unanticipated angle in order to maintain compatibility with the human view of the information it represents: there is no all-pervading, 'best' view. More recently, Brian Gladman has made the

† In fact, the entire Human Genome Initiative is pregnant with information-oriented challenges that have a considerable amount in common with the themes of this paper (Frenkel, 1991).

insightful observation (in the form of a comment to one of the authors) that 'information is the connection between raw data and purpose', thus making explicit the reason why we should expect the most appropriate view to vary from time to time.

8.3.3 Artificial intelligence view

Artificial Intelligence (AI) aims to throw light on human cognition by developing programs that exhibit ever more realistically human behaviour. The 'strong AI' view anticipates eventual development of a simulated human which, given the way some humans are already able to solve many of the problems mentioned above, would appear to address our desire to develop an open information system.

For a while, AI research relied on extensions to mathematical logic and database technology, but it has now incorporated neural models and other forms of novel machinery to try (unsuccessfully, so far) to overcome the limits on adaptable behaviour. While not achieving anything remotely like overall human behaviour, AI has developed programs that can mimic important components of the human system; for example, speech generation and (to a limited extent) recognition. Some databases nowadays can be accessed via a 'natural language' interface, and there have been several attempts to provide adaptive database interfaces (e.g. Heger *et al.*, 1991), although the degree of adaptability is very limited when compared with human behaviour.

Attempts to mimic the adaptability of 'real' human behaviour have foundered so far on issues such as *consciousness* and *common sense*. Programs have been developed that can 'plan' activities in relatively restricted scenarios, but learning and responding to change are extremely rudimentary. The state of the art in this area is captured pertinently in the July 1994 issue of the *Communications of the ACM*, on 'Intelligent Agents'. A paper in that issue on the Cyc system (Guha & Lenat, 1994) contemplates potential applications that are highly relevant to our quest, and the editor's interview with Marvin Minsky (Riecken, 1994) throws useful light on the practical barriers to be overcome in future research. This interview also echoes our view that progress in this kind of endeavour relies on integrated application of multiple technical approaches.

Distributed AI and Cooperative Distributed Problem Solving (Durfee *et al.*, 1989) are developments of this topic that seem pertinent to the GyPʃIS Challenge. Generalised languages and systems are being developed for support of 'multi-agent' computing, and there is interest in the creation of 'societies' of such computational entities (see, also, the comments on Huberman (1988) in subsection 8.3.4).

Of course, it is tempting to believe that achievement of 'strong AI' would offer a way of overcoming all of the problems in the GyP∫IS Challenge. It is certainly true that human beings are much more adaptable than any current form of computation when they have a source of information available to them and are asked to process it in new ways or provide new sorts of reports. Hence, the argument goes, if one can mimic human intelligence, one will solve all such challenges. However, we remain unconvinced that artificial intelligence on its own will offer a complete solution, and we note that the companion article in this volume by Alan Bundy, on 'Prospects for Artificial Intelligence', takes a similar view.

8.3.4 Computer architecture view

There is another computer science viewpoint that considers all difficult problems to be solvable by provision of sufficiently powerful computer hardware. This has led to the current attention being paid to massively parallel computer architecture. Is there any evidence that such research can meet the GyP∫IS Challenge?

In fact, the fundamentals of computer architecture are challenged by the requirement for a global view of information. Individual repositories in the GyP∫IS will be huge: furthermore, they will be widely distributed geographically. Many of the problems encountered when handling distributed computational objects have been studied in the field of distributed computing. The view is taken that computational *processes* can invoke other computational processes in physically distant processors. Naming conventions are necessary to locate remote processes and processors, and interface protocols have to be adhered to: as mentioned earlier, there is a major problem with identifying exactly which entity is being requested.

In terms of the system architecture, there are important questions about the way in which concurrent and distributed computations are created and managed, and how the necessary communication and synchronisation between them are achieved. The companion article in this volume by Roger Needham, on 'Computers and Communications', ponders on the way some of this technology might develop and also speculates amusingly on possible applications of the developing technology over the relatively short term.

The present state of the art in this field is exemplified by the Internet and the World Wide Web. These implement a truly global network of interacting computers, but the degree of sophistication implied by the GyP∫IS is far from being achieved. Nonetheless, there are clear signs that researchers (both implementers and users) are beginning to view this system as an information resource, as exemplified by some of the articles in the August 1994 issue of the *Communications of the ACM* on 'Internet Technology'. In particular, the paper on 'Resource Discovery' (Bowman *et al.*, 1994) describes situations similar to those expected in the GyP∫IS.

Access paths must be planned, with a view both to performing computation where it can be undertaken most efficiently and avoiding the transfer of huge volumes of data over expensive networks where most of the data will simply be rejected in subsequent processing, prior to delivery to the end-user. This has obvious resonance with the design of cache memory systems for massively parallel computer systems (see Tokoro (1990) for an interesting view on this). Huberman's book (Huberman, 1988) *The Ecology of Computation* has chapters on 'Agoric Systems', 'Deals among Agents' and 'Market-like Task Schedulers' which all relate to this topic†.

Some interesting effects emerge when the concepts of compiling and accessing of information are applied to distributed networks themselves (i.e., the subject of a database is the structure and operation of the network).

There can be no doubt that hardware architecture and distributed processing research tackle problems that are germane to searching for information, and will contribute to meeting the GyP∫IS Challenge. However, it is inconceivable that architectural research alone will provide all the answers. The cautionary tale about the original attempts to create integrated information systems *within* corporations should make us pause before imagining that the fact that computing power and data storage capacities are adequate is in itself a guarantee of success. At most, architectural research is investigating the nature of possible environments in which the GyP∫IS will have to operate.

An interesting parallel can be drawn with the situation in database technology, in that it is unreasonable to expect a 'best' architecture to emerge for the GyP∫IS. The fact that we need a multiplicity of views

---

† As a frustrating example of difficulty in accessing information, Bush (1967), Huberman (1988) and Kent (1978) are all out of print and two of these had to be obtained by the time-consuming 'Inter-Library Loan' process.

of data and information means that alternative forms of 'computation' could prove to be more effective than our currently predominant model. Indeed, in some conventional application areas, alternative architectures, such as neural networks, are already making an impact. It is not even clear that the current dominance of digital techniques will necessarily persist.

8.3.5 Formal methods view

The preceding sections present predominantly engineering-oriented views of potential responses to the GyP∫IS Challenge. Here we review the contribution which can be made by more theoretical research.

Abstract data types have received extensive discussion in the theoretical literature, and practical experience confirms that they form an excellent way of encapsulating data so that internal design decisions do not affect the users of such data. However, in the GyP∫IS, it is precisely the need to obtain data from behind a program interface which is the challenge for someone wishing to write a novel program which accesses that data in a way which was not envisaged by the original designer. So, while abstract data types may contribute from the theoretical (and even practical) point of view, it may now be necessary to move on and find more appropriate building blocks for a worldwide information network. In moving on, it is desirable to have the same kind of theoretical underpinning – as was present with abstract data types – for the new concepts which are to be used in future systems.

One natural extension of the abstract data type theme is found in object-oriented concepts (notably Tokoro (1993)). Already, considerable formal methods attention is being paid to such concepts, and it may prove possible to extend them to meet the global requirement of the GyP∫IS.

Reactive systems are those which go on executing for ever and whose behaviour is described in terms of *reaction* to *stimuli* rather than the input–output relation which may be used to specify a simple computation. The GyP∫IS will certainly have to be reactive and, therefore, one could look at the theoretical notations used to describe reactive systems. However, here again, we can see that future systems may have to go beyond what we currently view as a reactive system. In particular, it is difficult to see how anything can respond to the GyP∫IS Challenge if it cannot adapt its behaviour so as to answer queries (about information which is held internally) not in the form which the program was initially specified to handle. Hence we are facing a class of system in which its interactions cannot be pre-planned. There is relevant technical work here in the description of behaviours of systems which cope with mobile processes.

A conclusion from what has been discussed already is that it will be necessary for the system to store contextual information about the environment in which it runs. This is another form of information which will need to respond to interactions with the environment. More speculatively, there needs to be more research on 'semantic structures' and knowledge representation. And a final way in which formal methods may be able to contribute is to tackle the inherent complexity of search in the GyP∫IS.

Many of these topics are discussed elsewhere in this volume, most explicitly in the contributions of Robin Milner, on 'Semantic Ideas in Computing', Tony Hoare, on 'Algebra and Models', and Alan Bundy, on 'Prospects for Artificial Intelligence'. Tony Hoare takes the view that theory should be developed more or less for its own sake. However, in our view, the thing that formal methods cannot do on its own is to deliver acceptance by the general community of any particular theory. We shall return to this topic again later.

8.3.6 Summary

There are many complementary technical perspectives to the GyP∫IS Challenge. The ones identified above are by no means the only ones we could have mentioned. For example, as noted earlier, many applications of the GyP∫IS require it to deliver large quantities of information from remote repositories quickly. This raises further research issues, which are associated with the need for 'time-constrained' (more usually known as *real-time*) responses to information queries. There is an existing technology devoted to real-time numerical processing, for online process control, signal processing and interpretation (e.g., for radar), and so on, which can certainly contribute to solving the Challenge.

Another important technical aspect is the requirement for meaningful interaction, both among agents, and between human beings and agents. In a companion article in this volume, William Newman argues the case for 'The Place of Interactive Computing in Tomorrow's Computer Science', and this is another germane view of the GyP∫IS Challenge.

Our analysis of the technical states of the art suggests that no one of the existing technologies alone can solve all of the problems posed by the Challenge. Nevertheless, each technique has something to offer, and so an 'interdisciplinary' approach may pay off.

8.4 Pointers to a Response

If our prognosis for the 'information industry' is correct, the GyP∫IS is likely to provide the major source of challenges for informatics research in the coming decades. Hence, in this section (the final technical part of our contribution), we certainly do not aspire to offering a design which satisfies the challenge set out above. We can, however, attempt to identify at this stage a framework in which such a design could feasibly evolve.

In essence, the preceding sections express dissatisfaction with our present approaches to computer-based management and manipulation of information. As ever, there are two choices for improvement: either we develop a better approach from first principles, using more appropriate theoretical and practical bases (revolution), or we modify our current approach incrementally until it can handle the new challenges (evolution). We rule out revolution on two grounds. Firstly, prior investment is simply too large for the previous approach to be abandoned in its entirety (just think of the problems of 'upgrading' existing repositories – this problem already inhibits people from taking the far easier step of changing from one database technology to another). Secondly, in any case, we are not convinced that a 'better' overall approach can be found.

Hence we expect that existing information systems are going to evolve in such a way as to meet the needs of global-yet-personal information access. The main strategic objective will be to replace those parts of the overall 'system' that presently rely on human skills by some form of 'computational' activity. Of course, such 'computations' will need to be at least as effective as the human activity they replace. In order to achieve this, they will have to exhibit the new kinds of behaviour described in the remainder of this section.

8.4.1 Openness

Many systems are deliberately designed as object-oriented programs or abstract data types. In some senses, this is a technical advance over the 'control block' designs of the 1960s, but such abstract data types are deliberately designed to restrict the access to information. We must remember that the GyP∫IS Challenge relies on not pre-judging future modes of access to information, and try to achieve this while at the same time maintaining the discipline of structured design.

One can in fact propose a technical test for an open system. It is possible to decide whether, through interaction with a system, one can acquire (at some cost) enough information to completely reproduce the function of a particular repository (and its moderator). This is not true, for example, of the current machine-readable forms of the *Oxford English Dictionary*, where one can enquire about the meaning of a particular word, or all of the occurrences of a particular word in other definitions, but not obtain the whole text of the dictionary (except by an exhaustive listing of the entries, which would require prior knowledge of every word that is contained). Of course, open systems can also be abstract data types!

One might ask why the provider of a repository would wish to make available all of the information which has been gathered, perhaps at enormous cost. The answer is economic. In the first place, the acquisition of such detailed information might cost an enquirer so much that they would think twice about building their own version of the repository (and its moderator) rather than using the original one. Moreover, the original provider of the information has the opportunity to hone access paths in a way which makes it practical for them to provide most forms of information access at a lower cost than anyone who simply gets all of the basic entities and relations out of the repository. Finally, the originator is normally best equipped to undertake that the information will be kept up to date.

8.4.2 Adaptability

Many information systems today, whether or not they are officially listed as reactive systems, have extremely restricted protocols for interaction†. Not only must protocols be made more flexible, there must be parts of the protocol which are deliberately designed to permit the adoption of new behaviours.

8.4.3 Broad search capability

Remember that the primary motivation is to get as much relevant information as possible from distributed repositories into the hands of the decision-makers to some pre-defined schedule. In many cases, the desire to access information will involve elaborate searches through the repositories. Completing such searches in reasonable time will require sophisticated interactions, via seekers and presenters, between the 'end-users' of the information and the moderators providing the interface to

---

† But we must recognise that the same applies to some (obdurate) human beings.

the individual repositories (for the moment, we will assume that repositories are always 'moderated', if only to ensure that access is paid for).

In order to fit into the view of a geographically distributed information network, seekers must be responsive and have the ability both to communicate and to react to incoming stimuli. One could therefore think of a seeker having information which it 'owns' and some form of protocol handler which expresses its possible behaviours during interaction. But, as well as the information which is the *raison d'être* of the seeker, it will only be able to function if it has an effective (i.e., accurate and helpful) 'environment model' (which is itself information about the interactions which have been found or are expected to yield other sorts of information).

8.4.4 Mobility

It is our belief that sophisticated interaction, whether among humans, among machines, or between the two groups, demands physical proximity: dialogues with inordinate delays become unmanageable (e.g. long-distance telephone calls linked via satellite, as opposed to overland or submarine cable). Also, dialogues with minimal context can easily miss opportunities for 'short-cuts'; for example, a direct conversation with someone contains a considerable amount of 'non-verbal' communication ('body language') that is simply not available over, say, the telephone. Hence, in order to gain the required adaptability, it will be necessary to send the seekers to meet the moderators 'in person'.

We speak here of 'seekers' and 'moderators' and deliberately leave open the question of whether these are embodied in computer systems or whether they are human agents: if an end-user were prepared to pay enough for information that had not yet been gathered, the invoked interactions could ultimately initiate action by a human being who would gather it. However, our aim is to avoid such action if there is any stored source of the information sought.

It is open to debate whether the moderators should build their own internal model of the environment: it must be possible to operate without this. However, efficiency could well be improved if moderators were capable of pointing seekers 'in the right direction'.

8.4.5 Autonomy

Following from the above, seekers must be capable of operating autonomously, or at least semi-autonomously. First and foremost, each seeker will need to operate with some 'sense of purpose' (cf. the comment from Brian Gladman, cited in subsection 8.3.2), in a context that is 'inherited' from the end-user it is serving. Because it will be mobile and frequently away from its 'base', a seeker will at least need to 'touch base' every now and then for instructions, either 'in person' or via a (cheap) telecommunications link. More likely, for reasons of efficiency and cost, it will have to operate for prolonged periods without feedback from its end-user.

8.4.6 Economic and social dimension

There seems no reason to doubt that the information itself can be represented in something like the entity–relation view. Seekers, then, are involved in interactions whose behaviour is mediated by the protocols which they can conduct. In addition to the information sought, there must be economic information which indicates both the cost of, and time required for, access (searching, processing and moving) and, possibly, some knowledge of the constraints on access required by the law. Whenever a task is to be undertaken, some form of price will be established and thresholds set on queries or searches sent to other agents within the GyP∫IS.

Economic incentives will also serve to improve the general capabilities of the GyP∫IS. Repositories that do not adhere to the open philosophy will be vulnerable to competition from more market-minded systems: they must evolve to meet the demands of their 'customers', otherwise they will 'go out of business'.

8.4.7 Summary

Although the totality of these behaviours represents a big change in approach from current practices, no single step is frighteningly large. This would seem to support our contention that evolution towards the objectives of the GyP∫IS Challenge is at least conceivable.

8.5 On the Nature of Informatics

There is a danger that the reader could view the foregoing, especially section 8.3, as suggesting that all current computing research is germane, and that we should all carry on working the way we already are. But this is not the case. Quite apart from the need to focus on critically selected, key research issues (brought upon us by the inexorable tightening of budgets), we see a substantial disciplinary advantage deriving from *competitive* exploitation of the distinct results of fundamentally different approaches to such a Grand Challenge. In this 'bigger picture', underlying differences of opinion will increasingly tend to destroy the natural coherence of our discipline, unless the informatics research community takes specific steps to benefit from them. To help the reader understand this view, we have added the following, almost philosophical, 'epilogue' on the nature of research in the emerging discipline of informatics.

8.5.1 Informatics as science

Science is the process of gaining knowledge and understanding by means of methodical elaboration. The objective of scientific method is the construction of increasingly effective models (effective in the sense of facilitating ever more accurate *prediction*).

In informatics, we wish to understand the 'world around us' by constructing increasingly effective *information-based* models. The method we use for this follows the usual cycle of hypothesis (creation of a model) and test (using the model in some planned experiment and evaluating its validity, or otherwise, against the reality) that characterises the physical sciences. Several of the other contributions to this volume describe how this kind of cycle has driven the evolution of particular specialisations in the computing field; and these all make the point that it is the science of the field that is being advanced, not just the technology.

Note that non-trivial testing requires a substantial amount of high quality engineering, to construct the necessary experimental apparatus, as well as the observational and analytical skills more often associated with experimental science. This point is amplified in the article by Simon Peyton Jones elsewhere in this volume.

In common with the physical sciences, there are tensions between the groups that specialise in modelling (the 'theorists') and those that specialise in testing (the 'experimentalists'). There are also tensions between different 'theories' (and, hence, between the theorists). The latter are due to the vast number of ways there are of modelling 'reality', and the former are due to the frequent discoveries of inconvenient incompatibilities between modelling techniques and 'reality' (as well as the fundamentally different viewpoints inherent in the two groups)†.

Also in common with other sciences, informatics has started by investi-

---

† And this is quite apart from the tensions between these academic viewpoints and the views of industry and commerce that so dominate present-day research funding strategy. The potentially negative effects of such tensions are amply illustrated in Roger Needham's article in this volume.

gating simple phenomena, trying to understand small, bounded (closed) systems with few real-time constraints, before expanding into the more complex areas that are implicit in the GyP∫IS Challenge.

8.5.2 Historical influences

Of course, informatics is an *emerging* science, and not everyone who is working in it necessarily subscribes to the view presented above. Perhaps because they do not appreciate the existence of the tensions identified above, researchers argue about the relative merits of different models or experiments more 'blindly' than they would in an established science: after all, subjects such as physics and chemistry have had centuries of evolution in which to 'hammer out' their differences and develop a commonly agreed methodology for advancing their discipline. Whatever the reason, it is certainly the case that damaging competition and disparagement have been rife in certain prototypical areas of informatics (e.g., computer science).

In our opinion, it is much more fruitful to note how the differing approaches connect to one another and to related fields of science. We should be trying quickly to complete the 'hammering out' process and to agree the best methodology for advancement of our discipline. Analysing our 'roots', in the various fields of computer science and elsewhere, is one of the essential parts of this process: it helps to illuminate our collective scientific 'agenda'. At one level, this was the motivation for surveying possible approaches to the GyP∫IS Challenge in section 8.3.

In fact, one can see from section 8.3 that informatics is more than 'a science': for example, a great deal of its intellectual heritage belongs more naturally to the collective discipline of engineering. There is certainly a prevalent engineering view in informatics: many people wish to build systems that work and work efficiently. So we find discussion of an issue such as information processing in machines alongside comparisons with the way that human beings handle information; and we find a communications engineer looking at the way data flows through communication media such as wires or light pipes, while a social engineer investigates the ways in which humans react to the information they receive.

There is another view which is like that of an experimental scientist: people of this 'school' wish to make observations, develop models, and test whether those models are actually embodied in information systems. And there are the mathematically oriented informatics researchers who are interested in the abstract theoretical structure which underpins their subject. The latter particularly aim to provide the structure of an evolving science, and the recent publication of several series of 'Handbooks' which collect and record basic theoretical material is the first instalment of this promise.

Viewed from a suitable distance, all of these research activities can be seen to contribute to the scientific rationale offered in section 8.5.1. The great variety of approaches available is a huge asset; there is the potential to integrate diverse viewpoints and create a totality that far exceeds the sum of its parts†. The major question from a methodological point of view is how and when to deploy each of the various skills available to the advancement of the discipline. Petty wrangling simply delays progress, so the lesson to be learned from history is to cooperate more effectively.

8.5.3 Synthesis

With this background in mind, we propose that progress be made by deliberately looking at the GyP∫IS Challenge from successive, fundamentally different viewpoints, with the aim of finding the particular view that enables us to make an advance at the moment in question.

So, for example, computer architecture, programming and database design can be viewed most straightforwardly as engineering disciplines. Programs (and hardware systems) have to meet specifications and an important aspect of a programmer's task is to come up with an efficient product which satisfies the given specification. There is of course much established technology here. The notions of abstract data types, object-oriented languages and expert systems are all relevant to the sort of programming tasks needed in the GyP∫IS. What is important in facing the GyP∫IS Challenge is to carry forward the sort of engineering view which recognises that both ease of use and efficiency are vital considerations.

Elsewhere in this volume, Alan Bundy makes a strong case for present-day AI to be thought of as an experimental science. Viewing the GyP∫IS from this perspective, one might concentrate on the anthropomorphic qualities of the seekers and presenters, and on the 'fitness' of successive versions for service in 'society'.

What formal methods have to offer is the ability to model or describe

---

† Those readers who know the authors will realise that our backgrounds are very different. The fact that we are both able to subscribe wholeheartedly to this scientific rationale is significant.

complex computer systems and to reason about their implementation in a way that can, for example, show that design decisions satisfy their specifications. They do not necessarily solve the engineering problem of finding an efficient solution. Another important contribution of the formal methods point of view is that it can give analytic tools to designers of systems that allow them to simplify their architectures.

There is a major challenge in formulating the specification of the system(s) needed. The GyP∫IS contains information about the physical world. A physical scientist is concerned with building and animating *models* of physical reality, with as much veracity as possible. In order to avoid the pitfalls of earlier information systems (inaccuracy, incompatibility, inaccessibility, etc.), it is mandatory that the connection between physical and abstract world be adequate. In particular, the connection between the GyP∫IS and *its* model must be 'watertight'.

No one of these viewpoints is paramount – what is interesting is how an optimal solution can only be approached by balancing the tension between their diverse perspectives. In particular, there must be agreement across the representatives of all viewpoints on the nature of any compromises that have to be struck. Other contributions to this volume amply illustrate that progress in some fields has been made by shifting the collective viewpoint: take, for example, Alan Bundy's (slightly defensive) admission that the AI field spent much of its 'youth' in what he calls a 'scruffy' state of 'exploratory programming' before emerging into its present, 'respectable' persona. It is almost certain that the early state *had* to be endured in order to overcome the specific problems then being encountered.

Perhaps the penultimate word can be left to Keith Devlin (1991) who writes:

That there is such a thing as *information* cannot be disputed, can it? After all, our very lives depend upon it, upon its gathering, storage, manipulation, transmission, security and so on. Huge amounts of money change hands in exchange for information. ...But *what* exactly is it? The difficulty in trying to find an answer to this question lies in the absence of an agreed, underlying theory on which to base an acceptable definition.

If the 'agreed, underlying theory' is to be found, it will not be by theorists, or engineers, or experimental scientists alone. Notwithstanding the tensions between them, they must all work consciously together towards the discipline's common goal.

Acknowledgements

The authors are grateful for comments on earlier drafts of this article from Tim Clement, Ian Hayes, Robin Milner and Dave Snelling. One of the authors attended the *Software 2000* Workshop and wishes to express thanks to the attendees for stimulating some last-minute examples which have been added (the report of this meeting – Randell *et al.* (1994) – emphasises the key role of information in the future of the software industry).

9

Algebra and Models

C.A.R. Hoare

Summary

Science makes progress by constructing mathematical models, deducing their observable consequences, and testing them by experiment. Successful theoretical models are later taken as the basis for engineering methods and codes of practice for design of reliable and useful products. Models can play a similar central role in the progress and practical application of computing science.

A model of a computational paradigm starts with choice of a set of potential direct or indirect observations that can be made of a computational process. A particular process is modelled as the subset of observations to which it can give rise. Process composition is modelled by relating observations of a composite process to those of its components. Indirect observations play an essential role in such compositions. Algebraic properties of the composition operators are derived with the aid of the simple theory of sets and relations. Feasibility is checked by a mapping from a more operational model.

A model constructed as a family of sets is easily adapted as a calculus of design for total correctness. A specification is given by an arbitrary set containing all observations permitted in the required product. It should be expressed as clearly as possible with the aid of the full power of mathematics and logic. A product meets a specification if its potential observations form a subset of its permitted observations. This principle requires that all envisaged failure modes of a product are modelled as indirect observations, so that their avoidance can be proved. Specifications of components can be composed mathematically by the same operators as the components themselves. This permits top-down proof of correctness of designs even before their implementation begins. Algebraic properties and reasoning are helpful throughout development. Non-determinism is seen as no problem, but rather as a part of the solution.

9.1 Introduction

A scientific theory is formalised as a mathematical model of reality, from which can be deduced or calculated the observable properties and behaviour of a well-defined class of processes in the physical world. It is the task of theoretical scientists to develop a wide range of plausible but competing theories; experimental scientists will then refute or confirm the theories by observation and experiment. The engineer then applies a confirmed theory in the reverse direction: the starting point is a specification of the observable properties and behaviour of some system that does not yet exist in the physical world; and the goal is to design and implement a product which can be predicted by the theory to exhibit the specified properties. Mathematical methods of calculation and proof are used throughout the design task.

This article suggests a similar fruitful division of labour between theoretical and experimental computing science, leading to eventual application in the engineering of computer software and hardware. Theoretical computing scientists develop a wide range of plausible theories covering a variety of computational paradigms. The mathematical consequences of each theory are explored, and also relationships with other competing or complementary theories. The experimental computing scientist can then select some combination of related theories as the basis for the design of a software system or language, or an architecture for a computing device. The efficiency and effectiveness of this design are then tested by simulation or experimental implementation and application in representative case studies. Reliable use of the system or device or language will be further assisted by mathematical theorems, methods and heuristics derived from the original theoretical model.

Computing science is primarily concerned with discrete phenomena and therefore cannot take advantage of the large body of established knowledge of continuous mathematics, developed by applied mathematicians to the enormous benefit of physical science and engineering. It is rather from branches of pure mathematics that we obtain the concepts, notations, methods, theorems and proofs that are most relevant for computing. But in contrast to pure mathematics, potential relevance to computing is taken as a goal and a guide in the selection of directions for our research. Its achievement depends on a good general (but informal) understanding of practical computing science. This should cover

(i) a range of problems which may be solved by application of some computing device, and the terminology in which they are described,

(ii) the methods by which solutions to complex problems can be found by decomposition into simpler subproblems, so that these can then be solved by similar or even simpler methods,

(iii) the methods by which complex systems can be constructed by connecting subassemblies and components implemented in a similar or lower level technology.

(iv) the comparative cost and efficiency of alternative methods of design and implementation in hardware or in software.

Understanding of this wide range of topics should relate not just to the current computing scene (for which any new theory will come too late) but to some possible future evolution of it. As in all branches of physical science, success depends on a large element of intuition, insight, guesswork and just plain luck. That is why the community of theoretical scientists must be prepared to develop a large number of alternative theories, most of which will never achieve experimental confirmation or find practical application. This apparent profligacy is justified by simple economics. It is less expensive and risky to invent and develop ten new theories than it is to make even a prototype implementation of just one of them. And it is less risky and less onerous to design and implement ten prototypes than it is to invest in development of a new market for a genuinely innovative product. And not all new products that come to market will remain there. So theories are as numerous as the seeds scattered by the winds; only very few will settle and germinate and take root and reach maturity and propagate more seed to populate the forests of the future.

So let us postulate the wisdom or courage to select some general line of enquiry for a new theory. In its detailed development, the researcher would be well advised to lay aside all hope of future relevance, and adopt the attitude of pure mathematicians, engaged in the pursuit of truth wherever their curiosity may lead them. Avoid competitive promotion of one line of enquiry against another. Otherwise you lose the spirit of dispassionate scientific objectivity, so necessary for the health of science. Whenever choice arises between directions of pursuit, choose first the path of greater simplicity and of greater elegance. And that should be your second and third choice too, and especially your last one. An elegant theory will attract the attention of other theorists, and a simple one will attract the interest of teachers and students. This is the only way to reduce the risk that the theory will be forgotten before the time is ripe for its development and practical application. And finally, when the theory achieves widespread use or standardisation, the quality of elegance is the only hope we have of rescue from the quagmire of arbitrary complexity which is so pervasive, particularly in software of the present day. And elegance is a property that is needed not only for a mathematical model but also for the theorems and algebraic laws derivable from it.

It is the purpose of this article to encourage the development of new and simple theories with the aid of set-theoretic models. Such models permit easy derivation of algebraic laws, which in turn assist in derivation of efficient solutions to practical problems. Models also readily support a general method for deriving designs from specifications by top-down decomposition; in crossing levels of abstraction, we exploit a helpful correspondence between generality of specification at higher levels of design, and non-determinism at lower levels of implementation.

9.2 Observations

The first task of the theoretician is to decide on what kind of system to explore, and to characterise which of its properties are to be regarded as observable or controllable or otherwise relevant to the description and understanding of system behaviour. For each property, an appropriate name is chosen: for example in a mechanical assembly the name x may denote the distance of a joint along one axis, and $\dot{x}$ may denote its velocity. In mechanics, the observed values vary continuously with time, and they are often called measurements. In computing, observations usually yield discrete values, and they are made only at discrete points of time. For example, in the case of a fragment of program, x may denote the initial value of an integer variable before execution starts, and x' might denote its final value on termination. The fact that these observations are not continuous measurements in no way detracts from the mathematical and scientific quality of the theories which describe them.

Once the relevant observations have been named, the behaviour and properties of a general system or a particular one can be described or specified by mathematical formulae, equations, inequations or other predicates which contain these names as free variables (Hehner, 1984). Each predicate describes those systems in which the observed values of all its variables make the predicate true. In science, a general class of systems is often described by differential equations; and a specific member of the class by adding particular boundary conditions. For example, the predicate

$$x \geq k\dot{x} \quad \text{for} \quad 0 \leq t < 5$$

describes an initial segment of the behaviour of any joint which moves sufficiently slowly in the vicinity of the origin of the x axis. Similarly in the case of programs,

$$x' > x$$

describes the behaviour of any piece of code which increases the value of x. Such predicates may serve either as scientific predictions about the behaviour of known systems, or as engineering specifications of systems yet to be designed and implemented.

Sometimes the validity of a prediction R depends on the validity of some other condition P. This condition usually mentions variables whose values can be controlled by the experimenter, or the user, or in general by the environment within which the system described is embedded; and so it is often called a precondition. If the environment fails to make P true, no prediction at all can be made of the behaviour of the system; and, in the case of a specification, no constraint whatsoever is placed on the design of the product. In both cases, the precondition should be included as an antecedent of the conditional

$$P \Rightarrow R.$$

Observations which are described in user specifications are usually those which can be made directly, as it were with the naked eye. But in a mature branch of science the most important observations are those which can be made only indirectly by some more or less elaborate experiment. An experiment involves connection of its subject in some well understood manner with other processes whose behaviour is well understood, so that a more direct observation can be made of the behaviour of the combined system. Very often, the presumed understanding of the experimental apparatus itself depends on the very theory that is being tested. There is clearly a danger of circularity, a risk which attends research in all branches of science. But a successful choice of the right kind of indirect observation (for example, energy in physics) can provide a remarkably coherent and general explanation of a wide range of diverse phenomena. Such an indirect observation is often accepted as if it were a direct observation in some theory at a lower level of detail.

In a mechanical assembly, the most directly observable attributes are the positions of the various points of interest at any given instant of time. Their velocities are more indirectly observable as changes of position over arbitrarily short intervals of time; acceleration and force are even more indirectly observed. But accurate prediction and control of performance also requires knowledge of the coefficients of friction. These are investigated and measured as deviations from expectation in experiments whose validity depends on the simpler laws of mechanics.

In models of communicating processes (Brookes *et al.*, 1984), the most obvious and immediate observables are the events in which each process engages, and the order in which they occur. Much of the behaviour of a collection of interactive processes can be explained successfully in terms of event sequences (traces). But occasionally the system may reach deadlock; and this phenomenon can be explained only in terms of a more indirect observation of the events which the processes are *refusing* to engage in at the time that the deadlock occurs. Such indirect observations are usually more complex and abstruse (and even controversial) than direct observations, and they are not intended to appear in the user's specification of the completed product; but they are vital to the engineering soundness of the design, because they permit accurate specifications of interfaces and components that may then be designed and implemented separately by separate teams of engineers at separate times.

In a theory intended for engineering design, it is also important to include among the potential indirect observations all the possible ways in which a physical implementation may break or fail. It is only in a theory which includes such failures that it is possible to prove that a particular design or product will avoid them. Since all kinds of failure are to be avoided, there is no need to make fine distinctions between them, or to give accurate predictions of the behaviour after failure. For the same reason, there is no need to mention avoidance of failure explicitly in a user specification of a complete product. Let us describe all such universally undesirable observations by a predicate named *FAIL*.

A familiar example of failure in software is non-termination of a sequential program due to infinite iteration or recursion. This can be represented by introducing a special variable 'terminated', which is true when the program has terminated, and remains false if it never terminates. It is understood that the final values of the variables $x', y', \ldots$ are observable only when 'terminated' is true; this understanding can be coded in the mathematical theory by allowing these variables to take arbitrary values when 'terminated' is false. A specification never needs to talk about termination: one can take for granted that it is desirable. But implementations need to avoid it. So the first step in moving from specification to design notation is to introduce this extra variable.

Of course, in practice we can never wait the infinite time required to make an observation of a false value of the variable 'terminated'. This leads to philosophical objections against introducing a value which is so essentially unobservable; but they are the same kind of objection that can be made to zero as a number or empty as a set. Projective geometers never expect to observe their line at infinity, but their theory would not work without it. And in our case, the explicit introduction of non-termination and similar failures gives a similar advantage: it enables us to deal automatically with failure to meet 'liveness' conditions in the same simple way as we deal with 'safety' properties. To deal with 'fairness' conditions one must accept an even greater variety of indirect observations, which would take an infinite time to observe.

In summary, a theory intended for engineering design works with observations at two (or more) levels of abstraction. The direct observations are those which are described in a user specification S, and in a precondition P, placing constraints on the method and circumstances of use. The indirect observations are those mentioned in a description D of the actual behaviour of a delivered product, and in the description $FAIL$ of all the undesirable ways in which a product may fail if the precondition is violated. It is only a theory which includes the possibility of failure that can provide assistance in avoiding it. The fact that the product meets its specification is now encapsulated in a single mathematical theorem,

$$D \Rightarrow (P \Rightarrow \neg FAIL \ \& \ S).$$

This means that if the precondition P is satisfied, then every observation of the behaviour of the delivered product D will be a non-failing observation, and will also satisfy the specification S.

The last important message of this section is that an engineer never just delivers a product, but rather a product together with its specification, including operating instructions and preconditions for safe and successful use. Clarity and precision of specification are included among the most important qualities of a product; and mathematics provides excellent assistance in achieving them. Failure to realise this in software specification is notorious and leads to many of the other problems encountered in current software engineering practice.

9.3 Implementable Processes

The implication displayed at the end of the last section formalises a proof obligation which may be discharged after the design is complete. But it is far better to regard it as a mathematical statement of the designer's task, namely to find some design D which satisfies the implication and so meets the specification. Eventually, the whole design D must be expressed wholly within some limited set of design notations, which are known to be directly implementable in the available technology. The task is in principle no different from that of solving any other engineering problem which has been precisely formulated in mathematics.

An essential quality of the solution of a mathematical problem (for example a differential equation) is that it is expressed in more restricted notations than those used to formulate the original problem, – otherwise the solution could be just a trivial restatement of the problem. It is the notational restriction that makes the solution useful. In computing science, such notations can be designed to be translated automatically for direct implementation either in hardware or in the machine code of a computer. And, as in mathematics, it is very important that the notation of the solution should just be a subset of the notations used for specification. So the theorist must undertake to select from the class of all specifications those which are more or less directly implementable.

In the previous section we have assumed that specifications are written as mathematical predicates with free variables standing for observable values in a fashion generally understood by the educated professional. This is a style preferred by practising engineers and scientists, who tend to manipulate, differentiate or integrate the text of formulae rather than abstract functions: it is also the style adopted by the Z school of specification (Spivey, 1989), and in the specification-oriented semantics of programming languages. Pure mathematicians, on the other hand, tend to prefer closed mathematical abstractions like sets and functions and (more occasionally) relations. This is evident in the study of analysis and even more in topology. It is the style preferred in the denotational semantics of programming languages. Each style is more appropriate for the use to which it is put, and there is no conflict between them. Every predicate can be identified with a set, namely the set of those assignments of values to its free variables which make the predicate true. And the sets and functions of the pure mathematician can and should be translated into predicates and formulae before use by engineers and programmers. The important relation of set inclusion then translates to logical implication, defining precisely the designer's proof obligation. In the remainder of this article, it is more convenient to adopt the style of pure mathematics, dealing with sets and relations rather than variables and predicates.

Let us give the name OBS to the set containing mathematical representatives for all possible direct and indirect observations of all possible processes of interest. We can now represent a particular process P as that subset of OBS which contains all observations which could in any circumstances be made of that process. The set of all such processes, implementable in a particular envisaged language or technology, constitutes a family of subsets of OBS, to which we give the name of $PROC$. So the first two components of our model are similar to those of a topology – a carrier set OBS and a particular family $PROC$ of its subsets. It is already possible to formulate interesting questions about the family, for example does it contain the empty set, or the universal set OBS itself? Is it closed with respect to union or intersection? There are reasons for answering these questions by no, yes, yes, and no.

The family $PROC$ may be defined by describing the mathematical properties of each of its members. These commonly take the form of closure conditions, which force the sets to be 'large enough'. A closure condition can often be expressed in terms of a function or relation which maps members of the set to other members. A set S is closed with respect to a relation c if it contains its own image through c:

$$cS \subseteq S$$

where

$$cS =_{df} \{y \mid \exists x.x \in S \land x(c)y\}.$$

For example, if a communicating process has engaged in a long sequence of events, there must have been times at which it has engaged in only an initial subsequence of those events; and right at the beginning, the trace must have been empty. So each set in $PROC$ must contain the empty sequence, and be closed with respect to the prefix ordering on traces. Similarly, a process which is now deadlocked, refusing to engage in a large set of events, would also refuse any smaller subset of those events. Finally, a process that has already failed (perhaps by infinite recursion) cannot recover by engaging in further events – or at least it cannot be relied upon to do so. Different choices of closure conditions lead to a hierarchy of mutually related theories which invite exploration; each of them may be interesting or useful in different circumstances. The relaxation of closure constraints may lead to a more useful set of definable combinators which satisfy the closure conditions; but in general it will reduce the number of potentially useful algebraic laws. The selection of appropriate compromises may be influenced by understanding of the application domain as well as the implementation.

The conditions defining membership of $PROC$ are intended to ensure physical implementability. Like the laws of physics, they describe general properties such as conservation of energy that must be preserved in any physical system. So it is not surprising that their discovery and formalization are the first and most serious difficulty in the construction of realistic models; what is worse, their sufficiency and validity can be established only at the very last step in the evaluation of the model by practical use. That is why Dana Scott once characterised formalization as an experimental science. So when the experiment succeeds, when all aspects of the theory link together harmoniously, great satisfaction can be derived from the achievement, in addition to the possibility of more practical benefits.

The sets in $PROC$ are intended to represent exactly the implementable processes of the theory. But a specification of such a process does not have to be a member of $PROC$. Any other subset S, defined by any desired combination of mathematical predicates, can serve as a specification of requirements placed on a particular member P from PROC, which is yet to be designed. The design will be correct if and only if the eventually delivered P is a subset of S, i.e., all possible observations of the process (including even the undesirable ones) are permitted by the specification. So the subset relation between a process and a specification captures exactly the concept of satisfaction, as described in the previous section. Of course, it may be that there does not exist any P in PROC which satisfies the specification. It is then logically impossible to meet the specification within the given technology. The theory may help the engineer in avoiding the danger of promising to deliver such a product.

Consider a specification T, and let S be a subset of T. Then S is a stronger specification than T: it places more constraints on the product and may therefore be more difficult to implement. Indeed, because set inclusion is transitive, every product that meets specification S will serve also as an implementation of T, so implementation of T cannot possibly be more difficult than S.

The subset relation may also be used to define an ordering among the members of $PROC$. By transitivity of inclusion, $P \subseteq Q$ means that

P satisfies every specification satisfied by Q, and maybe more. Consequently for all relevant purposes and in all relevant respects P is better than Q (or at least as good). Thus if Q is a simple design or prototype which clearly meets its specification, then Q can be validly transformed to (or replaced by) P, without jeopardising correctness; the motive for doing so may be a reduction in cost or increase in efficiency. One of the main objectives of a mathematical theory is to provide a comprehensive collection of such correctness-preserving, but efficiency-increasing transformations. Notice that the interpretation of the relation $\subseteq$ as 'better than' depends on the fact that OBS contains all relevant ways in which a process may fail. It is this that ensures that the better process is the one that fails less often; and furthermore, because it gives rise to fewer non-failing observations, it is easier to predict and control what it is going to do. In this way 'better' also implies 'more deterministic'.

We can now single out from $PROC$ those processes which are the best of their kind, in the sense that none of them can be further improved. This subfamily will be called DET, because it contains those processes which are as deterministic and as free from failure as possible. For each process D in DET there exists a specification (namely D itself) which is met by D and by no other process:

$$P \subseteq D \Rightarrow P = D,$$

for all $P \in PROC$, and all $D \in DET$.

The size of DET is therefore indicative of the range of solutions provided by the theory, and therefore of the range of essentially distinct problems that can be solved by it. So a theory in which DET has only a few members is not likely to be widely applicable.

It is unusual for a general theory to include cost or speed among its observables, because these factors are highly variable between one project and another. However, if they are included in a more specific theory, it is important to ensure that the observations take the form 'it costs less than n' or 'it goes faster than m'. Then $P \subseteq Q$ means that Q can cost more and go slower, so the interpretation of inclusion as a merit ordering can be maintained. But such a theory can deal only with uniform improvement with respect to all criteria simultaneously; it becomes wholly inapplicable in the more frequent case when one criterion must be traded against another. That is another reason why these considerations are usually omitted from a general theory, and left to the good judgement of the engineer. No amount of mathematical theorising can ever replace that!

9.4 Some Simple Processes

Certain individual members of $PROC$ can be simply defined as sets of observations; and the simplest example would be the empty set of observations. But there are two devastating arguments against including the empty set in $PROC$. Firstly the philosophical one: it is wholly unrealistic to design and deliver a product which could never give rise to any observation whatsoever, either direct or indirect. Secondly the practical objection: the empty set would by definition satisfy every specification expressible in the theory. It would be the only member of DET, and even if there were other members of $PROC$, there would never be any need to use them. The empty set would be a miracle (Morgan, 1990) or panacea, and a mathematical theory which contains it can only be applied to a problem domain in which a panacea exists. But in such a domain, there is hardly any need for a mathematical theory. For this reason, it is essential to introduce enough indirect observations to ensure that no process is represented by the empty set.

Another easily defined process is the universal set OBS itself. This is called ABORT in Dijkstra's sequential programming language (Dijkstra, 1976), and CHAOS in CSP. It is the easiest of all processes to implement – in fact any process whatsoever will serve as an implementation. But it is the worst possible process to use; its behaviour is maximally uncontrollable and unpredictable, and it may go wrong in any or all possible ways. It is difficult to imagine a computational device that really behaves as badly as this; but perhaps one example would be a program which on receipt of an external interrupt executes a wild jump to a floating point number. But a true understanding of CHAOS comes from a recognition that a specification is an integral part of the delivered product. If somehow the specification becomes detached, say from a bottle of medicine, then the only safe thing to do with it is to throw it away unused. So also must one treat a product, say processed food, which has been stored in a manner which violates the stated preconditions for safe consumption. These are the most useless of products; and they are modelled in our theory by the weakest of all processes, namely the universal set OBS. These are good enough reasons for including OBS as a process in $PROC$; since OBS satisfies all possible closure conditions, it is mathematically convenient to do so. And since the responsible engineer should do anything to avoid such a dreadful process, mathematical convenience is a sufficient excuse for including it in the theory.

At the opposite extreme to CHAOS, which can give rise to arbitrary observable behaviour, there is a process which never does anything whatsoever, because it is deadlocked. This is known as STOP in CSP and Nil in CCS (Milner, 1989). Its trace is always an empty sequence, and it refuses to engage in any possible set of events that may be offered.

The behaviour of STOP is certainly highly undesirable, almost certainly the result of a design error or violation of a precondition. It is therefore tempting to make no distinction between STOP and the worst possible process CHAOS. Experience shows that it is wise to delay giving way to this temptation. Later we may wish to define a combinator that permits recovery from deadlock, but which cannot recover from other kinds of failure like non-termination. Premature identification of STOP with CHAOS would prevent introduction of this useful combinator.

Both of the processes STOP and CHAOS are useless, or worse. A useful process is one that starts by engaging in some event a. At the start, when its trace is empty it will refuse any set of events which does not contain a. All of its non-empty traces begin with a. After occurrence of a, its subsequent behaviour may be defined by a set P. This operation is known as prefixing, and is denoted in CSP by $(a \to P)$ and in CCS by $(a.P)$.

The single processes like those defined in the previous paragraphs are too simple to solve a real problem, even of the most trivial kind. They can only serve as primitive components, which need to be connected together and used in combination to exhibit more complex and useful behaviour. In order to prove in advance that such a combination will work as intended, we need to formalise by mathematical definition the various ways in which components and subassemblies can be combined into larger assemblies or can be adapted for new purposes. These combinators are usually denoted by mathematical operators, whose operands are written representations of the processes which they combine. The combinators are selected and designed to ensure that they map implementable processes to implementable ones; furthermore that they themselves are implementable by some kind of interconnection of components described by their operands. In this section we will introduce some combinators which can be defined with the aid of simple Boolean operators on sets.

Let P be a process and let S be some suitable subset of OBS, such that $P \cap S$ (P restricted to S) is also a process. Then $P \cap S$ is like P, except that its capability of giving rise to observations outside S has been removed. For example suppose P has a two-position switch, and S contains only observations taken when the switch is off. Then $(P \cap S)$ describes an object in which the switch (or at least the capability of turning it on) has been removed. This kind of restriction is used in CCS and ACP (Bergstra & Klop, 1985) to prevent external observation or interference with interactions occurring on internal communicating links in a network. It is immediately obvious that restriction distributes through set union. So do all the other combinators defined in the remainder of this article.

Conjunction might seem to be a useful operator for removing mistakes from a program, for example if S is the set of all observations that do not involve non-termination. Unfortunately the conjunction $(P \cap S)$ will usually fail the closure conditions for membership of $PROC$, except for very special sets S. Or perhaps this is fortunate, because in practice such a process would be impossible, or impossibly inefficient, to implement. For the same reason, a modeller should always take great care not to exclude accidentally the ways in which a combination of processes can in practice go wrong.

If P and Q are processes represented by sets, then their set union $(P \cup Q)$ is the strongest specification satisfied by both P and Q:

$$(P \cup Q) \subseteq S \text{ iff } (P \subseteq S \text{ and } Q \subseteq S), \text{ for all } S \subseteq OBS.$$

If the closure conditions for $PROC$ are expressed in terms of a relational image, $P \cup Q$ will be just the set union of the observations of P and of Q. This is extremely convenient, and explains why the standard semantics of CSP is given in terms of refusal sets, which are closed with respect to the subset relation, rather than acceptance sets, whose closure condition is not relationally definable.

This specification $(P \cup Q)$ presents no great difficulty of implementation. For example it can be implemented either by P or by Q, whichever is the easier; though the conscientious engineer will use his judgement to choose the one that is most cost-effective for the eventual user of the product. $(P \cup Q)$ can be thought of as a product delivered with two different operating instructions, one for P and one for Q, and no indication which is right. Of course it may be possible to decide between them by subsequent experiment; but until then the only safe thing is to use the product in a manner consistent with both its manuals. Or maybe there is a single manual, which is ambiguous, and does not state whether it will behave like P or like Q. Sometimes the supplier has good reason for the ambiguity – think of a restaurant which has fresh vegetable soup on its menu. Similarly, a designer may wish to keep options open for later decision, or a manufacturer may wish to retain freedom to deliver later variations of a product. In any case, the formula describing $(P \cup Q)$ may be simpler, more abstract, and easier to manipulate than either of the separate formulae for P or Q. So it is not unreasonable to regard $(P \cup Q)$ as a member of PROC, provided it satisfies the relevant mathematical closure conditions. And we do not have to decide the vexed question whether it is allowable (or even possible) to construct a genuinely non-deterministic process, whose behaviour is not determined even at time of delivery. We will return to this point in a later section.

If it is possible to take the union of two processes P and Q, what about their intersection $(P \cap Q)$? Such a process would engage only in observations on which both P and Q agree. If this is a member of PROC, it is better than both P and Q, although it is the worst process with this property. What is more, intersection can be very useful in meeting a specification expressed as a conjunction of a requirement S with a requirement T. For example suppose S requires that the final value of an array must be sorted in ascending order, and T requires that the final value must be a permutation of the initial value. With the aid of non-determinism it is easy to write a program P which assigns to the array an arbitrary ascending sequence of numbers, thereby meeting requirement S. Requirement T can be met similarly by a program Q that assigns to the array an arbitrary permutation of its initial value. Elementary propositional logic now guarantees that the intersection $(P \cap Q)$ will meet the conjunction $(S \cap T)$ of the requirements.

Unfortunately, in a conventional sequential language, the implementation of $P \cap Q$ would involve repeated execution of both P and Q, looking for an outcome possible for both of them. Such backtracking is excluded from most programming languages on the grounds of inefficiency. Intersection is such a useful and common combinator for specifications that it is highly desirable to explore special cases in which a conjunction of specifications can be efficiently implemented by some combination of processes, each of which meets only part of the specification. That is the main driving force behind research into non-conventional and non-sequential programming languages in which conjunction is a valid combinator, as well as motivating introduction of modular structures into more conventional languages.

If union is easy to implement but intersection infeasible, let us explore some further process combinators that lie between these two extremes.

Let S be some suitable subset of OBS. Then the conditional process $P\langle S\rangle Q$ (P if S else Q) is defined to exhibit an observation of P just when that is an observation in S; but each observation from outside S is an observation of Q:

$$P\langle S\rangle Q =_{df} (P \cap S) \cup (\neg S \cap Q).$$

Simple Boolean algebra gives

$$P \cap Q \subseteq P\langle S\rangle Q \subseteq P \cup Q.$$

In the case of a conventional sequential language, the set S usually takes the form of a computable test b to be applied to the initial state, independent of the final state:

$$B =_{df} \{(s,t)|s \text{ satisfies } b\},$$

so its complement also takes the same form:

$$\neg B = \{(s,t)|s \text{ does not satisfy } b\}.$$

This means that $P\langle B\rangle Q$ can be executed by a test on the initial state, before choosing between execution of P and of Q. Such a combinator is included in all general purpose procedural programming languages. But for other choices of S, it is very unlikely that the result will be a process. For example consider the relational converse of B, which tests the final state rather than the initial state. Such a conditional will not in general lead to consistent results; and even when it does, it could hardly be implemented without systematic backtracking.

The algebraic properties of $\langle S\rangle$, considered as an infix operator, are easily derivable by Boolean algebra. It is idempotent and associative; furthermore, it distributes through union and union distributes through it. Finally, $\langle S\rangle$ distributes through $\langle T\rangle$ for all S and T. Boolean algebra provides an extraordinary variety of mutually distributive operators: indeed, it seems that any operator which makes a selection between its operands, involving execution of exactly one of them, will distribute through itself and every other operator of the same kind.

I have encountered some resistance among algebraists to the idea of mutually distributive operators. To help overcome this prejudice, here is a whole new class of them. Let S be some suitable subset of OBS. Then the process $(P[S]Q)$ is defined to exhibit an observation in S just when both P and Q agree to do so; but each observation outside S may be either from P or from Q:

$$P[S]Q =_{df} (P \cap Q)\langle S\rangle(P \cup Q).$$

This is called the negmajority, because it gives the majority vote of P and Q and the negation of S. Simple Boolean algebra again gives

$$P \cap Q \subseteq P[S]Q \subseteq P \cup Q.$$

A useful special case is when S is STOP. So $P[\text{STOP}]Q$ will refuse only those sets which both P and Q refuse; if the initial event is impossible for P but not for Q, then the next and all subsequent transitions of $P[\text{STOP}]Q$ will be determined by Q and P will be ignored; and symmetrically, interchanging P with Q. In a state in which both P and Q can proceed, either of them may be selected for execution, thereby giving rise to non-determinism. In CCS this operator is written $+$ in CSP it is $[\![$, and it is called (external) choice because it allows the environment a degree of choice between its operands. The important distinction between external choice and non-determinism is often considered subtle or even controversial. The choice of refusal set as an observable property permits the distinction to be fully clarified by definitions of $\vee$ and $[\![$ in simple Boolean algebra.

By Boolean algebra $[S]$ clearly shares all algebraic properties common to both union and intersection (which are actually just the special cases $[OBS]$ and $[\{\}]$ respectively). Furthermore, $[S]$ has S itself as unit; this provides a method for averting deadlock in CCS or CSP by giving a better alternative:

$$\text{STOP}[\![P = P.$$

Finally, $[S]$ is highly distributive. Indeed, each of the operators $[S], [T], \langle U \rangle$ and $\langle V \rangle$ distributes through all of them (including itself). Most of the combinators of a process algebra have more complex and specific set-theoretic definitions; and the proof of algebraic laws is correspondingly more complicated.

As our last Boolean combinator, let us consider negation or complementation. Suppose we wish to define a process which behaves like P, except that it can never do anything that Q can do. Such a process could be very useful as a safety-critical control program. Let Q be a process whose observations include all erroneous or dangerous ones; thus $(P-Q)$ is guaranteed to be safe. Unfortunately, there is no general way to implement such a complementation operator: and mathematically it is very unlikely to satisfy the closure conditions which define processes. If physical and mathematical impossibility are not strong enough arguments, we will later find yet another reason for not admitting complementation as a combinator on processes. But of course, like all the Boolean operators, it remains extremely useful for specification. The characteristic feature of computational processes is that they involve many more steps than could ever be described explicitly in a program or other written representation of a design. This problem is solved by repeated use of parts of a program in some form of iteration, or more generally by recursion. We describe a simple but general form of recursion without parameters. Let X be a variable standing for an arbitrary subset of OBS. Let $F(X)$ be an expression of the programming language built up from X (and perhaps other process variables and explicitly defined processes) by means of combinators of the language. Consider the equation

$$X = F(X)$$

which states that X is a fixed point of F. Now subsets of OBS form a complete lattice under inclusion ordering, and F, being defined solely by relational images, is a monotonic function. A famous theorem by Knaster and Tarski proves the existence of a solution to the equation (Tarski, 1955).

In fact, there is a complete lattice of solutions: which one do we want? Since we want to be able to implement the solution, we want the easiest one, namely the greatest of them. Such a solution always exists as a specification; but in a general purpose programming language we would like it also to exist as a process. A general way of achieving this is due to Scott and Smyth (Scott & Strachey, 1971; Smyth, 1978).

   (i) Allow OBS to be a process.
  (ii) Suppose $\{X_i \mid i \in NN\}$ is any descending chain of processes. Ensure that $\bigcap_i X_i$ is also a process (in particular, it must not be empty). This requires exclusion of infinite non-determinism.
 (iii) Ensure that all combinators are continuous in the sense that $F(\bigcap_i X_i) = \bigcap_i(FX_i)$ for all descending chains. This is guaranteed if all combinators are defined in terms of relations that are finitary, in the sense that the inverse image of any finite set is also finite (or universal). Sometimes a non-finitary relation is allowable, as in the case of hiding in CSP.

Now the fixed point of F is just

$$\bigcap_i F^i(OBS),$$

where F^i is the ith iterate of F. This can be readily computed by unfolding the definition of F as many times as required. If no finite unfolding is adequate, the implementation will fail to terminate; but this is exactly what the theory also predicts. The existence of this simple general way of defining iterations or recursions is a great simplification of the task of the modeller, who can concentrate attention on the mathematical properties of finite processes, i.e., those that are defined without recursion. Another equally valid general method of explaining recursion is by metric spaces and contraction mappings: these always give a unique fixed point.

9.5 Calculus of Design

The previous sections have shown how to give a mathematical model of various ways in which processes may be combined into larger assemblies. The theory may be used predictively, as in science, to calculate the observable properties of a system whose components have known properties. But engineers have to work in the reverse direction. A specification is a description of the desired properties of an assembly that does not yet exist. The engineering task is to design and implement the components, and assemble them in a manner which meets the specification. For this we need a calculus of design. The calculus is based on the idea that a combinator defined on processes $P, Q, \ldots$ can be equally well applied to specifications, that is to arbitrary subsets $S, T, \ldots$ of OBS. This fact is heavily exploited (using predicates in the place of sets) by the schema calculus of Z.

Let us suppose that a designer is faced with a specification U. Judgement based on experience perhaps suggests an implementation in which (say) two components are connected by some combinator r. The further design and implementation of the components are to be delegated as separate tasks to two teams, or two persons, or even to one person working on the two tasks at separate times. Successful delegation requires careful formalisation of the correct specifications S and T of the two components. Their correctness should be proved before the first step of implementation, because detection and correction of design errors after delivery and assembly of the components may give rise to arbitrary unbounded expense and delay. The theorem that needs proof is formalised by using r to combine the specifications of S and T, showing this implies the original overall specification U:

$$SrT \subseteq U.$$

Because r is monotonic, any implementation of S, when combined by r

with any implementation of T, will assuredly satisfy U. This method of rigorous decomposition can be applied equally well to the design of the subassemblies too, and can be repeated until each component can be implemented by a primitive process or assembly already known to work. It is particularly effective in computing science, where the combinators available for connecting large assemblies are logically indistinguishable from those available for much smaller subassemblies, right down to the level of primitive components.

This design method can be adapted to assist in re-use of subassemblies that have already been designed, for example as a module in a library. Suppose T is a specification of such a module, which is to be connected into a system with specification U by means of a combinator r. The designer has to find and implement the specification S of the rest of the system, in a manner which satisfies the inequation

$$SrT \subseteq U.$$

The method described above requires discovery and formalisation of S followed by proof. If the proof fails, the formalisation of S must be repeated – a frustration familiar to many an engineer who does indefinite integration by guessing a formula and checking its derivative. Far better to calculate the correct result directly and immediately from T and U. Provided r is defined as a relational image, this can be done by the formula

$$S = \bigcup \{X \mid XrT \subseteq U\},$$

or better, by some simpler formula which has been proved equivalent to it. This gives the weakest specification of any product X which has the required property, namely

$$XrT \subseteq U \text{ iff } X \subseteq S.$$

So the choice of this particular S as a specification for the rest of the system involves no additional design commitment or loss of generality. The technical term for this situation is a Galois connection, a simple case of a categorical adjunction. In general, let r be any combinator. Then the weak inverse of r is defined as a combinator s with the property that

$$XrT \subseteq U \text{ iff } X \subseteq UsT.$$

The weak inverse of sequential composition has been called the weakest prespecification (Hoare & He, 1986); and in CSP the weak inverse of parallel composition has been called the weakest environment (Zhou,

1982). But in practice weak inverses give rise to complications that belie the simplicity of the general theory:

(i) S may in fact in unimplementable. In fact an early proof of this may save a lot of wasted effort, because it shows that the choice either of T or of r has been mistaken.

(ii) In practice, the size of the formulae derived by this method can be excessive. Nevertheless, the stepwise simplification of the formulae, with the aid of strengthening, may be a good guide to the further design decisions needed at this stage.

Further theoretical research to solve these problems is to be strongly recommended.

9.6 Non-determinism

The method of modelling a computational process as a set of observations is intended to deal in a uniform fashion with both deterministic and non-deterministic processes. It is possible to single out deterministic processes as a special case; it is possible to note informally when a combinator may fail to preserve determinism of its operands. But once non-determinism is accepted and taken for granted, there is no necessity to make these distinctions; and the mathematical theory develops most smoothly without them.

Many practising engineers are very reluctant to accept non-determinism, and rightly so. The only way that they have been taught to assess reliability of a product is to test it. But a non-deterministic product may very well pass every test, yet later fail in practical use, just when most reliance is placed upon it. The only known solution to this problem lies in mathematical design methods that inhibit the intrusion of error. Indeed, this is already coming to be accepted by some engineers as more effective than testing, even for deterministic products. Hence the slogan 'Design right – First time'.

Many mathematical computing scientists are also reluctant to accept non-determinism, and rightly so. They have been educated in a tradition that mathematics is about functions, and that its concepts are expressed primarily in functional notation. The use of functional notation for non-deterministic operations leads to immediate confusion: for example, one has to question the validity of the absolutely fundamental equation of mathematics, namely

$$fx = fx.$$

Similar difficulties arise for partial functions; and the solution is the same: go back to the foundation offered by set theory, and use relational notations wherever they are appropriate. This is a solution which is already being applied by abstract functional programmers, of the schools of FP (Backus, 1978) and squiggol (Bird, 1988); they have found it more effective to calculate with function composition rather than function application.

One important characteristic of our treatment of non-determinism is that it is not possible to specify that a delivered product must be non-deterministic at the time of delivery. Any satisfiable specification is satisfied by some member of DET. It is this that makes it possible to use the same mathematical model for non-determinism in products as for under-determination in designs and specifications; and full advantage is taken of this in the calculus of design.

Finally there is an interesting technical question, with strong philosophical overtones. Is it possible to make an observation of a delivered product that will reveal that the product was non-deterministic at time of delivery? In technical terms, could there be an observation of a non-deterministic process P which is not possible for any of the deterministic processes contained in P? Or is each process P equal to the union of all deterministic processes contained in it:

$$P = \bigcup \{D | D \in DET \ \& \ D \subseteq P\}?$$

One of the major differences between CCS and CSP is that CSP conforms to this principle of invisibility of non-determinism.

Of course, it is always possible to detect non-determinism if one can observe the internal structure of the implementation. For example a process known to have the structure $(P; P)$ could be observed to be non-deterministic if each instance of P were observed to behave differently. In the theory of testing which underlies the equivalence of CCS, it is permitted at any time to take a copy of the current state of the process, and conduct the same (or different) tests on each copy; and it is this that may make non-determinism visible. In many applications, of course, such wholesale copying is physically impossible – for example if the system to be copied is the whole universe, or some large or inextricable part of it, like you or me. Even at the level of a single particle, quantum theory tells us that no copy can be made: otherwise it would be possible to test momentum of one copy and position of the other. It is really only in the abstract world of mathematics that copying is possible, and so easy that it can be taken for free.

But enough of philosophy: there are also interesting technical and practical considerations. For example, if non-determinism is unobservable, it is possible to prove that a resource allocating process that chooses among free resources at the time of the request is just as good as one that gains efficiency by preselecting the next allocation at the time of the previous request. In CCS, these two processes can be distinguished, because one of them resolves its non-determinism later than the other; and this can be detected by cloning the whole allocator before the next request. But of course, a resource allocator is a prime example of a process that should never never be copied. So in this case at least there are good reasons for using the slightly more powerful proof methods available in CSP.

There is reason to suppose that will come to play an increasing role in computing science, both practical and theoretical. In practice, continuing miniaturisation of circuits will continue to favour highly parallel hardware, and provide increasing incentives to use it efficiently. But if parallel processes are to cooperate on the solution of a single problem, possibly sharing mechanical resources such as disc storage, they will certainly need on occasion to synchronise with each other. Each synchronisation will in principle delay at least one of the processes involved. Examples of the most significant delays are those arising from paging faults in a virtual memory, or from scheduling of arithmetic units in a dataflow architecture. Increase of processing speed can only increase the significance of these delays. The only solution is to allow the existence and duration of the delay to influence the course of the computation. For example the programmer can use the $\|$ combinator of CSP to allow the earliest possible selection of the first possible event that can occur. Since delays are essentially unpredictable, we are almost forced to accept non-determinism as an inherent property of programs and algorithms, and even of computer hardware. Learning how to cope with non-determinism is one of the most significant challenges and achievements of theoretical computing science, and still offers exciting challenges for the future.

9.7 Operational Semantics

The main danger in constructing mathematical theories about technological products is that they may in the end be unrealistic, impossible, or impossibly expensive to implement. The ultimate test of feasibility is widespread use by practising engineers and programmers, supported by mechanical design tools and compilers. For example, theoretical investigations into communication and concurrency have been validated by efficient implementation of the Occam programming language on the transputer (INMOS, 1988a, b), and by use of its algebraic laws in the design of the T800 floating point unit (Barrett, 1987). But the installation of theory in practice requires an enormous investment and usually takes more than fifteen years. So it is the duty of the theoretician to take every possible step to reduce the risk of unpleasant surprises at a later stage. Fortunately mathematics again provides methods of discharging this responsibility.

For a theory of hardware design, the justification for an abstract mathematical model, expressed say in Boolean algebra, is found by relating it to some more detailed model of implementation of the hardware components, say in terms of voltages on wires. And this too can be validated at an even lower level of abstraction by appeal to the relevant laws of physics. Only at this point, if there is any doubt, is the mathematical theorist entitled to hand over responsibility to the experimental scientist to confirm the physical accuracy of the theory.

In the case of software designs and programming languages, the mathematician can discharge more of the responsibility. For example consider the risk that a theory of processes is in principle unimplementable; perhaps because one of the operators requires a test whether its operand will fail to terminate; or because it is more subtly incomputable in the sense of Turing and Church. This danger can be averted by giving the language a denotational semantics (Scott & Strachey, 1971) expressed usually in a functional notation which is known to be Turing-computable. At one time this was the only known way of presenting an abstract formal semantics for a programming notation.

Apart from total incomputability, there is an equally serious danger, particularly for theories that include non-determinism: the language may contain an operator like conjunction whose implementation requires exploring all the possible non-deterministic behaviours of its operand, looking perhaps for one that terminates in some desirable state. Such an operator can indeed be implemented, but only by backtracking or similar techniques, which introduce an exponential increase in time taken or resources consumed. The way to check against this risk is to construct a mathematical model of a step-by-step implementation, for example as a Petri net (Petri, 1973), or by formalisation in Plotkin's structured operational semantics (Plotkin, 1981). Both of these techniques ensure that the permissible next steps in the evolution of a composite process can be determined by considering just the first possible step in the evolution of each of its components. Often at any given time only a small subset of the components needs to be considered, which increases the possibilities for parallel execution of many steps, and reduces the need for synchronisation. But once feasibility has been checked by an operational model, operational reasoning should be immediately abandoned; it is essential that all subsequent reasoning, calculation and design should be conducted in each case at the highest possible level of abstraction.

9.8 Process Algebra

The practical use of a model to assist in engineering design requires a significant use of mathematical reasoning of one kind or another. In principle, this reasoning can be based on the raw definitions of the operators involved; but the labour involved would be totally unacceptable – like solving partial differential equations by expanding the primitive definitions in terms of the epsilons and deltas of analysis. The only way that a branch of mathematics can be applied by engineers in practice is when it offers a range of useful theorems, symbolic manipulations and calculations, together with heuristics for their application. It is reasonable to expect a modeller to formulate and prove an initial collection of such theorems, because their proof may require changes in some aspect of the model, its operators, its processes, or even its observations.

The easiest kind of theorem to use is one that is expressed as a general equation, which is true of all values of the variables it contains. An equation which is needed in a particular application can often be deduced by a process of calculation: starting at either side of the desired equation, a series of substitutions is made until the other side is reached; each substitution is justified by a known equation of the theory. Each step is relatively easy to check, even with the assistance of a computer; and long sequences of steps may be carried out almost automatically by a term rewriting system. Such transformations are most frequently required to increase the efficiency of implementation by breaking down the more elaborate structure resulting from the top-down development. A very similar advantage can be taken of theorems (inequalities) using inclusion in place of equality, since all the operators involved in our theories are monotonic, and an engineer needs to exercise freedom to take design decisions which reduce non-determinism.

Of course, there is no limit to the number of theorems that may be derived from a model, and the mathematician needs good judgement in selecting the ones which are likely to be useful. Equally important, the chosen theorems should be reasonably memorable; for this, brevity and elegance are an important aid, as well as self-evidence to the operational understanding of engineers. Again, it is helpful if the theorems express familiar algebraic properties of combinators, for example, associativity, commutativity, idempotence, or distribution of one operator through another. In fact the best possible way of educating an engineer in a new computational paradigm is by an elegant collection of algebraic laws, together with examples and exercises combining theory with practice. This is the way in which pupils at school are taught to reason about the various kinds of number – integers, fractions, reals, complex numbers. The study of the sophisticated and widely differing models for these number systems is more the province of theoretical pure mathematics, and is a topic of specialist study in universities.

An important goal in the derivation of algebraic properties of a model is to find enough laws to decide whether one finite process (defined without recursion) is equal to another, or below it in the relevant ordering. In some cases there is a decision procedure which applies the laws in a particular direction to eliminate the more complex operators, and produce a simple normal form. This procedure is applied to both sides of an equation or inequation, and a simple comparison is then made of the two normal forms. The symbolic calculations are easily mechanised by a term rewriting system (Goguen & Winkler, 1988), though in many cases the normal form (or some intermediate expression) is so much larger than the original formula that it may exhaust the available resources of a machine, or at least the patience of its user. Except in the case of rather small finite universes, there is rarely any hope of an effective decision procedure for processes defined by recursion: in general, an inductive proof is necessary to reason about them.

The practical benefit of deriving laws strong enough for a decision procedure is that thenceforth it is known that all necessary equations (or inequations) can be proved from the laws alone, without expanding any of the definitions or even thinking about any of the observations. This is so valuable that it does not matter if the normal form contains notations which are not in fact implemented, or perhaps not even implementable. But even then, the task of the mathematical modeller is far from over. In each particular application area for a computational paradigm, there are likely to be more specialised theorems, which can help in reliable use of the paradigm; and sometimes the theorems will be of more general utility, and so deserve a place in the central core of the theory. The constant illumination of practice by theory, and the constant enrichment of theory by practice over many years and centuries, have led to the current maturity of modern mathematics and its applications in science and engineering; and they show the direction of future advance for the comparatively immature discipline of theoretical computing science.

Algebraic laws have proved their value particularly in the design and implementation of general purpose programming languages. They are most valuable in transforming a program from a structure which clearly mirrors that of its specification to one which most efficiently matches the architecture of the machine which will execute it. Such transformations may be carried out automatically, by an optimising compiler. Sometimes the motive is to transform a program into some smaller subset of a language, so that it may be implemented in some more restricted technology, for example by silicon compilation. Finally, algebraic transformations seem quite effective in verifying aspects of the design of the compiler itself (Hoare *et al.*, 1993).

The value of algebraic laws and equations is so great that there is a great temptation to avoid the laborious task of modelling, and simply to postulate them without proof. As Bertrand Russell has remarked (Russell, 1919): 'The method of postulation has many advantages: they are the same as the advantages of theft over honest toil.' In the case of a computational paradigm, the honest toil of linking algebra with an operational model is required to help implementation of the paradigm; and the link with a more abstract observational theory of specifications is essential for an effective calculus of design.

But of course, in spite of Russell's remark, the study of abstract algebra, independent of all its models and applications, has a most important role. A complete and attractive algebra (Bergstra & Klop, 1985; Roscoe & Hoare, 1988; Hoare *et al.*, 1987) can stimulate the search for applications and models to match it. A cramped and awkward algebra can give warnings about problems that are best avoided. When two models obey exactly the same complete set of algebraic laws, there is no need to choose between them; each can be used for the purpose it suits best. But the most important role of algebra is to organise our understanding of a range of different models, capturing clearly those properties which they share, and those which distinguish between them. The various number systems share many familiar algebraic properties – a useful fact that is totally concealed by the radical differences in the structure of their standard models. The variety of programming languages is subject to a similar algebraic classification.

My discussion of the relationship between models and algebra suggests future directions of research for pure algebraists.

(i) An algebra usually starts with a collection of primitive constants and operators (the signature), in terms of which other useful concepts and notations can be defined.

(ii) The derived notations are often as useful as the primitive ones; and their algebraic properties should be explored with at least as much enthusiasm.

(iii) As in other branches of algebra, alternative but equivalent choices of primitive signature and axioms should also be explored.

(iv) Preference should be given to operators which preserve interesting properties of their operands. For example, the parallel combinator of CSP preserves determinism, and the more complex chaining operator preserves responsiveness; both of these properties help in avoiding deadlock.

(v) Many useful laws can be expressed as inequations using some preorder representing improvement or implementation of specifications. All operators must be assumed monotonic in this order.

(vi) The most useful advances in pure and applied mathematics have been made by postulating inverses for more primitive operators, especially when this is counter to engineering intuition.

(vii) Where exact inverses are impossible or otherwise undesirable, weak inverses may be a very useful substitute, even if they are not directly implementable.

(viii) The existence of normal forms is a good test of the completeness and consistency of an algebra. There is no need for the normal form to consist wholly of implementable notations.

(ix) Limits and recursion can be introduced by standard techniques, using the ordering defined by set inclusion, or some suitable complete metric space.

(x) If possible, the algebra of implementable processes should be embedded into a complete Boolean algebra, which can then serve as a specification language.

(xi) The eventual goal of research is the development of a family of related algebras, suited to a wide range of application areas and implementation technologies. The more powerful and expressive members of the family will be more useful for specification and design; and methods of symbolic calculation will be available to transform designs to more directly implementable notations.

But the most important message of this article is one that we know already: that the interplay between models and algebra is constantly fruitful; and each of them provides guidance in taking rational decisions between otherwise arbitrary lines of development in the other.

9.9 Outlook

I have described the ways in which both models and algebras can contribute to the solution of practical design problems in computing; and I have illustrated my points by examples which may have given the impression it is easy. This is not so. The construction of a single mathematical model obeying an elegant set of algebraic laws is a significant intellectual achievement; so is the formulation of a set of algebraic laws characterising an interesting and useful set of models.

But neither of these individual achievements is enough. We need to build up a large collection of models and algebras, covering a wide range of computational paradigms, appropriate for implementation either in hardware or in software, either of the present day or of some possible future. But even this is not enough. What is needed is a deep understanding of the relationships between all the different models and theories, and a sound judgement of the most appropriate area of application of each of them. Of particular importance are the methods by which one abstract theory may be embedded by translation or interpretation in another theory at a lower level of abstraction. In traditional mathematics, the relations between the various branches of the subject are well understood, and the division of the subject into its branches is based on the depth of this understanding. When the mathematics of computation is equally well understood, it is very unlikely that its branches will have the same labels that they have today. The investigations by various theoretical schools, now labelled by a variety of Three Letter Acronyms (Bergstra & Klop, 1985; Brookes *et al.*, 1984; Milner, 1989), will have contributed to the understanding which leads to their own demise.

The clarification of the interfaces between complementary theories has important practical advantages. In most branches of engineering, product design requires mixture of a number of differing materials and technologies. Each separate technology must be well understood; but most of the difficulties and misunderstandings and unpleasant surprises occur at the interfaces between the technologies. And the same is true in computing, when attempting to put together a system from programs written, perhaps for a good reason, in different languages, with equipment of differing architectures, and perhaps increasingly in the future, with highly parallel application-specific integrated circuits. An appropriate theory can help in each individual aspect of the design; but only an understanding of the relationships between the theories, as branches of some more abstract theory, can help to solve the really pressing problems of overall system integration.

The establishment of a proper structure of branches and sub-branches is essential also to the progress of science. Firstly, it is essential to the efficient education of a new generation of scientists, who will push forward the frontiers in new directions with new methods unimagined by those who taught them. Secondly, it enables individual scientists to select a narrow specialisation for intensive study in a manner which assists the work of other scientists in related branches, rather than just competing with them. It is only the small but complementary contributions made by many thousands of scientists that have led to the achievements of the established branches of modern science. But until the framework of complementarity is well understood, it is impossible to avoid gaps and duplication, and achieve rational collaboration in place of unscientific competition and strife.

The same views have been expressed more strongly in a different context by Andreski (Andreski, 1972):

... the reason why human understanding has been able to advance in the past, and may do so in the future, is that true insights are cumulative and retain their value regardless of what happens to their discoverers; while fads and stunts may bring an immediate profit to the impresarios, but lead nowhere in the long run, cancel each other out, and are dropped as soon as their promoters are no longer there (or have lost the power) to direct the show. Anyway let us not despair.

10

Real-time Computing

Mathai Joseph

Abstract

Real-time computing has been the domain of the practical systems engineer for many decades. It is only comparatively recently that very much attention has been directed to its theoretical study. Using methods originally developed for use in operations research and optimization, scheduling theory has been used to analyse characteristic timing problems in the sharing of resources in real-time computing systems. Independently of this, specification and verification techniques used in sequential and concurrent programming have been extended to allow definition of the timing properties of programs. In terms of effectiveness, the two approaches are still limited and experimental, and neither on its own can yet be used to provide an exact timing analysis or to verify the timing properties of even modestly complex real-time programs of practical size. But if restricted classes of program are considered, they are rapidly approaching the point of practical usefulness. This suggests that the development of a discipline of real-time programming would allow the construction of programs with analyzable and verifiable timing properties. Such a discipline will need to be built upon on a well integrated framework in which different methods are used where appropriate to obtain timing properties to which a high level of assurance can be attached.

10.1 Introduction

A real-time computer system interacts with an environment which has time-varying properties and the system must exhibit predictable time-dependent behaviour. Most real-time systems have limited resources

188

(e.g. memory, processors) whose allocation to competing demands must be scheduled in a way that will allow the system to satisfy its timing constraints. Thus one important aspect of the design and analysis of a real-time system is concerned with resource allocation.

Job sequencing, timing, scheduling and optimization are problems that have been studied in operations research for many decades. By the early 1970s, similar techniques were being used to analyse the timing properties of simple classes of real-time programs. In a seminal and influential paper, Liu & Layland (1973) derived a sufficient condition for guaranteeing that a set of independent, periodic processes with fixed computation times could be scheduled without any processing overruns. This condition provided a useful guideline (though in general it is stronger than necessary) and, together with their identification of a *rate-monotonic* order of the periods of the processes as 'optimal', remained the most important outcome of scheduling theory for the next 10–12 years.

At the same time, the definition of axiomatic proof systems for programming languages led to the development of techniques for proving the correctness of programs with regard to what would now be called their 'functional' properties: producing results with the right values. Wirth (1977) pointed out the need for a distinction between this kind of program correctnessidxprogram correctness and the satisfaction of timing constraints and argued that ensuring the latter was considerably more difficult. Wirth was considering a very restricted class of real-time programs, but even so a more general class than would be susceptible to Liu & Layland's analysis; Mok (1983) gave a good account of the extent of the gap in the early 1980s between timing properties that could actually be calculated using scheduling theory and what was needed for practical real-time programming. Since that time, there have been many advances in scheduling theory and in program specification and verification, and both are approaching the point where they will be able to consider comparable classes of programs of significant size.

The imperatives in real-time computing come from the nature of the application and the capabilities of the hardware. Despite predictions of saturation in circuit speed and complexity, there has in fact been a fairly regular increase in processor speed and throughput for many years now. This has made it possible for most real-time programs to be sequential programs with altogether simpler timing properties than would be the case for concurrent or distributed programs. If this were to remain the case, there would be very little need for further work in the area. But not only is this unlikely, the demands of more complex applications will themselves lead to the need for better understood and more effective ways to specify, verify, analyze and validate the timing properties of real-time systems.

10.2 Timing in a Real-time Program

There has been much interest in the mathematical representation of time and there are few models of concurrency that do not incorporate some theory of time. In terms of requirements, the problem is to specify and verify a program which† must meet functional as well as timing requirements, i.e. producing results with the right values at the right time. If computer systems were sufficiently fast (though how that can be determined is itself a major question), the necessary computations could be done in any order with no significant delays. Systems whose speed is a constraint require other ways of planning the order in which computations are performed. Adding timing requirements to a program specification can make verification of program properties much harder and so different ways have been devised to keep designs simple.

10.2.1 Real-time without time

The need for simplicity and the dangers of overspecification both suggest making as little use as possible of explicit values of time in a real-time program specification. Turski (1988) has argued that time may be an issue for an implementation but should never appear in a specification; observable time in a program's execution can differ to an arbitrary extent from universal or absolute time so the correctness of a program is more easily proved if its actions are based on observable events, rather than apparent values of time. Hehner (1989) incorporates time in the semantics of programs as an auxiliary variable (using an explicit time variable) and shows how values of time can be used in assertions and for reasoning about simple programming constructs; even with this, he argues that where there are timing constraints, it is always better to construct a program with the required timing properties than to try to compute the timing properties of an arbitrary program.

---

† There are other definitions of a real-time system, such as the one given by Le Lann (1990): 'A computing system where initiation and termination of activities must meet specified timing constraints. Time dependent activities are associated with activity terminations. System behaviour is determined by algorithms designed to maximise a global time-dependent value function.'

Where programs can be constructed with these relatively simple restrictions, there seems little reason to make any more complicated assumptions. Thus for programs that can be implemented with fixed schedules on a single processor, or those with restricted timing requirements which can be efficiently met by relatively simple programming constructs, these assumptions provide a good basis for reasoning about real-time programs without reasoning about time.

10.2.2 Synchronous real-time languages

Some of the most interesting recent work in real-time programming has made use of the *synchrony hypothesis*: external events are ordered in time and the program responds to each event as if instantaneously. The synchrony hypothesis has been used in the *ESTEREL* (Berry & Cosserat, 1985), *LUSTRE* and *SIGNAL* family of languages, and in *Statecharts* (Harel, 1987). Programs can also be represented in terms of their behavioural properties using theories called process algebras and time can be made part of the behaviour. In these timed process algebras, time is often made to progress following the synchrony hypothesis.

The synchrony hypothesis is elegant and very effective, where it is applicable. The idea that a response can be 'instantaneous' is of course an idealization and can be approximated by any time of response which is smaller than the minimum time between external events. Moreover, what is apparently instantaneous to the external viewer does not need to be mirrored internally, and this makes it possible for the expected computational properties of order and causality to be preserved.

Under this hypothesis, external time is modelled by a discrete representation and internal actions are deterministic and ordered and can be converted into the actions of an automaton. The 'natural' implementation is for a single processor; a distributed or multiple processor implementation must emulate this.

If an application can make highly variable computing demands, the synchronous hypothesis is difficult to sustain because it would require unreasonably powerful processing capacity. Also, if the nature of the application leads to a distributed implementation and the external time delays are sufficiently small, it becomes difficult for a single processor implementation to be emulated. And the dedicated commitment of computing resources needed to support the synchrony hypothesis can make it hard to satisfy restrictions that may apply to the cost, weight or power consumption of a practical real-time system. *Strong synchrony* is a more general form of synchrony applicable to distributed systems where non-determinism is permitted but events can be ordered by a global clock.

10.2.3 Asynchronous real-time

In an asynchronous system, external events are 'timed' by external clocks (typically with time expressed as a value from a dense domain) and internal events must closely follow external timing. From a simple real-time system with a single processor and a set of devices seeking its attention at intervals using interrupts, to a complex distributed system with varied control, processing and fault-tolerance requirements, the assumption of asynchrony has often been a starting point.

Communication has been studied in terms of asynchrony because it allows an interpretation of phenomena that is close to what can actually be observed and implemented. Other reasons for introducing asynchrony include the need to combine good average case responsiveness with effective bounded response to infrequent (but perhaps critical) external events, to allow less restricted implementation on multiple processor or distributed systems, or even because of a belief that 'it's more natural'.

There is at least one practical reason to favour the use of a dense time domain, which is that the execution time of an instruction typically lies in a real interval rather than having a fixed value. But there are technical reasons relating to compositionality as well, for example as shown in the denotational semantics of Roncken and Gerth (1990). Thus in terms of both theory and practice, specification of time in some dense domain can be justified, though the reasons for choosing between different dense domains (e.g. the reals or the rationals) are less compelling.

There are many areas where restrictions must be imposed (or further assumptions made) if the timing properties of an asynchronous system are to be fully determined: e.g. the use of discrete rather than continuous time, the imposition of determinism, and approximating cyclic behaviour and aperiodicity by periodic behaviours. Few of these restrictions are really compatible with the asynchrony hypothesis: they must be justified because without them the analysis of the timing behaviour may not be possible by a particular method.

10.3 Real-time Logics and Algebras

A number of real-time logics have been proposed within the last 15 years and a few of them have continued to provide influential examples of how timing properties can be specified and verified. The earliest of these is Koymans' metric temporal logic MTL (Koymans, 1989) which uses dense time and adds time bounds to the temporal operators $\Diamond$ and $\Box$. Thus instead of $\Box$ standing only for 'henceforth', as in temporal logic, it can be given a time attribute t so that it denotes 'henceforth for t units of time'; likewise, the timed version of the 'eventual' operator $\Diamond$ can denote 'eventually within t time units'. By comparison, in explicit clock temporal logic (e.g. Ostroff, 1989) there is a (usually discrete) clock value associated with each state of a program execution. Following Lamport, program properties are often divided into safety properties ('nothing bad will happen') and liveness properties ('something good will eventually happen'). In MTL, some timing properties are safety properties and others are liveness properties, while in explicit clock logics all timing properties are safety properties (Pnueli & Harel, 1988). Pnueli has shown that specifications in MTL have equivalents in explicit clock temporal logic, and Hooman (1991) has suggested that they may still be distinguishable in terms of their utility: high-level specification is better done in MTL while program-level specifications need explicit reference to a clock.

A great deal of current interest centres on specification and verification of *hybrid* systems which contain discretely as well as continuously varying components. A lot of this is centred around the use of the duration calculus (Zhou *et al.*, 1991), which is derived from an interval temporal logic and allows specification of integrals over system states by interpreting formulae over bounded intervals.

Timed process algebras usually provide ways of explicitly manipulating time: e.g. CSP has been extended into Timed CSP with timed models (e.g. Schneider (1990), Davies (1991)) to match each of the untimed CSP models (Reed & Roscoe, 1988), and CCS has been extended into TCCS ('Timed CCS'). Among other process algebras extended with time are ACP, ATP and LOTOS (see Ostroff (1994) for a short account). A specification is treated as a program in a process algebra, so timing properties can be examined algebraically or by the usual techniques of bisimulation, or testing, or in terms of a denotational domain.

10.3.1 Verification and model-checking

Most real-time properties of practical significance are finite (e.g. 'either action a occurs before time t or action b occurs at time t') even if the programs they are embedded in have nonterminating executions. Verification of such properties should therefore be no more difficult than verification of other program properties, i.e. as a problem of *satisfaction* between a specification S and an implementation I, and this is usually stated in terms of a logical implication $I \rightarrow S$. However, a number of difficulties can be introduced by the choice of a model of time (dense or discrete) and the kind of logic used for specification. For example, with a linear temporal logic using discrete time and simple operations ($\leq$ and addition with integer constants) on time, the satisfiability problem is decidable, but with dense time it is not. But Henzinger *et al.* (1991b) show how if a specification is independent of a model of time (i.e. is 'digitizable') then continuous time can be used for specification while verification can still be done using deductive techniques (i.e. using proof rules) applicable for discrete time.

Alternatively, a semantic model of states produced during the execution of a program can be constructed and program properties verified using this model. By their nature, such models quickly grow in size and a modestly sized program, or one that executes for even a relatively short time, can require a model with 10^{20} states or more. To use model-checking for verification of a real-time program requires an algorithm to test whether all the possible unfoldings of a finite state timed transition system representation of the program satisfy a specification S. Due to the large state-spaces, model-checking is applicable only for small, often hardware-level, systems (Ostroff, 1994). Alur *et al.* (1991) show that simple syntactic restrictions over the logic can make it possible (decidable in EXSPACE) to verify real-time specifications by model-checking.

10.4 Program Models for Scheduling Analysis

Scheduling theory has typically considered the problem of determining whether an implementation of a program is feasible, i.e. whether it meets timing deadlines. The first models of programs used for analysis were very simple: each program had multiple, independent processes with fixed computation times and these were executed periodically on a single processor; the deadline for each process was equal to its period. This model was studied under different scheduling disciplines: e.g. fixed priority pre-emptive execution with processes ordered in ascending order of period (i.e. rate-monotonic order) (Liu & Layland, 1973), and dynamic priority allocation according to earliest deadline (Dertouzos, 1974) or least slack ordering (Mok, 1983), each of which was shown to be optimal in that if it did not provide a feasible schedule then no other scheduler in the same class would provide a feasible schedule.

Making the model more realistic and representative brings in many difficulties; Mok (1983) showed that if processes needed to synchronize with each other at arbitrary points, then every synchronization point must be known *a priori* if feasibility is to be determined, and that in general the problem of determining if such a schedule is feasible is NP-hard. Simpler solutions are possible if process synchronization takes place in a more structured (and restricted) way. The *Priority Ceiling Protocol* and its variants introduced by Sha *et al.* (1990) allow processes to synchronize through a mechanism like a procedure call (called a remote procedure call, since it takes place between processes). A process making the remote procedure call is blocked until the callee responds to its request and there may be several such waiting calls. The protocol preserves the relative priority order of processes and allows computation of the maximum blocking time for each such call and analysis of feasibility. However, it does require processes to be periodic and deterministic and for their interactions to be through nested remote procedure calls (for example) which are completed before a process completes execution.

To complement the accuracy with which scheduling analyses can take account of processor speeds, it is important to be able to include other factors, such as communication delays, that can affect program performance and implementation issues such as the effective use of multiple processors. Tindell and Clark (1994) provide an analysis which covers end-to-end communication delays and Tindell *et al.* (1992) show how feasible multiprocessor allocations can be made. A good survey of past and present work on fixed priority scheduling is given in Audsley *et al.* (1994).

10.5 Verification versus Scheduling Analysis

Given that logical and algebraic specification of real-time programs considers similar problems to those studied by scheduling theory, it is interesting to consider how results from one field (e.g. necessary and sufficient feasibility conditions (Joseph & Pandya, 1986)) may be interpreted in the other. But there are many reasons why this is far from easy.

(i) There is a wide variety of architectures on which a real-time program may be implemented and it is difficult to represent their

timing characteristics in a sufficiently abstract way to be of use
in a verification method.

(ii) The timing characteristics of programs are so varied that unless they are vastly simplified, it is difficult to predict timing
behaviour when executed on a particular system.

(iii) Effective use of the hardware requires efficient scheduling of the
use of resources by the program; if this is functionally transparent
to the programmer, no resource dependencies will be encoded
into the program and the performance of the scheduler can be
predicted.

In terms of both levels of abstraction and the objects of abstraction
it would be attractive to find a meeting ground. Scheduling theory is
able to make limited use of the control and dependency structure of the
program and verification methods are able to consider simple systems
with particular scheduling policies (Davies, 1991; Hooman, 1991). If
deadlines are specified as timing properties and scheduling is treated as
a transformation of the program to be scheduled, then feasibility can be
defined as the preservation of deadlines between a specification and its
implementation (i.e. the transformed program) (Liu *et al.*, 1993; Zheng
& Zhou, 1994).

10.6 Timing and Fault-Tolerance

The problem of constructing fault-tolerant programs can similarly be
considered as one of transforming a program written for execution on a
fault-free system into a *fault-tolerant* program for execution on a system
which is susceptible to failures. For this to be possible, the fault environment must be specified and interference by the fault environment on the
execution of a program can then be described as a *fault-transformation*.
A recovery transformation transforms the program by adding a set of
recovery actions, called a *recovery program*.

In practice, fault-tolerant systems usually have real-time constraints.
So it is important that the timing properties of a program are refined
along with the fault-tolerant and functional properties defined in a program specification. If the model used in the transformational framework
is extended by adding timing properties with respect to some *time domain*, the recovery transformation and refinement can be defined with
timing constraints. The implementation of a fault-tolerant program can
then be required to satisfy conditions such as 'after a fault occurs, the

system is restored to a consistent state within a time bound which includes the delay caused by the execution of the recovery action'.

This formal treatment of fault-tolerance assumes that faults are *detected* by some underlying mechanism and establishes the required fault-tolerant properties for detected faults only. It has been argued (Cristian, 1990) that if time is added to the specification, then it can also be used explicitly to detect both transient and permanent faults. However, it is then also necessary to make recovery actions explicit and this can make it more difficult to obtain compositionality.

10.7 Conclusions

One part of the problem of designing a correct real-time program is that of specifying its properties; another is to prove that its implementation satisfies these properties. If the system architecture is complex (and this may be necessary due to the nature of the application), the second part of this task is non-trivial and there is at present no single method which satisfactorily encompasses both tasks for programs of meaningful size. In this chapter we have briefly examined what can be achieved in terms of specification and verification, and in terms of scheduling theory. There is still a gap between the kinds of programs considered in these two frameworks but it is decreasing and further work should make it possible to use different analytical methods within a common framework.

10.8 Acknowledgements

I am grateful to Zhiming Liu and Tomasz Janowski for their comments on an earlier draft.

11

Evaluation of Software Dependability

Bev Littlewood

11.1 On Disparity, Difficulty, Complexity, Novelty – and Inherent Uncertainty

It has been said that the term software engineering is an aspiration not a description. We would like to be able to claim that we engineer software, in the same sense that we engineer an aero-engine, but most of us would agree that this is not currently an accurate description of our activities. My suspicion is that it never will be.

From the point of view of this essay – i.e. dependability evaluation – a major difference between software and other engineering artefacts is that the former is pure design. Its unreliability is always the result of design faults, which in turn arise as a result of human intellectual failures. The unreliability of hardware systems, on the other hand, has tended until recently to be dominated by random physical failures of components – the consequences of the 'perversity of nature'. Reliability theories have been developed over the years which have successfully allowed systems to be built to high reliability requirements, and the final system reliability to be evaluated accurately. Even for pure hardware systems, without software, however, the very success of these theories has more recently highlighted the importance of design faults in determining the overall reliability of the final product. The conventional hardware reliability theory does not address this problem at all.

In the case of software, there is no physical source of failures, and so none of the reliability theory developed for hardware is relevant. We need new theories that will allow us to achieve required dependability levels, and to evaluate the actual dependability that has been achieved, when the sources of the faults that ultimately result in failure are human intellectual failures.

The importance of human activity, and human fallibility, in the design process shows itself in several ways. One of these is the enormous disparity that is concealed under the name of 'software'. Since much of the difficulty of writing software arises from the particular nature of the application domain, it seems unlikely that software engineering will ever be a coherent discipline in the way that civil and electrical engineering are. Rather we should look to differences in the tasks that face the software designer in different applications for an explanation of the varying success – particularly varying dependability – with which systems are built.

Secondly, the question of 'difficulty' of the problems we tackle in software is not well understood. It is intuitively obvious that some problems are intrinsically harder than others: real-time problems such as aircraft flight control are probably harder to solve than, say, those involving accountancy, word-processing, etc., or those involving rigorously expressed mathematics. Models of human intellectual ability, particularly propensity to failure, are not effective in other disciplines – we do not have good ways of characterising difficulty in mathematics, for example. We should not be surprised that we have a poor understanding of what makes software problems hard, but equally we should be aware that it is this variation in hardness that explains much of the variation in the observed dependability of the systems we produce.

The issue of difficulty, or hardness, of a problem is distinct from the notion of the complexity of its solution. Complexity has been recognised as an important factor in determining the dependability of software products. It is generally agreed that we should avoid complexity if we desire to achieve high dependability, particularly in the case of safety-critical systems. Similar arguments have also been used for dependability evaluation. Certainly it has been said that the utmost simplicity is a prerequisite for being able to have a sufficiently complete understanding of a system that one could claim that it was absolutely free of design faults. Intuitively, it seems plausible that, even when we cannot make such a strong claim as complete perfection, nevertheless keeping things as simple as possible will be 'a good thing'. Unfortunately, there are no satisfactory measures of complexity; there is not even an agreed means of deciding incontrovertibly that A is more complex than B. The few proposed 'measures' of complexity turn out in practice to be merely measures of 'size' (Fenton, 1991). More seriously, no useful relationship has been established between such measures and system attributes such as dependability.

Finally, the typically high degree of novelty of software systems distinguishes them from more conventional engineering. At the most mundane level this is manifest in a tendency to reinvent the wheel. In spite of much rhetoric about software re-use, this is still quite rare compared with the reuse of tried and tested design in other engineering disciplines. When we do not learn from previous experience, we run higher risks of failure from design faults. The most serious source of novelty, however, arises from the very success of software-based systems in delivering extensive functionality. It is clear that technological 'progress' has accelerated sharply with the widespread use of computer-based systems, and it is now commonplace to see systems that it would be unthinkable to implement purely via conventional hardware engineering: fly-by-wire and unstable aircraft control systems; railway signalling and control systems that provide greater track utilisation by allowing less physical separation of trains, etc. If we consider the evolution of civil aircraft over the past fifty years, it could be argued that the greatest discontinuity in terms of design novelty occurred with the introduction of computers in engine controllers and flight control systems. In certain industries there seems to be an almost cavalier attitude to the use of software – if it can be done it will be done. Unfortunately, knowing that certain novel functionality can in principle be delivered by software is not the same as knowing that it will be delivered with the required dependability.

If disparity, difficulty, complexity and novelty are so important, why do we not have adequate theories that account for their roles in software engineering and allow us to control their impact? One reason lies, I think, in our aspiration to be a 'proper' engineering discipline, with a genuine scientific underpinning. This laudable aim is too often taken to mean that we must only engage with that which is objective and external to the human – preferably, in fact, with mathematics. Unfortunately, the human element in what we do seems paramount, and any theories that discount it will be doomed to failure. Thus exhortations to 'mathematicise' software engineering, so as to stay in the world of the logical and deterministic, will at best only address a vanishingly small class of problems, and at worst may give a false confidence to the designers faced with those other real-world problems. My point here, in singling out (some would say caricaturing) a view of formal methods, is not to argue that it has no merit as a means of aiding system design. Rather it is to claim that for almost all real systems the problem of evaluating dependability involves an inherent uncertainty that arises from the potential fallibility of humans when they are faced with solving difficult, novel problems.

I cannot claim that the probabilistic approach to software dependability is a solution to the problems I have described. On the other hand, notwithstanding its considerable limitations, it does recognise the uncertainty present in much of what we do. A better understanding than we currently have will only come about by acknowledging the inevitability of this uncertainty.

11.2 The Need for Evaluation Methods

It has become a truism that society depends more and more upon the correct functioning of software. For the most part the trust we have so far placed in computer systems has been vindicated: instances of catastrophic system failure, and consequential loss, arising from software faults are surprisingly rare. Unfortunately, system complexity continues to rise, and the extent of our dependence increases. It would be rash merely to assume that future systems can be depended upon – rather we need to be able to decide in each instance whether such dependence is justified. The subject of this essay, then, is the evaluation of dependability in the possible presence of design faults, particularly software faults.

The most dramatic issues in dependability arise in safety-critical applications when human life can be at risk in the event of failure. I shall begin by briefly listing some examples of real and proposed systems, with their required levels of dependability:

- Flight-critical avionics for civil aircraft require a failure rate better than 10^{-9} per hour (RTCA, 1992). Examples include the existing 'fly-by-wire' system in the Airbus A320 (Rouquet & Traverse, 1986), and similar systems planned for aircraft such as the Boeing 777. Such requirements may be several orders of magnitude beyond what can actually be achieved but, more importantly, they pose insurmountable problems to those responsible for their validation.

- The software-driven Primary Protection System (PPS) of the Sizewell B reactor originally required a better than 10^{-4} probability of failure upon demand (pfd) (Hunns & Wainwright, 1991). As a result of concern expressed about the likelihood of being able to demonstrate such a level, an analysis of the overall reactor safety case was carried out which showed that, in fact, 10^{-3} pfd would be sufficient. There is general agreement that such modest levels are probably achievable, even for complex systems such as this. These levels can also, in principle, be validated.

- The Advanced Automation System (AAS), the new US air traffic control system, has a dependability requirement expressed as an availability: better than 3 seconds down-time per annum (Avizienis & Ball, 1987). It is curious that there does not appear to be a reliability or safety requirement, i.e. that safety-related events will only occur at an acceptably low rate.

- Computer control is becoming increasingly common in medical applications. Examples include radiation therapy machines (Jacky *et al.*, 1991) (this application area is noteworthy for providing one of the few well documented examples of computer failure resulting in loss of human life), heart pace-makers (Mojdehbakhsh *et al.*, 1994), and even robotic surgeons.

These examples illustrate several things. In the first place, even for safety-critical systems there is great variation in the levels of dependability that are required. Some systems seem to need levels that are probably several orders of magnitude from what we can actually achieve – and are certainly orders of magnitude beyond what it is possible to evaluate quantitatively in a scientifically convincing way. Some safety-critical systems, on the other hand, have surprisingly modest requirements. Certain types of heroic surgery upon terminally ill patients may only be possible with computer assistance; in such cases even a low probability of success may be better than the status quo.

Secondly, the nature of the requirement varies from one application to another. In systems that need to be working continuously, such as an air traffic control system, availability and reliability are both important. Even in those cases where reliability is the most important issue, the precise way in which this is specified needs some care.

Consideration of these examples of safety-critical systems should not deceive us into thinking that it is only here that the validation of acceptable dependability levels is of importance. There are many other circumstances where, although human life might not be at risk, nevertheless a high dependability needs to be assured because the consequences of failure can be catastrophic: some tightly coupled financial systems come to mind in this context. And of course in more mundane applications, although ultra-high dependability is not required, users will still demand that a system is sufficiently dependable. The fallibility of my word-processor, together with my tendency to forget to save documents, results in frequent minor crises. It could be argued that vendors who are prepared to demonstrate that a software product achieves a particular level of reliability, even though this is relatively modest, will gain the same market advantages that accrued to Japanese manufacturers of electronic consumer goods in the past couple of decades. Certainly this approach would be preferable to some current software 'warranties' which are textbook examples of *caveat emptor*.

Adjudication between different competing software development methods is another area where dependability evaluation is important. If we can demonstrate that a particular approach delivers more reliable software for a given cost we would be well disposed to use it. At present, recommendations about good practice are at best based on anecdotal evidence, at worst are dishonest special pleading with no empirical support.

The above are some of the reasons why we need to be able to measure the dependability of software. In the next section we shall look at the problem of how this can be done, briefly describing the current state of the art before going on to consider some issues that need further research.

11.3 Where we are Now

The word dependability has come to embrace all those aspects of behaviour upon which the user of a system might need to place dependence: it thus includes reliability, safety, availability and security. Measures of dependability are necessarily probabilistic because of an inherent uncertainty. In the case of reliability, for example, this uncertainty in the failure behaviour arises directly from two main sources.

In the first place, there is uncertainty about the program itself, inasmuch as we do not know which of the inputs will, when executed, cause failure.

Secondly, the operational environment is variable in a non-deterministic way: we cannot say with certainty which inputs will be presented to a program in the future. The net result is that we cannot predict with certainty when failures will occur in the future.

These remarks concern the failure behaviour of a system with constant reliability. There is a further cause of uncertainty when we debug programs and thus cause reliability growth. When we identify a fault, as a result of experiencing a failure, we cannot be certain that an attempt to fix the fault will be successful – indeed, it is common to introduce novel faults at such fix attempts. This is another aspect of the human fallibility that was discussed earlier. Even if the fix is successful, we do not know the 'size' of the fault that has been removed, i.e. there will be uncertainty about the magnitude of the improvement in reliability that will take place even in the event of a perfect fix.

A great deal of work has been carried out on the problem of estimating and predicting the reliability of a program as it is being debugged during test: the reliability growth problem. There are now many stochastic models which purport to be able to provide such predictions (Goel & Okumoto, 1979; Jelinski & Moranda, 1972; Littlewood, 1981; Littlewood & Verrall, 1973; Musa, 1975; Musa & Okumoto, 1984); see Xie (1991) for a useful survey of this work. Although none of these can be relied upon always to give reliability measures that are accurate, recent techniques allow us to check whether they are providing accurate results on a particular software system (Abdel-Ghaly *et al.*, 1986; Littlewood, 1988). It is often possible to use these techniques to allow a model to 'learn' from its past errors and so recalibrate future reliability predictions (Brocklehurst *et al.*, 1990). The bottom line is that it is usually possible to obtain accurate reliability measures from software reliability growth data, and to know that confidence in such figures is justified.

Another area where modelling has had some success is in the incorporation of structural information about the program into the reliability estimation process. These models aim to emulate the classical hardware procedures which allow the reliability of a system to be computed from knowledge of the reliabilities of its constituent components, together with information about the organising structure (Barlow & Proschan, 1975). Whilst these hardware theories are essentially static, the software approach must be dynamic and emulate the way in which software components (modules) are successively exercised in time. This is done by assuming Markovian (Littlewood, 1976; Siegrist, 1988, b) or semi-Markovian (Littlewood, 1976, 1979) exchanges of control between modules. Each module can itself fail with its own unique failure rate, and the exchanges of control between modules are failure-prone in the most general formulation. The potential advantage of this approach is that it allows the reliability of a system to be predicted before it is built, in the event that it is to be built of modules whose failure history in previous use is known.

Other structural models have been studied in order to model the failure behaviour of fault-tolerant software based on the idea of design diversity. The great difficulty here is that we know from experimental studies Eckhardt *et al.*, 1991; Knight & Leveson, 1986) that it would be too optimistic to assume that diverse software versions fail independently.

This precludes the simple modelling assumptions that are sometimes made in the case of hardware redundancy. Estimating the actual degree of dependence in failure behaviour between two 'diverse' software versions seems very difficult; indeed, it seems as hard as simply treating the whole fault-tolerant system as a black box and estimating its reliability directly by observing its failure behaviour (Miller, 1989).

These are some of the areas where there have been advances recently in our ability to measure and predict the reliability of software. It must be admitted, however, that this success story relates only to those cases where the reliability being measured is quite modest. It is easy to demonstrate that reliability growth techniques are not plausible ways of acquiring confidence that a program is ultra-reliable (Littlewood & Strigini, 1993; Parnas, 1990): the testing times needed become astronomically large as a result of a law of diminishing returns, and the issue of whether the test inputs are truly representative of those the system will meet in operational use becomes a serious one. Similarly, as we have seen, the effectiveness of fault-tolerance is limited by the degree of dependence in the failure processes of the different versions, and experiments (Eckhardt *et al.*, 1991; Knight & Leveson, 1986) suggest that this will be significant.

Arguments about the reliability of a software system based upon the efficacy of the development methods used will probably remain weak, even when we have good evidence for such efficacy – and this is not the case at present.

If we really need an assurance of ultra-high system reliability, and this seems inescapable in some safety-critical applications, it seems that this will have to be achieved without depending upon software to be ultra-reliable. In fact, of course, the problem is even worse, since everything we have said about software applies to design faults in general.

Any claims that particular systems are safe because their control systems are ultra-reliable must take note of these unpalatable facts. The only possible exceptions are those systems that are so simple that it can be argued that they are completely correct (and are a complete and accurate embodiment of their high-level requirements, which must also be extremely simple)†. This observation may give us some leeway to build

---

† It may seem contradictory at first that I would believe your claim that the failure rate is zero, but regard as untenable your assertion that this was a system with a failure rate of 10^{-9} per hour – after all, the former is the stronger claim. In fact, the reasoning in the two cases will be very different. In the first case it will be completely logical and deterministic: you will be asserting that the system is sufficiently simple that you have convinced yourself, and are trying to convince me, that it contains no design faults and thus cannot fail (at least as a result of design faults). In the second case, you are acknowledging the possible presence of design faults, and thus are in the realm of probability, but you are claiming that their impact upon the reliability is incredibly small. I might accept the first argument, but I would not accept the second.

computer-based systems, with the extra non-safety functionality that these can deliver, that are nevertheless measurably safe, by confining the safety-critical functionality in a tightly controlled kernel.

11.4 Future Work: Needs and Practicalities

Dependability modelling is an area of research which is largely driven by the problems of system validation that people meet in real life. Rather than pretend that there is a coherent organising framework, then, this section will be presented in terms of the different problems that need to be addressed.

It seems inevitable that social and political concerns about safety-critical systems will continue to play a large role in deciding which problems are important. However, it may be the case that some of this work will find its widest application in more modest applications. The success of manufacturers of fault-tolerant hardware in selling systems for applications such as financial services, for example, might suggest that software fault-tolerance techniques might also move out of their present ghetto of safety-critical applications. Although we shall begin with some problems of dependability evaluation that presently concern safety-critical systems, it should be borne in mind that solutions to these problems may have much wider applicability.

11.4.1 Safety-critical systems and the problem of assuring very high dependability

It seems clear that computers will play more and more critical roles in systems upon which human lives depend. Already, systems are being built that require extremely high dependability – the figure of 10^{-9} probability of failure per hour of flight that has been stated as the requirement for recent fly-by-wire systems in civil aircraft is not exceptional. There are clear limitations to the dependability levels that can be achieved and assured when we are building systems of a complexity that precludes us from making claims that they are free of design faults.

Although a complete solution to the problem of assessing ultra-high dependability is beyond us, there is certainly room for improvement on what we can do presently. Probabilistic and statistical problems abound in this area, where it is necessary to squeeze as much as we can from relatively small amounts of often disparate evidence. The following are some of the areas which could benefit from investigation.

Design Diversity, Fault-Tolerance and General Issues of Dependence

Clearly, one promising approach to the problem of achieving high dependability (here reliability and/or safety) is design diversity: building two or more versions of the required program and allowing an adjudication mechanism (e.g. a voter) to operate at run-time. Although such systems have been built and are in operation in safety-critical contexts, there is little theoretical understanding of their behaviour in operation. In particular, the reliability and safety models are quite poor.

For example, there is ample evidence that, in the presence of design faults, we cannot simply assume that different versions will fail independently of one another. Thus the simple hardware reliability models that involve mere redundancy, and assume independence of component failures, cannot be used. It is only quite recently that probability modelling has started to address this problem seriously (Eckhardt & Lee, 1985; Littlewood & Miller, 1989). These new models provide a formal conceptual framework within which it is possible to reason about the subtle issues of conditional independence involved in the failure processes of design diverse systems. They provide a link between informal notions such as 'common fault', and precise formulations of the probabilistic dependence between the failure behaviours of different versions. The key novel idea here is that of variation of 'difficulty' over the input space of a particular problem: those inputs that are most 'difficult' are ones that will tend to have highest chance of failure when executed by all versions.

The notion of difficulty in these models is an abstract one, but it is an attempt to represent the intuitive concept of difficulty discussed earlier.

In the work of Eckhardt and Lee it is assumed that something that is difficult for one team will also be difficult for another; our own work, on the other hand, allows there to be differences between the teams in what they find difficult (perhaps because they are using development tools that have different strengths and weaknesses).

There is possibly a subtle and important distinction to be made here between identical mistakes and common faults. In experiments like that of Knight and Leveson, the different teams sometimes made exactly the same mistakes (for example in misunderstanding the specification). In the Eckhardt and Lee model, there is a propensity for different teams to make a mistake in similar circumstances, but not a requirement that the nature of the mistakes be the same. It is an open question worthy of investigation as to whether this distinction is important. For example,

what are the implications for the shapes of individual fault regions in
the input space? (An interesting experiment by Amman and Knight
explored the shapes of 'faults' in subsets of the input space (Amman &
Knight, 1988).) Further probabilistic modelling is needed to elucidate
some of the other complex issues here. For example, there has been little
attention paid to modelling the full fault-tolerant system, with diversity
and adjudication.

In particular, we do not understand the properties of the stochastic
process of failures of such systems. If, as seems likely, individual program
versions in a real-time control system exhibit clusters of failures in time,
how does the cluster process of the system relate to the cluster processes
of the individual versions? Answering questions of this kind requires
information about the shapes of the fault regions, discussed above, and
about the nature of execution trajectories in the input space.

Although such issues seem narrowly technical, they are of vital importance in the design of real systems, whose physical integrity may be
sufficient to survive one or two failed input cycles, but not many.

Judgement and Decision-making Framework

Although probability seems to be the most appropriate mechanism for
representing the uncertainty that we have about system dependability, there are other candidates such as Dempster–Shafer (Shafer, 1976)
and possibility (Dubois & Prade, 1988) theories. These latter might be
plausible alternatives in those safety-critical contexts where we require
quantitative measures in the absence of data – for example, when we
are forced to rely upon the engineering judgement of an expert. Further
work is needed to elucidate the relative advantages and disadvantages of
the different approaches for this specific application. There is evidence
that human judgement, even in 'hard' sciences such as physics, can be
seriously in error (Henrion & Fischhoff, 1986): people seem to make consistent errors, and to be too optimistic in their own judgement of their
likely error. It is likely software engineering judgements are similarly
fallible, and this is an area where some empirical investigation is called
for. In addition, we need formal means of assessing whether judgements
are well calibrated, as well as means of recalibrating those judgement
and prediction schemes (humans or models) which have been shown to
be ill calibrated. This problem has some similarity to the problems of
validation of the predictions emanating from software reliability models, in which the prequential ideas of Dawid have proved very useful
(Brocklehurst *et al.*, 1990; Dawid, 1984).

It seems inevitable that when we are reasoning about the fitness for purpose of safety-critical systems, the evidence upon which we shall have to make our judgements will be disparate in nature. It could be failure data, as in the reliability growth models; human expert judgement; evidence of efficacy of development processes; information about the architecture of the system; evidence from formal verification. If the required judgement depends upon a numerical assessment of the dependability of the system, there are clearly important issues concerning the composition of evidence from different sources and of such different kinds. These issues may, indeed, be overriding when we come to choose between the different ways of representing uncertainty – Bayes, for example, may be an easier way of combining information from different sources of uncertainty than possibility theory.

A particularly important problem concerns the way in which we can incorporate deterministic reasoning into our final assessment and judgement of a system. Formal methods of achieving dependability are becoming increasingly important, ranging from formal notations to assist in the elicitation and expression of requirements, through to full mathematical verification of the correspondence between a formal specification and an implementation. One view would be that these approaches to system development remove a certain type of uncertainty, leaving others untouched (uncertainty about the completeness of the formal specification, the possibility of incorrect proof, etc.), in which case we need to factor into our final assessment of the dependability of a system the contribution that comes from such deterministic, logical evidence, keeping in mind, though, that there is an irreducible uncertainty about the failure behaviour of a system arising from different sources.

Systems Issues

Designers need help in making decisions throughout the design process, but none more so than those at the very highest level. For example, the allocation of dependence between computers, hardware and humans often seems to be carried out rather informally. In addition, real systems often pose difficult problems of assessment because of these early trade-offs. In the Airbus A320, for example, an early decision was to take certain responsibilities out of the hands of the pilot, and place a great deal of trust in the computerised fly-by-wire system. Furthermore, most of the hardware was removed that would have allowed a pilot, *in extremis*, to fly the aircraft manually: in the event of complete loss of the computer control system only rudder and tail trim can be activated

manually. In the Sizewell B nuclear reactor, the software-based Primary
Protection System (PPS) is backed up by a very much simpler hard-
wired secondary system (SPS), which in the event of failure of the PPS
can handle most but not all demands. This decision was taken early
in the development. Quite late in the day it became clear that it was
going to be very difficult to justify a claim of having met the original
requirement for the PPS of 10^{-4} probability of failure upon demand (or
better) – by which time it was too late to increase the coverage of the
SPS without considerable delay to the project. A recalculation of the
overall reactor safety case then showed that in fact a PPS requirement
of only 10^{-3} pfd would satisfy the overall plant safety requirement –
at the time of writing this seems to have saved the day, but somewhat
fortuitously.

In taking these very early decisions, designers need help in two ways.

Firstly, they need to be able to set realistic targets for the dependability of the various system components in order that there will be a good
chance of the overall system meeting its reliability and safety targets.
In particular, this means that they need to be able to set such targets
for software. The example of the A320 illustrates the problem: here
the 10^{-9} comes not from a reasoned view of what is achievable with
software, but from a crude allocation of responsibilities among many
critical subsystems in order to arrive at an overall figure of 10^{-7} for
the aircraft as a whole. Most of us would agree that 10^{-9} is far beyond what is actually achievable in software for a system as complex
as this.

The 10^{-4} goal for the PPS, on the other hand, is a more considered
judgement: it was devised as a general claim limit for critical software
in UK nuclear power stations (CEGB 1982a, b).

The second area where designers need help is in designing for eventual validation. It may be that here formal methods and probability
modelling can work together. For example, in certain cases it may be
possible to argue deterministically about safety – essentially prove that
certain classes of safety-related events cannot occur – and leave only
reliability to be treated probabilistically. This may have been possible in the Sizewell example, where a software-based, highly functional
PPS could have been completely backed up by a simple SPS, guaranteed free of design faults. Such a solution provides the advantages of
the software functionality most of the time, but *in extremis* provides
the required system safety without unreasonable dependence upon the
software.

11.4.2 The role of evaluation at modest levels of dependability

In this subsection I will examine a few of the more important general issues concerning dependability evaluation and its relationship to software engineering. I have attempted here, not to be exhaustive, but rather to pick out some areas where a probabilistic and statistical approach could be helpful.

Experimentation and Data Collection, General Statistical Techniques

Software engineering is an empirical subject. Questions concerning issues such as the efficacy of software development methods ought to be resolved by observation of real practice or by experiment. Instead, a dearth of data has been a problem in much of this area since its inception. There are still only a handful of published data sets even for the software reliability growth problem, and this is by far the most extensively developed part of dependability modelling. Sometimes the problem arises because there is no statistical expertise on hand to advise on ways in which data can be collected cost-effectively. It may be worth while attempting to produce general guidelines for data collection that address the specific difficulties of the software engineering problem domain.

Confidentiality issues are a problem here – industrial companies are reluctant to allow access to failure data because it is thought that this will cause people to think less highly of their products. More use could be made of anonymous reporting methods to overcome such difficulties: even in the case of safety-critical system failures it might be possible to adopt confidential reporting as has been done successfully for air miss incidents. An alternative would be to make reporting of safety-related incidents mandatory.

Experimentation, with notable exceptions, has so far played a low-key role in software engineering research. The most extensive research involving experiments has been, somewhat surprisingly in view of its difficulty and cost, in investigation of the efficacy of design diversity (Anderson *et al.*, 1985; Eckhardt *et al.*, 1991; Knight & Leveson, 1986). There are other areas where experimental approaches look feasible and should be encouraged. The most obvious question to address would be the general one of which software development methods are the most cost-effective in producing software products with desirable attributes such as dependability. Statistical advice on the design of such experiments would be essential, and it may be that innovation in design of experiments could make feasible some investigations here that presently seem too expensive to contemplate. The main problem in this kind of statistical approach to evidence arises from the need for replication over many software products. On the other hand, there are some areas where experiments can be conducted without the replication problem being overwhelming. These involve the investigation of quite restricted hypotheses about the effectiveness of specific techniques.

An example concerns questions related to software testing: are the techniques that are claimed to be effective for achieving reliability (i.e. effectiveness of debugging) significantly better than those, such as operational testing, that will allow reliability to be measured? Such evidence as we have suggests that testing in a way that allows reliability measurement can also be efficient at debugging (Duran & Ntafos, 1984): if this can be shown to be generally true, it would be an important factor in encouraging practitioners to obtain numerical estimates of product reliability.

The Influence of the Software Development Process, and Other Factors, on Dependability

Some of the most important and contentious issues in software engineering concern the efficacy of different practices and methods. There is surprisingly little real evidence to support even the most widely accepted claims, for example about the effectiveness of structured programming. In more contentious areas, such as formal methods, the picture is even more bleak. But some tools for such investigations are largely in place. Issues of comparative effectiveness are largely ones of costs and benefits; costs are relatively easy to track, and product reliability is one benefit that is now generally measurable with reasonable accuracy.

The main difficulty in such investigations, when they are based upon real product development, is to identify and control those confounding factors which can interfere with the simple hypothesis under test. Thus if we want to examine whether process A can deliver a given level of reliability more cost-effectively than B, we need to be able to exclude the influence of factors such as quality of personnel, difficulty of problem being tackled, and so on. The simplest way of doing this involves comparisons where all these factors are kept constant, with only the process factors under examination being allowed to vary. Unfortunately, this requires replication of the entire development, which is usually prohibitively expensive for realistic software products (even where this has been done, at great expense, in investigations of the effectiveness of design diversity, the problems tackled have been somewhat artificial).

There are other statistical approaches to these problems. If we could identify all the confounding factors, and measure them, we could build larger regression models. The problem here is that we would require quite large samples of different software product developments, which brings us back to the data collection difficulties of the previous section.

Because of all these difficulties, most investigations of the efficacy of software development processes have involved case studies: essentially just single developments in which measurement of interesting factors takes place. Clearly there are strong limitations to what can be concluded from such studies, particularly the extent to which the conclusions generalise outside the immediate context. Nevertheless, realism suggests that this may be the best we can hope for. Even here, it is vital that investigation proceeds within a proper measurement framework (Fenton, 1991), and is not reduced to mere anecdote.

The Influence of the Operational Environment on Dependability

It can be misleading to talk of 'the' reliability of a program: just as is the case in hardware reliability, the reliability of a program will depend on the nature of its use. For software, however, we do not have the simple notions of stress that are sometimes plausible in the hardware context. It is thus not possible to infer the reliability of a program in one environment from evidence of its failure behaviour in another. This is a serious difficulty for several reasons.

In the first place, we would like to be able to predict the operational reliability of a program from test data. The only way that this can be done at present is to be certain that the test environment – i.e. the type of usage – is exactly similar to the operational environment. Real software testing regimes are often deliberately made different from operational ones, since it is claimed that in this way reliability can be achieved more efficiently: this argument is similar to hardware stress testing, but is much less convincing in the software context.

A further reason to be interested in this problem is that most software goes out into the world and is used very differently by different users: there is great disparity in the population of user environments. Vendors would like to be able to predict how different users will perceive the reliability of the product, but it is clearly impractical to replicate every different possible operational environment in test. Vendors would also like to be able to predict the properties of the population of users. Thus it might be expected that a less disparate population of users would be preferable to a more disparate one: in the former case, for example, the problem reports from the different sites might be similar and thus involve less costs in fault fixing.

The data requirements for studies of operational environments are much less severe than for those investigating the relationship between process and product attributes. Manufacturers of, say, operating systems should have considerable quantities of information about the different environments in which a particular product operates. If we could identify interesting explanatory variables – a problem for software engineers rather than statistical modellers – it should be possible to use standard statistical techniques to predict reliability in a novel environment, and other things of interest. There may be other ways of forming stochastic characterisations of operational environments. Markov models of the successive activations of modules, or of functions, have been proposed (Littlewood, 1979; Siegrist, 1988a, b), but have not been widely used. Further work on such approaches, and on the problems of statistical inference associated with them, seems promising.

Stochastic Models for Security Evaluation

Ideally, a measure of the security of a system should capture quantitatively the intuitive notion of 'the ability of the system to resist attack'. That is, it should be operational, reflecting the degree to which the system can be expected to remain free of security breaches under particular conditions of operation (including attack). Instead, current security levels (NCSC, 1985) at best merely reflect the extensiveness of safeguards introduced during the design and development of a system. Whilst we might expect a system developed to a higher level than another to exhibit 'more secure behaviour' in operation, this cannot be guaranteed; more particularly, we cannot infer what the actual security behaviour will be from knowledge of such a level.

Clearly there are similarities between reliability and security and it would be desirable to have measures of 'operational security' similar to those that we have for reliability of systems. Very informally, these measures could involve expressions such as the rate of occurrence of security breaches (cf. rate of occurrence of failures in reliability), or the probability that a specified 'mission' can be accomplished without a security breach (cf. reliability function). Recent work (Littlewood *et al.*, 1993) has started to investigate this analogy between reliability and security and a number of important open questions have been identified that need to be answered before the quantitative approach can be taken further.

Empirical investigation of these issues is difficult: problems of data collection here are even more acute than in the rest of software engineering. Partly this is because security events, by their very nature, are incompletely observed. Another reason is that the security community has tended to concentrate on the problems of ultra-high security, since much of the research funding here comes from military and other government sources. Evaluating operational security at these very high levels is likely to be even more difficult than the problems of evaluating ultra-high reliability – and we have seen that these are essentially insurmountable. Work on stochastic models of security should therefore concentrate on systems which have more modest requirements – analogous to the work that has been successful in reliability modelling.

One approach to the data problem that might be worth pursuing involves experimenting with instrumented systems and sanctioned attackers. Some tentative steps have been taken in this direction (Brocklehurst *et al.*, 1994) with qualified success.

11.5 Conclusion

In this essay I have tried to make clear what I believe to be certain unpalatable truths, and to sugar this pill with some suggestions as to where modest progress might be made.

The first point I wanted to make was that there is an inherent uncertainty about the behaviour of the systems we build, which forces us to talk about their dependability in the language of probability and statistics. This is unpalatable to many computer scientists, who conclude from the deterministic predictability of the machine itself that we can have similar determinism at the macroscopic level of the behaviour observed by a user. Whilst I will concede that arguments of fault-freedom are *possible*, at the price of only building systems of great simplicity, I think that in practice such simplicity will rarely be achieved. Certainly, I have never seen a computer system used in a context where it would be plausible to claim that the software could never fail.

If readers concede this first point, it seems to me that questions about whether a software-based system is fit for its purpose become questions about whether a particular probabilistic dependability level has been achieved – a problem of numerical evaluation. It is easy to show that we can only answer such questions when the level required is quite modest:

we *cannot* gain confidence in ultra-high dependability without obtaining (literally) incredible amounts of evidence.

I think these difficulties have serious implications for the builders of safety-critical systems, and for society at large. It is easy to be seduced by the extensive functionality that can be provided by software, without the constraints of ensuing hardware unreliability. Some of the benefits from this functionality may indeed be claimed to bring enhanced safety. But at the end of the day we have a right to demand that the system is sufficiently safe, and this cannot be demonstrated for some of the systems that we are building even now. Perhaps now is a time to take stock and consider some retrenchment – for example, deciding that an unstable civil airliner is not a good thing.

All is not gloom. Systems with these dramatic requirements are not that common. For more modest systems, with modest dependability requirements, evaluation is possible. Further research will extend this achievement – but only relatively modestly.

Acknowledgements

My work in this area has been funded over the years by many agencies, too numerous to name here. Most recently, my thinking about the limitations to the evaluation of software dependability has been supported by the CEC ESPRIT programme under project number 6362, PDCS2, and by EPSRC and DTI under the DATUM project, which is part of the Safety-Critical Systems Research Programme.

12
Engineering Safety-Critical Systems
John A. McDermid

Abstract

Society is becoming increasingly dependent on safety-critical computer-based systems where the operation or failure of these systems can lead to harm to individuals or the environment. There are many individual technical innovations that can be made to improve the processes of developing and assessing safety-critical systems, but perhaps the biggest need is for a coherent and integrated set of methods; narrow technical innovation is not sufficient. Thus we stress here a broad engineering approach to the development of safety-critical systems, identifying research directions which we believe will lead to the establishment of an effective, and cost-effective, development process.

12.1 Introduction

Society is becoming increasingly dependent on automated systems; in many cases the operation or failure of these systems can lead to harm to individuals or the environment. If the behaviour, or failure, of a system can lead to accidents involving loss of life, injury or environmental damage then it is *safety-critical*. States of the system, classes of system behaviour and failure modes of the system which can potentially lead to accidents are referred to as *hazards*. Our concern here is with safety-critical systems where the computing and software elements can potentially contribute to hazards.

12.1.1 Technical background

Safety-critical systems are found in a wide range of applications including aircraft flight control, reactor protection systems, fire protection systems

217

on oil and gas platforms, and medical electronic devices. Increasingly these systems contain a substantial programmable element, using either conventional computers, or programmable logic controllers (PLCs). The large-scale systems such as the Sizewell B reactor protection system (140,000 lines of code) and the Boeing 777 (reportedly 5 million lines of code†) attract the greatest attention, although the vast majority of safety-critical systems are much smaller and are based on the more humble PLCs. PLCs are typically used as local controllers in more complex overall systems, e.g. for traffic light sequencing, or control of a small part of a process plant.

Fundamentally the issues in designing, assessing and managing the safety of both classes of system (PLC or conventional computer) are the same:

- requirements – determining the set of hazards pertinent to the system, and identifying the requirements on the system and software to do with hazard avoidance and mitigation;
- design – to design the system so that the likelihood of a hazard arising is acceptably low;
- assessment – to show convincingly that the design is safe (not just that it meets its requirements), including evaluating the risks associated with the hazards;
- management – to achieve control over the process so that safety is achieved in a cost-effective manner.

There are many technical innovations that can be made to improve the processes of developing and assessing safety-critical systems. Our focus is on the technical issues associated with development, as this seems most appropriate for a book concerned with research in computer science, but we briefly discuss some broader issues.

12.1.2 Philosophical and social context

There are many philosophical issues associated with the development of safety-critical systems. Often the failure rates required are very low, e.g. 10^{-9} per operational hour, which is about once every 114,000 years (for a single system). It is questionable whether or not such a figure is meaningful, and whether or not we can ever measure, or predict, such failure rates (see the article by Littlewood in this volume).

---

† Similar figures are quoted for other aircraft of this generation, e.g. the Airbus Industrie A330/340.

A related problem is the difficulty of knowing how much a particular technology contributes to achieving or assessing safety. There are many different standards relating to the development of safety-critical software†, and often they give directly contradictory guidance on which development and assessment technology to use. This situation exists, in part, because it is so difficult to measure the effects of a particular technology – a well designed system will probably not give rise to a fatal accident in its life and, even if it does, it is hard to say which aspects of technology helped, and which hindered the achievement of safety. As a consequence we are, to some extent, operating 'open loop' in choosing technology for developing safety-critical systems. Thus the suggestions made regarding research directions, even in a technical field, must be seen as firmly in the realm of value judgement.

There are also difficult sociological questions about the acceptability, or tolerability, of risk. It is well-known that people are more averse to accidents involving multiple simultaneous deaths – for example we are generally more willing to accept the much higher probability of death from road travel – than we are from the rare (but often horrendous) accidents associated with air travel. There are similar biases associated with nuclear power – many people are more influenced by the enormity of the worst-case accident than the average-case expectations of death and injury, even though they are much lower than with conventional power plants. These are very important issues, and they can have a major impact when eliciting requirements, and when making trade-offs between design approaches and technologies.

These issues also have broader impact, and may lead to decisions that it is inappropriate to build or deploy certain sorts of system‡. Software engineers involved in the development or assessment of safety-critical systems should be aware of these issues, but we choose not to follow the associated research directions here.

12.1.3 Scope and focus

In order to keep the scope of this article reasonable, we focus on technical issues in developing systems, specifically covering requirements and design (including implementation). It is widely recognised that safety

---

† Over 100 the last time I checked, spanning a large range of industries and countries.
‡ Readers may recall that Dave Parnas withdrew from providing advice on 'Star Wars' due to this form of concern.

is a systems†, not a software, issue and our discussion of requirements takes a systems perspective. Further it should be noted that very many safety-critical systems are also real-time systems, i.e. systems which have to operate in time-frames dictated by the environment. Inevitably we touch on real-time issues, but we exclude detailed discussion of those issues on the grounds of scope. Our views on real-time aspects of the future of the development of safety-critical systems are set out in Burns & McDermid (1994).

We also deliberately take an engineering view, covering all aspects of the constructive processes‡, because individual innovations are likely to be ineffective unless they form a component of an effective process. Thus we try to look at what constitutes the 'complete' set of issues, at requirements, design and implementation, rather than focus on particular technical issues, e.g. fault-tolerance strategy or program proof. Inevitably the material is therefore broad and somewhat shallow, but it is hoped that this will complement the other articles in this volume.

The remainder of the chapter gives an overview of the process of developing safety-critical computer-based systems highlighting current practice and indicating key research issues. Section 12.2 briefly describes the model of the life-cycle which we are assuming for the rest of our discussion. Section 12.3 considers requirements, particularly how requirements for computing systems emerge from the broader engineering design process. Section 12.4 discusses high-level design, which we refer to as the 'architectural' level, covering a wide range of issues, not just considering functionality or timing. In section 12.5 we discuss implementation, proposing a somewhat radical view of how to construct safety-critical systems. In section 12.6 we discuss trends and present conclusions.

12.2 System Development

There are many different life-cycle models which we could use in discussing system development. We choose a simple model which emphasises the three main concerns for safety-critical systems, and the reader is referred to McDermid & Rook (1991) for a more extensive treatment of development processes. This model is based on assessment of good

---

† The term 'systems engineering' is widely used. Here it is used to mean analysis and design work where the concern is with multiple technologies, including choice of, and allocation of functions to, different technologies.

‡ Testing, safety analysis, and many other techniques are important, but space does not permit us to do them justice – we would need a handbook, not an article, to cover all these issues adequately.

industrial practice, but this does not mean that any particular system developer follows this model exactly (throughout any reference made to industrial practice refers to the author's view of those organisations who are operating at or near the 'state of the practice'). The three primary stages are:

- *requirements and system concept* – the development of the requirements for the overall system (of which the computing element is just a part) and a high-level design (system concept) capable of satisfying those requirements, including choice of technologies and allocation of function to technology;
- *computing system architecture* – the logical and physical structure of the computing and software system intended to implement part of the system concept, and to satisfy part of the requirements;
- *software production* – the generation of executable programs intended to realise part of the architecture.

We do not assume a 'waterfall' style development process and accept that, in practice, most safety-critical systems are developed in a concurrent engineering environment, with some design iterations in one technology (e.g. software) being caused by changes in another (e.g. hydro-mechanical). At each stage we stress the constructive aspects of system development, and briefly identify the evidence which needs to be produced from that stage to show that the system is safe.

For each of these stages of development we consider how:

- the system is described/represented;
- the description is generated;
- the description is verified;
- the description is validated.

Following Boehm, we use verification to mean 'doing the thing right' and validation to mean 'doing the right thing' (Boehm, 1981). We consider both internal verification, i.e. internal consistency, and external verification, i.e. against other descriptions. In discussing each stage we follow the same basic schema: we define the key concepts associated with the stage, outline current industrial practice, then present a view of a more radical approach to that stage of the process and indicate the research directions which follow from a desire to realise that more radical process.

12.3 Requirements and System Concepts

At this stage of the process three main descriptions are developed:

- fundamental requirements;
- system concept;
- derived requirements.

We amplify on these notions below. The development of these three descriptions is tightly interwoven, so we treat them as one stage in the development process. We take a broad view of the issues, as safety has to be achieved as part of the overall systems engineering process, and cannot be considered in isolation.

12.3.1 Basic concepts

It has long been recognised that requirements and design are intrinsically interwoven (Swartout & Balzer, 1982). This is especially true with safety, where some requirements, e.g. for acceptable rates of failure in particular hazardous failure modes, can only be determined once we have a design and we know what the possible failure modes are, and which components can give rise to particular failure modes. Thus the fundamental requirements are amplified or re-interpreted to produce derived requirements, and these are articulated in terms of a system concept.

In more detail we characterise the three forms of description as follows:

- *fundamental requirements* – the primary goals for the system as defined by the stakeholders† who have legitimate concerns about the behaviour of the system (this may include the public, or representatives of the public, such as licensing bodies, for some safety-critical systems);
- *system concept* – a high-level system design, allocating functionality to different technologies, e.g. hydro-mechanical, computing and electronic;
- *derived requirements* – detailed requirements, e.g. for functions or failure rates, which are consequences of the fundamental requirements, given the chosen system concept.

Often the fundamental requirements will be articulated in terms of

---

† The term is used in the literal sense – an individual or organisation who has a stake (in the new system). This term originated in 'soft systems' work, but is now becoming widely accepted in requirements engineering.

some form of risk or risk exposure, e.g. 10^{-6} deaths per passenger kilometre for a transport system, which is deemed to be socially acceptable. The derived requirements then include failure rate targets for particular components, e.g. 10^{-4} failures (in some particular mode) per operational hour. We illustrate these ideas with a brief example in subsection 12.3.3 below.

12.3.2 Current practice

The above concepts are well understood in industrial practice, and many development processes and some standards recognise these distinct issues, e.g. SIRT discusses derived requirements (SIRT, 1994). However, they are not always reflected in distinct notations and documents, nor are the same terms always used. In some disciplines, e.g. structures and aerodynamics in aircraft design, there are good computer-based models for developing and validating the requirements and concept. The situation is much poorer for computer-based systems and the associated systems engineering. Indeed the concept of computer-based systems engineering has only recently begun to be accepted, although the difficulties of developing requirements in a systems engineering context have been recognised (White, 1993).

The norm in developing even complex systems is to use natural language text and to use structural models, e.g. structured analysis style data flows, to show the overall functional decomposition of the system. The distinction between fundamental requirements, system concept and derived requirements is often blurred and it is not uncommon for a system concept and a set of requirements to be produced and the fundamental requirements 'lost'. This is unfortunate, as these are the ultimate arbiter when making trade-offs between conflicting requirements. Considerable stress is placed on traceability, especially traceability from the requirements through the design in to the implementation to show that the requirements have been met.

There are few good methods and tools for this stage of development, although a number deal with specific aspects of the problem (and are often claimed to deal with more of it than they do). For example, Statemate (Harel *et al.*, 1990) and RDD-100 (Alford, 1994) deal with some classes of state-based specification effectively, and animation facilities can be used for validation. Other systems, e.g. RTM (James, 1994), support traceability from textual requirements. Methods such as CORE stress the need to analyse systems from different (stakeholders') viewpoints (Mullery, 1979).

We are aware of no method or tool which properly addresses the broader systems engineering issues, e.g. dealing with multi-technology systems. Some of the existing methods are, individually, very effective at dealing with some aspect of requirements, but they are currently poorly integrated, have little process support, and much of the verification and validation is by human review, and thus prone to error.

12.3.3 Research directions

The primary research direction which we see is to provide support for the process identified above, including making trade-offs, analysing conflicts between stakeholder's fundamental requirements, and handling change (arising from actions by stakeholders, changes in other engineering arte-facts, or difficulties found in implementation). We briefly describe an approach currently being taken towards this objective, to provide a context within which to articulate some more detailed research direc-tions.

The design of a safety-critical system inevitably involves trade-offs. Safety requirements are often in conflict with other requirements, e.g. for availability or performance, and suitable compromises have to be found. The identification of conflicts between requirements, and their resolution, is thus a central part of the design process which we shall refer to as the spine. We have previously proposed the use of 'goal-structuring' as a way of making the spine of the process clear, focusing on the structuring of requirements (Coombes *et al.*, 1994), and others have adopted a similar approach to requirements-structuring, e.g. Dar-denne *et al.* (1993), Mylopoulos *et al.* (1992). It is our contention that these concepts help structure and explicate the complex processes of developing safety-critical systems, particularly showing the relationship between safety analysis and design. We briefly review the key concepts of goal structures which provide the spine of the process. The two most fundamental concepts are:

- *goal* – is something that a stakeholder in the design and assessment process wishes to be achieved; it encompasses fundamental and de-rived requirements;
- *strategy* – a strategy is a (putative) means of achieving the goal or goals, e.g. a system concept, which will often generate sub-goals; *meta-strategies* can be used to represent the fact that a choice exists between two or more strategies.

Goals are decomposed through the strategies, and we will refer to sub-goals where this is helpful. Where there is a single goal, the structure is a hierarchy. Where we have conflicting goals, or multiple goals which need to be satisfied at once, the strategies will be introduced to resolve conflicts or to represent other forms of trade-off, and the structure will not be a strict hierarchy as a strategy can satisfy more than one goal.

Some goals may be satisfied directly, e.g. by carrying out an action, or providing a product with the right properties, but others cannot be achieved in this way. We use the term *solution* for the action or product which satisfies a goal. Goals with solutions are *leaves* of the goal structure, i.e. they have no strategy or sub-goals.

We use the term *constraints* to refer to those goals which are not solved directly, but which restrict the way in which other goals are solved, i.e. which restrict the set of allowable strategies (and models, see below). The satisfaction of constraints must be checked at multiple points in the goal hierarchy. Common safety requirements such as 'no single point of failure shall lead to a hazard' are representative of this class.

It is intended that goals and strategies will provide the main structure in developing requirements and safety cases (see McDermid & Wilson (1995) for their use in safety cases) – informally they provide the spine of such developments, and are the basis for traceability (a key issue when dealing with complex designs). However, there are other important facets of the structure which are not related to goals or strategies. These include:

- *models* – these represent part of the system of interest, its environment or the organisations associated with the system; goals will often be articulated in terms of models, especially when the model is an abstraction of the system design; models may be the (putative) solutions to goals, and will often be introduced by strategies (see the illustration of the approach, below);
- *justification* – a justification is an argument, or other information, e.g. the results of a safety analysis, presented to explain why a strategy is believed to be effective; this may justify the strategy either at the time the choice is made, or retrospectively once solutions to the sub-goals have been provided.

The standard simplifying assumption in any engineering endeavour is that we can have a 'top down' process, starting with the most abstract requirements, moving through layers of decomposition until the system is realised. We illustrate the above concepts by considering just such a 'simplistic' process involving the development of a safety case. Treatment of 'real' processes is outside the scope of this chapter.

To illustrate the use of the process model we describe a fragment of the process of decomposing requirements. For this example we take the scope of our concern to be the development of a civil aeroplane engine.

One fundamental goal will, in many cases, be to do with the licensing or certification of the equipment or system of interest. Thus, for an aeroplane engine, the top-level safety goal might be to 'certify the engine to the requirements of JAR E' (JAR E is the Joint Aviation Regulation pertinent to civil aeroplane engines). Other fundamental goals will be concerned with performance, cost, etc. The first level of decomposition will typically introduce a system concept, i.e. a high-level design and allocation of function amongst technologies, and the individual top-level safety (and other) requirements for the systems under consideration. Thus we might get goals such as 'show that failure mode X does not occur more frequently than 10^{-Y} times per flying hour', and this might be demonstrated by applying hazard analysis to the system concept. The example is illustrated in Figure 12.1. Two fundamental goals are introduced – one concerned with performance, the other with safety. The goals may be articulated directly, or in terms of a model of the situation in which the engine will be used – the environment. A strategy for attaining the goals is introduced which identifies a system model. This model introduces some direct safety goals, e.g. about allowable rates of failure modes. It also introduces a constraint (the box with two horizontal lines at top and bottom) which restricts the way that all the remaining goals are satisfied, i.e. it restricts lower-level designs and strategies. In general the strategy will be constrained by the relevant standards, and the views of the certification and licensing body. In this specific example, JAR E identifies safety targets for engines, including allowable failure rates for particular failure modes, and constrains the means of compliance with those requirements, including calling up standards and guidance such as DO 178 B (RTCA, 1992). The justification will probably be by appeal to accepted practices or the requirements of the prevailing standards. Decomposition of the safety goals will parallel the decomposition of the system design, and failure rates will be allocated to different components and their failure modes in such a way that satisfying the component-level goals will satisfy the system-level goals. This is carried on to the bottom-level of the design decomposition where

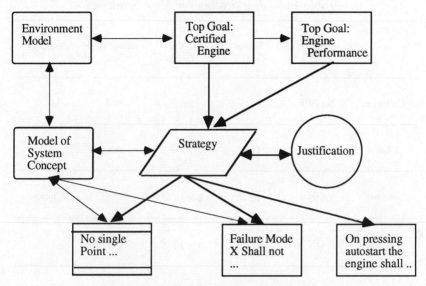

Fig. 12.1. Fragment of Goal Hierarchy

the goals have to be satisfied by safety analysis, or other means of compliance†.

In choosing a strategy, trade-offs will have to be made and these may include availability against safety, against performance, and against cost. (Implicitly, most trade-offs reflect cost and time-scale issues.) These trade-offs are typically negotiated between the stakeholders. For example, consider a simple safety system with the following properties:

- one lane‡– unacceptable, one failure could lead to an accident;
- two lanes – safe, but low availability;
- three lanes – safe, higher availability, but *lower* overall reliability, hence more spares are needed, etc.

We may choose two lanes (the choice is selecting a strategy from a meta-strategy), but this depends on the relative weights of the goals, see Table 12.1.

Tables such as that shown in Table 12.1 are used to represent the

---

† The term 'means of compliance' has a specific meaning in the certification of civil aircraft and includes safety analysis, flight testing, laboratory testing, etc. In practice means of compliance for particular goals use a combination of these methods and are agreed with the certification authorities.

‡ A set of components, to perform a given function, connected in series.

Table 12.1. *Justification for Meta-Strategy*

	Safety Goal 1	Safety Goal 2	Rel'ty Goal	Avail'ty Goal	Verdict
Criterion	No SPF	10^{-3}	10^{-2}	99%	
1 Lane	X	10^{-2}	10^{-2}	99%	
2 Lanes	OK	10^{-4}	2×10^{-2}	98%	Choice
3 Lanes	OK	10^{-6}	3×10^{-2}	99.99%	

trade-offs (these would form part of the justification for a meta-strategy). We can use a similar approach to represent justifications within a single strategy, where we are evaluating the design proposal against multiple goals, see Table 12.2, where FSD stands for full-scale deflection of some instrument.

This is a variant of Gilb's design by objectives (DBO) (Gilb, 1988) where the minimum is the minimum acceptable level for that goal, the target is what we aim to achieve, and the ideal is the best we can reasonably hope to achieve. In general, we would expect to iterate the design step if a particular design is not acceptable. Thus, in our approach:

- the models represent the design, its environment, and perhaps alternative designs;
- the goals and strategies identify the requirements and associated means of meeting those requirements, and also provide the structure of the development process;
- the use of safety analysis (and other techniques) provides solutions and justifications 'prove' the design, thus providing the information needed to provide rationale for the approach, and ultimately to verify that the requirements have been met.

We can see a number of research directions, or research challenges, in

Table 12.2. *Justification for Strategy*

	Goal 1 Maintainability	Goal 2 Accuracy	Goal 3 Reliability	Goal 4 Mass
Value	Medium	0.1% FSD	10^{-2}	5 kg
Minimum	Low	0.5% FSD	10^{-3}	12 kg
Target	Medium	0.2% FSD	3×10^{-2}	5 kg
Ideal	High	0.1% FSD	10^{-2}	3 kg

the context of this model of the development process. These include (in no particular order):

- *refinement of approach* – the above approach is tentative and, although we have used some non-behavioural properties in the examples above, much more needs to be done to deal effectively with broad systems issues; in particular we need to know how to analyse different classes of properties, and this requires having a suitably broad range of models and analysis techniques;
- *requirement categorisation* – categories are important, as different classes of requirements should handled (justified, analysed) in different ways; the direct/constraint distinction above is weak, and we need a much better way of categorising requirements to know how to meet them, and show how they have been met; the work of the KAOS project (Dardenne *et al.*, 1993) is relevant here, although their categorisation seems incomplete;
- *trade-off analysis* – we need better ways of representing weights, etc. in carrying out trade-off analysis, including sensitivity analysis; work in economics on multi-variate utility theory may be relevant; the notions of 'design space analysis' (MacLean *et al.*, 1993) may also be of value here;
- *change management* – in practical engineering situations, require-

ments are always subject to change; techniques are needed for carrying out impact and sensitivity analysis, and propagating the effects of change through the design†;

- *requirements representation* – almost inevitably, an eclectic approach to representation will be required, and natural language will remain relevant, as will state-transition and control representations; however, there is some evidence that a causal approach to modelling behavioural requirements is relevant (Coombes *et al.*, 1994) as embedded systems are essentially concerned with cause and effect, as are safety analysis techniques; other notations such as MAL, developed by the FOREST project (Maibaum, 1987) may also be relevant within this framework.

With the model we have presented, it is reasonable to ask 'when are requirements complete?' The answer would have to be 'when the perceived risk is such that it is acceptable to start building the artefact, not just models of the artefact'. Note that this is primarily process risk, not product risk. Thus we also need to place notions of risk management on our research agenda, even within the technical context, although further discussion of these issues is outside the scope of this article.

12.4 Computing System Architecture

Having established a set of requirements and a system concept, some of the requirements will have been allocated to the computing system, for realisation in software. Within the process articulated above, the computing system architecture is the design model proposed to meet these allocated requirements. The primary focus of the architecture is on the software, but it also covers the computing hardware necessary to execute the software. Here we are normally in the domain of real-time systems (although some safety systems are not real-time), but we will keep the treatment of timing issues brief. A much more extensive treatment of research directions in the real-time aspects of safety-critical systems can be found in Burns & McDermid (1994).

12.4.1 Basic concepts

The aim at the architectural level is to specify the structure of the software system as it will be built, and to define the properties of the system components, e.g. processes, communication mechanisms and data repositories. It must be possible to analyse the architectural-level specification

† The SafeIT PROTEUS project is addressing this problem.

to show that the required functions and properties will be achieved by the implementation, and it is desirable to generate the implementation (at least significant parts of it) from the specification (see section 12.5). In general the components at this level will only implement part of a requirements-level function, e.g. an integrator for a control law, or an action from a state-transition description. Thus the mapping between the requirements and the architecture may be complex, and it must be possible to extract from the architecture 'transactions', i.e. the interaction of a set of components generating an output from an input to the system, which correspond to requirements-level functions. In many cases the transactions will simply amount to sequential execution of a set of components in the architecture. The basis of verification is to compare the architectural-level transactions with the required functions, although we will also need to verify failure modes and rates.

In specifying systems at the architectural-level we are concerned with identifying the components, and specifying the properties of the components, as well as determining the properties of the system as a whole. We need to consider two aspects of component structuring:

- *dynamic* – the system as it executes – components are processes/tasks and their inter-communication mechanisms;
- *passive* – the system as it is implemented and built – components are modules/packages and their interconnections;

In general these structures will not be the same as processes may have a common set of (re-usable) packages to implement them, processes may be replicated, and so on. For brevity, we focus mainly on the dynamic structure, as this is the most important for analysing the architecture and showing that it meets its requirements. We can divide the dynamic structure into two parts (Burns & Lister, 1991):

- *logical* – structure of processes† excluding replication and their inter-communication, independent of hardware mapping, independent of replication for performance or fault-tolerance, etc.;
- *physical* – structure of processes including replication and their inter-communication, structure of the hardware, plus the mapping of the processes and communications to the hardware.

---

† We will refer to processes, but the concepts are still relevant where code fragments are called by a cyclic scheduler, or a hybrid approach as adopted on a number of real-time systems where a low-level scheduler calls 'packages' which do their own local scheduling.

For our present purposes, we can view the logical architecture as an abstraction from the physical architecture† which helps in determining transactions, and thus verifying them against the requirements. Thus we will focus on the physical architecture, and on describing the software components of the physical architecture. The hardware structure can be represented in a conventional way, and there are no technical difficulties in representing the software–hardware mapping.

The core of the software part of the physical architecture is an identification of the processes, the inter-communication between the processes, and the nature of the inter-communication. We need to identify the required functionality (and timing properties) of the individual processes and inter-communication functions in the software architecture. In addition we need to know the behaviour of the computing system in both the resource and failure behaviour domains. Thus the characterisation of the system in the functional, timing, resource and failure domains gives a 'complete' description of the software system at the architectural level (McDermid, 1993), sufficient to enable it to be verified against the requirements. In the model set out in section 12.3, the justifications for an architecture would include the results of the analyses to show it had the right timing properties, functional properties, etc.

12.4.2 Current practice

In discussing current practice we will consider both industrial norms and some of the relevant academic research work.

Industrial practice is mixed, and we briefly characterise the extremes of industrial practice, as we see it. The weakest practice is to focus entirely on the passive structure of the software architecture, identifying software modules, and to trace back from these to the requirements. In such an approach there is no explicit model of the behaviour (dynamics) of the system at this level, and it is difficult to verify the software against the requirements. In practice, most of the verification is done through testing, and testers reconstruct the transactions in order to show that the set of functions provided meet the requirements (or not as the case may be). This approach is quite common even for safety-critical systems, and the evidence and confidence in the system arises primarily from discipline and simplicity in software design and construction, and from the quality of the testing.

---

† In fact, it should be possible to generate the physical architecture from the the logical architecture, but this is a research issue, see below.

At the other extreme, effective structural techniques are used to define the system at the physical level, and a mixture of formal and informal techniques are used to define the behaviour of the individual system components. Techniques such as MASCOT (JIMCOM, 1987), DORIS/DIA (Simpson, 1990) and ECSAM (Lavi & Winokur, 1992) are perhaps the best examples of this approach, from the structural perspective. These approaches identify clearly individual processes, their communication, the form of data communication, e.g. destructive write – non-destructive read, and the decomposition of the primary system components. With these approaches definition of functional and timing properties tends to be informal. It is unusual for resources to be specified in detail and, instead, general requirements such as '50% spare capacity' are quoted (but rarely met). It is unusual for failure behaviour to be specified separately within such approaches and, in practice, much of the failure behaviour has been 'functionalised' by the time this stage is reached, i.e. the response to known failure modes of the hardware has been incorporated into the functional specification.

In the context of MASCOT and DORIS, the structure of the implementation (templates for processes, etc.) can be generated from the design. With other approaches, e.g. the SAO sheets used on the Airbus family (Briere *et al.*, 1994), functional code is also generated. We return to this issue in section 12.5.

Perhaps the biggest weakness with these practices is that verification activities are limited to review and testing, because the formalism used does not give an adequate basis for analysis. These weaknesses affect timing, resource usage and failure behaviour, not just functionality, although some extensions have been made (Burns *et al.*, 1993). The strongest part of the approaches, used to aid verification, is the traceability back to the requirements.

The contrast between industrial practice and academic research is quite sharp and, in some regards, there appears to be little common ground. Much academic research which is relevant to this part of the development process has focused on process algebras, most notably CSP (Hoare, 1985) and its derivatives, and CCS (Milner, 1980) and its derivatives. These approaches represent the process structuring from the dynamic part of the architecture, and focus on specifying behaviour (functionality). Extensions to CSP and CCS have been produced which deal with time, e.g. TCCS (Moller & Tofts, 1989) and TCSP (Davies, 1991).

These techniques are well understood, and some research directions are given elsewhere in this volume, so we restrict attention to some observations about the use of the techniques in the context of developing safety-critical systems. The techniques, in their current form, seem to have a number of limitations for this application:

- *decomposition of processes* – the decompositional approach means that the bottom-level processes will not normally correspond with what will be implemented as a single schedulable unit, and this gives poor engineering intuition about the way in which the system will work; this arises because it is often necessary to represent state by decomposing processes, as the algebras have no notion of state;
- *models of time* – the techniques typically assume instantaneous transitions or communication; whilst this may be a valid abstraction in some cases, it is dubious for distributed systems, where failures can arise due to time delays, mis-ordering of events, etc.;
- *failure behaviour* – it can be difficult to deal with failure behaviour (in the safety sense, not the technical sense) within the computational models;
- *resources* – the techniques tend to assume adequacy of resources, and do not assist in determining whether or not some resource-limited architecture will satisfy its timing requirements.

These comments are contentious, and it is not intended to say that process algebras are irrelevant. Instead these observations should be seen as posing some challenges for research in this area and the development of process algebras. In particular, some of the more recent work on action systems is promising as a way of alleviating such problems. We can now turn to research directions and, although we will focus on one approach, we will try to set out requirements for the approach which could also be met by an alternative approach based on process algebras.

12.4.3 Research directions

The primary research direction which we see is providing an approach to architectural specification which has three main properties:

- gives a 'complete' description of a system and its components in the functional, timing, resource and failure domains;
- allows analysis of the properties of the architecture and prediction of the properties of the implementation with a high degree of confidence;
- allows formal verification against requirements, at least with respect to functionality and timing properties.

The approach which we advocate is integrative, drawing on work on structured and formal methods, schedulability/real-time analysis and safety analysis. It is also aimed towards synthesis of implementations from specifications. As before, we illustrate the approach, then articulate some lower level research goals.

We advocate an approach building on the MASCOT/DORIS-style model of the dynamic structure of the architecture, complemented by more precise (formal) definitions of the required properties of the computational components. In this approach the communication mechanisms are abstract data types with well-defined access interfaces and supporting particular communication protocols†. The behavioural requirements will specify what each component does, and where it obtains and delivers its data. They may take a number of forms, most likely:

- *control components* – e.g. an integrator, with data transfer implicit, e.g. by the data names corresponding to the procedures in the communication packages;
- *state-transition* – a simple state-transition system with no internal concurrency, and with data transfer appearing as actions on transitions corresponding to the calling of procedures in the communication packages;
- *'pure' functional* – a single function (perhaps including table look-ups) with data transfer implicit, as for control components.

These describe the components in the functional domain, but more is needed to show the overall behaviour, and the mapping back to requirements. We need:

- *transactions* – sequences of component activations to implement some high-level functions;
- *transaction timings* – identification of whether the transactions are periodic or aperiodic, and response times, deadlines, jitter and other requirements;
- *component timings* – allocation of timing requirements to the components, including adding timing requirements to transitions in the state transitions (Henzinger *et al.*, 1991a);
- *failure modes* – acceptable failure modes of the components, and of the transactions;

† Typically they will be 'monitor-like' and of a form that could be implemented, say, as protected objects in Ada9X.

- *resources* – allowable memory, etc. utilisation for the components, and other transactions.

This gives a 'complete' description of the system, at this level.

The specification can be analysed for certain consistency properties, e.g. of the timing requirements on the transactions against the components' allocated properties. In principle, the consistency of the failure behaviour of transactions can be checked against those of the components, in a similar way, although there are some difficulties in doing this, see below. Knowledge of the component properties and the structure of the transactions enables end-to-end functionality to be derived, which can then be verified against the requirements. This is straightforward for 'pure' functional requirements (essentially function composition), but more complex for control and state-based requirements. Scheduling analysis can be used to show that the timing requirements are satisfied on a transaction-by-transaction basis, assuming that the components are implemented to satisfy their timing requirements. This can be done as the architecture is produced to verify the overall design, and reconfirmed once the implementation has been produced and the actual code timings are available.

There are some existing relevant research results (see below), but there are a number of research issues involved in making it a practical reality, and there are some very valuable extensions which define research directions:

- *accurate and flexible timing analysis* – existing scheduling theory gives a basis for analysing system architectures, but it tends to produce conservative results, which are inefficient in their use of resources; this is particularly problematic when it comes to integrating non-deterministic software, e.g. AI components, into the system, as the worst-case behaviour of such software will be very much worse than the average; a research direction for this important topic is articulated in detail in Burns & McDermid (1994);
- *resource analysis* – there are currently few techniques for resource analysis, although this is covered by some timing analysis techniques, e.g. bus bandwidth usage in the MARS approach (Kopetz *et al.*, 1989); a more comprehensive approach is needed covering all system resources including buses, main memory, and file-store; this work can build, at least in part, on current research into timing analysis;
- *semantics and functional analysis* – analysis of simple transaction structures for 'pure' functional components is straightforward, but

a richer semantic basis and set of composition rules are needed for the range of notations outlined above; this is a subtle technical issue, although it may be relatively tractable for safety-critical systems, as they tend to be functionally simple;

- *failure analysis* – issues here include the application of safety analysis techniques to software systems, development of compositional techniques enabling the failure behaviour of transactions to be derived from those of components (Fenelon *et al.*, 1994), and integration of quantitative failure analysis into the architectural design process; this also requires the ability to relate the functional and failure behaviour as recovery actions taken by system components can affect the fault propagation through the system; there is much relevant research, especially in the fault-tolerance and reliability communities, see for example Ciardo *et al.* (1994), McDermid & Pumfrey (1994);

- *re-use* – re-use is potentially important for safety critical systems; reuse of well-established components is accepted as good practice in other engineering disciplines, but has not been widely established in software engineering; most progress seems likely to be made by identifying domain-specific components (see section 12.5), or domain-specific architectures†, e.g. an architecture for a range of aeroplane engine controllers; this would have the added advantage of facilitating re-use of analysis results;

- *design synthesis* – it is possible to synthesise lower levels of the design from more abstract levels; here we are concerned with the structure of the implementation and scheduling information, not the application functionality (code); in particular the physical architecture can be generated from the logical architecture, given a hardware structure, in some circumstances (Burns *et al.*, 1993); current work has shown how to synthesise systems which satisfy timing properties and resource constraints, and it is a research issue to generate designs with the appropriate failure behaviour properties; this is a specific case of a more general optimisation problem, so such approaches are likely to use heuristic search techniques such as simulated annealing (Johnson *et al.*, 1989) and genetic algorithms (Goldberg, 1989);

- *tool integrity* – to gain benefit from the use of the above technology we need to be able to trust the tools, and to reduce or remove some testing

---

† There has been DoD-funded work on domain-specific architectures in the USA, but we are not aware of similar activities in the UK or elsewhere in Europe. It seems to us that this is potentially another very important research direction, as the commercial pay-back could be very large.

activities (this gives a cost benefit); this means that the tools have to be of high integrity, and this suggests they should be constructed using formal methods (it might suggest we use well established tools, but the evidence shows that this is insufficient for the required levels of trust); there are some challenges here, not the least being the complexity of the tools, but it may be possible to construct analysis and synthesis tools to an appropriate degree of rigour, using formal methods.

We believe that it should be possible to move to a situation where much of the physical architecture is generated from the logical architecture, although there are a number of difficulties in doing this. One is the issue of sensitivity – do small changes in the design lead to large changes in the implementation? If they do, then this will be a major problem as previous validation testing may be rendered nugatory as a consequence. Another important issue is predictive accuracy. The architectural-level analysis will not give good results unless the computational model in the implementation is reflected accurately in the architectural specification. This is a key issue for semantics work, and one of the underlying reasons for feeling current process algebras to be inappropriate for use in this application domain.

12.5 Software Production

Software production is a relatively well understood process, although the best principles are not always applied so the results can be of questionable quality, even for safety-critical systems. In the terms we introduced earlier, this stage of the process is concerned with implementing the components of the passive physical architecture, and integrating them (together with run-time support programs and data) to provide a software system which will execute according to the dynamic properties given in the architectural specification. Because it is well understood, we deal with the concepts and current practice briefly, and then turn to research directions.

12.5.1 Basic concepts

We are interested in the properties of the software, as at the architectural level, in the functional, timing, resource usage and failure domains. In general, software is developed by a manual creative process, and analysed or tested to show that it has the relevant properties, i.e. those specified in the architecture. The main distinction from the architectural level is that we need to analyse a component for its contribution to the system properties, and the component properties have to be combined with others to show that the requirements are met.

In the functional domain, behavioural requirements will be mapped down to more classical pre–post style specifications. End-to-end timing requirements will be reduced to worst-case execution time (WCET) requirements on the components, and similarly with resource usage (if resources are allocated at this level). Failure behaviour will tend to be reduced to a functional specification of response to hardware failure events, but see subsection 12.5.3.

12.5.2 Current practice

Current industrial practice is that code is produced manually, and its properties evaluated by a mixture of review and testing. There is an increasing usage of static analysis tools such as SPARK (Carre *et al.*, 1992) for functional properties, but this is not yet widespread. Testing is carried out systematically, with measurement of code coverage to ensure that testing is thorough (although, of course, it cannot normally be exhaustive)†. WCETs are normally determined by a combination of review of the code to find the worst-case path (and to determine the path traversal conditions), and testing to exercise that path, by setting up the path traversal conditions. If failure behaviour is assessed at all, then it is carried out by separate procedures, such as software fault-tree analysis (Taylor, 1982; Leveson & Harvey, 1983; Clarke & McDermid, 1993) which is essentially a form of '*wp*-calculus for failure modes'.

From a more academic perspective, formal approaches to program development are well established, and experimental program proving systems such as GYPSY (Good, 1984) have existed for many years. Whilst such approaches have been used 'in anger' they have not scaled well, and tend only to be used on small, critical components. More modern formal program development systems, e.g. those based on refinement such as Morgan's (1990) may be more effective, given appropriate tool support (Jordan *et al.*, 1994).

Tools are beginning to emerge which can evaluate program WCET statically (Shaw, 1989; Park, 1993; Chapman *et al.*, 1993). The use of such systems should become more widespread in the near future.

---

† Coverage analysis is supported for a number of languages by commercially available tools, e.g. the LDRA Testbed, AdaTEST from IPL.

12.5.3 Research directions

We believe that the trend will be towards code generation, i.e. producing source language programs from the architectural-level specifications, with the analytical techniques used to show that the generated code has the right properties (analysis may be applied to the generated code, and/or used in construction of the generators). The architectural specification can be used to generate the source code for the system, and the information needed by the scheduler to meet the timing requirements. Whilst some code will be generated 'directly' we anticipate that much will be produced by linking together re-usable components. There are four major aspects of the generated code:

- *structure* – the process framework and inter-communication areas that come directly from the software architecture – see section 12.4;
- *control components* – re-usable generic software, instantiated with the relevant gain parameters, rate limits, etc.;
- *state-transition components* – a set of nested case clauses; the top level reflects the set of states; the next level the transitions out of each state; actions are represented as separate procedures, called from the arms of the case clauses;
- *simple functions* – directly generated code, or re-use of generic packages.

Assuming we had a complete repertoire of re-usable components, of sufficiently high integrity, this produces all the source code which can then be compiled and linked (but see below).

Work is needed to analyse the software in the timing domain. Each code fragment should be analysed for worst-case execution time (WCET) and checked to see that the actual WCET satisfies the requirements on the component. Further, the scheduler data (execution lists) are produced to ensure the timing properties are met, based on the actual WCETs, rather than the specified ones (this makes the process rather more robust than insisting that all the WCETs are as specified). Note that, in terms of the model introduced in section 12.3, the justification for the timing properties of the architecture produced at the architectural stage will be supplemented with the analysis here – thus the justification expands as the process proceeds, finally containing the low-level detail necessary to gain certification. The intermediate justifications provide a basis for controlling the process.

The above approach is viable for situations where we have the necessary re-usable packages. However, where new classes of functionality are required, it is insufficient. We propose the use of a fairly classical formal development to produce the re-usable packages, and then to extend the repertoire of the design tools to use these new packages. Thus, for example, a package supporting matrices, together with the basic matrix operations†, might be introduced and made available to the specifiers of the functions and the actions in the state-transition notations. Thus the scope of the approach could be extended to deal with the matrix type and basic operations, or other types appropriate to the domain. This gives the basis of an extensible approach to the development of safety-critical software, which enables a high degree of rigour to be used and maintained even as the scope of the method is expanded. Within this approach there are a number of research issues which mirror those at the architectural level:

- *accurate and flexible timing analysis* – analytical techniques for determining WCETs tend to be pessimistic, as they allow for paths which are syntactically feasible, but which are not semantically feasible; work is needed to combine counts of instructions and instruction times from assembler level with source-level control flow information to give more accurate information, and to extend the subset of the programming language which can be handled (Chapman *et al.*, 1994);
- *resource analysis* – analytical tools for other aspects of resource analysis, e.g. memory and stack usage, are needed; these can be based on WCET analysis tools;
- *functional analysis* – this is well understood and the research issues are mainly engineering concerns, e.g. to make the techniques more widely applicable, and more cost-effective;
- *failure analysis* – if failure behaviour is specified functionally, then functional analysis can be used in this role; however, it is interesting to see whether or not failure analysis techniques, e.g. fault-trees, can be applied to software analysis to provide cost-effective methods of safety verification (there is some evidence that they are cost-effective, in some circumstances (Leveson & Harvey, 1983; Fenelon, 1993);
- *re-use* – the overall approach assumes re-use, but it also poses challenges for re-use of analysis results, e.g. WCETs; we require much

† The example is not particulary significant, but matrix-based approaches might be appropriate if we are to implement modern control algorithms, e.g. those proposed for multi-variable control.

better compositional calculi for properties such as failure behaviour and resource usage if we are to re-use known component properties in deriving overall system properties;

- *design synthesis* – whilst it will be possible to construct much of the code by re-use, *de novo* code generation will always be required; more work is needed on efficient code generation, especially on the ability to generate code against WCET requirements.

Most of the concerns at the architectural level apply here also, especially those concerned with the integrity of the tools (work on compilation verification (Pavey & Winsborrow, 1992) is also germane). The theory to support much of what we have described here already exists. The major research issues seem to be more at the engineering level – providing sufficiently effective algorithms and tools that the approach can be supported cost-effectively.

12.6 Overall Trends and Conclusions

We briefly identify trends from the above discussion, consider some non-technical issues affecting the achievement of the above research aims, and finally consider the difficulty of validating research in this area.

12.6.1 Trends

We believe that there are four major trends which will influence research directions in this area. These are the desire to achieve better:

- *analysis* – there is the need to provide better analysis of notations at all stages, ranging from trade-off analysis in early requirements and concept formulation to low-level code timing analysis;
- *integration* – it is increasingly clear that a number of approaches and techniques have to be integrated to produce effective system design tools, and this means a broader spectrum of techniques than just formal and structured methods;
- *tool integrity* – the desire to achieve and demonstrate tool integrity, and the need to provide 'end user' capabilities, will lead to an increasing trend to see the currently available formal methods as tool-builders' tools, not 'end user' tools;
- *synthesis* – there will be an increasing trend to use synthesis techniques for part, if not all, of a system design and implementation, and this will foster greater re-use in safety-critical systems.

Examples of these trends should have been apparent in the preceding three sections. The view expressed here that the current sorts of formal methods will be used more as 'tool-builders' tools' in future is perhaps the least apparent, and the most contentious.

12.6.2 Conduct of research

The research directions we have identified reflect challenging technical goals, but there are further, non-technical, impediments to achieving the goals arising out of the way research is usually conducted in the UK, many of them reflecting poor collaboration between universities and industry. Of course this is not to say that there is no effective collaboration – just that there appears to be many fewer effective interchanges than is possible and desirable.

To meet the above goals, and in particular to show that the ideas are effective, requires effective co-operation between academia and industry. There are several reasons for this. Perhaps the most important is to ensure that the research produces results which can fit into industrial processes – if it does not it won't be used, and its utility cannot be validated. In part this is an issue of dealing with problems of scale, but it also includes providing effective ways of handling change, providing techniques which are amenable to inspection and review, providing techniques which are usable by industrial software engineers under project pressures, and so on. Perhaps it is not essential to have collaboration to address these problems – but in my experience it is hard to appreciate these problems if you cannot experience them, at least at second hand. In effect, this means that more stress is needed on *engineering* research (which is not to decry the value of the underlying science).

However, there are many barriers to effective collaboration arising out of differences in objectives between industry and academia, commercial sensitivity, attitudes to rate of return on research investment, and so on – the problems lie with both 'sides' in the collaboration (McDermid, 1994). These barriers are, to some degree, intrinsic, due to the interests and motivations of people who choose to work in industry or universities, but I believe are exacerbated by current and recent research funding mechanisms. Historically, research funding has not stressed industrial collaboration. The more recent collaborative research programmes, such as SafeIT, tend to 'throw together' industry and academia for a period of time, but the links are often broken at the end of the project. It takes considerable time to build up mutual understanding and *trust*, and a long-term commitment is needed to achieve really effective interaction. Some large industrial companies recognise this, e.g. Rolls-Royce with their long-running programme of University Technology Centres in a range of disciplines, but such arrangements are the exception, not the rule.

It is to be hoped that the recent White Paper on 'Realising our Potential' might prompt some change in attitudes, and lead to the funding for more long-lived working relationships between industry and academia, but the omens do not look too promising. I believe that a change in mechanisms is needed to enable universities to undertake research which is academically valuable, stimulating and rewarding, whilst providing useful results for industry. These changes might include, for example, support for industrially linked lectureships, more support for exchange (staff secondments) between industry and academia, recognition of the need to support tool development and experimental applications.

None of these issues are peculiar to work on safety-critical systems, but the difficulties are exacerbated by the sensitivity surrounding such applications.

12.6.3 Validating research results

Finally, returning more directly to the theme of safety, there is one major difficulty in conducting any line of research – determining whether or not the research hypotheses, or research directions, are valid and the research results effective. The failure rates demanded for many systems, e.g. in aerospace, are so low that the expectation value is for zero failures in the lifetime of all the deployed systems of a given type. For example, some controllers† on the most widely used aeroplane engines have achieved about 10^7 hours of operation without failure, against a target of 10^{-9} failures/hour. This is good news for aero-engine manufacturers and the flying public, but not a basis for drawing conclusions about the effectiveness of the technology deployed, or for making comparative analyses of development techniques.

Consequently, there is a need to collect experiential data to assess the effectiveness of current technology and to set research directions. Further, it seems necessary to investigate incidents and accidents where software was a causal factor, to gain some insight into the effectiveness of the techniques used, and into the sources of the most serious problems‡.

† Usually referred to as FADECs – full authority digital engine controllers.
‡ Long reputed to be requirements.

This is inevitably an imperfect and difficult process, but one which is necessary to put our research on a sounder footing. Some work has been done in this area (Jackson *et al.*, 1994), but a major programme of data collection and analysis is needed to provide the necessary understanding of the problems that arise in practice, and the effectiveness of the techniques developed. In order to get sufficient data, and data which reflects current practices, it seems necessary to analyse current development and test programmes. Historically it has been hard to gain access to this data for reasons of commercial sensitivity, but there seems to be a growing recognition by industry of the need for openness. It is to be hoped that this indicates a new trend and facilitates an important research direction.

Acknowledgements

Over the last five years I have been fortunate to work with a number of major aerospace companies in the UK, and companies in a number of other industries, including transport and nuclear power, in Europe and the USA. I gratefully acknowledge the financial support I have had for my research over the years. The collaborative research has also given me a particular perspective on the problems of developing safety-critical systems. I hope that I now have a fairly balanced view of how to establish a development process which has technical rigour (the academic view) together with practicality (the industrial view). If I have achieved this happy state, then I owe much to my industrial sponsors and collaborators.

I am also deeply indebted to my research colleagues in York, and elsewhere. All the staff in my research group deserve thanks for their support, and tolerance of an over-full diary. I would especially like to thank Alan Burns in York, and John Dobson in Newcastle, who have been particularly influential in the development of my thinking over the last few years. Finally, thanks should go to Ian Wand who persuaded me to move to York in 1987 and thus provided me with the opportunity to develop the above ideas.

13
Semantic Ideas in Computing
Robin Milner

13.1 Introduction

Are there distinct principles and concepts which underlie computing, so that we are justified in calling it an independent science? Or is computing a resource or commodity – like water – which is perfectly well understood in terms of existing science, for which we merely have to find more and better uses?

In this essay I argue that a rich conceptual development is in progress, to which we cannot predict limits, and whose outcome will be a distinct science. This development has all the excitement and unpredictability of any science. We cannot predict how the conceptual landscape will lie in a decade's time; the subject is still young and has many surprises in store, and there is no sure way to extrapolate from the concepts which we now understand to those which will emerge. I therefore support my argument by explaining in outline some semantic ideas which have emerged in the last two or three decades, and some which are just now emerging.

I try to present the ideas here in a way which is accessible to someone with an understanding of programming and a little mathematical background. This volume aims to give a balanced picture of computer science; to achieve this, those parts which are mathematical must be presented as such. The essence of foundational work is to give *precise* meaning to formulations of processes and information; clearly, we should employ mathematics in this work whenever it strengthens our analytical power. Thus, rather than avoiding equations, I try to surround them with helpful narrative.

It is a somewhat arbitrary matter to decide when a scientific discipline is mature and stands significantly on its own. Important criteria are that

246

its ideas have distinctive character compared with those of other disciplines, that these ideas have a well-knit structure, and that they have some breadth of application. As far as distinctive character is concerned, many of the notions discussed here are new; moreover a unifying theme pervades them which we may call *information flow* – not only the volume or quantity of the flow, but the structure of the items which flow and the structure and control of the flow itself. As for breadth of application, there are clear signs that the field of computing spans a wider range than many would have predicted thirty years ago. At that time, the main concern was to *prescribe* the behaviour of single computers or their single programs. Now that computers form just parts of larger systems, there is increasing concern to *describe* the flow of information and the interaction among the components of those larger systems. Another paper in this volume (Gurd & Jones) draws attention to this trend at the level of system engineering and human organizations, while Newman argues that interactive computing should be installed in the mainstream of computing as an engineering discipline. At the fundamental level, the concepts of computing can increasingly be seen as abstractions from the phenomena of information flow and interaction. One may even claim that computing is becoming a science to the extent that it seeks to study information flow in full generality.

In section 13.2, I distinguish between two sources of ideas for computing. One source is the theoretical core of mathematical logic, whose long development (most intense in the last hundred years) makes it a firm basis for our subject. The other source is computing practice itself, as made possible by the digital computer; I claim that this practice is not merely the application of already established science, but also an activity from which scientific concepts are distilled. The remainder of the essay indicates how this occurs, with specific examples; I try to show that software engineering not only exposes the need for a scientific basis, but even provides the germs of the ideas of that science.

In section 13.3, I consider the practical business of making sure that a computing system meets its specification. I pay particular attention to the problem of software maintenance, since the difficulties are most acute there. We see that this activity, and more generally the software design and development process, demand the use of formal descriptions and specifications, and formal methods of analysis and design.

While this need has gained a degree of acceptance in software engineering, I argue in section 13.4 that formalism is not the most important part of the story. Consider the specification of a complete computer system S; it is formal because we need rigour, but every formal expression has a meaning, and this meaning has conceptual content. This content will vary from the mundane to the esoteric. The specification of the *complete* system S will express its intended behaviour in terms of concepts drawn from its field of application (e.g. money if the field is banking; geometry and mechanics if the field is robotics); on the other hand the specification of a *component* deeply situated within S will employ concepts which are inherently computational, and pertain to information flow in general.

Section 13.5 is devoted to identifying some of the concepts which have emerged from the challenge to understand conventional programming languages, which provide the raw material for software engineering. Many of these ideas are now stable, and form a considerable part of the foundation of computing. Despite their fundamental character, they have emerged through application experience which has only been possible since the programmed computer was invented. Thus computing is a science which not only informs an engineering discipline, but uses that very discipline as its laboratory for experiment.

Section 13.6 deals with some concepts which are currently emerging, and less stable. Due to the shift of emphasis which I mentioned above from prescribing computer behaviour to describing system behaviour, these emerging concepts are more and more concerned with the interaction of system components, with the flow of information among them, and with the dynamic reconfiguration of the systems to which they belong. Despite the more tentative status of these ideas, they appear to belong to the same large conceptual development as the more stable ideas in section 13.5, and I try to present this continuity of progress.

13.2 The Nature of Computation Theory

At the outset, we should recall that computation has for long had a hard theoretical core closely linked with mathematical logic. Around 1900, the famous mathematician David Hilbert mounted a programme, or issued a challenge, to show that every mathematical truth is deducible – i.e. mechanically derivable – from a set of axioms; the challenge was to find those axioms. This programme was overthrown by the work of Gödel, Kleene, Church and Turing. It was found that any reasonably expressive axiomatic system will inescapably be either *inconsistent*, meaning that one can deduce some proposition and its negation, or *incomplete*, meaning that there are some propositions P for which one can deduce neither P nor the negation of P. This even occurs in cases where we intuitively regard P as true. In other words, there will always be truths which are not deducible; and this amounts (via the work of these pioneers) to saying that certain mathematical functions cannot be computed by any computer program.

It may appear that this has nothing to do with computing, except to show that it has limitations. But this hard core of computation theory soon ramified into a *classification* of what is computable; that is, there are *degrees* of computability. The ramification began with recursion theory, where it is shown that certain things are essentially harder to compute than others. Within computer science, the theory known as computational complexity carries on this programme; it is reviewed by Atkinson in this volume. We now know that a lot of useful things can be computed in linear time, others take non-linear but polynomial time, still others almost certainly take exponential time and some definitely do. Tasks are also classified in terms of the memory space they require, and in terms of the extent to which parallelism can speed their computation.

Some people, even computer scientists, regard this difficult and unfinished study as essentially the mainstream of computation theory. According to this view, the rest of computer science consists largely of engineering, either of hardware or of software. It is understood that physical science will continue to develop new and more powerful kinds of hardware; on the other hand, software is seen as a resource or commodity whose scientific basis is already established, like water; our task is not to probe further into its nature, but to exploit it by pouring it into everything. It is admitted that this development, or pouring, amounts to a new and intricate engineering discipline; it is hardly allowed that new scientific concepts are needed to underpin the development.

This negative view is at best unproven, as long as we admit that science is concerned with the rigorous understanding of the world about us. There is no doubt that large computer systems exist in the world about us; they are orders of magnitude more complex than anything made before, probably as complex as many natural systems (e.g. ecologies), and their complexity is steadily increasing. Further, there are new kinds of system, containing parts which are not computers and may even be human, which exist only because of the computers they contain; a modern banking system is a good example. In the light of this growth, the negative view seems not only unproven but shortsighted. The surge of interest in object-oriented programming shows that new ideas are entering the very nature of software, though they are imperfectly understood.

Further, as computing is extended to include communication and information flow in distributed and heterogeneous systems, we are faced with the need to understand a newly identified group of phenomena which are indeed pervasive.

In the following sections I argue that this understanding will have broad application; I also show that it employs a well knit body of concepts, some developed in the last few decades in studying programming languages, others newly emerging and more concerned with interaction. Thus the criteria for a significant scientific discipline which I mentioned earlier are met, and the negative view which I have described is refuted. To the extent that the phenomena of computing and communication are man-made, we have a substantial new 'science of the artificial', as Herbert Simon (1980) has recognised.

How do we arrive at these new concepts? In the natural sciences, observation plays a central rôle. A large part of computer science is about man-made phenomena, and we therefore expect engineering practice to play a large part in suggesting new ideas. Computer science is not unique in this; it is hard to imagine that engineering practice (building things) did not play a strong part in the development of 'natural philosophy', i.e. mechanics, including Newton's laws of motion. What is surely unprecedented in computer science is the enormous rate at which we have acquired engineering experience over a few decades. This experience or experiment (in French the word is the same!) is our means of observation.

All experiment is done against an already accepted scientific background, an established body of concepts. In computer science, mathematical logic has always figured largely in this background. (For Turing, the Turing machine and the Ace computer were conceptually close.) This reflects the distinctive part which computer systems play in our environment; they act as extensions of our mental power, in other words as prosthetic devices of the mind. Any prosthetic device is controlled somehow, and in the case of computers the means of control is formal language. Mathematical logic is concerned with the structure and meaning of formal languages, and thus provides essential background to our experiment; it underlies not only *deductive* languages (logics as commonly understood), but also *imperative* or *effective* languages such as programming languages. In studying the way we control systems, or interact with them, we are therefore broadening the field of mathematical logic; we may expect computer science and logic to grow intimately together.

In the next section we shall look at a particular example of systems engineering experience, namely *software maintenance*. The problems encountered there, and our progress in dealing with them, rather clearly illustrate the need for – and the difficulty in arriving at – concepts which help to understand computer systems.

13.3 Understanding a Software System

One of the most important reasons for understanding a software system is to change it. There are two reasons why one may wish to change it; it may be wrong, or it may be required to work in a changed environment. Both of these reasons apply in many cases! But they are not the only reasons for needing to understand software; even if a system is perfect and working in a perfectly unchanging environment, we shall want to build other systems, for different but similar tasks, without starting again – and we can at least hope to use a lot of its pieces unchanged.

What kind of understanding helps in making this sort of adaptive change? This is the problem of *software maintenance*, an activity which is claimed to absorb 80–90% of software effort. Even for experienced computer scientists a simple everyday analogy may be useful in answering this question.

Suppose that you want to adapt your bicycle, when you leave the city to live in the country, so that it will cope with hill paths. How do you know what to change? Your first idea might be to fit fatter tyres which grip the surface better, so you try to find out how to do this. A bicycle is largely open; you can see a lot of the 'code' of a bicycle. Imagine that you've never really looked at any wheeled vehicle properly before; you've only used them. So looking at the bicycle for the first time is like looking at the raw code of a software system. It's all there, but you cannot see all its joins; for example, you can't see whether or how the tyre comes off the wheel – it might be riveted on. In fact you don't even know that there is a separable thing called the 'tyre', a component of a thing called 'wheel'; this structure is not completely manifest.

This problem is met again and again in software engineering, because big systems exist without any, or without enough, structural description. The reason can be completely mundane; perhaps it was written five years ago, by someone who has now left, and written in such a hurry that there was no time to describe it. The only way to solve the problem, if you have not enough time to start again, is what is known as 'reverse engineering'

(Walters & Chikofsky, 1994). At its crudest level this consists in poring over the code for days, weeks or months in order to intuit its structure.

Reverse engineering is important, and it is a serious professional activity. Much has been written on it, and this is not the place to describe it in detail. Because systems engineers are repeatedly confronted with the problem of adapting large inscrutable software systems, it would be pointless to criticize them for using reverse engineering. But we must resist the inference that software engineering will always involve makeshift activity, which – in its crude form – reverse engineering undoubtedly is. More positively, we should try to arrive at means by which this activity will be found unnecessary.

To get an idea of how to avoid reverse engineering, it is useful to take the bicycle analogy two steps further. First, the situation is not usually so bad as suggested above; instead of poring over unstructured low-level code, the reverse engineer will often pore over code written in a high-level language such as Ada or Pascal. This makes the job a lot easier; the modular structure of the system is manifest in the code because these languages are designed to express precisely the interfaces between system components. This is like not only having the bike to look at, but also having the exploded assembly diagram of the bike, showing how the tyre fits on the wheel, and the wheel on the bike.

With this knowledge, perhaps you fit tougher tyres and take the bike on a hill-path. It then collapses; the wheels buckle and the spokes break. Why? The reason cannot be found in the exploded assembly diagram (i.e. the high-level program text). What is missing is any information about the bike *in action*; for example, about the stress which can be transmitted from the road through the tyre (now tough enough) to the wheel. In software terms, the high-level code – though it may be beautifully structured – tells you nothing about how a new user interface (for a tougher environment) can place extra demand on an inner software component which it wasn't made to bear.

A good reverse engineer will, all the same, avoid many of these traps. Mostly this will be because he or she has a good feel for the behaviour of software modules and for their interaction; it may also be because the original Ada code was well adorned with useful comments. Equally, the man in the bike shop was not trained in the strength of materials, or in dynamics, but he too could have told you that new tyres would not be enough for hill riding; you would certainly need new wheels and he might even wonder about the frame.

But we must not be reassured by this sort of horse sense. Software is unboundedly complex; new situations will always arise in which know-how from previous experience is little help. What is needed is a theory of software dynamics, and a conception of the strength of software material. So this is the second step in the development of our analogy.

What kind of thing is the 'strength' of a piece of software? One way of expressing the strength of a piece of steel is

If you apply a force of no more than 100 newtons to it, and let it go, it will spring back.

For a piece of program we may say analogously

If you give it a quadratic equation with coefficients no bigger than 15000, and let it go, it will compute the roots.

Such a statement – call it S – is usually known as a *specification*. It is precise, and it is not a program; many different programs P may satisfy S. A specification S may be called a contract between the designer of P and the designer of the system environment which will use P. The designer of a complete system has a contract to meet with his or her customer; he must not only ensure that his design meets the contract but he must present an argument that it does so, in a way which others can follow. This second requirement more or less forces him to design in a modular way. Then his argument can be modular too; at each level it will show that if a module can rely upon its parts P_i meeting their subspecifications S_i then the module composed of those parts in turn meets its specification.

The point is that reverse engineering just isn't necessary if good enough specifications are available for each module in a software system, because the specification represents just the knowledge that the reverse engineer is trying to recover. If his customer contract changes, this may mean that the subcontract S for P has to be strengthened – replacing the bound 15000 by 20000 say; this in turn means that P itself may have to be reprogrammed.

I do not wish to imply that this is easy. Specifications can be extremely complex and subtle. But academics are working alongside the software industry to bring about this sea-change in methodology. An early success is VDM (Vienna Development Method) (Jones, 1986), a logic-based methodology which originated in IBM's laboratory in Vienna a quarter of a century ago; another notable example is Oxford University's collaboration with IBM, using the medium of the specification language Z (Spivey, 1992). Every effort must be made to develop the applied mathematics of specifications, because without it software design – and in particular software maintenance – will remain a black art, full of black holes into which human effort and financial resource are inexorably drawn.

13.4 Underlying Concepts

The previous section amounts to a case for the use of *formal methods* in system engineering. The argument is particularly important for the upgrading of reverse engineering into a more rigorous and less chancy exercise; it will be familiar to many readers. In recent years there has been a fairly widespread acceptance that, at least in principle, specifications should be expressed in a formal language and the reasoning about them conducted with computer assistance where possible.

The problem we now confront, which is central to this essay, is: What do these formalisms express? Most people will reject the extreme formalist view that a formalism expresses nothing! Let us first consider the formal specification of a *complete* computing system; that is, a system which is embedded not in another computing system but in some 'real-world' environment. Then most software engineers (who admit formal specification at all) will agree that this top-level specification should not express anything to do with the internal structure of the system, but should be solely concerned with how the system must behave in its environment. (This may include how much power it consumes, and how long it takes, i.e. its costs.) The specification is therefore written in terms of concepts which pertain to the environment – not to computer science. So far then, concepts which are peculiar to computer science won't show up in the specification of a complete computing system, any more than the concept of a magnetic field shows up in the specification of an electrically driven food-mixer.

But if we admit that a specification of a system expresses behaviour using concepts relevant to the system's environment, then this holds also for incomplete systems – i.e. the modules and submodules within complete ones. By any reasonable count there are more such modules than there are complete systems! So most of the time, a system engineer will be dealing with concepts which refer to the internal working of computing systems. We then naturally ask whether concepts with which we are already familiar – from mathematics, logic, or the external world – will be enough for this purpose. If so, then computer science does not really deserve to be called a science in its own right – though computer systems engineering will still be a distinct branch of engineering.

I believe that an emphasis on *formal methods*, necessary though it is for systems engineering, may lead to a false conclusion: that familiar mathematical notions, such as the calculus of sets and relations, are enough to specify the behaviour of internal modules of a system, and that we get all the understanding we need – as well as the rigour – by wrapping these up in a suitable logic. Therefore, before discussing some of the new semantic ideas in computer science, I shall give two examples to support the need for them. Other examples can easily be found.

First, consider a computing system at the heart of a communications network which allows links between different pairs of sites to be formed, used and broken. (We need not be concerned whether these are voice links, or links for textual traffic.) The external specification of the system will be something like this: The system accepts requests for links to be formed, forms them, allows interaction across them, takes action if they break accidentally, etc. All this can be specified in terms of external behaviour. Now consider a piece of software within the system whose job is to re-route an existing link (perhaps under certain traffic conditions) while it exists, without in any way affecting the interaction occurring on the link. (Two people having a telephone conversation need not be concerned whether their connection is via one satellite or another, or via none, nor should they be able to detect changes of route in mid-call.) How is this piece of software specified? It must be in terms of some concept of *route*. What is this concept? It is not only a concrete route through hardware; it is also mediated by software, so it has abstract elements too. Whatever it is, it is unlikely to be a concept specific to this one application, nor a concept familiar to users of the system. One can only conclude that it is a concept specific to computer science; in fact, it pertains to the structure of information flow.

As a second example, consider a software-development suite for an industrially used computer language – say Ada. Part of this suite of programs is the *compiler* for the language. The compiler – itself a program – translates the Ada language into basic machine code, or perhaps into some intermediate language close to the machine code, so that the machine can execute it. What is the specification which this compiler is to meet? Among other things (e.g. how errors should be reported) the specification must demand that the translation be correct.

What, precisely, does it mean to say that the translation from one language to another is correct? First, this assertion presupposes a precise (and therefore formal) definition of the behaviour of a program in each language. Recently, there have been several formal definitions of programming languages; Ada itself was the subject of a monumental attempt, partly successful, at formal definition. Therefore we are reaching the situation that the assertion of compiler-correctness is at least about well defined entities. But this success in formal definition is not the whole story. For, as I said above, every formalism expresses something; in this case, the formalism in which the language is defined should express the *behaviour* of computer programs. To assert that the compiler is correct is to say that, in every case, the behaviour of an Ada program is equivalent to that of its translation. But computer scientists are still not agreed upon the nature of these behaviours; *a fortiori*, it is not settled what constitutes *equivalence* among them! This is partly because Ada tasks run concurrently; the concept of *concurrent process* is unsettled, and there are many different candidates for the notion of equivalence of processes.

Even for languages which have no sophisticated communicational features, indeed no concurrency, the study of equivalence of meaning has generated some of the most striking concepts in computer science, which are even new to mathematics. These concepts are not only concerned with programming languages; they are also about the behaviour of computing and communicating systems in general. After all, this is what our languages are supposed to describe! I shall now go on to discuss some of the concepts which are emerging from the need to understand not only the external specification of computing systems, but also what goes on inside them. I hope that the foregoing discussion has convinced the reader that a conceptual framework is needed for this understanding, and that we cannot assume the concepts to be familiar ones.

13.5 Programs and Functions

I earlier alluded to computers as 'prosthetic devices of the mind'. This may be a fanciful description, but it pinpoints exactly what software is. Just as we control any tool, we control computation and use it for our own purposes, and the *means* of control is just programming. One might hope for a once-and-for-all discipline of control; but this leaves out of account the growing variety of the purposes to which we put computing. Few people would now claim that there can be a universal programming language, or even a small number of them, though the claim has been made in the past.

We may, of course, choose to stay with our current repertoire of half-understood languages, and inhabit Babel for ever. A (rather weak) argument for this is that, after all, we are not doing badly; computer systems do more or less what we intended – and if not, we can adapt to them. But the situation will not stay still; we need only look at the current growth of object-oriented languages to see that new, less understood, languages are emerging – and we have no reason to think that this growth of language will cease. Babel is not stable!

A more insidious argument for continuing to inhabit Babel is that we have no choice, for the following reason: The only alternative is to find a way of understanding languages which does not depend upon language, and this is literally impossible; all descriptions must be expressed in some symbolism – and we are back to the impossibility of a universal language.

This argument ignores the power of mathematical understanding. Certainly mathematics uses formalism, but its essence lies in its *ideas* – expressed using minimal formalism. Thus we seek not a universal *language*, but a universal *understanding* of languages. Indeed, one of the greatest advances in computation theory over the past thirty years has been the development of mathematical theories which explain (i.e. give meaning to) a very wide range of programming languages, including virtually all those which do not involve parallel or interactive computation. With such theories we see the variety among languages in its proper sense – not as prolix symbolism but as variation of methodology within an understood space.

In this essay I cannot do full justice to the theoretical development. But in keeping with my main theme, I want to show how it has led not just to formal or logical definitions, but to a repertoire of concepts which arise *inevitably*, from phenomena of programming which are simple and familiar. So, though we shall end up with a new and significant branch of mathematics, we shall now begin with the most familiar programming ideas, and ask what meaning lies behind them.

13.5.1 Computational domains

We shall look at several well-formed pieces of program, in a familiar kind of programming language. For each one of them, we shall see that it *expresses* or *denotes* an abstract object; for each one we shall ask in what *space* of objects it lies.

Let us begin with a piece of program which declares a procedure for computing the nth power of a real number x:

```
PROCEDURE power(x:REAL, n:INTEGER):REAL
    RESULT = x^n
END PROCEDURE
```

After this declaration, the name **power** has a meaning which it did not have before; it denotes a *function*. But it is not just any function; it is a function which takes objects in one space, the *argument* space, and gives an object in another space, the *result* space. We call the argument space REALS × INTEGERS; it contains all pairs consisting of a real number and an integer. This space is constructed as the *product* (×) of two simpler spaces; the real numbers REALS, and the integers INTEGERS. The result space is just REALS again.

Another way of saying this is that **power** itself denotes an object in a space: the *function space*

$$\text{REALS} \times \text{INTEGERS} \ \rightarrow \ \text{REALS} \ ,$$

where '→' is another way of constructing new spaces from old. In general, for *any* spaces D and E, $D \times E$ is the space containing pairs (one member from D, one from E), while $D \rightarrow E$ is the space of functions from D to E.

It is important to speak generally, in this way, because then we see opportunities for generality of usage. For example, we see that the result space E of the function space $D \rightarrow E$ may itself be a function space; this reflects the fact that in some languages a procedure can deliver a result which is another procedure.

To introduce a third space-construction, we consider how to model a realistic situation, namely that an arithmetic operation can cause overflow; this may make **power** *raise an exception*, i.e. exit abnormally, rather than return a normal result. To model this we can use *summation* (+) of spaces; we say that **power** denotes an element of the space

$$\text{REALS} \times \text{INTEGERS} \ \rightarrow \ \text{REALS} + \{\text{overflow}\} \ ,$$

meaning that it will return sometimes a real number, and at other times the special result 'overflow'. (In general, + can be used for richer alternatives.)

As we consider further program features, we find phenomena which determine more precisely the nature of these spaces. Consider first the

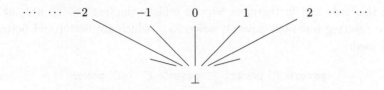

Fig. 13.1. The flat domain of integers

execution of a piece of program which sometimes loops (fails to terminate). We have to give meaning to such programs, even if people shouldn't write them, since we have to describe bad as well as good programs. Suppose someone writes

```
PROCEDURE power0(x:REAL, n:INTEGER):REAL
    IF n>0 THEN ...
    RESULT = x^n
END PROCEDURE
```

where '...' is some looping program; then `power0` no longer denotes a *total* function (one which always gives a result), but a *partial* one. Partiality can be represented by allowing domains to contain a spurious element $\perp$ (pronounced 'bottom'); we write $D_\perp$ for the domain $D + \{\perp\}$, and then we can allow for looping by saying that `power0` denotes an element of the function space

$$\text{REALS} \times \text{INTEGERS} \;\rightarrow\; \text{REALS}_\perp,$$

meaning that when applied it will sometimes 'produce' the result $\perp$ – i.e. it will loop without giving any result.

This element $\perp$ is special; intuitively, it is 'less well defined' than every other element. So a space is not, as we might have thought, just a *set* of objects of a certain kind; for its members are *ordered* according to how well defined they are. This ordering is written '$\sqsubseteq$'; in the space INTEGERS$_\perp$ for example, we have that $\perp \sqsubseteq n$ for every integer n, but we don't have either $1 \sqsubseteq 2$ or $2 \sqsubseteq 1$ because no integer is *better defined* than any other. We draw INTEGERS$_\perp$ as in Figure 13.1. It is a very 'flat' space (though it does have $\perp$ below everything else), but more interesting spaces quickly arise. Consider REALS $\rightarrow$ REALS$_\perp$; this space contains functions, and we can say that one function is less defined than ($\sqsubseteq$) another if it gives a defined result less often. Thus the ordering of functions is defined in terms of the ordering of REALS$_\perp$; writing $\sqsubseteq$ to stand for '⊑ or =', we define $f \sqsubseteq g$ to mean that $f(x) \sqsubseteq g(x)$ for every real number x. The meaning of power0 is below the meaning of power in this ordering; furthermore we can replace the test n>0 by n>1, n>2 etc., getting functions power1, power2,... which are better and better defined:

$$\text{power0} \sqsubseteq \text{power1} \sqsubseteq \text{power2} \sqsubseteq \cdots \sqsubseteq \text{power} \ .$$

Thus the meaning of a procedure reflects how ill defined is its *result*. But suppose you give the procedure an *argument* which is ill defined; is it forced to give an undefined result? The following two simple (and stupid) procedures indicate that a procedure may or may not be sensitive to an ill defined argument:

```
PROCEDURE nought(x:REAL):REAL
    RESULT = 0
END PROCEDURE

PROCEDURE zero(x:REAL):REAL
    RESULT = x-x
END PROCEDURE
```

In the space REALS → REALS⊥ nought and zero will denote the same function: that which returns 0 whatever real number you give it as an argument. So this isn't the right space, if we want to reflect that they may differ if you apply them to an ill defined argument! They *do* differ, in some languages. If you execute the two procedure calls

$$\text{nought(power0(0,1))} \qquad and \qquad \text{zero(power0(0,1))}$$

then one will loop but not the other. The argument to both calls is power0(0,1), and this (if executed) will loop. But the first call will return 0 because the procedure nought doesn't *need* to execute its argument, while the second loops (i.e. 'returns' ⊥) because the procedure zero *does* need to work out its argument. We need a space of meanings to reflect this difference; so we assign each procedure a meaning in the space REALS⊥ → REALS⊥ (instead of REALS → REALS⊥), where they indeed denote *different* functions.

We now go beyond the cosy world of procedures which only compute functions, and consider programs which can change the state (value) of a variable. Suppose that a program consists of a sequence of commands which are executed one by one. One such command is a procedure declaration, such as we have shown above. Another kind of command is an *assignment* such as

```
z := power(y+z, 2)
```

which changes the value of the variable z to be the square of the sum of the (current) values of y and z. Commands are executed in a *state* in which each name (y, z, power, ...) has a value. So a state is just a function from names to values, and again we can use a space; a state is a member of the space

$$\text{STATES} = \text{NAMES} \rightarrow \text{VALUES}$$

where in turn the space VALUES is supposed to contain every kind of meaning which a name can have:

$$\text{VALUES} = \text{REALS}_\perp + \text{INTEGERS}_\perp + \cdots .$$

Now, since each command has the effect of changing the state – i.e. creating a new state from the current one – a command takes its meaning in the space

$$\text{COMMANDS} = \text{STATES} \rightarrow \text{STATES} ;$$

for example, the meaning of the assignment z := z+1 is a function which, given any state $s \in$ STATES, creates a state s' identical with s except that $s'(z) = s(z) + 1$.

Let us return to procedures. They may take as arguments and return as results all kinds of values, so we may use the larger space VALUES $\rightarrow$ VALUES for their meanings (rather than REALS$_\perp$ $\rightarrow$ REALS$_\perp$). But, since we are now considering state-change, this space is not enough. For our language may allow assignments such as z := z+1 to appear *inside* procedures; then each call of a procedure not only returns a value but may also change the state. To reflect this, we take the meaning of a procedure to lie in the more complex space

$$\text{PROCEDURES} = (\text{STATES} \times \text{VALUES}) \rightarrow (\text{STATES} \times \text{VALUES}) .$$

As a final twist, we must remember that a state must record not only the association between a variable name z and its value, but also the meaning of every procedure name. This means that the space of procedure–meanings has to be included in the space of values, so finally we take

$$\text{VALUES} = \text{REALS}_\perp + \text{INTEGERS}_\perp + \cdots + \text{PROCEDURES} .$$

We have now explored enough programming features. We have captured the character of each feature by associating with it a specific space of meanings. We have naturally expressed each space in terms of others. The striking thing is that, without dealing with very complex features, we arrived at three spaces – STATES, PROCEDURES and VALUES – each of which depends upon the others; there is a cyclic dependency! Do we have any right to suppose that spaces – whatever they are – can be found to satisfy such equations? The answer is not trivial, and the need for the answer led to the concept of a *domain* (Gunter & Scott, 1990).

13.5.2 Semantic concepts

The preceding paragraphs read like the first few pages of a textbook on programming semantics. But this is essentially the way in which, in 1969, Christopher Strachey identified many of these challenges for a semantic theory of programming. In that year his fruitful collaboration with Dana Scott (Scott & Strachey, 1971) inspired Scott's invention of domain theory. We shall now use the word 'domain' instead of space; we proceed to identify a handful of key concepts which arise inevitably from this short exploration.

Solving domain equations From the simple assumption that every well-formed piece of program should stand for an object in some semantic domain, we have arrived at equations which such domains should satisfy. The exercise would be abortive if there were no solution to these simultaneous equations; we would have failed to find suitable spaces of meanings. But the equations connecting the domains STATES, PROCEDURES and VALUES show a cyclic dependency among them; the existence of solutions is therefore not obvious.

We have to face this fact: If the function domain $D \to E$ contains *all* the functions from D to E, then there *can be no solution* to our equations! This can be shown by a direct adaptation of Cantor's argument that the infinity of the real numbers is strictly larger than the infinity of the integers. For this argument also implies that the size of the function domain $D \to E$ is strictly larger than that of D (if D and E have more than one element); using this fact we can trace around our equations to show that the size of VALUES would be greater than itself!

This paradox is resolved below by making sure that the function domain $D \to E$ actually does *not* contain all functions. This is no contrivance; the omitted functions have no computational significance. Once this functional domain construction is settled, a theory emerges

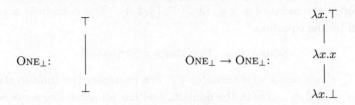

Fig. 13.2. The two-element domain and its function space

which guarantees that *any* family of equations using suitable domain constructions has a solution. Such an equation-set arises in the mathematical description of any programming language; from our simple illustration above it should be clear that it not only lies at the heart of a semantic definition of the language, but gives a clear grasp of the ontology of the language.

Monotonicity From an intuitive understanding of program execution it is easy to accept that, for any procedure which we can define in a reasonable language, any increase in the definedness of its arguments can only lead to an increase (or no change) in the definedness of its result. Such a statement can, indeed, be formally proven if the rules of execution of the language are formally given. We therefore require of the function domain $D \to E$ that it contain not *all* functions, but only those functions f which are *monotonic*, i.e. such that

whenever $x \sqsubseteq y$ holds in D, then $f(x) \sqsubseteq f(y)$ holds in E .

Take for example the domain ONE with only one element $\top$, so that ONE$_\perp$ has two elements. Then ONE$_\perp$ $\to$ ONE$_\perp$ will not contain the function $f^?$ which exchanges $\perp$ and $\top$, since this function is not monotonic. The omission of $f^?$ from the space is justified because any procedure written to compute $f^?(x)$ from x would have to loop if and only if the computation of x *doesn't* loop, and no procedure could ever be written to do this. The ordering diagrams are shown in Figure 13.2. In the diagram we use λ-*notation* for functions; if M is any expression, then $\lambda x.M$ means 'the function f given by $f(x) = M$'.

Completeness and continuity An interesting domain is one consisting of *streams* (sequences) of some kind of value, say integers. A stream can be finite or infinite. For streams s and s' we define $s \sqsubseteq s'$ if s' is a proper extension of s, e.g. $(3,2) \sqsubset (3,2,4)$. The domain is actually given by the equation

$$\text{STREAMS} = (\text{INTEGERS} \times \text{STREAMS})_\perp .$$

If $s \sqsubseteq s'$ we say s *approximates* s'. For example, the infinite stream $evens = (0,2,4,\ldots)$ is in the domain, and has an ascending sequence of finite approximants

$$evens_0 \sqsubseteq evens_1 \sqsubseteq evens_2 \sqsubseteq \cdots$$

where $evens_k = (0,2,4,\ldots,2k)$. We naturally think of the 'complete' stream $evens$ as the *limit* of this sequence of streams; this notion of limit is mathematically precise, and we write $\bigsqcup x_i$ for the limit of an ascending sequence $x_0 \sqsubseteq x_1 \sqsubseteq x_2 \cdots$ in any domain.

The following fact is (after some thought) intuitive, but needs careful proof: If a function f from streams to integers can be defined by a program, and if $f(evens)$ is well defined – say $f(evens) = 14$ – then there is some approximant $evens_k \sqsubseteq evens$ for which also $f(evens_k) = 14$. (For $j < k$ we may have $f(evens_j) = \perp$.) In other words: To get a finite amount of information about the result of applying a function to a stream, we only need supply a finite amount of the stream. This is a general phenomenon of information flow in computations; it is not confined to functions over streams. It justifies a further constraint upon the functions f which are included in the domain $D \to E$, that they be *continuous*; this means that for any ascending sequence $x_0 \sqsubseteq x_1 \sqsubseteq \cdots$ in D, if $f(x_i) = y_i$ for each i then

$$f(\bigsqcup x_i) = \bigsqcup y_i .$$

This condition is usually accompanied by the *completeness* condition that every ascending sequence in a domain has a limit in the domain. These conditions ensure that the function domain $D \to E$ is small enough to avoid the Cantor paradox, and thereby also ensure that solutions exist to the equations among domains which we have met.

Types One of the most helpful concepts in the whole of programming is the notion of *type*, used to classify the kinds of object which are manipulated. A significant proportion of programming mistakes are detected by an implementation which does *typechecking* before it runs any program. Types provide a taxonomy which help people to think and to communicate about programs. Certain type-disciplines have a simple mathematical theory which guides the algorithms used for typechecking;

thus even a simple theory (much simpler than that of the underlying semantics) can lead to good engineering practice.

An elementary example of typechecking is this: by analysing the procedure body, the implementation can discover that the procedure power has type (REAL,INTEGER)->REAL, as its header line suggests; knowing this, the implementation can disallow the procedure–call power(2.3,0.5) because 0.5 isn't an integer.

It is no accident that the type of the procedure 'looks like' a domain. Ignoring the presence of states, the meaning of every procedure lies in the domain VALUES → VALUES. The theory of domains provides an elegant story of how the domains REALS$_\perp$ and REALS$_\perp$ × INTEGERS$_\perp$ 'lie inside' the domain VALUES, and then how the function domain REALS$_\perp$ × INTEGERS$_\perp$ → REALS$_\perp$ also lies inside VALUES. Thus we may say that the type-taxonomy of programs is mirrored by a mathematical taxonomy of the 'subdomains' of a domain of values. These remarks only touch upon the rich subject of type-disciplines (Mitchell, 1990), but we have shown that the mathematical framework reflects the computational intuition of types.

Further concepts We cannot treat properly all the computing notions reflected in domain theory, but should mention a few more.

First, some programming languages involve non-determinism, either explicitly by allowing the programmer to choose one of several execution paths at random, or implicitly, e.g. by leaving undefined the order of evaluation of certain phrases (when the order may affect the outcome). There is a domain construction called the *powerdomain* (Plotkin, 1976) of D, written $\mathcal{P}(D)$, whose elements are *sets* of elements drawn from D. If a procedure takes a real argument x and non-deterministically returns either x or $-x$, we can think of it returning the set $\{x, -x\}$; its meaning therefore lies in the domain REALS$_\perp$ → $\mathcal{P}$(REALS$_\perp$).

Second, domains provide an understanding of the flow of *information* in a computation. This is already suggested by our definition of a continuous function; it turns out that any function which can be programmed, since it lies in a function domain, only needs a finite amount of information about its arguments in order to deliver a finite amount of information about its result. Indeed, to say *how much* information is needed in all cases, and *when* it is needed, is tantamount to defining the function! In fact a domain can be seen as a partial ordering of *amounts of information*, and domain theory can be presented entirely in terms of information flow; domains viewed in this way are called *information systems* (Winskel, 1993).

Third, there is a more subtle point connected with information flow. The elements of a domain which represent finite chunks of information are naturally called *finite*, so what we have seen is that for a finite result you need only compute with finite values. (This is obvious if you are just dealing with numbers, or streams, where the term 'finite' has a familiar meaning. Its meaning is not so familiar when we deal with higher domains.) It also seems to be true, for all computations we can imagine, that even if you are trying to compute an infinite object you can approach this object as close as you like by a succession of finite elements. (Again this is obvious for familiar objects like streams, e.g. the stream of digits in π, but less obvious for higher computational objects like functions.) This property of approximability by finite elements is precisely defined in domain theory, and a domain is said to be *algebraic* if every element has the property. It turns out that all the domains of common interest are algebraic.

Finally, domains have a rich connection with the use of mathematical logic in explaining programming. A well-known method of defining the meaning of a programming language is the so-called *axiomatic method* (Hoare, 1969); a logic is defined in which one can infer sentences of the form $\{P\}A\{Q\}$, where P and Q are logical formulae expressing properties of program variables, while A is a piece of program. The sentence means 'if A is executed with P initially true, then Q will be true when and if the execution is complete'. These *program logics*, as they are called, have special inference rules, and the soundness of these rules can be established by domain theory. A second, more intrinsic, rôle for logic in domains arises from the information flow discussed above; if the quanta of information flowing from argument to result (of a function) are thought of as logical propositions, then the laws of flow can be understood as logical entailments. This leads to yet another presentation of domain theory, known as *domains in logical form* (Abramsky, 1991).

13.5.3 Sequentiality

I shall now discuss an important concept which has been exposed with the help of domain theory, but which may well go beyond that theory.

The reader may not be surprised to learn that, in general, many of the elements in a function domain $D \to E$ are not expressible as the 'meaning' of a procedure in any programming language. It is well-known that there are just too many (too large an infinity of) functions, if D or E is infinite. But if D and E are both *finite*, we may naturally think that every one of the functions in $D \to E$ can be computed by some procedure. It may seem that the only necessary constraint is monotonicity, which we have already imposed.

But this is not so! To see why, let BOOLS be the set $\{t, f\}$, the truth-values, and consider the domain $\text{BOOLS}_\perp = \{t, f, \perp\}$. Here is a simple procedure to calculate the 'or' $a \lor b$ of two truth values:

```
PROCEDURE or(a:BOOL, b:BOOL):BOOL
    IF a THEN RESULT = true
    ELSE RESULT = b
END PROCEDURE
```

Because $\text{BOOLS}_\perp$ contains $\perp$, this procedure may express one of several functions in the domain $\text{BOOLS}_\perp \times \text{BOOLS}_\perp \to \text{BOOLS}_\perp$, all giving the usual values when both arguments are defined. Here are three of them, with their differences underlined:

$a \lor_1 b$	$b = t$	$b = f$	$b = \perp$
$a = t$	t	t	$\perp$
$a = f$	t	f	$\perp$
$a = \perp$	$\perp$	$\perp$	$\perp$

$a \lor_2 b$	$b = t$	$b = f$	$b = \perp$
$a = t$	t	t	$\underline{t}$
$a = f$	t	f	$\perp$
$a = \perp$	$\perp$	$\perp$	$\perp$

$a \lor_3 b$	$b = t$	$b = f$	$b = \perp$
$a = t$	t	t	$\underline{t}$
$a = f$	t	f	$\perp$
$a = \perp$	$\underline{t}$	$\perp$	$\perp$

The first function, $\lor_1$, gives $\perp$ if either of its arguments is $\perp$; this is the one expressed by our procedure, if the rule of evaluation requires that both arguments of any procedure-call $\text{or}(\cdots, \cdots)$ must always be evaluated. But some procedure-call disciplines require an argument to be evaluated only when needed in the execution of the procedure body; in that case our procedure expresses the second function $\lor_2$ because it needs b only when $a = f$, not when $a = t$. Note that $\lor_2$ is not symmetric. The third function $\lor_3$ is symmetric (like $\lor_1$), and has been called the 'parallel-or' function.

Thinking in terms of information flow, $\lor_1$ delivers a quantum of information only when *both* arguments deliver one, while $\lor_3$ delivers the quantum t if *either* argument delivers this quantum. How could any procedure $\text{or}(a,b)$ be written to behave in this way? It must somehow evaluate both its arguments *in parallel* – hence the nickname 'parallel-

or' – since it has no means of knowing which argument may provide
a quantum, or of stopping when the first quantum arrives (ignoring or
aborting the possibly looping evaluation of the other argument).

In fact no conventional programming language such as Fortran, Algol,
Cobol, Lisp or C provides control features with this power. This is
not a vague statement; once the evaluation rules of these languages
are formally given (as they can be) then one can prove the foregoing
assertion. Loosely speaking, the evaluation-discipline of these languages
is inherently *sequential*.

When this was first observed, it seemed that using domain theory
one should be able to define the notion of *sequential function* mathematically; one could then exclude the non-sequential functions from any
function domain $D \to E$, and finally claim that domain theory corresponds perfectly to the evaluation mechanisms of a well defined class of
languages – the sequential ones. Large steps have been made in this direction. The so-called *stable* functions (Berry, 1978) are a restricted class
of the continuous functions which excludes the 'parallel-or' function, but
includes all functions definable by ordinary programs; unfortunately it
also includes some which are intuitively non-sequential! On the other
hand there is an elegant notion of *sequential algorithm* (Berry & Curien,
1982), more abstract than a program but less abstract than a function.
These ideas apparently converge upon the elusive notion of 'sequential
function', but they have still not isolated it.

Results have recently been obtained which suggest that, to explain
sequentiality properly, one has to deal with ideas not intrinsic to domain
theory. An intuition for this can be expressed as follows. Think of the
result $z = f(x, y, \ldots)$ of a function being computed in 'demand mode';
that is, if the caller demands more information about z, then f will
supply it – if necessary by in turn making demands upon one or more of
its arguments $x, y, \ldots$. Several kinds of event occur repeatedly, in some
order: The caller may ask f for a quantum of the result z; f may ask
any of its arguments $x, y, \ldots$ for a quantum; f may receive a quantum
from an argument; f may deliver a quantum to the caller. Then we may
say loosely that f is operating *sequentially* if whenever it has requested
a quantum from some argument, say x, it will remain idle until that
quantum arrives; in particular, it will not request any quantum from
another argument.

This is, of course, a very mechanical explanation; the aim of theoretical
research in this area is to find concepts of information flow which underlie
such mechanical disciplines. Recently, it has been observed that this

sequential discipline is highly significant in *game theory*, and in terms of that theory a new approach to understanding sequentiality (Abramsky *et al.*, 1994; Hyland & Ong, 1994) has been found. While it is too early to judge with certainty, a mathematically convincing account of sequentiality does appear to be emerging.

13.5.4 Summary

My brief survey of semantic ideas for sequential programming is now complete. I spent some time on the idea of sequentiality itself; it is a prime example of an idea which is intrinsic to computing, or to information flow, and which was analysed nowhere in mathematics or logic before computers and their languages forced us to study computation in its own right. The difficulty in isolating sequentiality as a concept has surprised most people who work in semantics; this leads them to expect the emergence of further deep insights into the structure of information flow.

Sequentiality is a pivotal idea, for its understanding will contribute also to the understanding of *parallel* computation; it will help us to describe more clearly what is *lacking* in sequential programming languages, preventing them from expressing a whole class of parallel computations exemplified by the 'parallel-or' function. We now turn to parallel processes.

13.6 Interaction and Processes

With the advent of multiprocessing and computer networks, computer science could no longer comfortably confine itself to the building and understanding of single computers and single programs. This is a formidable activity, but it must be carried on now in the context of the broader field of computing systems – and indeed systems with non-computer (even human) components. Terms such as 'computer', 'program', 'algorithm' and 'function' will be less dominant, beside new terms such as 'system', 'information', 'interaction' and 'process'. All the same, it will be fatal to have one set of concepts for the lower (older) level, and one for the upper (newer) level; we have to expand our ideas and theories, not just increase their number.

In this section I shall try to view these levels, at least for the purpose of discussion, as instances of one kind of structure which I shall call a *communicating system*. We call the behaviour of such a system a

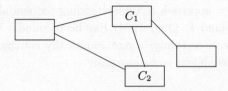

Fig. 13.3. The structural diagram of a system

process, and we shall limit ourselves to *discrete* processes – those whose behaviour is made up of atomic (not continuous) changes of state.

When we build or study a communicating system, we often draw a diagram such as Figure 13.3 to show how it is composed of subsystems such as C_1 and C_2. If we know what happens on the arcs of such a graph, i.e. we know the way in which the components react one with another, then we can build an understanding of the system from an understanding of its components (the nodes). Indeed, such a diagram remains vacuous until we make precise what kind of traffic occurs between components; the nature of this traffic determines the concepts which shape our understanding of a whole system.

We shall now explore a variety of computational models which differ in a fundamental way just because their concepts of traffic between components differ. We shall begin with the *functional* model, which has already been powerfully exploited in understanding programming languages; this topic was explored in section 13.5. In this way we see that the functional model, and the languages based upon it, represents an especially disciplined form of interaction in a hierarchical system. We may then contrast it with models which pay increasing attention to the autonomy of the separate components and their concurrent activity.

13.6.1 The functional model

Let us begin by assuming that a computer program starts by reading in some arguments and finishes by yielding a result, remaining obediently silent in between. This is the situation which we modelled in the previous section. Our model was abstract; we represented a program as a mathematical function, which captures just the external behaviour of a program but says nothing about how it is constructed, nor how it behaves during execution.

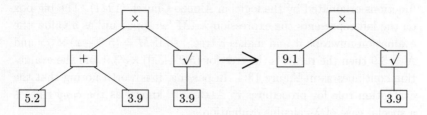

Fig. 13.4. Evaluating an expression

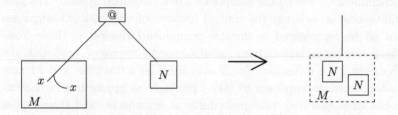

Fig. 13.5. The λ-calculus evaluation rule: $(\lambda x.M[x])@N \longrightarrow M[N]$

But a program does behave in a precise manner, and it serves our purpose to consider it as a communicating system with a certain discipline for traffic between its components. At its very simplest, a program is like an automated desk calculator evaluating complex expressions. We think of the system diagram as a tree, each node as an operator, and the traffic consists of the passage of values – representing completed evaluations – along arcs. A step of evaluation is shown in Figure 13.4.

Though it is hardly apparent from this simple example, highly complex programs can be treated as functions evaluated in this way. An important feature of the functional model – many would call it the essence of the model – allows the very values computed by components to be *themselves* programs, understood as functions. A (still simple) example is the procedure which, for any argument x, will evaluate the expression $(5.2 + x) \times \sqrt{x}$. In λ-notation, which we touched upon earlier, the function computed by this procedure is written $\lambda x.\,(5.2+x) \times \sqrt{x}$. Now, using an operator @ which applies a function to an argument, we can represent procedure-call as an evaluation step as shown in Figure 13.5, where $M[N]$ means that N is substituted for x in M. This is in fact a picture of the single evaluation rule of the λ-*calculus*, the calculus of

functions originated by the logician Alonzo Church (1941). The big box
on the left represents the expression $\lambda x.M$ 'wrapped up' as a value; the
evaluation unwraps it and makes a tree – so if $M = (5.2 + x) \times \sqrt{x}$ and
$N = 3.9$ then the result is the tree for $(5.2 + 3.9) \times \sqrt{3.9}$ and the evaluation continues as in Figure 13.4. In passing, it is worth noting that the
evaluation rule for procedures in ALGOL60, known as the *copy rule*, is
a special case of λ-calculus evaluation.

Just as we saw that any program or procedure (in a conventional language) can be represented as a value in a domain, so we can represent the
evaluation of programs and procedures by this hierarchical discipline of
communication among the components of a (tree-like) system. The generality here is striking; the control features of conventional languages
can *all* be represented as suitable components (nodes) in these trees.
The power comes largely from the *higher-order* nature of λ-calculus; the
argument x for a function $\lambda x.M$ may itself be a function, and M may
contain function applications (@) – precisely as procedures in conventional languages may take procedures as arguments, and their bodies
may contain procedure-calls. This challenge to understand programming languages has greatly deepened the study of the λ-calculus in the
last two decades (Barendregt, 1984).

The simple hierarchic discipline of interaction which I have described
allows very little autonomy for its components; we now proceed to develop it and to increase the autonomy.

13.6.2 The stream model

It may strike the reader that the components, or operators, in our evaluation trees could perform a more interesting rôle, suggested by the
information flow which we discussed in section 13.5. We may think of
such a tree operating in demand mode; in response to a request for a
quantum from its parent node, each node may respond or may trans-
mit requests to one of more of its children. Though still arranged in a
hierarchy, the components are now interacting more subtly; indeed, the
distinction between sequential and non-sequential computation can be
analysed in terms of the tree structure.

If we relax the hierarchy by allowing arbitrary – even cyclic – connectivity among components, we arrive at the *stream model* (Kahn,
1974; Broy, 1987). This is a model of the well-known interaction
discipline known as *pipelining*; each arc in a system diagram has an
orientation, and is interpreted as a *pipeline*, along which a stream of

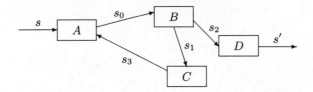

Fig. 13.6. A typical pipeline system

data (quanta) can flow. Moreover, such systems are truly heterarchic, or distributed; no single component maintains central control. A typical system is shown in Figure 13.6. Now let us imagine that a quantum of information is an integer. The total history of the system's behaviour is characterized by the stream of quanta which flow along each of its arcs. But each stream is a finite or infinite sequence of integers, which as we saw in section 13.5 is just an element of the domain

$$\text{STREAMS} = (\text{INTEGERS} \times \text{STREAMS})_\perp .$$

A common situation is that each component (node) behaves as a continuous function over STREAMS. In that case, it can be shown that the whole system also behaves as such a function. To find this function, we first write down equations which all the streams satisfy; in this case they are

$$s_0 = A(s, s_3), \quad s_1 = B_1(s_0), \quad s_2 = B_2(s_0),$$
$$s_3 = C(s_1), \quad s' = D(s_2) .$$

Eliminating s_1, s_2, s_3 yields $s' = D(B_2(s_0))$ where $s_0 = A(s, C(B_1(s_0)))$. The latter equation expresses s_0 in terms of itself and the given s. Domain theory ensures that this 'recursive' equation has a solution for s_0; moreover, there is a solution which is *least*, in terms of the information ordering $\sqsubseteq$. Moreover, this solution agrees exactly with what is expected from an operational description of stream computations; this agreement provides another justification of the theory.

The stream model not only is mathematically pleasant, but also is realistic for systems in which communication occurs only via 'pipelines'; as this term suggests, this kind of information flow is by no means restricted to computers. The model has stimulated much study, aiming at a more general model. For example, if the behaviour of any node is critically dependent upon which of its input streams supplies quanta more quickly, then the situation is much more delicate. It is also natural to examine the case in which the data structure connecting two nodes

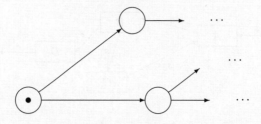

Fig. 13.7. A transition diagram

(i.e. the 'traffic' structure) is other than a sequence. This has given rise to the study of *concrete domains* (Kahn & Plotkin, 1993), which contributed to the growing understanding of sequentiality discussed in section 13.5.

The stream model and its variants are appropriate whenever systems are loosely connected, in the sense that an event at one node need never be synchronized with an event elsewhere.

13.6.3 The reactive model

Let us now contrast the functional and stream disciplines of communication with a more intimate one, where an arc between two components represents their contiguity. Contiguity is a physical concept; a wooden block is contiguous with the table on which it rests, so a movement of the table is immediately felt by the block. But contiguity makes sense with respect to information too. If neighbouring components are a human and a workstation, then the pressing of a key on the keyboard is simultaneously sensed by the human and by the workstation; one can say that they *change state* simultaneously.

One of the earliest ways to model change of state was the basis of *automata theory*, developed mainly in the 50s. The theory made use of *state transition diagrams* such as in Figure 13.7. In these diagrams each circle represents a state, and each arc (arrow) represents a possible transition between states. In the diagram, there are two *alternative* transitions from the left-hand state, and the token • indicates that the left-hand state is the *currently holding* state.

In the early 60s, Carl-Adam Petri (1962) pointed out that automata theory (as it was then) cannot represent the *synchronized* change of state in two contiguous systems. His idea for repairing this weakness is

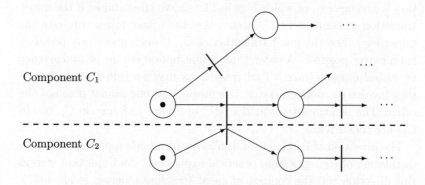

Fig. 13.8. A Petri net, or diagram of shared transitions

simple but far-reaching; it allows transitions which are *shared* between separate components of a system. Suppose that Figure 13.7 represents the possible transitions for component C_1, and we want to indicate that the lower transition of C_1 may not occur independently, but must coincide with a certain transition in component C_2. This would appear as in Figure 13.8. The tokens represent the *concurrent holding* of two states, one in C_1 and one in C_2, and transitions are drawn no longer as arcs but as another kind of node (here a bar); thus a shared transition typically has more than one ingoing (and more than one outgoing) arc, representing *how* it is shared.

This apparently mild development has opened a new and complex world. In this new interpretation the traffic upon the arc between C_1 and C_2 is no longer merely the passage of the result of a (functional) computation by C_1 as an argument to C_2, as it was in the stream model. Behaviour can no longer be expressed just in terms of arguments and results; C_1 in its behaviour requires (or suffers) repeated interaction with its neighbours. The transition shared across the dotted line in the diagram is just one of these interactions.

The behaviour of such communicating systems has been extensively analysed in terms of a handful of important concepts. The most obvious of these is *non-determinism*, or *conflict*. This is present already in Figure 13.7, where either but not both of the two possible transitions takes place. It is unrealistic to expect rules and details (e.g. priorities, timing) to be included in a system model which will determine its behaviour completely.

Allied to non-determinism are other important notions. One such notion is *preemption*, of which Figure 13.8 shows an example; if the upper transition in component C_1 occurs (i.e. the upper token traverses the upper bar) then the lower transition of C_1, though previously possible, is no longer possible. A second important notion is that of *concurrency* or *causal independence*. Two transitions may be called concurrent if they involve no common states; this means that one cannot preempt the other. The two transitions at the right of Figure 13.8 (one in C_1, one in C_2) are concurrent.

The invention of Petri nets and subsequent models represents the slow distillation of concepts from practical experience. An important step in this direction was the concept of *event structure* (Nielsen *et al.*, 1981). In a Petri net each pair of transitions is either *in conflict*, or *concurrent*, or *in causal dependence*; an event structure consists of a relational structure in which these three binary relations satisfy certain axioms. Event structures are somewhat more abstract than Petri nets; the study of stronger or weaker axioms for event structures has contributed to the development of the concept of process.

13.6.4 Process constructions

Much analysis of practical systems has been done using the ideas which we have mentioned. However, when we leave the stream model we are no longer dealing with mathematical functions. We are dealing with operational or behavioural properties of computational processes, but we have no agreed *concept of process* at the same level of abstraction as mathematical functions, nor a *calculus of processes* as canonical as is the λ-calculus for functions. Several steps have been taken in this direction, but the study is far from complete.

An important step was to notice the striking coincidence between a (simple) notion of process and the mathematical idea of a *non-well-founded set* (Aczel, 1988). In mathematical set theory, sets are traditionally well-founded; this excludes, for example, a set S which satisfies a recursive equation such as

$$S = \{a, b, S\}.$$

If S satisfies this equation, then it can be depicted as in Figure 13.9, where the nodes are elements (which may be sets) and an arrow $S_1 \longrightarrow S_2$ means that S_1 contains S_2 as a member – i.e. $S_2 \in S_1$. This 'set' might be written $S = \{a, b, \{a, b, \{a, b, \ldots\}\}\}$; but most of us have been

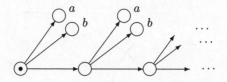

Fig. 13.9. A process which is a non-well-founded set.

so thoroughly 'well-founded' by our education that we think it is cheating to allow it as a solution to the equation, because it has an infinite containment chain $\ldots \in S \in S$. Why are we so suspicious? It is perhaps because we are biassed towards static notions; we think of a set almost as a box *containing* its elements – and of course boxes can't nest infinitely! But think of an arrow representing *procession* rather than containment; think of S as proceeding (non-deterministically) either to the terminal state a, or to the terminal state b, or to a state in which it has exactly those three alternatives again. We may say that a process is constructed from its possible futures, exactly as a set is constructed from its members.

If you object that processes are one thing and sets another, then you may keep them distinct if you wish; but their mathematics has a lot in common. The topic of discrete processes is of growing importance; children in the first decades of the twenty-first century may become as familiar with the mathematics of processes – complete with infinite procession! – as we are with sets. In this way computer science even makes some contribution to the foundations of mathematics.

We shall now look at some other constructions of processes. We may not know what processes *are*, abstractly, but we do know ways of combining them. It is typical in mathematics that the objects of study are nothing by themselves; it is the operations upon them, and the mathematical behaviour of those operations, which give them status. This is the attitude which gave birth to *process algebra* in the late 70s; if we can (with the benefit of practical experience) find some small distinguished class of operations by which interacting systems are built, then to agree upon the algebraic properties of these operations is a necessary step towards the concept of process.

In seeking such operations we may follow the paradigm of the calculus of functions (the λ-calculus), but we must be wary. Consider first the familiar operation of *function application*, @; if M and N are functional objects, then $M@N$ stands for the application of M as a function to the

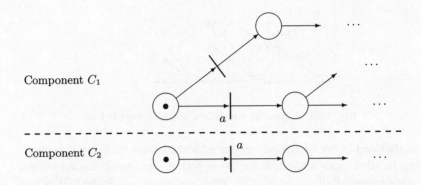

Fig. 13.10. Two components of an interactive system before assembly

argument N. We may look for an analogue of application over processes.
But note that application is non-commutative; $M@N$ is quite different
from $N@M$.

By contrast, if the arcs of Figure 13.3 are to be interpreted as interaction, which is a *symmetric* concept, then the operation of composing
two systems – by connecting them to allow interaction – must be a commutative one. We find a clue to the nature of process composition if
we first separate out the two components from which Figure 13.8 was
formed, as shown in Figure 13.10. Notice that the separate transitions in
C_1 and C_2 are labelled. In Hoare's process algebra CSP and other process algebras (Hoare, 1985; Milner, 1989; Baeten and Weijland, 1990),
this labelling dictates where the interactions will occur when we combine C_1 and C_2 by *parallel composition*, $C_1 \parallel C_2$. (This operation is
indeed commutative, and also associative.) The result is not quite the
system of Figure 13.8, because if we further combine with C_3, forming
$C_1 \parallel C_2 \parallel C_3$, then C_3 may also be able to take part in the transition
a. If we wish this transition to be shared only between C_1 and C_2,
we must write $(C_1 \parallel C_2)\backslash a$. The unary operation $\backslash a$, called *hiding* in
CSP, has this localizing effect; it is really just a local declaration of (the
name of) a transition. (In passing, this is another example of something
distilled from programming practice into a theory: every programmer
knows about local variable declarations.)

These two operations, composition and hiding, give us some idea of
what process algebra is. Through the 80s there has been considerable
progress in using algebra to express and analyse communicating systems,
and considerable theoretical development of the algebra. Full agreement

on the algebraic operations has not been reached, but enough to indicate a consensus of understanding.

It is central to the argument of this essay that process algebra is not the application of an *already known* abstract concept to the study of computation. The real situation is more untidy, and far more exciting. The algebraic method acts as a guide along the difficult path towards *discovering* an abstract notion of process which matches the way we construct discrete systems, or which helps us to analyse existing systems. This discovery is occurring incrementally, via definition and experiment, not all at once.

13.6.5 Mobility

When do we have enough operations for constructing processes? That is, when can we claim that we truly know what kind of thing a discrete process is, because we know all the operations by which it can be constructed? This may never occur with certainty; but our algebraic experiments can give evidence that we *lack* enough operations, for example if they do not allow the construction of systems with some desirable property. This has indeed occurred with the property of *mobility*, as we now show.

If we are content to model the behaviour of a concrete interactive system, whose processors are linked in a fixed topology, then we expect the shape of the system graph (Figure 13.3) to remain fixed throughout time. Many communicating systems – software as well as hardware – have a fixed connectivity.

We have already seen one model where the connectivity is flexible – the λ-calculus. It also turns out that the various process algebras explored during the 80s all admit a controlled kind of mobility; they allow that an agent may divide itself into a collection of subagents which are interconnected, or may destroy itself. These capabilities have made it possible to build theoretical models for many real concurrent programming languages, as well as to analyse distributed systems and communication protocols.

But something is lacking in this degree of mobility; it does not allow *new* links to be formed between *existing* agents. This simple capability is, in fact, crucial to the way in which we think about many systems of widely differing kinds. Consider a multiprocessing system supporting a parallel programming language; if we model the implementation, we have to consider the mechanism by which procedures of the (parallel) program

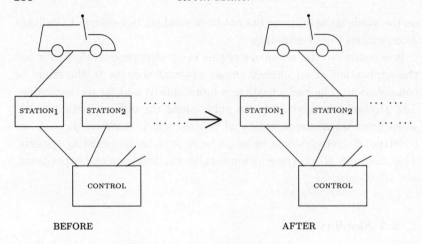

Fig. 13.11. A mobile telephone network

are relocated upon different processors, to achieve load balancing. If we represent both the procedures of the program and the processors of the machine as agents in the model, then relocation of procedures is an instance of mobility among agents. As a second example, consider the resources allocated by an operating system to different jobs; this allocation varies dynamically, and is naturally modelled by the creation and destruction of links. Third, consider the cars of a mobile telephone network; as a car moves about the country it will establish (by change of frequency) connection with different base stations at different times. This is shown in Figure 13.11.

These examples suggest that dynamic reconfiguration is a common feature of communicating systems, both inside and outside the computer. The notion of a *link*, not as a fixed part of the system but as a datum which it can manipulate, is essential to the understanding of such systems. Indeed, we need the notion at the very basic level of programming, when we consider data structures themselves. If a data structure is mutable (and most realistic programs deal with at least some mutable data) then we may consider it to be a process with which the program interacts. This makes particularly good sense if it is a structure which is shared among subprograms running in parallel. An instance of dynamic reconfiguration occurs when one subprogram sends the *address* of a mutable data structure to another subprogram.

We then naturally ask: Is there a common notion of link which subsumes *pointers*, *references*, *channels*, *variables* (in the programming

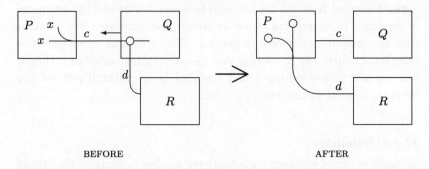

BEFORE   AFTER

Fig. 13.12. The π-calculus interaction $cx.P[x] \parallel \bar{c}d.Q \longrightarrow P[d] \parallel Q$

sense), *locations*, *names*, *addresses*, *access rights*, ..., and is it possible to take this notion as basic in a computational model? To put it another way: What is the mathematics of linkage?

In searching for this, it is quite reasonable to look first for a *calculus* which treats linkage and mobility as basic, in much the same way as the λ-calculus treats function application as basic. For the λ-calculus was invented and put to considerable use before it was understood in terms of abstract functional models such as domain theory. A recent calculus for mobile processes is the π-*calculus* (Milner *et al.*, 1992); it is in some ways more primitive than the λ-calculus (which can indeed be embedded in it), and takes interaction at a link as its *only* basic action. This is not the place to give its details, but some idea of it is given by the diagram in Figure 13.12. To understand the diagram, let us compare its constructions with those of the λ-calculus and its evaluation mechanism, as shown in Figure 13.5. In the λ-calculus, the *function* $\lambda x.M[x]$ can receive any argument N and then compute $M[N]$; in the π-calculus, the *process* $cx.P[x]$ can receive along the channel c any channel d, and then proceed as the process $P[d]$. The π-calculus also has the process $\bar{c}d.Q$, which sends the channel d along the channel c and then proceeds as Q. Finally, in place of the application @ of a function to an argument, the π-calculus (like CSP) has parallel composition $\parallel$ of two processes. We may now compare *evaluation* in λ-calculus with *interaction* in π-calculus; in Figure 13.5 the agent N is moved into the places held in M by the variable x, while in Figure 13.12 it is not the agent R but a *link* d to R which moves; it travels along a link c and occupies the places held by x in P.

This calculus is simple, and it directly models a number of phenomena. The three examples discussed earlier – including the mobile telephone network – yield to it, and it has also been used to model the exchange of messages in concurrent object-oriented programming. The calculus thus appears to be sufficiently general; if its technical development is satisfactory (here the λ-calculus provides a valuable paradigm), then it will provide strong evidence that mobility is an essential part of any eventual concept of process.

13.6.6 Summary

We have explored different computational models in terms of the idea of interaction; emphasis is placed upon concurrent processes, since interaction presupposes the co-existence of active partners. In the previous section, we found that the domain model can be understood in terms of amounts of information, and also that *sequential* computation corresponds to a special discipline imposed upon the flow of information. In the present section, we have found that a key to understanding *concurrent* or interactive computation lies in the structure of this information flow, i.e. in the mode of interaction among system components; this attains even greater importance in the case of mobile systems where the linkage does not remain fixed, a case which arises naturally both in computer systems and in the world at large.

There is no firm agreement yet on the properties which an *abstract* concept of concurrent process should possess. I hope to have shown that we may advance towards the concept by distillation from practice, via models which are somewhat *concrete* and *formal*, but nonetheless mathematical. The formalisms of computer science are not only important as a vehicle for rigorous description and verification of systems; they are also a means for arriving at a conceptual frame for the subject.

13.7 Conclusion

At the beginning of this essay I argued that the science of computing is emerging from an interaction between mathematics, especially logic, and practical experience of system engineering. I discussed the difficulties experienced in software maintenance, a branch of system engineering which clearly illustrates the need for formality and conceptual clarity in software design. I stepped from there into the realm of software itself, i.e. the programming languages in which software is written; the remainder of the essay has been devoted to explaining concepts which underlie software, since these are at the core of the emerging science.

Before concluding this discussion of concepts, let us put them into perspective. In July 1994, the British press reported yet another fiasco in computer system engineering; a failed design for a system for the Department of Social Security, which may cost the tax-payer fifty million pounds. Software engineers are likely to blame the failure on mis-application of the *software development process*, the managerial and technical procedures by which the specification of software is elicited and its manufacture conducted. They will be wrong to lay the blame wholly at this door; this would be to presume that software is, like water, a commodity which certainly demands a high standard of engineering and management, but which is well understood in itself. I hope to have shown in the preceding two sections how ill founded this presumption is. I believe that advances in software science will change the very nature of software engineering processes; the obsolescence of reverse engineering (discussed in section 13.3) will be one example.

Throughout the essay I have discussed semantical concepts with some degree of informality. In some cases, particularly in section 13.6, the informality is *necessary* because the concepts themselves have not yet been fully distilled from practice; this is particularly true of the concept of process. In other cases there is a well developed theory (e.g. domain theory), and the informality is *possible* because the concepts are intuitively compelling, in the same way that the notion of force in mechanics is compelling. It is a test of the scientific maturity of a discipline that its conceptual framework is robust enough to allow precise but informal communication of ideas. On this criterion, computer science has made strong progress, but has much further to go.

In the introduction two other criteria of scientific maturity were mentioned: broad application, and a well knit body of ideas. I have shown that these two criteria are being met, not separately, but by two trends which are closely linked. First, the field of application of computer science has enlarged from the study of single computers and single programs to the far broader arena of communicating systems; so increasingly the field is concerned with the flow of information. To match this, we have seen in sections 13.5 and 13.6 above a progression in the way computation theories are presented, leading from the notions of *value, evaluation* and *function* towards notions of *link, interaction* and *process*. Thus both applications and theories converge upon the phenomena of information flow; in my view this indicates a new scientific identity.

14
Computers and Communications

R.M. Needham

Progress in the computer and communication industries has run in parallel for a great many years, and convergence or even unity has often been predicted. Do they not, after all, both use digital circuits and the associated logic? The present chapter seeks to investigate why the convergence has not happened, and to look into the future.

The earliest contacts, at any rate in the civil sphere, were in some sense casual. Data transmission, as the subject was known, was not in any way regarded as an integral part of computing but rather as an added facility that one was well advised to have some understanding of – rather like air-conditioning.

14.1 Early Contacts

What started to bring the two activities into more serious contact was the development of time-sharing systems. As soon as it was demonstrated that these systems were very valuable means to improve the human convenience of using computers it was obviously necessary to connect terminals in considerable numbers. At first these tended to be in the same buildings as the computers they served, and the physical connections were wholly under the control of the computer people. There was not much, if any, suitable equipment one could go and buy; accordingly computer engineers learned about transmission, designed multiplexors, and so on. They found it not unfamiliar, and not too difficult. Before long, however, it became necessary to communicate off site, or off campus. This revealed that in most if not all countries there were legal restrictions on who could provide telecommunication facilities outside a single site. The rules varied. Maybe it was a matter of crossing a highway, or of going to land in different ownership. But usually one had to use the facilities offered by a monopoly provider who was firmly of the belief that it knew what was right for the customer, it was better informed about what the customer needed as against what he thought he wanted, and anyway it was going to decide what the customer got and when. The final point was important. Telecommunication administrations were not accustomed to moving fast, and this was a great contrast to the computer industry which, then as now, behaved as if yesterday were too late for whatever people needed.

The ensuing difficulties were not the same in every country, but were in one form or another almost universal. The frustration experienced, in particular, by companies setting up time-sharing bureaux were extreme and led in the UK to some level of political agitation. A particular feature was that discussions or negotiations between providers and consumers, or rather would-be consumers, were difficult and characterised by mutual incomprehension. An example is the way the UK Post Office discouraged the use of acoustic modems for remote access to computers. It was never at all clear to the writer what the problem was. The Post Office had a duty to carry sounds round the country and it was no business of theirs how the sounds were made or what they were used for. A possible concern may have been that the Post Office were used to providing and indeed owning everything used for communication except the people talking, and thus had complete responsibility for the quality of service rendered. Failure to communicate properly between a portable terminal and the host computer would be a mixed responsibility between the vendor of the acoustic modem and the provider of the wires, and this was an untidy situation that the provider of the wires did not like at all.

While these battles were being fought an entirely new set of developments occurred. It was clear that there was scope for much more general interconnection of computers than simple terminal links. The invention of packet-switching and the very far-sighted development in the USA of the Arpanet showed the way to computer networks in the modern sense. It needed the money and power of the US Government, and it was revolutionary. It also led to the development of a great deal of expertise in this style of communication in the advanced computing community, quite separately from anything the communication industry did. This is not surprising, for packet-switching is a way of multiplexing trunk lines for data that is quite irrelevant to the carriage of voice. Voice cannot stand jitter (variance in transit time) to any noticeable extent. Data, at any rate as conceived at that time, was more or less immune to it. The response of computers at the far end was sufficiently slow and variable that jitter in the network was neither here nor there, at any rate for the present polemical purpose.

At about the same time the communications industry was making computer-managed telephone exchanges. This was an immensely challenging and difficult job of real-time computing and raised, not for the first time, the possibility that the two industries had so much in common that they would become very close. This seems not to have happened. Anecdotal evidence from many sources suggests that the structuring techniques developed in computing to improve the reliability and comprehensibility of large programs were (and may even continue to be) very slow to be applied in a circumstance to which they seem to be ideally suited. It appears that it is so unusual to make any sort of clean start in switching office software that there are great obstacles to major methodological changes.

14.2 Local Area Networks

Local area networks were an advance of the mid-70s. A serious initial motivation was to make it possible for a number of relatively cheap computers to share exotic or relatively expensive peripherals. It is important to remember this, because the development of contemporary distributed computing, still based largely on 10 Mb/s infrastructure, did in fact come later and was not the initial motivation for LAN development. In fact the data rates at which LANs worked were determined as much by what was natural to the technology employed as by any considerations of bandwidth requirements. Various numbers emerged, all in the multiple megabit range, and this attracted unfavourable comment from the communications industry which thought that it was grossly excessive and wasteful. The fact that the higher date rates did not cost anything seemed to escape them; the fact that even if lower data rates had been sufficient the communications industry did not have suitable products available certainly did not escape the computer people.

At that time a whole variety of network types were put forward, differing in topology. The main contenders were rings, stars, and line segments. Line segments eventually won, in the shape of the well-known 10 megabit Ethernet, but for a considerable time the controversy raged with the peculiar intensity which occurs when engineering disputes and questions of commercial interest coincide. The matter in question is important; reliability, ease of maintenance, ease of management are all significant topics and the various approaches do indeed differ in these regards. The topology debate, however, obscured an issue that from today's perspective seems to be more fundamental.

How should one think of a local area network? One view is that it is a microcosm of the wide area network and should be treated as such. In the extreme version of this view, the fact that the LAN tends to work faster is epiphenomenal and not to be relied on. The other view is that it is a system bus writ large, to be treated in the same way as the backplane of a computer. Its behaviour is as intrinsic to the behaviour of a distributed system as the behaviour of a bus is intrinsic to the behaviour of a computer.

The reason these distinctions matter is that they give one totally different views about errors. In wide area networks of the time, transmission rates were low and error rates were high. It is only a slight exaggeration to say that it was something of an achievement to get large quantities of data through correctly at all, and protocol design was heavily concerned with control of error and disorder, retransmission strategies, and so forth. The families of protocols used for ethernets came from that stable, because their architects did. It seemed natural to stay within the tradition, which did indeed have appropriate elements when communication was between stations on different Ethernets connected by a wide area system. It also was appropriate since ethernet was not, by design, intended to be a highly reliable medium. This remark is not intended to be critical; it reflects the designers' intentions.

By contrast some other networks were designed with high reliability in mind. To speak of one with which the writer had a close connection, the 10 Mb/s Cambridge Ring was designed to test itself continuously when otherwise idle, to check the parity of every 38-bit cell at every station it passed rather than only at the destination, and to make it easy to locate faulty equipment by central monitoring. The net result was that bit errors were very unusual. They were measured at a rate of 1 in 10^{11}, a very low rate indeed in the days of copper communication. The combination of this observation with the fact, regretted at the time, that Cambridge Rings were typically not connected to the outside world, led to a very different approach to their use. They were used like buses.

The relevant characteristic of a bus is that it is expected not to make errors, and if it does it is not considered very important that a system will degrade gracefully or recover automatically. Most computers do not behave in a particularly helpful manner if they have bus errors. To make the point about style of use, we may consider an approach taken in Cambridge to the matter of archiving the file store for an experimental computer. The file store lived on a 28 Mbyte disc, then considered substantial, and the way it was archived was to copy it to another similar disc across the ring. This should be done as fast as possible, and the job was done by copying all of the disc contents to the other drive, followed by a single checksum. The entire operation would be repeated from the beginning if the checksum failed. There was no provision for identifying a failed packet or cell, so restart was the only option. It never happened, and performance was excellent. This approach permeated the way in which that network was used. A file server was constructed in the late seventies which has as its fundamental read protocol a message 'give me b bytes of file f starting at file offset a' and these would be returned without intermediate acknowledgement or any kind of flow control. If the recipient could not receive and process the material at the rate the file server sent it, then the request should not have been made. A complementary approach was used for writing to the file server.

The protocol stacks used in most local distributed systems did not, and do not, take advantage of the characteristics of local networks, and this is why it is relatively recently that computers have been able to exploit the full bandwidth of even 10 Mb/s communications. All the time went in being prepared to control errors and disorders that were not, or should not have been, present. Only recently, as the limits of the media are reached, has it seemed appropriate to look to protocol simplification. One can imagine successful attempts to optimise communications by transparently using simpler protocols locally and more complex ones globally though this is certainly not a fashionable line.

This may seem to be an ancient and worn-out controversy but it has its relevance today, as we shall now see.

14.3 Increasing the Bandwidth

There are two possible reasons for wanting to increase the performance of a network. One is lack of point-to-point bandwidth, and the other is lack of system bandwidth. In an ethernet these are the same, so the difference is not very evident. In a slotted ring, for example, they are very different. The 10 Mb/s Cambridge Ring had a system bandwidth of around 4 Mb/s net of overheads, but a point-to-point bandwidth of only about 1 Mb/s. This meant that it was very much less suitable for the page swapping traffic associated with discless workstations than an ethernet, though its architectural bandwidth sharing meant that it was much more suitable than an ethernet for continuous medium traffic such as digital speech. Discless workstations have also had their effects on ethernets; although 10 Mb/s is a perfectly adequate point-to-point bandwidth for this purpose, enough such workstations quickly exhaust the ethernet's system bandwidth.

As time went on proponents of architecturally shared media such as slotted rings sought to increase point-to-point bandwidth in order to compete, and proponents of ethernets saw a need for more system bandwidth as discless workstations ate up capacity and backbones ran out. This is a chapter on communications and computing, rather than purely on networking, so it is fortunately unnecessary to pursue shifts and expedients such as FDDI.

Continuous media have already been mentioned, and they have led to developments which have been instructive in relation to the computing/communications interface. The requirements of continuous media are twofold. One is that bandwidth demands tend to be substantial. The other is that jitter (variance of delay) can only be tolerated to a very limited extent. The former is sometimes true of pure data communication; the latter very rarely is. Furthermore packet networks are not at all well adapted to jitter avoidance. Large packet sizes reduce overhead, but also cause longer waits for medium access or for the opportunity to exercise priority judgments about use of switches. A homely analogy is that a police car may have total priority at a junction, but if there is a 30 m truck crossing it the car just has to wait.

14.4 ATM Networking

A combination of the various needs just mentioned has led to the present very high level of interest in Asynchronous Transfer Mode (ATM) networking. The characteristic of ATM networks is that communication is based on the transmission of cells of equal (and rather small) size, individually routed. The smallness of the cells (in the international standard 53 bytes including overheads and a 48 byte payload) means that the time that will elapse until a new priority decision can be taken is never very long. At 100 Mb/s it is under 5 μs. The individual routing means that the cells that compose a packet do not have to be kept together. The idea is not new; the slotted Cambridge Ring was an early implementation of the principle, and the advantages for the handling of continuous media were appreciated very soon. Contemporary ATM networks are virtual-circuit-based, so all the cells belonging to a particular logical flow pass through by the same route and disordering does not happen. As bit rates have increased so has the cell size; since the physical transmission rate is constant increasing the bit rate simply makes the bits

shorter and with a fixed cell size the overheads mean that end-to-end
performance is not improved as much as one would wish. Although the
ATM principle is speed-independent the cell size evidently is not. The
53 byte cell will do up to about 1 Gb/s, after which it is likely to be
awkward to take routing decisions fast enough. At that speed there will
be less than 0.5 μs to take and act upon decisions, and that is not much.

Most ATM implementations are switch-based in the sense that the
routing component is an $n \times n$ switch capable of routing an input cell
on any line to any output. Typically space division switches are used,
though there is no need for this; ATM rings of up to 512 Mb/s have been
successfully deployed, and some designs for switches are ring-based internally. The paradigmatic transmission medium is optical fibre although
coaxial cable is still used too for economic reasons.

A main argument for ATM is that it offers an opportunity for a com-
promise between the purely circuit-switched communication characteristic of the telephone industry, which is not good for data, and the packet-
based communication of the computer industry, which is not good for
steady circuits. It is possible to ensure that continuous-media traffic
flows smoothly through an ATM network that allows capacity that is
not, at a particular time, being used to function efficiently for regular
data traffic.

14.5 The Past Revisited

Although now there is little argument about topologies the other aspect
of local net design, the one that was underappreciated before, has come
back into attention. Optical fibre is a very reliable transmission medium,
and the silicon that is found at its ends is very reliable too. We are back
in the position of having to decide whether we are dealing with a network
or a bus, that is to say whether we should expect a system with an ATM
network at its heart to be able to recover gracefully from communication
errors.

A standard comment to make at this point is that transmission errors
are not the only way data gets lost. In switched networks data, in our
case cells, may get lost because of congestion or buffer overflow. Practically all designs for ATM switches have in fact got buffering to deal with
fluctuations in demand for particular output lines; the precise locus of
the buffers is dependent on switch design details. It is possible to design
an ATM switch in such a way that in a properly functioning network
buffer overflow never occurs, though to do so adds some complication to
the design. Is it worth while? The answer presumably is 'If it enables

us to use simple protocols and take the chance that in an extremely rare circumstance there will be an ungraceful failure, then perhaps yes. If the context is such that ungraceful failures, or ones for which recovery even if automatic is ungainly cannot be allowed at all, then perhaps no.'

This is not a topic on which one can give a definitive answer. The reason for discussing it is that it brings us back to the relations between communications and computers. The kind of network under discussion, working in ATM mode at speeds up to 1 Gb/s, will be mainly computer networks. It would be inappropriate to design them in ignorance of the needs and preferences of the people who will program those machines. In particular, if computers are going to use robust protocols anyway, it may be wasteful to put complication into the network to make it very nearly lossless.

This is a suitable time to come back to our earlier theme of the relationships between the computer industry and the communications industry. One could expect that this would now be close. After all the 53 byte ATM standard came from the communications world as a CCITT standard, and was adopted by the computer industry voluntarily. It seems to be the case that both sides are working not merely on analogous things but on the same thing. The convergence would seem to be almost there; but curiously it isn't. Working on the same thing has brought out some of the deep cultural differences between the two activities in a way that remained obscure when subject matter was more different than it is now.

The communications industry is used to regulation; heavy long-term investment; high utilisation of plant; striving for good uniform quality of service. The computer industry is the most unregulated there is; it sees five years hence as infinity; most of the things it sells are heavily underutilised; it depends on maximum speed to market. These differences make for widely divergent cultures. They give impressions of each industry to the other of being quite deplorable. To the computer person the communications industry is ponderous; slow; overcautious; congenitally fussy. To the phone company man the computer industry is anarchic; has a throw-away culture; is wasteful; peddles unreliable trash.

14.6 The Future

Will this position change? Somebody said that it is always difficult to foretell the future, particularly before it happens. My guess is that there will be furious competition between traditional communications companies and computer companies for the equipment market, particularly the equipment market for use inside large enterprises. One may perhaps wonder why, since the value of switches and so forth is likely to fall fast. The reason is that along with a physical network go name servers, file servers, print servers, and other assorted infrastructure. The telephone companies would dearly like to be suppliers of these things as value-added services – and so would the computer companies. We may expect that this competition will be greatly to the advantage of the customer. As the industries compete one may guess that they will become more similar.

The communications industries are realising that they are now deregulated and that they had better keep up with the needs of the market because otherwise their competitors will. Bakers bake bread in pieces of a shape, size, and so forth that their customers are prepared to pay for; phone companies will move bits about at rates and in bundles of sizes that their customers are prepared to pay for. Computer companies are realising that the vast volumes that their products, both hardware and software, are sold in are themselves motivations for the pursuit of quality and reliability. A computer company which it would be unkind to name was once said to have as its motto 'data processing equipment of all descriptions designed and constructed on your own premises'. Today's companies certainly cannot do that, and it costs them a huge amount of money to have to alter something that is installed all over the world. They are feeling some of the pressures that forced the communications companies to fuss so much about uniformity and so forth. Computer hardware, in particular, especially when considered in conjunction with its operating software, is in fact becoming very standardised, as are its environmental demands in terms of distributed services availability.

Perhaps one may hazard a guess that in future there will be three kinds of players in the industry rather than two. There will be communications companies moving bits around. They will not necessarily know what the bits are for, and it may become unusual to charge by the bit for the service. They will be expert at moving bits cheaply with acceptable performance, just as soup companies are expert at using the least possible tomato to make acceptable tomato soup. They will not provide much in the way of value-added services; phone companies have never been very good at that. It is debatable how much of the total of digital communication will be the province of communication companies. Local area networking probably will not be, and there are many questions over radio/infra-red support for mobile computers. Then there will be companies that make the computers that make the bits that have to be moved. They will make very similar looking products which compete on price and performance. General purpose processors will be used for all sorts of purposes that presently often use special hardware; to name a couple that are much associated with communication, they will be used for compression and encryption. The computer companies will probably not be big in value-added services either; though they have perhaps been better at it than phone companies it has never really been in their ethos.

In this scenario one would not expect either the communications companies or the computer companies to be hugely profitable, because their markets would be too competitive and their products too undifferentiated. Bits are bits and additions are additions, and either they are the same or they are wrong. The real adders of value will be the providers of useful services. Access to data, performance of transactions, games, entertainment of various sorts – all of these will generate vast revenues. As a colleague working in that field said recently, video on demand is being done first simply because it is something financiers understand. The real profits will be from much more elaborate applications. No service provider will wish to be in pawn to a single communications company or a single computer company, and they will make sure that they are not.

14.7 Research

These developments will have a considerable influence on research in computer and communications technology. It is possible to guess at some aspects, though attempting to do so is necessarily pretty speculative.

It is commonplace in distributed computing to place emphasis on problems of scale. In due course the developments outlined will really extend scalability features, and it is almost certain that more work will be needed. In some ways similarly, bodies of data will be subject to concurrent access on a scale never before attempted, stressing the technology for managing that too. The price advantages of general purpose equipment will make it so attractive by comparison with special purpose equipment that research will be needed in the provision of high and predictable performance in operating systems. These changes, and doubtless many others of the same general sort, will be substantial but incremental.

Where we may expect to see a lot of very serious action is in a general area difficult to name which includes aspects of security, authorisation, management, and accounting. Pervasive and powerful communications provide opportunities for all kinds of *bona fide* debate and decision which need to be conducted by people and in decent privacy. Consider for example the conduct of an electronic ballot by a political organisation of half a million members, in a manner that shall be independent of where the members are when they vote, secure against interlopers, and confidential. Consider the preparation and planning of a political agitation designed to constitute a (perfectly legitimate) elephant trap for the Government of the day, including perfecting potentially embarrassing video material to be released at the appropriate time. Consider exercising the privileges of membership in a society with numerous local instances, such as teleshopping wherever you happen to be. Consider running the affairs of a gambling syndicate with members using hand-portable equipment on each of numerous racecourses. Consider a totally computerised stock exchange with a distributed implementation. All of these examples require access control, some degree of confidentiality, and good management. They could be on a vast scale. Many of the services provided will require to be billed for, and to have their use audited, as for example if they are paid for by advertising. It would be intolerable for all of them to be managed and accounted *ad hoc*; we would all be carrying a mountain of cards, keys, passwords, and so on. It would be intolerable for all these functions to be centralised, for both anti-monopoly and security reasons. The bishop is entitled to watch porn films without being blackmailed, for example.

These subjects may appear to be, or actually be, not very elevated topics. There is some real computer science in finding out how to do them properly though. It will require fresh system understanding to set up a lean, certifiable, and well scalable set of systems for the future.

15

The Place of Interactive Computing in Tomorrow's Computer Science

William Newman

Introduction

Three decades ago the Sketchpad system was presented to the public, an event that did much to put interactive systems on the computing agenda (Sutherland, 1963). I remember the event well. The Sketchpad film, shown at a conference I was attending in Edinburgh, ran for only about ten minutes, but this was quite long enough for me to make up my mind to abandon my faltering career as a control-systems engineer and seek to become a computer scientist. I have never regretted that decision.

Thirty years later, interactive systems have established themselves across society, in a fashion that I and my 1960s contemporaries never dreamed of. Today we interact with computers in TV sets, telephones, wristwatches, ticket machines, kitchen scales, and countless other artefacts. The range of human activities supported by interactive technology is still expanding, apparently without limits. Demand for interactive systems and artefacts has fuelled the growth of today's computer industry, which now treats interactive computing as the mainstream of its business. Thus a technology that was startlingly radical in 1963 has become part of normal practice today.

My concern here is not with the amazing change, during three decades, in the way computers are used, but with a disappointing lack of change in the ways computing is taught and computer science research is carried out. I am concerned that interactive systems, having gained a place on the computing agenda in 1963, are still little more than an agenda item as far as computer science is concerned. While interactive computing now represents the mainstream of the industry's business, it plays hardly any part in the mainstream of computer science. It continues to be treated as a special case.

My interest in 'computing tomorrow' focuses on this anomaly in the treatment of interactive computing, and on the question of how it is to

Table 15.1. *HCI course offerings by a selection of leading US computer science departments. Source: World Wide Web.*

College or University	No. of HCI courses
Cornell, Columbia, Dartmouth, MIT, Northwestern, Princeton, UC Irvine, UCLA	0
Brown, Carnegie Mellon, George Mason, Purdue, U. of Colorado	1
Georgia Tech.	2
Stanford	4

be resolved. A great deal of money and effort have gone into trying to resolve it already, but to little effect. For example, Guy *et al.* have described the difficulties experienced during the 1980s by the British government's Alvey research initiative in structuring a Human Interface programme; in their view the problem lay with the Alvey Directorate's inability to integrate a Human Interface component into other research progammes (Guy *et al.*, 1991). In the US, the ACM and IEEE identified human–computer communication as one of nine main subject areas for inclusion in their 1991 Computing Curricula but, as can be seen in Table 15.1, few of the leading departments have done much in response (ACM/IEEE, 1991).

My purpose here is, first, to demonstrate that there is indeed a serious problem to be solved, and then to try to develop a course of action that might solve it. I will try to show that interactive computing lacks the engineering foundations that would make it appealing to the mainstream of computer science. I will provide evidence that interactive computing is, nevertheless, acquiring stronger engineering credentials, and I will argue that there is a case for trying to establish it as a topic in its own right, within the computing mainstream. I will finish with some suggestions on how this might be achieved.

I will be using the term 'mainstream computing' to refer to the collection of topics that form the foundations of computer science, as it is presently taught and researched. These are topics such as discrete mathematics, algorithms and data structures, computer architecture, operating systems, distributed computing, programming languages and software engineering. I will use the term 'interactive computing' to refer to an overlapping set of subtopics that underpin the design and development of interactive systems, and I will summarize at the end what these subtopics are. A third term that I will refer to is *Human–Computer Interaction* or HCI; this is the set of topics that deal specifically with the interactive elements of computer systems, such as their user interfaces. It might appear that the sidelining of interactive computing can be overcome simply by treating HCI as a mainstream topic. This is certainly a popular point of view, espoused by many others besides the ACM/IEEE Curriculum Committee. I do not believe it offers a solution to the overall problem, however, for reasons that I will explain.

The Situation of Concern

The purpose of this article is to address a real problem, and my first task is to clarify what I perceive to be the problem, or the *situation of concern* to use Checkland's phrase (Checkland & Scholes, 1990). As I see it, the established field of mainstream computing provides adequate support to the engineering of non-interactive or embedded computer systems, but its support to the engineering of interactive systems leaves much to be desired. Trained computer scientists often do not know how to design interactive systems, or where to go for guidance. There is a need to extend the domain of mainstream computing to support the engineering of all categories of computer system, both interactive and non-interactive, with equal thoroughness.

There is evidence of progress towards helping system developers out of this situation. For example, a wide range of tools now exist for developing interactive systems, including prototyping systems like HyperCard and Visual Basic, and product development tools like the Macintosh Programmers' Workshop and Visual C^{++}. These tools often come with excellent design guides, such as the original handbook written for the Apple Macintosh, or the more recent and voluminous work for Microsoft Windows (Apple, 1987; Microsoft, 1992). Taken together, these tools and guidebooks come to the rescue of the interactive system designer.

It is also true that many computer science students gain experience in using HyperCard and other interactive programming systems during their degree courses. Some universities teach these skills to those who are not majoring in computer science; for example, Alan Biermann describes a course for non-majors that includes programming assignments such as interactive tree-searching and text editing (Biermann, 1994). Employers who need graduates with interactive systems experience no longer face the bleak situation that pertained five years ago or more.

On the other hand, the scientific content of mainstream computing, as it is taught and researched, has hardly shifted at all towards supporting interactive system design. As I showed in Table 15.1, few leading departments are yet offering courses on any aspects of interactive system design. Of course, the ACM recommended a mere four lecture hours on user interfaces out of a total of 271 hours of 'common requirements', hardly a significant shift! Computer science students are still, therefore, being taught to think about system design as non-interactive system design.

Further evidence of the sidelining of interactive computing is to be found in the industry's attitudes, exemplified by its reactions to crises. When interactive systems go disastrously wrong, and inquiries are conducted, attention usually turns towards failures on the non-interactive side. For example, when the London Ambulance Service's dispatch system failed a few days after its introduction, a major inquiry was conducted, but its focus was almost entirely on the management and software engineering of the project (London Ambulance Service, 1993). No studies were done of the user interfaces of the dispatchers' workstation or of the in-cab console, although it is clear from careful reading of the inquiry report that these contributed to the failure.

Likewise Leveson and Turner's well-known report on accidents with the Therac-25 radiation therapy machine focuses on design flaws in internal software which enabled an essential time-delay to be bypassed during rapid operation (Leveson & Turner, 1993). The user interface, according to Leveson and Turner, was a side-issue in the accidents. But an alternative assessment could be that the user interface was itself seriously flawed due to the unprincipled hiding of some of the functionality of the underlying machine while making the rest visible†. A better user interface design would have led to a different implementation that might, conceivably, have avoided the risk of bypassing the time-delay. This is of course largely guesswork on my part, but the point is that failures of in-

---

† I refer here to the decision by Therac-25's designers to expose most of the functions and features of the underlying X-ray machine to the operator, but to hide crucial other features including the time-delay during the setting of bending magnets. This was bound to encourage operators to form an inadequate mental model of the system. Either the time-delay should have been made explicit, as part of the 'system image' presented via the user interface (Norman, 1986), or a different conceptual design should have been developed that supported safe operation of the machine.

teractive systems can often be understood better if their user interfaces are included in the analysis, yet this is rarely done.

For me, a major source of concern is the common practice of publicly delineating topics in computer science as if interactive computing did not exist. For example, when the topic of software testing is discussed, it is quite acceptable to ignore the question of how to test interactive properties (Ostrand, 1994; Zage & Zage, 1993). Likewise the reliability of computer systems is often treated as if it were synonymous with the reliability of the hardware and software, taking little or no account of the errors (sometimes disastrous) that users may make due to poor system design (Neumann, 1994). I am therefore glad to see Bev Littlewood, in a companion article in this book, taking a broader view of software dependability. This kind of view is not adopted often enough.

This sidelining of interactive computing should not, I think, be viewed as a failure or oversight on the part of people in mainstream computing. As I shall explain, there are serious scientific obstacles in the way of finding a place for interactive computing in the mainstream. The solution does not lie in simply 'adding more HCI.' There is, as Newell and Card have eloquently pointed out, an almost total lack of overlap between the engineering sciences of mainstream computing on the one hand and of HCI on the other (Newell & Card, 1985). This makes it difficult to introduce HCI to the curriculum. Mainstream computing and HCI employ different sets of analytical models in order to find explanations for design failures, and these can give conflicting answers which muddy the picture. Mainstream topics have adopted benchmarks and requirements that enable a high degree of mutual understanding within each topic; in HCI the benchmarks and requirements are quite different. So we must look deeper for an explanation for the situation, and for a possible way of resolving it.

The Foundations of Engineering Disciplines

Computer science is an engineering discipline. Although it is labelled as a science, and is sometimes talked about as an art or as a craft, it fits the engineering mould better than it fits anything else. This mould has been described by Rogers as 'the practice of organizing the design and construction of any artifice which transforms the physical world around us to meet some recognized need' (Rogers, 1983). If we want to change computer science, e.g., by bringing interactive computing into the mainstream, we should therefore try to understand what it means to change an engineering discipline.

As it matures, an engineering discipline builds ever stronger foundations. These enable the discipline in question to develop faster and further, but they also limit the directions of development. Sometimes, therefore, it is necessary to re-examine the foundations, and this is what I propose to do here. I find it helpful to consider the foundations of engineering disciplines under the following six headings:

- *Domains of application* As Rogers points out, engineering artefacts are designed to transform the physical world around us. One of the essential components of any field of engineering is, therefore, a thorough understanding of the domain within which tranformations and changes are to take place. For example, traffic engineers need to understand the domain of road vehicles and their drivers. Herbert Simon has called such domains the 'outer environments' of design (Simon, 1969). Engineering designers need to understand the outer environment well enough to make predictions of the changes to the environment that their designed artefacts will bring about. And they must share this understanding in the interest of strengthening the discipline.

- *Benchmarks* Since engineers cannot test engineering designs on every conceivable situation that pertains in the domain of application, they must choose a representative set of situations, or benchmarks. Thus traffic engineers will often choose certain traffic patterns when testing designs for road intersections. If benchmarks are chosen well, they can provide an adequate basis for sampling the quality of the design. However, they must be reviewed from time to time, and this means referring back to the domain of application.

- *Forms of solution* The basic stock-in-trade of an engineering discipline is the set of functional designs, or forms of solution, that it can apply to design problems. Thus a traffic engineer can choose among several forms of solution for a light-controlled crossroads. The cycle of iterative design involves selecting a form of solution from among those available, modifying it to address the problem, testing it on suitable benchmarks, assessing the impact on the domain of application and, if this impact falls short of what is needed, repeating some or all of the steps (Rogers, 1983). Solution forms are thus constantly undergoing modification and enhancement; the process by which they acquire maturity, and thus become a part of normal practice, is synonymous with the process of innovation (Constant, 1980).

- *Requirements* The primary purposes of requirements are (a) to identify any special functional features to be included in the chosen form of solution, and (b) to set performance targets (DeMarco, 1979; Vincenti, 1990; Newman & Lamming, 1995). Requirements thus help the engineer to manage the iterative process of design: they indicate where the initial solution may need functional modification, and they also indicate when to stop iterating. A traffic engineer will set requirements for certain lane configurations, e.g., early cut-off of traffic across the opposing flow, and for a performance of, say, 2,000 units per hour westward under saturation conditions. In a well established engineering domain, well supplied with solutions, requirements will tend to vary only in terms of established performance factors and minor functional features, both of which are familiar to experienced engineers. In an immature field, where there is often a lack of well established targets and forms of solution, requirements may need to be worked out more or less from scratch for each design problem.

- *Representations* During the design phase, engineers must work on the solution in the abstract, developing its form, analysing its behaviour and describing it to other engineers. They have a consequent need for representations that can support exploration, analysis and communication (Ferguson, 1992). These need to cover all aspects of the artefact's design and construction, from the domain of application to the form of solution. In traffic engineering, for example, there is a need to represent not only the form of an intersection, but also its benchmark traffic patterns and the timing of its control systems. When engineers lack adequate representations, their ability to work in the abstract is hampered, and they must rely more on prototyping.

- *Analytical models* In almost every branch of engineering, designs are tested against requirements analytically, using predictive models. These models are derived from engineering research, both theoretical and empirical. They generally incorporate simplifications and abstractions that make them easier to apply in the design context. A simple model used by traffic engineers states that drivers joining a main road at a T-junction will, on average, give way to vehicles on the main road, if these are due to reach the intersection in five seconds or less (Salter, 1989). Often analytical models are built into simulators and other computer-based design tools. To verify that the analysis has been adequate and that requirements have been met, it is common practice to build and test a prototype of the completed design (Rogers, 1983).

In the practice of engineering we can see how these six foundational components link together to support the engineer's work. Thus an understanding of the application domain leads to the establishment of benchmarks which, in conjunction with forms of solution, generate requirements, all of them suitably represented in the abstract. Solutions can then be analysed, and the results checked against requirements.

Mainstream Computing as an Engineering Discipline

How well does mainstream computing measure up against the six essential components? I do not find this question easy to answer, because mainstream computing topics vary widely, especially in their choice of domains, benchmarks and solutions.

One property, however, is shared by almost all topics in mainstream computing, a property that greatly helps these topics to function in the engineering mould. I am referring here to the emphasis on *embedded* computer artefacts† – on artefacts designed to support other forms of computer artefact. This is manifestly the case with discrete structures, algorithms, data structures, computer hardware, operating systems, distributed systems and programming languages. Just a few mainstream topics, including software engineering, do not deal entirely in embedded technology. Ironically, they adhere less closely to the engineering mould. But I will defer discussing the special case of software engineering until later.

As regards the bulk of mainstream computing, my general impression is that it has the hallmarks of a mature engineering discipline. In most of its topics the domain of application – construction of computer systems – tends to be well understood and this understanding to be widely shared. Benchmarks usually consist of computing processes capable of testing the level of support; these are often made widely available in the form of standard programs. Forms of solution tend to become well established and well known, partly because they export well defined interfaces into the domain of application. Mainstream topics are supported by a comprehensive and widely used set of notations and formalisms. And because so many mainstream topics are concerned with the construction of software, they can share a range of mathematically based modelling techniques.

---

† I am applying the term *embedded* more broadly than is perhaps usual in computer science. I regard an embedded computer artefact as something that may not be wholly inaccessible to human users, indeed it may need to be accessible to the system developer so that it can be configured for the system it supports. In this sense it supports the human activity of developing the supported system, but only as a means of achieving its primary purpose of providing system support.

I have left till last the issue of requirements, because mainstream computing appears to adopt a rather unconventional attitude here. Basically, requirements – as defined above – have the appearance of a non-issue, rarely mentioned in textbooks or research papers. I have sometimes tried to get discussions going with my mainstream computing colleagues on how they deal with requirements, but with little success; they admit to having nothing much to say on the matter. It appears that mainstream computer scientists are able, for the most part, to go about their work without the need to consider requirements as such.

I have come to believe that this tacit approach to requirements is in fact yet another hallmark of an engineering discipline. When the performance measures and features of solutions become well established, the need constantly to spell them out gradually goes away. Walter Vincenti (1990) has written a classic book (Vincenti, 1990) about developments in aircraft engineering during the inter-war years, in which he describes how aircraft flying- quality requirements were established (my own italics):

Looking back after forty-five years, Gilruth [Robert R. Gilruth of NASA] says, 'I boiled that thing down to a set of requirements that were very straightforward and very simple to interpret. The requirements went right back to those things you could design for.' Thanks to the extensive testing, quantitative limits could now be stated for the designer with some certainty. The seemingly remarkable result that the same requirements could be applied (with minor exceptions) to all current types and sizes of airplanes, however, *was nowhere explicitly mentioned*. If anyone had ever debated the point, *by now it was taken for granted*.

Mainstream computing takes the same approach, tacitly applying the same quantitative measures to virtually all systems: speed, reliability, ease of re-use, ease of maintenance, and so on. There is no need to remind designers that these requirements apply; they are ingrained in the practice of mainstream computing.

The mainstream of computing thus operates very largely as an engineering discipline should. Indeed it has a particular degree of coherence and stability about it, for most of its artefacts are built from the same material – from software. The only serious fault I can find with it is its inability to find a place for interactive computing. As a step towards understanding how it might adapt in this way, I will now take a look at the field of HCI, and assess whether it offers a set of foundations for interactive computing.

The Foundations of HCI

The field of HCI is concerned with interactive computer systems and their design. It focuses on situations where there is human *activity*, because where there is no such activity there can be no interaction. It also focuses on technologies that support human *interaction* with computers. These technologies include the user interface and its constituent parts: they include devices such as displays, pointing devices and virtual-reality headsets; and they include windowing systems and other software that supports interaction.

The domains of application of HCI thus include any domain of human activity where computers can play a supporting role. Right away we have identified one of the challenges facing HCI, namely its endless variety of domains of application. Activities that are supposed to be similar, such as placing a telephone call, can vary so much that they need a variety of different supporting systems. Even a single individual cannot be expected to perform a particular activity the same way every time. To overcome this problem, interactive system designers focus their attention on small goal-oriented units of activity, or tasks, that can be seen to recur in similar forms. They design systems so as to support the tasks that make up the user's activity.

The endless variety of domains of application gives rise to an almost endless variety of forms of solution, i.e., of user interfaces. The user interface must be designed to fit the task, rather than vice versa. To cater to the variety of ways in which specific tasks are performed, user interfaces need to be tailorable; for example, users need to be able to define their own abbreviations for frequently used commands. There is, admittedly, some movement towards standardizing user interfaces, partly to reduce training costs, partly just to reduce the enormous task of building and supporting so many different designs. But meanwhile the development of new forms of solution continues, fuelled by the changing and expanding needs of users, by the source of new interactive technologies, and by developers' search for new product identities.

Any engineering discipline saddled with such a vast array of application domains and forms of solution will need an underlying science base of considerable strength and breadth. HCI has by tradition drawn on cognitive science for its scientific foundations, and has attempted to develop cognitive models for use in system design. Two examples of useful predictive modelling tools are the keystroke-level model of Card, Moran and Newell, which can produce accurate speed predictions for the performance of repetitive tasks, and the cognitive walkthrough technique of Polson and Lewis, useful in identifying problems with walk-up-and-use systems such as automated teller machines (Card *et al.*, 1983; Polson & Lewis, 1990). Progress towards developing a wider range of tools has been hampered, however, by the sheer difficulty of making predictions about the way human beings will perform tasks.

In recent years the science base of HCI has broadened to include contributions from anthropology and sociology (Suchman, 1987; Hughes *et al.*, 1993). These have helped to get the subtopic of Computer-Supported Cooperative Work (CSCW) off the ground. They provide explanations for some of the social processes that are observed in work settings where interactive systems are used, e.g., the social process of interaction between doctor and patient described later in this chapter. These bodies of theory should one day provide a basis for developing models for use in designing organizational and multi-user computer systems. In the few years since CSCW research began, however, there have been no significant developments of this kind.

HCI thus has a long way to go towards establishing itself as an engineering discipline. The profusion of application domains and forms of solution means that benchmarks are rarely, if ever, established, and this makes it difficult for designers to tell whether they are achieving improvements. Not surprisingly, the engineering tradition of slow enhancement has failed to establish itself in HCI – designers prefer to develop something new rather than improve on something that exists (see Figure 15.1). In these circumstances there are few opportunities for tacitly agreed requirements to develop around established forms of solution. Instead designers must work to vague requirements for ease of use, ease of tailoring, etc., and must try to take advantage of the multitude of guidelines that have been compiled on the basis of designers' past experience.

Prospects for HCI's Integration with the Mainstream

As I have already mentioned, HCI could simply be declared to be a mainstream computing topic. But is this the right way to proceed? Can mainstream computing and HCI be integrated successfully into a single discipline?

While this model, 'add more HCI', has its attractions, I suspect it is quite impossible to achieve by intent. After all, if it is achievable, why has it not happened in response to all the efforts made during the last

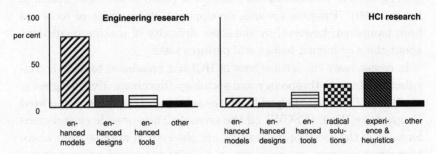

Fig. 15.1. Distribution of the products of research, showing the percentage of products devoted to enhanced models, enhanced designs and enhanced tools: (a) in established engineering disciplines, (b) in HCI, where most research is devoted to inventing radical solutions, and to studying them with a view to gaining experience or defining heuristics (Newman, 1994).

fifteen years? I am not even sure I know what it means to merge two disciplines in this way.

What I do believe can occur, however, is a gradual process of change within an established discipline. Indeed this is constantly occurring within all live disciplines, including mainstream computing and HCI. I am therefore very interested in how an engineering discipline, such as mainstream computing, can make a gradual transition towards truly representing a wider territory, in this case interactive computing. I am quite sure it can happen only if members of the discipline want it to happen. In particular, I am sure that any future changes to mainstream computing must meet the following criteria:

(i) It should remain equally easy to measure scientific progress. If progress becomes harder to measure, scientific excellence is harder to maintain. The introduction of new topics of a more subjective nature, e.g., the design of new tools for building software, needs to be balanced with theory-based work.

(ii) It should remain possible to show benefit to industry. This is how mainstream computing retains its relevance to real-world application domains, and is how it justifies continued funding for teaching and research.

(iii) There should still be plenty of interesting, challenging, lasting problems to tackle. Even in a field as active as computer science, this cannot be guaranteed for every new topic. With technology continuing to develop at breakneck speeds, attention can suddenly shift to topics that have recently become fashionable. If these have insufficient depth, it can shift away again.

(iv) There should be no increase in dependence on other disciplines. The range of topics now covered by mainstream computing is already very broad, and it is hard for anyone to be knowledgeable about a wide range of them. However, the mainstream topics do at least all draw on related bodies of theory in mathematics and physics, which creates a sense of community. It may be hard to branch out in directions that involve hiring scientists from other disciplines.

These criteria suggest that it may be quite difficult to move the mainstream in the direction of interactive computing. As Figure 15.1 shows, HCI is greatly concerned with inventing new solutions and studying their impact, two kinds of research whose progress is hard to measure. HCI also has perennial problems in proving its value to the computer industry; there is a lack of evidence that people will recognize good interactive system design and pay extra for it. While there are plenty of challenging problems in HCI, many of them are simply too difficult to enable rapid progress; this certainly applies to the problem of developing generalized models of human behaviour. As a result, those who want to get their research published must resort to inventing or to conducting studies. And finally, HCI depends heavily on the discipline of cognitive psychology. It is unrealistic to expect all computer science departments to hire psychologists in order to support a transition towards interactive computing.

Taken together, these factors help to explain why past attempts to introduce HCI to the mainstream have met with resistance. They suggest, moreover, that HCI will continue to be rejected in the future. The two disciplines appear destined to develop in isolation from each other.

I believe this deadlock can be broken. However, I think it involves treating with great care any proposals for changes to mainstream computing. There is no point in trying to introduce material that weakens the engineering foundations of the mainstream; this material will be discounted and rejected. The only approach that can succeed is, I believe, one that maintains or even strengthens computer science as an engineering discipline. This means being highly selective about the application domains, the forms of solution and the analytical models that are put forward. In the next section I will present a few examples of what I mean. I will conclude by addressing the question 'where can this new material find a home?' and will discuss two alternatives: expanding the current role of software engineering to include interactive computing, or trying to build up interactive computing as a separate mainstream topic.

Extending the Mainstream: some Examples

The examples I will present in this section have one thing in common: they are all concerned with specific, well established application domains. In several cases the form of solution is also well established, and some of the applications are supported by modelling techniques for predicting performance. In other words, they are all partially or fully supported by engineering science. These properties make them very different from the high-tech, ground-breaking examples that are usually quoted as representative of interactive computing. Nevertheless they are, I would claim, typical of the applications and solutions that earn interactive systems their place in society.

Support of general medical practice

During the last few years general practitioners have begun to use computer systems for storing patient records, assisting preparation of prescriptions, and accessing databases of drugs and treatments. The crucial human activity that these systems support is the consultation between doctor and patient – a complex, varied and often lengthy process. Consultations involve a delicately balanced social interaction between doctor and patient. The doctor needs to establish the patient's trust and cooperation during a consultation that lasts only a few minutes; during the same brief period of time the patient must find words for all of the symptoms that are causing him or her concern, and must enter into a constructive partnership with the doctor to diagnose the illness and agree a plan for treating it. All in all, this is a challenging application domain for computer systems.

Many of the systems that have been designed and installed for use during consultation have come in for criticism. It appears that doctors feel uncomfortable using the computer during the actual consultation, and uncertain whether to allow the patient to see what they are doing with it. Yet if they do not use it during the consultation, they are faced with the task of updating records after the patient has left. It is also clear, from studies conducted by Greatbatch *et al.*, that patients react adversely to the presence of these systems; they appear more hesitant in their interactions with the doctor (Greatbatch *et al.*, 1993). Why do these problems occur?

I find this particular case offers a fascinating opportunity to apply different means of investigation and analysis. It invites us to 'debug' the design in much the same way that a malfunctioning computer program invites us to start probing for software bugs. Consider, for example, the implications of the following theories drawn from anthropology and psychology:

- *Gaze direction affects the flow of conversation.* Goodwin has shown, on the basis of extensive studies of videotaped conversations, that a speaker's flow of conversation tends to falter, restart or pause when the hearer's gaze turns away (Goodwin, 1981). This would suggest that a patient will become hesitant in describing symptoms if the doctor's gaze is constantly diverting towards a computer terminal.
- *During data entry, pauses occur between certain types of keystroke.* This has been found by Card *et al.*, who incorporated their findings into their keystroke-level model (Card *et al.*, 1983). Principally, they found that users will pause for 'mental preparation' before they type a command string (e.g., AGE), and between typing an operand (e.g., 55) and confirming it (e.g., with RETURN). As a result, the keyboard activities of the doctor will be punctuated with pauses, and these are visible to the patient even if the actual text entered is not.
- *Pauses may be seen as opportunities to speak.* Studies by Greatbatch showed a tendency on the part of patients to start or restart speaking – even if the doctor's gaze was on the workstation – when the doctor paused between keystrokes, and especially during the longer pause that preceded termination of data entry (Greatbatch *et al.*, 1993). This observation led to theorizing that the patient saw this pause as an indication of an opportunity to take a turn in the conversation, and regain the doctor's attention. Unfortunately for the patient, the computer had a tendency simultaneously to do the equivalent thing, displaying a screenful of text that caused the doctor to pay little or no attention to what the patient then said.

I mention these nuggets of theory to demonstrate that this may be an application domain suitable for inclusion in the mainstream. I accept that this is a complex domain, but perhaps not so complex as to defy analysis. There is a predictable structure to the typical consultation, by which it progresses from the initial pleasantries to eliciting symptoms, through testing hypotheses, arriving at an explanation and testing it, to choosing a treatment, writing a prescription and instructing the patient on what to do. There is an opportunity here to identify a useful set of 'benchmark consultations'. There is an absence, unfortunately, of established solutions that support the activity well. However, there are some useful theories that could help the designer to analyse designs in terms of their support for benchmark consultations. Taken as a whole, this application domain offers a rich set of opportunities for computer science research, whose results would probably be applicable to other similar domains in which experts make use of computers in the course of dispensing advice to clients.

The negotiation and recording of equity deals

This next example concerns the provision of computer support to dealers in equity stocks and shares in the City of London. Unlike general medical practice, this is an application domain that few people are likely to experience first-hand, and so I will start by describing how the dealer's activity is carried out, and then discuss the engineering problem of supporting it.

Equity dealers handle a constant stream of deals, primarily in response to telephone calls from other buyers or sellers. Each deal involves negotiating a price for a certain quantity of stock, and then recording the deal. During the negotiation stage, the dealer interacts primarily with the caller, meanwhile reading price information off computer displays and sometimes checking with fellow dealers working nearby. Here, for example, is a typical negotiation by an equity 'market-maker' recorded by Jirotka *et al.* (1993).

(caller): Eh, Glaxo for Hambros please

J (dealer): [after peering at screen] Ehhh ... ninety five nine

    C: Ninety five nine

    J: [answers another phone call while waiting]

    C: Eh ... thirty seven thousand gets at six nine five, seven one six

    J: Thirty seven thousand I buy at six nine five?

    C: That's right, John

    J: Thank you [continues talking on phone]

Here the dealer, J, has agreed to buy thirty-seven thousand shares in Glaxo at a price of 6.95 from the caller, C, whose customer number is 716. Details of this purchase must now be recorded in the dealer-room computer system, within sixty seconds of closing the deal. For a variety of reasons, this is currently done in two stages, the dealer writing details of the deal by hand on a paper 'ticket', and a deal-input clerk then collecting the ticket and entering the details into the system. In other words, the overall system provides direct support to the dealer only during the negotiation stage, through the provision of up-to-date price information.

The problem of supporting the equity dealer lends itself to an engineering approach. The application domain is well established and has been described on a number of occasions in the computing literature, e.g., by Heath *et al.* (1993). Benchmark tasks, similar to the one transcribed above, are easy to identify. The use of computer systems in the recording and settling of deals is also well established, although it is an arena of relatively rapid change. Not much has been made public about the internal design of these systems, but this situation is changing; see CREST (1994) for example. Requirements are quite clear: the dealers' information displays must offer adequate levels of legibility, currency and information content; and the recording of the deal must minimize errors and use of dealers' time, and must be completed within sixty seconds.

There are opportunities to apply engineering methods to the design of improved systems for dealer support. The two-stage structure of deal-making and recording makes it possible to tackle the improvement of each stage independently. Models of human perception and interpretation can be employed in designing enhanced information displays. Meanwhile keystroke-level models such as that of Card *et al.* can be used to estimate the performance of other deal-recording user interfaces, e.g., direct key-in by the dealer.

The two stages of dealing can also be treated in conjunction. Both Jirotka *et al.* (1993) and Heath *et al.* (1993) have discussed a number of interesting alternative ways of supporting the dealer, including the use of voice recognition. They point out some of the difficulties posed by the complex combinations of verbal and computer interactions taking place as deals are made, such as the conduct of several deals in parallel as illustrated in the example above. They show how techniques of conversation analysis can help the designer understand how to model the impact of new technologies. This application domain lends itself to mainstream computing, as a context both for exploring uses for new technologies and for conducting research into better models of how the dealer's work is carried out.

Project Ernestine: the case of the Toll-and-Assistance Operator's workstation

The final example I will quote is already well known in HCI circles as one of its most convincing demonstrations of true engineering research. It concerns a mundane but vitally important application, the handling of calls to the telephone operator for assistance, e.g., for placing credit-card calls, charging calls to a third party, reversing the charge, etc. The phone company operators who handle these calls – known in the US as Toll-and-Assistance Operators or TAOs – have been supported by interactive systems for a number of years. From time to time new equipment is introduced to enable them to handle calls more efficiently.

In a quest for cost savings and improved service, New England Telephone began a project in the late 1980s to replace its TAO workstations. The new design they selected offered potential savings of two seconds or more per call handled, gained by rearranging the keyboard, speeding up data transmission and taking keystrokes out of the TAO's keyboard procedures. Given that the average call is handled in about 20 seconds, this speed-up translated into large overall savings, amounting to millions of dollars per year.

Before committing to the project, the company prudently conducted a field trial of 24 new workstations. This showed, to everyone's amazement, that the new workstation was *slower* than the current design, by about two-thirds of a second per call. On this basis, it was likely to cost the company over a million dollars per year in lost efficiency. Worse still, the field trial offered no clues as to why the new workstation, outwardly superior to the current one in several respects, was inferior in performance.

Explanations for the loss in performance were gained from a programme of HCI research that began at the time the field trials were getting under way, and gradually built up a model of how the new workstation was affecting call handling. This programme, known as Project Ernestine, has been described by Gray *et al.* (1992, 1993) and also in Newman & Lamming (1995). Looked at as an engineering research project, it had all of the necessary ingredients:

- The domain of application was extremely well established. Most TAO services have been available to the public for years; they are so well known, and so heavily depended upon, that there is little or no scope for radical change. 18 different types of call (credit-card call, collect call, etc.) account for the vast majority of operator calls. The application has also come to be very well understood by the phone companies, although not completely so, as this project demonstrated.

- The basic form of solution was well established also. Call-handling involves a standard sequence, in which the TAO establishes who should pay for the call, determines what rate should be charged, and concludes by handing off the call. The workstation provides efficient ways of following this sequence whatever the type of call. It displays status information, and provides a numeric keypad and a set of function keys for the TAO's input of data and commands.

- Requirements were tacitly understood. The basic performance requirement for TAO workstations is speed of task performance; in this case a target was set for a two-second improvement overall.

- Benchmarks could be identified. Phone companies do not employ benchmarks as such in measuring TAO performance, but they were needed in support of the analyses conducted during Project Ernestine. They were identified by videotaping the performance of TAO tasks and choosing examples that represented typical calls within all of the 18 common categories.

- Suitable representations were available. One of the challenges in analysing TAO tasks is the number of parallel streams of ongoing activity. During a collect call, for example, the TAO is writing down the name of the caller while waiting for the number to answer and watching for a displayed response from the billing system showing that the number can receive collect calls. In Project Ernestine a PERT-chart notation was used to document all of the different streams of activity. These included the TAO's cognitive, perceptual and motor operators and the computer system's responses (see Figure 15.2).

- Analytical models were capable of predicting performance. A modelling technique called CPM-GOMS (John, 1990) was used to arrive at estimated performance times for the 18 benchmark tasks. This involved assigning empirically determined times to each of the operators in the PERT chart, and plotting the critical path, as shown in Figure 15.2. The resulting predictions, showing an average increase of 0.63 seconds in performance times for the 18 benchmarks, were within 0.02 seconds of the differences actually observed during the field trial.

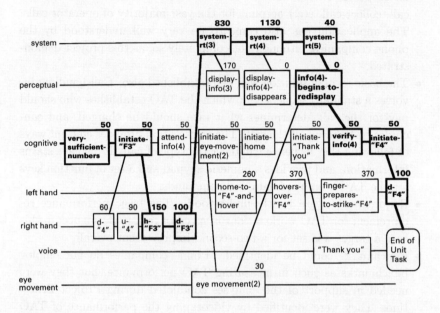

Fig. 15.2. Portions of the CPM-GOMS model of a credit-card call, showing the final stages of the call. The critical path, shown emphasized, includes two F3 operators which contributed to increasing the task time. Home, down and up-strokes are abbreviated as 'h-', 'd-' and 'u-'. Based on Gray *et al.* (1993).

The reasons for the workstation's poor performance eventually emerged from the analysis. Each of the 'improvements' had, in its own way, caused a performance degradation. The rearrangement of the keyboard, bringing all of the frequently-used keys together, had forced TAOs to do most of the keying with their right hands, rather than interleave left- and right-hand keying. The faster communication lines had made the workstation slower because they added a half-second packet transmission time that preceded every display of data. And the new procedures for data entry, although they involved fewer keystrokes overall, had been achieved by unwittingly adding keystrokes at points on the critical path while removing them from non-critical sequences.

For the purposes of our discussion here, the TAO application represents a strong candidate for inclusion in mainstream computer science. Not only does it have all of the necessary engineering foundations; it also has the potential for exploration of enhanced solutions. For example, the CPM-GOMS model suggests that real performance improvements could be gained from using pre-recorded announcements (e.g., 'New England Telephone, can I help you?') and a faster billing-system response to TAO queries. In other words, there are opportunities here to show the benefits of improvements in embedded computing components, in terms of improved performance of human activities.

On the introduction of application domains to mainstream computing

There is nothing very special about any of the three activities I have described, or about the technology that supports them. The reason for selecting them is that they have been studied and documented in some depth, to a point where it is possible to develop models of the user's activity, which in turn can support the analysis of proposed solutions. The only example that has been taken to this final stage is the TAO application, but the others have the potential to do the same, thus helping to build up a set of cases supporting an engineering discipline of interactive computing

The principal remaining question is, I believe, how to introduce this new material into the mainstream in a manner that computer scientists will find acceptable. I have no neat answer to this question, but will offer two possible routes forward. The first is to try to find a place for interactive computing within the topic of software engineering. I am doubtful whether this will be possible, for reasons that I will now explain. This leaves one other possibility, to try to establish and grow a new topic of interactive computing within the mainstream. The quoted examples, and others like them, could act as building blocks for creating this new topic.

Software engineering: a home for interactive computing?

Of all of the topics in mainstream computing, software engineering would appear to have the most direct concern with supporting the 'real world' of human activity. Its express concern is with methods for constructing large, complex software systems. Many of these systems are interactive, and there is a consequent need for methods that help in dealing with systems' interactive elements. There are statements of concern within software engineering about addressing this need, but I sense that HCI is being relied upon to deliver the required goods. For reasons I have already given, I do not think software engineers can just stand back and wait for this to happen.

As a comparative outsider, I see in software engineering some clear opportunities to strengthen its methods for dealing with interactive systems, and also some formidable challenges. The most obvious opportunity lies in providing methods of the kind that software engineers currently lack, for representing and analysing the interactive properties of systems. Darrel Ince was kind enough to say several years ago that 'human–computer interface researchers seem to be solving many of the problems associated with the naive user' (Ince, 1988). Whether or not that is over-optimistic, I do think there are methods, such as the cognitive walkthrough technique mentioned earlier, that should become part of the software engineer's stock-in-trade.

The most obvious challenge I see in current software engineering practice is its tendency to treat interactive and embedded software in the same way. Until recently the situation was even worse – interactive systems were ignored entirely. Now I find that the interactive–embedded distinction is starting to be made, but as a relatively minor one. It is not brought out as a single general issue, but is buried within each subtopic of software engineering. Thus we find treatment of interactive systems under the headings of reliability, re-use, requirements, formal methods and so on (Littlewood, this volume; Sommerville, 1994; Davis, 1990). In other words, interactive computing is sidelined here as in other mainstream topics.

I am concerned about this lack of discrimination between interactive and embedded software because I believe it is important to treat interactive and embedded software systems as different kinds of artefacts, using different representations and different analytical tools. This is easier said than done, of course, for there is a severe shortage of good methods for describing and analysing interactive solutions. However, I would suggest that the answer lies in making software engineers fully aware of the methods that do exist, and meanwhile encouraging research into new methods, rather than continuing to treat interactive and non-interactive software the same way.

I perceive a second challenge, of a more awkward nature, in software engineering's preoccupation with the process of software development rather than with the systems – interactive or otherwise – that are being developed. This makes me doubt whether software engineering can provide a sympathetic ear for interactive computing's preoccupation with designing systems to support human activity. The foundations of software engineering are skewed towards supporting its interest in the development process: its domain of application is the software industry, its benchmarks are problems in software development, its solutions take the form of methodologies, its tacit requirements are for reduced development costs, timescales, etc., and its models are oriented towards predicting what these costs, timescales and other properties will be. The only contributions from HCI that I would expect to be of real interest to software engineering are the various methods for prototyping user interfaces and some of the methods for modelling and evaluating usability. A prime example of an HCI method that should be taken up by software engineers is Nielsen and Molich's heuristic evaluation method for efficiently finding problems with user interface designs (Nielsen, 1992).

The examples of applications that I have quoted earlier are not, I fear, the kind that would greatly interest software engineers, for they are relatively mundane and their supporting technologies are in most instances quite simple. In most of the examples, the form of solution is not really in question. In contrast, the applications that interest software engineering, and that have a need for software engineering processes, are those that are large and complex, and whose form of solution is unknown. As Alan Davis puts it, 'problem [or requirements] analysis is applicable to only new, difficult or yet-unsolved problems. Why waste time analyzing a problem that is already understood?' (Davis, 1990). My interest is in exposing the mainstream to design problems that are understood, more or less, and I am worried that software engineers would consider them a waste of their time.

Interactive Computing as a Mainstream Topic

I perceive no other mainstream topic besides software engineering that could easily provide a home for interactive computing. The only mainstream topic that shows any real interest in the design of end-user applications is artificial intelligence, but it is committed to a particular technical approach and to applications that can take advantage of that approach. I do not see how AI could accommodate applications such as telephone operation that offer little or no scope for the use of its technologies.

Therefore I believe we are left with the option of trying to form a new topic, interactive computing, within the mainstream. What might be the content of such a topic? I suggest it could contain five subtopics:

- *Application domains* The emphasis here should be on gathering well documented studies and analyses of application domains, such as the domains mentioned in the examples. A second activity should be the development of taxonomies of application domains; this would be valuable in identifying areas where studies and analyses were needed.

- *Solutions* This complementary subtopic would be the gathering of well documented solutions. These are, I fear, hard to come by – those in possession of documented solutions know they own a valuable commodity. I would hope that this culture of hoarding design knowledge can be dispelled, because it is a serious impediment to engineering progress.

- *Requirements* The study of solutions and their evolution would help to identify underlying requirements, in the form of performance factors and functional variations influencing the design. This body of knowledge would fill a crucial void, complementing the work of software engineers on methods for defining the requirements of large, complex systems.

- *Representations* The need for this subtopic would follow naturally from the need to describe and analyse application domains and solutions.

- *Analytical models and tools* The theoretical base of interactive computing will inevitably lie in its repertoire of models, and principally in its models of the human activities found in the application domains. These will be based on psychological and sociological theories, but they will need to be cast into the form of engineering tools that computer scientists can use without the need to educate themselves in these theories. The keystroke-level and cognitive-walkthrough models, mentioned earlier, are good examples of theory cast into the form of useful tools.

These would form a topic that could, I believe, gain a place in the computing mainstream. It would share the interest that mainstream topics have in forms of solution and how to enhance them. It would help build tacit knowledge of requirements relevant to particular solutions. It would also help create a range of analytical tools capable of supporting the designer. Research would tend to focus in these areas, and would help generate results of the kind shown on the left-hand side of Figure 15.1 – enhanced models, solutions and tools.

This new topic of interactive computing would thus take a complementary approach to HCI. Its focus on established solutions and their requirements would complement HCI's emphasis on the development and study of novel applications. Its need for analytical models, and for in-depth studies of application domains, would provide an outlet for HCI research in these areas. It would depend on a flow of research materials from HCI but would not, I believe, require the recruiting of qualified psychologists or sociologists into computer science departments. I would expect to see the two topics establishing mutual dependence, one of them within the computing mainstream, the other operating as an independent discipline.

Conclusion

What I have been working towards here is a possible strategy for building up an interactive computing topic within the mainstream of computer science. I have discussed the possibility of merging HCI with mainstream computing, and have explained why I think this must fail. I have explored the possibility of using software engineering as a stepping stone, but I am not convinced this approach would succeed either. I am therefore recommending that attempts be made to create a new topic. This would involve gathering together material on application domains where human activities play a crucial role. These would need to be documented to much greater depth than is currently the practice. There would be a need also to document solutions to design problems in these domains, and to provide analyses of the designs. This is turn would enable software designers to test the feasibility of enhancements, in the way that Project Ernestine made possible the testing of new designs for TAO workstations. There would be a need to make explicit the features and performance factors governing requirements for solutions, thus making public what would normally be tacitly understood between experienced designers.

I recommend an approach such as this, because I believe it meets all of the essential criteria for introducing changes to an engineering discipline. The introduction of new, fully documented application domains would mean that scientific progress would be relatively easy to measure, both in developing new solutions and in conducting more exact analyses. The range of applications of mainstream computing would be extended, making it easier to show commercial benefit. The introduction of well established applications and solutions might help mainstream computing to resist being dragged along by the latest technological developments and swayed by this year's marketplace fashions. And it might be possible to avoid increasing the dependence of mainstream computing on other disciplines, by creating conduits into computer science from psychology and sociology, along which could be transferred recent studies and newly developed analytical models and tools. I am sure that others in the computing field will see how to proceed in these directions more clearly than I have, but I hope some of these ideas will prove useful.

Acknowledgments

I wish to thank the editors of this volume, and also Peter Brown and Michael Underwood, for their helpful comments on earlier versions of this chapter. I am also grateful to Walter Vincenti for his amplifications of the points made in his book about the nature of engineering requirements.

16

On the Importance of Being the Right Size: the Challenge of Conducting Realistic Experiments

Simon Peyton Jones

16.1 Introduction

As Milner eloquently argued in a submission to the Fairclough review of the Science and Engineering Research Council, computer science is a unique synthesis of a scientific and an engineering discipline. On the one hand, computer scientists seek to abstract unifying ideas, principles and techniques. On the other, the construction and evaluation of artefacts – software and/or hardware systems – is part of the essence of the subject. Both aspects are necessary. Without the ideas and principles, each artefact is constructed *ad hoc*, without taking advantage of lessons and ideas abstracted from earlier successes and failures. Conversely, without artefacts, it is impossible to know whether the ideas and principles are any use.

Unless we are aware of the symbiotic relationship between science and engineering, there is a danger that we will unconsciously construct the equations

$$
\begin{aligned}
\text{science} &= \text{research}, \\
\text{engineering} &= \text{development}.
\end{aligned}
$$

No researcher in a traditional engineering discipline would make such an identification, because engineers realise that there are substantial research challenges in building artefacts. Alas, computer scientists (sic) are prone to do so.

Perhaps one reason for this is that computer programs, unlike bridges or electric motors, are built from a particularly malleable medium. Unlike wood or steel, computer programs do not break merely because they have become too large, nor do they rot or rust. It is simply our own frustrating inability to deal with complexity which limits our 'reach' in building computer systems. In truth, though, the challenges of dealing

321

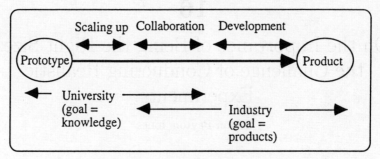

Fig. 16.1.

with complexity are at least as great as those facing engineers working with physical media.

In short, the process of building and stressing systems plays a critical, and undervalued, role in computing in general, and in computer science research in particular. In this article I argue the case for valuing system-building more highly than the UK academic research community generally does.

16.2 Research in Computing

Much research in computer science is, quite rightly, carried out by teams of one or two people. Where a grant is involved, the time-scale is usually three years. This small-scale approach is a very cost-effective way to carry out research. The participants are highly motivated, the work is tightly focused, and little time is spent on project-management overheads.

What is interesting is what happens next, or rather what does not happen next. The results of a three-year study are generally in the form of papers, and perhaps a prototype of a promising piece of software. Sometimes the plain fact is that the results are not very encouraging, and a new approach is needed. But sometimes, especially when a particular area has received attention from several small-scale projects, the appropriate next step is to 'scale up' the prototype into a larger, more robust system. The difficulty is that such a scaling-up enterprise often falls between the two stools of academic respectability on the one hand (since it can readily be dismissed as 'just development work') and industrial relevance on the other (since the prototype is often a long way from a commercial product). Figure 16.1 illustrates the dilemma.

Once a company perceives that an idea offers benefits (especially products or productivity) in less than three years or so, there is a reasonable chance that a collaborative project can be established which, if successful, will lead on to subsequent development work funded entirely by the company. The difficulty is that the gap between a prototype and a product is often much longer than three years. The result is the oft-cited 'British disease' of producing lots of good ideas, but failing to take enough of them through to successful commercial products. Somewhat more support for scaling-up work might contribute to a cure.

It is reasonable to ask, then: is scaling up a task appropriate for a university research department? The answer is a resounding yes! My main thesis is this:

The twin exercises of

(i) scaling up a research prototype to a robust, usable system, and

(ii) studying its behaviour when used in real applications,

expose new research problems which could not otherwise be identified and studied.

Scaling up is not a routine development process. New technical were challenges come to light when building a 'real' system, that either not apparent, or were relatively unimportant, in the prototype stage. Identifying and solving these problems constitutes a durable contribution to knowledge, provided of course that the knowledge is abstracted and published, rather than simply being encoded into the scaled-up prototype.

Scaling up also provides a new opportunity: that of establishing a symbiosis between the emerging robust system on the one hand, and some realistic applications on the other. These applications can give much more 'bite' and focus to the scaling-up effort, and make sure that effort is being directed to where it will be of most use. This interplay often cannot be established at the prototype stage, because the prototype is too small and fragile to handle a real application.

It is not difficult to think of examples of successful scaling-up projects: the York Ada compiler, the Edinburgh LCF system, the HOL theorem-prover, Wirth's Pascal and Modula compilers. A contemporary example is the Fox project at Carnegie Mellon University, which is aimed at implementing the complete TCP/IP protocol stack in Standard ML, to see whether the job can be done in a more modular and robust manner than using the conventional technology. To illustrate the ideas outlined so far, the remainder of this article describes another scaling-up project with which I have been closely involved.

16.3 Functional Programming and the Glasgow Haskell Compiler

I am fortunate to have been supported by a succession of SERC grants to work on the implementation of non-strict functional programming languages, on both sequential and parallel hardware. The most visible outcomes of this work are the Glasgow Haskell Compiler (GHC), and the GRIP multiprocessor. I believe that these are useful artefacts, but probably their most lasting value lies in the research issues their construction exposed, the collaborations they have enabled, the informal standardisation they have nourished, and the framework they have provided for the research of others. I elaborate on these in the following sections. (I use the first person plural throughout, since the work was done with a number of colleagues.) In order to makes sense of what follows, one needs to have some idea of what functional programming is, so I begin with a brief introduction.

16.3.1 Functional programming

Anyone who has used a spreadsheet has experience of functional programming. In a spreadsheet, one specifies the value of each cell in terms of the values of other cells. The focus is on *what* is to be computed, not *how* it should be computed. For example:

- we do not specify the order in which the cells should be calculated – instead we take it for granted that the spreadsheet will compute cells in an order which respects their dependencies;
- we do not tell the spreadsheet how to allocate its memory – rather, we expect it to present us with an apparently infinite plane of cells, and to allocate memory only to those cells which are actually in use;
- for the most part, we specify the value of a cell by an *expression* (whose parts can be evaluated in any order), rather than by a *sequence of commands* which computes its value.

An interesting consequence of the spreadsheet's unspecified order of re-calculation is that the notion of *assignment*, so pervasive in most programming languages, is not very useful. After all, if you don't know exactly when an assignment will happen, you can't make much use of it!

Another well known nearly-functional language is the standard database query language SQL. An SQL query is an expression involving projections, selections, joins and so forth. The query says what relation should be computed, without saying how it should be computed. Indeed, the query can be evaluated in any convenient order. SQL implementations often perform extensive query optimisation which (among other things) figures out the best order in which to evaluate the expression.

Spreadsheets and databases, then, incorporate *specialised, not-quite-functional* languages. It is interesting to ask what you get if you try to design a *general-purpose, purely-functional* language. Haskell is just such a language. To give an idea of what Haskell is like, Figure 16.2 gives a Haskell language function which sorts a sequence of integers using the standard Quicksort algorithm, and an explanation of how the function works. For comparison, Figure 16.3 gives the same function written in C. It is interesting to compare the two:

- The Haskell function is a great deal shorter. Once one has overcome the initial unfamiliarity, it is also much, much easier to convince oneself (formally or informally) that the Haskell function is correct than it is for the C version. Indeed, it is so easy to make a small but fatal error when writing the C version that I copied it out of a textbook.
- On the other hand, the C version incorporates Hoare's very ingenious technique which allows the sequence to be sorted without using any extra space. In contrast, the Haskell program deliberately leaves memory allocation unspecified. As a direct result, functional programs usually use more space (sometimes much more space) than their imperative counterparts, because programmers are much cleverer than compilers at optimising space usage.

Functional languages take a large step towards a higher-level programming model. Programs are easier to design, write and maintain, but the language offers the programmer less control over the program's execution. This is a familiar tradeoff. We all stopped writing assembly-language programs, except perhaps for key inner loops, long ago, because the benefits of using a high-level language (which provides an arbitrary number of named, local variables instead of a fixed number of registers, for example) far outweigh the modest run-time costs. Similarly, we willingly accept the costs of a virtual memory paging system, in exchange for the more supportive programming model of an infinite virtual address space; the days of explicit memory overlays are over. The interesting question is, of course, whether the benefits of a higher level of

```
qsort []        =       []
qsort (x:xs)    =       elts_lt_x ++ [x] ++ elts_greq_x
                where
                elts_lt_x   = [y | y <- xs, y < x]
                elts_greq_x = [y | y <- xs, y >= x]
```

Here is an explanation of how qsort works. The first line reads: 'The result of sorting an empty list (written []) is an empty list.'

The second line reads: 'To sort a list whose first element is x and the rest of which is called xs, just sort all the elements of xs which are less than x (call them elts_lt_x), sort all the elements of xs which are greater than or equal to x (call them elts_greq_x), and concatenate (++) the results, with x sandwiched in the middle.'

The definition of elts_lt_x, which is given immediately below, is read like this: 'elts_lt_x is the list of all y's such that y is drawn from the list xs, and y is less than x.' The definition of elts_greq_x is similar.

The syntax is deliberately reminiscent of standard mathematical set notation, pronouncing '|' as 'such that' and '<-' as 'drawn from'. When asked to sort a non-empty list, qsort calls itself to sort elts_lt_x and elts_greq_x. That's OK because both these lists are smaller than the one originally given to qsort, so the splitting-and-sorting process will eventually reduce to sorting an empty list, which is done rather trivially by the first line of qsort.

Fig. 16.2. Quicksort in Haskell

abstraction outweigh the costs of extra run-time resource consumption. In order even to begin to answer that question, one has to build an implementation which

(i) is sophisticated enough to have reduced the run-time costs to a minimum,

(ii) is robust enough that real programmers can use it for real problems.

The Glasgow Haskell compiler aspires to being such an implementation.

16.3.2 Standardization

While one is building throwaway prototypes, there is little or no incentive to contribute to standardisation. On the other hand, when one contemplates investing substantial effort in a (hopefully) long-lived system, the picture changes entirely. Without some sort of standard interface (a pro-

```
qsort( a, lo, hi )
int a[], hi, lo;
{
  int h, l, p, t;

  if (lo < hi) {
    l = lo;
    h = hi;
    p = a[hi];

    do {
      while (l < h) & (a[i] <= p) do
        l = l+1;
      while (h > l) & (a[h] >= p) do
        h = h-1;
      if (l < h) {
        t = a[l];
        a[l] = a[h];
        a[h] = t;
      }
    } while (l < h);

    t = a[l];
    a[l] = a[hi];
    a[hi] = t;

    qsort( a, lo, l-1 );
    qsort( a, l+1, hi );
}}
```

Fig. 16.3. Quicksort in C

gramming language in our case) nobody will use the system, or want to
invest their own efforts in developing it further.

Until about 1990 there was a fairly anarchic situation in the non-
strict-functional programming community, in which each research group
had its own language, and no common standard had emerged. (This
contrasted with the strict-functional language community which had by
then adopted Standard ML.) Our interest in scaling up led us to become involved in an international effort to agree a common language,
which successfully developed the Haskell language. Many researchers
participated in this process, and most were motivated by a desire to get
non-strict-functional programming into a state where it had some hope
of escaping from the computer lab and into the real world – in short,
scaling up. Haskell is not a formal standard, but now that many research

groups around the world are using Haskell, it has certainly become a *de facto* standard.

16.3.3 Benchmarking

Nowadays, computer systems usually come rated with their 'SPEC-marks'. This relates to the speed at which they can execute the SPEC benchmark suite. Unlike earlier synthetic benchmarks (such as Whetstone), SPEC consists of a collection of real application programs, across a variety of application domains. Small programs with dominant inner loops, which are susceptible to special pleading in an implementation, have been weeded out. As a direct result, more of the designers' creativity has been focused on solving the problems which matter, rather than merely on making Whetstone go fast.

Our focus on practical system-building has led us to attempt, in a modest way, to achieve the same goals for the non-strict-functional programming community. We have collected a variety of large, real application programs, written by people other than ourselves who were simply trying to get a job done (not benchmark a compiler). The resulting suite, the `nofib` suite, is now directly available to others. We use the `nofib` suite on a daily basis as a stress test for our compilation technology. Doing so keeps us honest: deficiencies in our compiler quickly become painfully obvious. A second important use for the suite is as a basis for making detailed quantitative measurements of the behaviour of 'real' functional programs. The fact that these programs were written in the first place was due, in turn, to the existence of a standard language (Haskell in this case), and to the existence of implementations of Haskell which were robust enough that programmers could treat them as a tool rather than as an object of study.

16.3.4 Application

Some four years ago we set up the FLARE project, whose goal was to study the effectiveness (or otherwise) of functional programming in real applications, using the compilers and other tools produced by the Glasgow team. The FLARE participants were deliberately not functional programmers; rather, they were application-domain experts who were prepared to try their hand at functional programming. The applications included a theorem prover, numerical hydrodynamics, data-compression utilities and graphical user interfaces. In retrospect, we were much too ambitious. From our point of view as implementers, FLARE was an enormous success, serving as a major source of direction and focus for our work. But our tools and implementations were, until the final stages of FLARE, embarrassingly immature, especially those for our parallel implementation on the GRIP multiprocessor. As a result our poor application partners had a frustrating time of it. The lessons we would draw from this experience are these:

- using a collection of applications as a 'test load', to guide (or even govern) priorities, is extremely beneficial;
- the application partners must be aware from the start that they are participating in an experiment, not in a product development. Even then, they need a saintly disposition.

16.3.5 Research benefits

Earlier, I mentioned that a most important outcome of the scaling-up exercise is the research payoff, in the form of research issues identified and solved. Our Haskell compiler illustrates the point well. Here are a number of examples:

- **Input/output**. Purely functional languages have in the past provided input/output mechanisms which are rather inconvenient to use, because input/output is inherently a side-effecting activity, rather alien to an otherwise purely-functional setting. As we distributed our compiler more widely, it became clear that difficulties with I/O were a major obstacle to many potential users.

  This painful realisation led us to focus our attention on the I/O problem. Serendipitously, this coincided with work done by one of our colleagues (Wadler) on so-called monads. We discovered how to apply monads to allow I/O-performing computations to be expressed much more easily than before, and to be implemented rather efficiently.

  A neat generalisation allowed direct calls from Haskell to C, a mechanism on which we built the whole of the new I/O system in GHC. Based on the demands of our users, we are now developing the ideas further, to include interrupts, timeouts, and call-backs.
- **Encapsulated state**. An obvious variation of an I/O-performing computation is a computation which performs some side effects on state which is entirely internal to a program. Some (though not many) algorithms appear to be expressible only using mutable state – depth-first search, for example.

Driven by this observation, we have recently succeeded in generalising the I/O-monad idea to accommodate securely-encapsulated computations which manipulate internal mutable state in the program, while presenting a purely-functional external interface to the rest of the program.

- **Profiling** We have always known that functional programs (especially non-strict ones) sometimes consume much more space and/or time than expected. But the advent of real applications turned this issue from a general awareness into a pressing problem.

  Measuring where the time is spent in a non-strict, higher-order language is quite tricky. For example, if one part of a program produces a list which is consumed by another part, the list is only produced as the consumer demands it. This means that execution alternates between producer and consumer, so it becomes much harder to measure how much time is spent in each part of the program.

  The existence of higher-order functions makes things worse: in a higher-order program it is hard to say just what a 'part' of a program, to which execution costs should be attributed, means any more.

  We have succeeded in developing a profiler which solves these problems, the first to provide accurate time profiling for a compiled, non-strict, higher-order language. Its implementation in the GHC provides a convincing demonstration that the ideas work, and do so with an acceptably low overhead. Indeed, many developments of the profiler followed directly from experience of its use.

- **Unboxed data types**. In a non-strict language, a function which takes an integer argument will usually be passed a heap-allocated *suspension* which, when evaluated, produces the integer. To support this argument-passing convention, all integers, whether evaluated or not, are represented by a heap-allocated object or 'box'. In order to do any operations on an integer, it must first be evaluated, extracted from its box, operated on, and then boxed again.

  These boxing and unboxing operations are usually implicit, and handled by the code generator. Unfortunately, that forces into the code generator an important class of optimisations, which aim to manipulate a value in unboxed form for as long as possible. For example, there is little point in adding one to an integer, boxing the result, and then unboxing it again before performing some subsequent operation on it. Getting the code generator to do a really good job of avoiding redundant operations is possible, but it is not easy.

We have developed an alternative approach, in which unboxed values become an explicit part of the language, with a well defined semantics. The boxing and unboxing operations thereby also become explicit, and a set of generally useful program transformations can be used to eliminate redundant operations. The desire for a tidier, more modular implementation led us to develop a useful new theory, whose applicability goes well beyond our own compiler.

This catalogue is not intended as a demonstration of research prowess. The point is simply that most of these issues are either unimportant or inaccessible in a small prototype implementation, but become pressing matters when writing and compiling large Haskell programs. The exercise of scaling up remorselessly exposed new challenges. (The glory of working in a university is, of course, that every new problem can become the object of a new research project, rather than simply being an obstacle to be circumvented.)

16.4 The Compiler as Motherboard

There is a second major crop of research payoffs from the scaling-up exercise. Often individual researchers in functional language implementations have an idea, perhaps a good idea, that they want to try out. For example, they might have devised a new way of analysing programs which should improve the implementation, or a new technique for code generation, or a new program transformation. The difficulty is that to try out their idea they have to build a great deal of scaffolding: often this takes the form of a complete implementation of a very small functional language, complete with front end, symbol table, code generation, and so on. It has to be a very small language in order to make the scaffolding feasible at all, and even then it is quite an effort. The outcome of such work is often extremely unconvincing. Even if the idea gives good results on the half-dozen tiny programs on which its behaviour is measured, what does that say about its behaviour when given a 30,000 line program?

A major goal of our compiler was to resolve this dilemma by providing a well structured 'motherboard' into which researchers can 'plug in' their incremental improvements. The front end, back end, and (most important) suite of benchmark programs, are all provided. The effort of integrating one's ideas into a large existing compiler is still not small, but it is much smaller than that of making a complete new implementation for even a small language, and the results are incomparably more convincing. Not only that, but if the project is successful, its results can be used immediately by others. Here are some examples of the ways in which our compiler has already been used as a 'motherboard', mostly by PhD students:

- **Generational garbage collection** has been used for languages such as Lisp and Standard ML for some while. The folklore was that it would work badly for *non-strict* languages such as Haskell, because suspensions are continually being updated, an operation which is relatively expensive for generational collectors.

  Based on measurements of substantial Haskell programs we have been able to show that, on the contrary, generational collectors work very well for non-strict programs, because objects are almost always updated when they are very young. The compiler we distribute now has a generational collector as standard.

- **Deforestation**. Functional programmers tend to make heavy use of lists (and other data structures) as intermediate values connecting a pipeline of computations together. For example, consider the expression

  ```
  map f (map g xs)
  ```

  The function `map` applies a function (its first argument) to each element of a list (its second argument). The expression given above therefore first applies `g` to each element of `xs`, builds a list of those results, and applies `f` to each element of this list. An intermediate list is built, only to be consumed immediately. The program is easier to understand in this form, but less efficient to execute than one in which the computations are entwined together with no intermediate structures. For example, here is an equivalent expression:

  ```
  map (f.g) xs
  ```

  A single map suffices to apply the function f-composed-with-g, `(f.g)`, to the list `xs`. It is well known that the intermediate lists can often be transformed out, a process known as deforestation, but the process has so far been too complex, or incomplete, to automate. We have recently developed two new approaches to deforestation which can be completely automated, and are incorporating them in the compiler. As in other cases, the motivation was provided by the need for practical, rather than idealised, solutions. Our experience with implementing our deforestation techniques in GHC led directly to new developments.

- **Strictness analysis** is a static program analysis that aims to discover when a given function is sure to evaluate its argument(s), and to what degree. Using this information it is often possible to derive a more efficient calling convention for the function. A very large number of papers have been written about strictness analysis, but only a tiny minority report the effectiveness of the analysis on any but minute examples. The reason is exactly that outlined above: they lack adequate scaffolding.

  We have used our compiler to make detailed measurements of a fairly simple strictness analyser, and we know of others who are building more sophisticated analysers for the compiler.

- **Compilation by transformation** A unifying theme of the compiler is the use of program transformation as the major compilation technique. The program being compiled is translated into a simple 'Core' language, and is then extensively transformed, before being fed to the code generator. This is not, of course, an original idea, but having the transformation system embedded in a substantial compiler has enabled a PhD student to make extensive quantitative measurements of the effectiveness of a variety of transformation strategies. These, in turn, led him to propose, implement, and measure a variety of new transformations which we had not at first thought of.

16.4.1 Research vs. development

A major tension in this kind of project is between the research goals on the one hand, and the care and maintenance of the artefact itself on the other. It is all too easy for the compiler to take on a life of its own, and to absorb all the limited effort we have available. We come under pressure from our users to enhance it in one way or another, and it is, in any case, all too easy to become addicted to adding 'one more feature'. One can address each such demand in one of three ways:

- **Resist it**, on the grounds that it isn't research, involves too much work, or that it opens up too big a research area. Examples of desirable developments we have not undertaken for these reasons are: an interactive version of our compiler, a persistent store, and a dynamic data type to allow run-time type checking where required.
- **Try to satisfy it as directly and economically as possible**, because it will make a real impact on the usefulness and acceptability of the system. Requests that fall into this category include porting to

other machine architectures, improving compilation speed, reducing compiled code size, and allowing Haskell to manipulate pointers into malloc'd C space.

- **Treat it as a new research opportunity**. We took this approach with input/output, mixed-language working, profiling, and graphical user interfaces. The important thing is to recognise and embrace the third option: a major justification for the whole scaling-up exercise is, after all, to expose new research problems.

16.5 Conclusions

I have argued that the exercise of scaling up a research prototype into a robust implementation, if carefully undertaken, is a legitimate, fruitful and important form of research. When it goes well it can set up a virtuous circle of benefits:

- it exposes new research challenges which could not otherwise be identified and studied;
- it makes available a useful tool for others to use, which may in turn open up new areas of application for the technology, leading to new challenges;
- it provides valuable scaffolding to support the research of others in the same area;
- it contributes to standardisation;
- it allows credible quantitative measurements to be made;
- it bridges an important part of the gap between a proof-of-concept prototype and a commercial product.

So far as funding policy is concerned, I would argue that those who fund research should be willing to support some well thought-out scaling-up projects. They are likely to be more expensive than the more common 'develop-an-idea' project, and should be rigorously scrutinised to make sure that the objectives concern research rather than artefacts. The whole argument is really directed more towards modifying the cultural assumptions of referees than towards changing any official funding policy.

Building things is tremendously exciting; and much research lies in the building, as well as in the original vision.

Postscript

Papers describing all the work mentioned above can be found in my World Wide Web home page:

http://www.dcs.glasgow.ac.uk/~simonpj

References

Abbott, J.A., R.J. Bradford & J.H. Davenport (1985) 'A remark on factorisation'. *SIGSAM Bulletin* **19**, 31–33, 37.

Abdel-Ghaly, A.A., P.Y. Chan & B. Littlewood (1986) 'Evaluation of competing software reliability predictions'. *IEEE Trans. Software Eng.* **12**, 950–967.

Abramsky, S. (1991) 'Domain theory in logical form'. *Ann. Pure Appl. Logic* **51**, 1–77.

Abramsky, S., P. Malacaria & R. Jagadeesan (1994) 'Full abstraction for PCF'. In Springer Lecture Notes in Computer Science **789**, 1–15.

ACM/IEEE (1991) *Computing Curricula*.

Aczel, P. (1988) *Non-well-founded Sets*, CSLI Lecture Notes **14**, CSLI, Stanford University. Distributed by Cambridge University Press.

Aho, A.V., J.E. Hopcroft & J.D. Ullman (1974) *The Design and Analysis of Computer Algorithms* Addison Wesley.

Aiken, Peter, Alice Muntz & Russ Richards (1994) 'DoD legacy systems'. *CACM* **37**, 26–41.

Alford, M.W. (1994) 'Attacking requirements complexity using a separation of concerns'. In *Proc. 1st International Conference on Requirements Engineering, Colorado Springs* IEEE Computer Society Press.

Alur, R., T. Feder & T. Henzinger (1991) 'The benefits of relaxing punctuality'. *Proc. ACM Conference on Principles of Distributed Computing*.

Alvey Committee (1982) *A Programme for Advanced Information Technology* HMSO.

Amman, P.E. & J.C. Knight (1988) 'Data diversity: an approach to software fault tolerance'. *IEEE Trans. on Comp.* **37**, 418–425.

Anderson, T., P.A. Barrett, D.N. Halliwell & M.R. Moulding (1985) 'An evaluation of software fault tolerance in a practical system'. In *Proc. 15th IEEE Int. Symp. on Fault-Tolerant Computing (FTCS-15)*, Ann Arbor MI, 140–145.

Andreev, A.A. (1985) 'A method of proving lower bounds of individual monotone functions'. *Soviet Math. Dokl.* **31**, 530–534.

Andreski, S. (1972) *Social Science as Sorcery* Pelican Books.

Anon (1994) 'Critical technology assessment of the US artificial intelligence sector'. Technical Report PB93-192409, US Department of Commerce.

ANSI (1975) 'Interim report of ANSI/X3/SPARC study group on data base management systems'. *ACM SIGFIDET* **7**, 3–139.

Appel, K.I. & W. Haken (1977a) 'The proof of the Four Color Theorem I: Discharging; II: Reducibility'. *Illinois J. Math.* **21**, 421–490; 491–567.

Appel, K.I. & W. Haken (1977b) 'The solution of the Four-Color-Map problem'. *Sci. Am.* **237**, (4) 108–121.

Appel, K.I. & W. Haken (1986) 'The Four Color proof suffices'. *Math. Intelligencer* **8**, (1) 10–20.

Apple Computer (1987) *Apple Human Interface Guidelines* Addison Wesley.

Atkinson, M.D. (1987) 'An optimal algorithm for geometrical congruence'. *J. Algorithms* **8**, 159–172.

Atkinson, M.D & J.-R. Sack (1992) 'Generating binary trees at random'. *Inform. Proc. Letters* **41**, 21–23.

Atkinson, M.D & R. Beals (1994) 'Priority queues and permutations'. *SIAM J. Comput.* **23**, 1225–1230.

Atkinson, M.D., M.J. Livesey & D. Tulley (in preparation) 'Permutations generated by token passing in graphs'.

Audsley, N.C., A. Burns, R.I. Davis, K.W. Tindell & A.J. Wellings (1994) *Fixed Priority Scheduling: an Historical Perspective* Technical Report, Department of Computer Science, University of York.

Avizienis, A. & D.E. Ball (1987) 'On the achievement of a highly dependable and fault-tolerant air traffic control system'. *IEEE Trans. on Comp.* **20**, 84–90.

Baayen, Harald (1991) 'A stochastic process for word frequency distributions'. In *Proc. 29th Annual Meeting of the Association for Computational Linguistics*, 271–278.

Baayen, Harald, R. Piepenbrock & H. van Rijn (1993) *The* CELEX *Lexical Database (CD-ROM)* University of Pennsylvania, Philadelphia, Linguistic Data Consortium.

Bachmann, C.W. (1973) 'The programmer as navigator'. *CACM* **16**, 653–658.

Backelin, J. & R. Fröberg (1991) 'How we proved that there are exactly 924 cyclic 7-roots'. In *Proc. ISSAC 1991* ACM Press 103–111.

Backus, J. (1978) 'Can programming be liberated from the von Neumann style? A functional style and its algebra of programs'. *CACM* **21**, 613–641.

Baeten, J.C.M. & W.P. Weijland (1990) *Process Algebra*, Cambridge Tracts in Theor. Comp. Sci. 18, Cambridge University Press.

Balcazár, J.L., J. Diáz & J . Gabarró (1988) *Structural Complexity I* Springer Verlag.

Barendregt, H. (1984) *The Lambda Calculus*, revised edition North Holland.

Barlow, R.E. & F. Proschan (1975) *Statistical Theory of Reliability and Life Testing* Holt, Rinehart & Winston.

Barrett, G. (1987) *Formal Methods applied to a Floating Point Number System* Monograph PRG–58, Oxford University Computing Laboratory, Programming Research Group.

Bassiliades, N. & P.M.D. Gray (1994) 'Colan: A functional Constraint Language and its implementation'. *Data Knowl. Eng.* **14**, 203–249.

Bates, J.L. & R.L. Constable (1985) 'Proofs as programs'. *ACM Trans. Program. Lang. Syst.* **7**, 113–136.

Bergstra, J.A. & J.W. Klop (1985) 'Algebra of communicating processes with abstraction'. *Theor. Comp. Sci.* **37**, 77–121.

Berry, G. (1978) 'Stable models of typed λ-calculus'. In Springer Lecture Notes in Computer Science **62**, 72–89.

Berry, G. & L. Cosserat (1985) 'The ESTEREL synchronous programming language and its mathematical semantics'. In Springer Lecture Notes in Computer Science **197**, 389–449.

Berry, G. & P.-L. Curien (1982) 'Sequential algorithms on concrete data structures'. *Theor. Comp. Sci.* **20**, 265–321.

Biber, Douglas (1993) 'Using register-diversified corpora for general language studies'. *Comp. Ling.* **19**, 219–241.

Biermann A.W. (1994) 'Computer science for the many'. *IEEE Computer* **27**, (2) 62–73.

Birch, B.J. & H.P.F. Swinnerton-Dyer (1963) 'Notes on elliptic curves I'. *J. für Reine und Angew. Math.* **212**, 7–23.

Bird, R. S. (1986) *An Introduction to the Theory of Lists* Technical Report PRG-56, Oxford University Computing Laboratory, Programming Research Group.

Bird, R.S. (1988) 'Lectures on constructive functional programming'. In *NATO ASI Series F (55) Constructive Methods in Computer Science* Springer Verlag, 151–218.

Black, E., F. Jelinek, J. Lafferty, D.M. Magerman, R. Mercer & S. Roukos (1993) 'Towards history-based grammars: using richer models for probabilistic parsing'. In *Proc. 31st Annual Meeting of the Association for Computational Linguistics*, 31–37.

Black, E., J. Lafferty & S. Roukos (1992) 'Development and evaluation of a broad-coverage probabilistic grammar of English-language computer manuals'. In *Proc. 30th Annual Meeting of the Association for Computational Linguistics*, 185–192.

Bobrow, D.G., R.M. Kaplan, D.A. Norman, H. Thompson & T. Winograd (1977) 'Gus, a frame-driven dialog system'. *Artif. Intell.* **8**, 172.

Bobrow, R.J. (1991) 'Statistical agenda parsing'. In *Proc. February 1991 DARPA Speech and Natural Language Workshop* Morgan Kaufmann, 222-224.

Bod, R. (1992) 'A computational model of language performance: data oriented parsing'. In *Proc. 15th International Conference on Computational Linguistics (COLING-92)*, Volume III, 855–859.

Bod, R. (1993) 'Using an annotated corpus as a stochastic grammar'. In *Proc. 6th Conference of the European Chapter of the Association for Computational Linguistics*, 37–44.

Boehm, B. (1981) *Software Engineering Economics* Prentice Hall).

Bowman, C.M., P.B. Danzig, U. Manber & M.F. Schwartz (1994) 'Scalable Internet resource discovery: research problems and approaches'. *CACM* **37**, 98–107.

Brassard, G. & P. Bratley (1988) *Algorithmics: Theory and Practice* Prentice Hall.

Brent, Michael R. (1993) 'From grammar to lexicon: unsupervised learning of lexical syntax'. *Comp. Ling.* **19**, 243-262.

Briere, D., D. Ribot & D. Pilaud (1994) 'Method and specification tools for airbus on board systems'. In *Proc. 1994 Avionics Conference and Exhibition* ERA Technology.

Brill, E. (1992) 'A simple rule-based part of speech tagger'. In *Proc. 3rd ACL Conference on Applied Natural Language Processing*, 152-155.

Brill, . & M.P. Marcus (1992) 'Automatically acquiring phrase structure using distributional analysis'. In *Proc. February 1992 DARPA Speech and Natural Language Workshop* Morgan Kaufmann, 155–159.

Brill, E., D.M. Magerman, M.P. Marcus & B. Santorini (1990) 'Deducing linguistic structure from the statistics of large corpora'. In *Proc. June 1990 DARPA Speech and Natural Language Workshop* Morgan Kaufmann, 275–281.

Briscoe, E. & J. Carroll (1993) 'Generalized probabilistic LR parsing of natural language (corpora) with unification-based grammars'. *Comp. Ling.* **19**, 25–59.

Briscoe, E., V. de Paiva & A. Copestake (eds.) (1993) *Inheritance, Defaults, and the Lexicon* Cambridge University Press.

Brocklehurst, S., P.Y. Chan, B. Littlewood & J. Snell (1990) 'Recalibrating software reliability models'. *IEEE Trans. Software Eng.* **16**, 458–470.

Brocklehurst, S., B. Littlewood, T. Olovsson & E. Jonsson (1994) 'On measurement of operational security'. In *COMPASS 94, 9th Annual IEEE Conference on Computer Assurance* IEEE Computer Society, 257–266.

Bronstein, M. (1990) 'The transcendental Risch differential equation'. *J. Symb. Comp.* **9**, 49–60.

Brookes, S.D., C.A.R. Hoare & A.W. Roscoe (1984) 'A theory of communicating sequential processes'. *JACM* **31**, 560–599.

Brouwer, L.E.J. (1907) *Over de grondslagen der wiskunde* Doctoral Thesis, Amsterdam.

Brown, P.J. (1992) 'UNIX Guide: lessons from ten years' development.'. In *Proc. ACM Conference on Hypertext, Milan*, D. Lucarella *et al.* (eds.) ACM Press, New York 63–70.

Brown, P.F., S.A. Della Pietra, V.J. Della Pietra, & R. Mercer (1991) 'Word-sense disambiguation using statistical methods'. In *Proc. 29th Annual Meeting of the Association for Computational Linguistics*, 264–270.

Brown, P.F., V.J. Della Pietra, V. de Souza, J.C. Lai & R. Mercer (1992) 'Class-based n-gram models of natural language'. *Comp. Ling.* **18**, 467–479.

Broy, M. (1987) 'Semantics of finite and infinite networks of concurrent communicating agents'. *Distrib. Comp.* **2**, 13–31.

Buchberger, B. (1970) 'Ein algorithmisches Kriterium für die Lösbarkeit eines algebraischen Gleichungssystem'. *Aeq. Math.* **4**, 374–383.

Buchberger, B. (1979) 'A criterion for detecting unnecessary reductions in the construction of Gröbner bases'. In *Proc. EUROSAM 79*, Springer Lecture Notes in Computer Science **72** 3–21.

Buchberger, B. (1985) 'Gröbner bases, an algorithmic method in polynomial ideal theory'. In *Recent Trends in Multi-Dimensional System Theory*, N.K. Bose (ed.), Reidel, 184–232.

Burns, A. & A. Lister (1991) 'A framework for building dependable systems'. *Comp. J.* **34**, 173–181.

Burns, A. & J.A. McDermid (1994) 'Real-time, safety-critical systems: analysis and synthesis'. *Soft. Eng. J.* **9**, 264–281.

Burns, A., M. Nicholson, K. Tindell & N. Zhang (1993) 'Allocating and scheduling hard real-time tasks on a point-to-point distributed system'. In *Proc. Workshop on Parallel and Distributed Real-Time Systems, April 1993*.

Burstall, R.M. & J. Darlington (1977) 'A transformation system for developing recursive programs'. *JACM* **24**, 44–67.

Bush, V. (1967) *Science is Not Enough* William Morrow.

Cade, J.J. (1985) 'A new public-key cipher which allows signatures'. *Proc. 2nd SIAM Conf. on Applied Linear Algebra, Raleigh NC*.

Cannon, J.J. (1984) 'An introduction to the group theory language Cayley'. In *Computational Group Theory*, M.D. Atkinson (ed.), Academic Press.

Card, S.K., T.P. Moran & A. Newell (1983) *The Psychology of Human Computer Interaction* Lawrence Erlbaum Associates.

Caron, T. & R.D. Silverman (1988) 'Parallel implementation of the quadratic sieve'. *J. Supercomp.* **1**, 273–290.

Carre, B.A. *et al.* (1992) *SPARK – The Spade Ada Kernel (Edition 3.1)* Program Validation Limited.

CEGB (1982a) *Design Safety Criteria for CEGB Nuclear Power Stations*, HS/R167/81 Central Electricity Generating Board.

CEGB (1982b) *Pressurised Water Reactor Design Safety Guidelines,* DSG2 (Issue A) Central Electricity Generating Board.

Chapman, R.C., A. Burns & A. J. Wellings (1993) 'Worst case execution time analysis of exceptions in Ada'. In *Ada: Towards Maturity: Proceedings of 1993 Ada UK Conference,* L. Collingbourne (ed.), IOS Press.

Chapman, R.C., A. Burns & A. J. Wellings (1994) 'Integrated program proof and worst-case timing analysis of SPARK Ada'. In *Proc. Workshop on Languages, Compilers and Tools for Real-Time Systems* ACM Press, Orlando, FL.

Checkland P. & J. Scholes (1990) *Soft Systems Methodology in Action* Wiley.

Cheng, Y.C., D.J. Houck, J.M. Liu, M.S. Meketon, L. Slutsman, R.J. Vanderbei & P. Wang (1989) 'The AT&T KORBX system'. *AT&T Tech. J.* **68**, 7–19.

Chitrao, M.V. & R. Grishman (1990) 'Statistical parsing of messages'. In *Proc. June 1990 DARPA Speech and Natural Language Workshop* Morgan Kaufmann, 263–266.

Church, A. (1941) *The Calculi of Lambda Conversion* Princeton University Press.

Church, K.W. & R.L. Mercer (1993) 'Introduction to the special issue on computational linguistics using large corpora'. *Comp. Ling.* **19**, 1–24.

Church, K.W. & R. Patil (1982) 'Coping with syntactic ambiguity or how to put the block in the box on the table'. *Am. J. Comp. Ling.* **8**, 139–149.

Churchhouse, R.F. (1988) 'Some recent discoveries in number theory and analysis made by the use of a computer'. In *Computers in Mathematical Research,* N.M. Stephens & M.P. Thorne (eds.) IMA Conference (NS) **14** Clarendon Press, Oxford, 1–14.

Ciardo, G., J. Muppala & K. Trivedi (1994) 'Analysing concurrent and fault-tolerant software using stochastic reward nets'. *J. Par. Distrib. Comp.* (to appear).

Clarke, S.J. & J.A. McDermid (1993) 'Software fault-trees and weakest pre-condition analysis: an evaluation and comparison'. *Soft. Eng. J.* **8**, 225–236.

Cohen, P.R. (1991) 'A survey of the eighth national conference on artificial intelligence: pulling together or pulling apart'. *AI Magazine* **12**, 16–41.

Coleman, D., P. Arnold, S. Bodoff, C. Dollin, H. Gilchrist, F. Hayes & P. Jeremes (1994) *Object-Oriented Development: the Fusion Method* Prentice Hall.

Collins, N.E., R.W. Eglese & B.L. Golden (1988) 'Simulated annealing – an annotated bibliography'. *Amer. J. Math. Management Sci.* **8**, 209–307.

Constant, E.W., II (1980) *The Origins of the Turbojet Revolution* Johns Hopkins University Press.

Cook, S. (1971) 'The complexity of theorem proving procedures'. In *Proc. 3rd Annual ACM Symposium on Theory of Computing* 151–158.

Cooley, J.W. & J.W. Tukey (1965) 'An algorithm for the machine calculation of complex Fourier series'. *Math. Comp.* **19**, 297–301.

Coombes, A., J.A. McDermid & P. Morris (1994) 'Causality as a means for the expression of requirements for safety critical systems'. In *COMPASS 94, 9th Annual IEEE Conference on Computer Assurance* IEEE Computer Society.

Copestake, A. & K. Sparck Jones (1990) 'Natural language interfaces to databases'. *Knowl. Eng. Rev.* **5**, 225–249.

Coppersmith, D. & S. Winograd (1990) 'Matrix multiplication via arithmetic progressions'. *J. Symb. Comp.* **9**, 251–280.

Cormen, T.H., C.H. Leiserson & R.L. Rivest (1992) *Algorithms* McGraw Hill.

Cowie, J., J.A. Guthrie & L. Guthrie (1992) 'Lexical disambiguation using simulated annealing'. In *Proc. 15th International Conference on Computational Linguistics (COLING-92)* Volume I, 359–365.

CREST Project Team (1994) *CREST: Principles and Requirements (revised)* Bank of England.

Cristian, F. (1990) *Understanding Fault-tolerant Distributed Systems* IBM Research Report RJ6980.

Curry, H.B. (1963) *Foundations of Mathematical Logic* McGraw Hill.

Daelemans, W. (1994) 'Memory-based lexical acquisition and processing'. Tilburg: ITK Research Report 49, May 1994. To appear in *Machine Translation and the Lexicon*, Petra Steffens (ed.), Springer Lecture Notes in Artificial Intelligence.

Daelemans, W. & G. Gazdar (eds.) (1992) *Comp. Ling.* **18**, parts 2, 3, special issues on inheritance.

Dagan, I. & Itai, A. (1994) 'Word sense disambiguation using a second language monolingual corpus'. *Comp. Ling.* **20**, 563–596.

Dagan, I., S. Marcus & S. Markovitch (1993) 'Contextual word similarity and estimation from sparse data'. In *Proc. 31st Annual Meeting of the Association for Computational Linguistics*, 164–171.

Dardenne, A., A. van Lamsweerde & S. Fickas (1993) 'Goal directed requirements acquisition'. *Sci. Comp. Progr.* **20**, 3–50.

Darlington, J. & M. Reeve (1981) 'A multi-processor reduction machine for the parallel evaluation of applicative languages'. In *ACM Conference on Functional Programming Languages and Computer Architectures* 65–74.

Darlington, J. & H.W. To (1993) 'Building parallel applications without programming'. In *Leeds Workshop on Abstract Parallel Machine Models 93* Oxford University Press.

Darlington, J., Y. Guo, H.W. To, & J. Yang (1995) 'Functional skeletons for parallel coordination'. In *Proc. EuroPar* Springer Verlag.

Davenport, J.H. (1981) *On the Integration of Algebraic Functions* Springer Lecture Notes in Computer Science **102**.

Davenport J.H., P. Gianni & B.M. Trager (1991) 'Scratchpad's view of algebra II: A categorical view of factorization'. In *Proc. ISSAC 1991* ACM Press, 32–38.

Davenport, J.H. & B.M. Trager (1990) 'Scratchpad's view of algebra I: Basic commutative algebra'. In *Proc. DISCO '90*, A. Miola (ed.) Springer Lecture Notes in Computer Science **429** 40–54.

Davies, J. (1991) *Specification and Proof in Real-time Systems* DPhil thesis, Programming Research Group, University of Oxford. Published in *Distinguished Dissertations in Computer Science* Cambridge University Press.

Davis A.M. (1990) *Software Requirements Analysis and Specification* Prentice Hall.

Dawid, A.P. (1984) 'Statistical theory: the prequential approach'. *J. Roy. Statist. Soc., A* **147**, 278–292.

de Bakker, J.W. & J.-J.Ch. Meyer (1988) 'Metric semantics for concurrency'. *BIT* **28**, 504–529.

de Bruijn, N.G. (1980) 'A survey of the project Automath'. In *To H.B.*

Curry: Essays on Combinatory Logic, Lambda Calculus and Formalism, J.P. Seldin & J.R. Hindley (eds.), Academic Press, 579–606.

Delaunay, Ch. (1860) *Théorie du mouvement de la lune* CR l'Acad. Sci. **LI**.

DeMarco T. (1979) *Structured Analysis and System Specification* Prentice Hall.

Dertouzos, M. (1974) 'Control robotics: the procedural control of physical processes'. In *Information Processing* **74**, J.L. Rosefeld (ed.) North Holland.

Devlin, Keith (1991) *Logic and Information* Cambridge University Press.

Dijkstra, E.W. (1972) 'Notes on Structured Programming'. In *Structured Programming*, O. Dahl, E.W. Dijkstra & C.A.R. Hoare (eds.), Adademic Press, 2.

Dijkstra, E.W. (1976) *A Discipline of Programming* Prentice Hall.

Dubois, D. & H. Prade (1988) *Possibility Theory: An Approach to Computerised Processing of Uncertainty* Plenum Press.

Dunning, Ted (1993) 'Accurate methods for the statistics of surprise and coincidence'. *Comp. Ling.* **19**, 61–74.

Duran, J.T. & S. Ntafos (1984) 'An evaluation of random testing'. *IEEE Trans. Soft. Eng.* **10**, 438–444.

Durfee, Edmund H., Victor R. Lesser & Daniel D. Corkill (1989) 'Cooperative distributed problem solving'. In *The Handbook of Artificial Intelligence IV*, Avron Barr, Paul R. Cohen & Edward A. Feigenbaum (eds.), Addison Wesley, 85–147.

Eckhardt, D.E. & L.D. Lee (1985) 'A theoretical basis of multiversion software subject to coincident errors'. *IEEE Trans. Soft. Eng.* **11**, 1511–1517.

Eckhardt, D.E., A.K. Caglayan, J.C. Knight, L.D. Lee, D.F. McAllister, M.A. Vouk & J.P.J. Kelly (1991) 'An experimental evaluation of software redundancy as a strategy for improving reliability'. *IEEE Trans. Soft. Eng* **17**, 692–702.

Edmonds, J. (1965) 'Paths, trees, and flowers'. *Canad. J. Math.* **17**, 449–467.

Ehrig, H., B. Mahr, I. Classen & F. Orejas (1992) 'Introduction to algebraic specification. Part 1: Formal methods for software development. Part 2: From classical view to foundations of systems specifications'. *Comp. J.* **35**, 451–459; 460–467.

Embury, S.M., P.M.D. Gray & N. Bassiliades (1993) 'Constraint maintenance using generated methods in the P/FDM OODB'. In *Proc. 1st Workshop on Rules in Database Systems*, N.W. Paton & M.H. Williams (eds.), Springer Verlag, 364–381.

Erdös, P. (1932) 'Beweis eines Satzes von Tchebyschef'. *Acta Litt. Ac. Sci. (Szeged)* **5**, 194–198.

Faugère, J.C., P. Gianni, D. Lazard, & T. Mora (1993) 'Efficient computation of zero-dimensional Gröbner bases by change of ordering'. *J. Symb. Comp.* **16**, 329–344.

Fenelon, P. (1993) 'Towards an integrated toolset for software safety analysis'. *J. Syst. Soft.* **21**, 279–290.

Fenelon, P., D.J. Pumfrey, J.A. McDermid & M. Nicholson (1994) 'Towards integrated safety analysis and design'. *ACM Comp. Surveys* **2**, 21–32.

Fenton, N.E. (1991) *Software Metrics: A Rigorous Approach* Chapman & Hall.

Ferguson E.S. (1992) *Engineering and the Mind's Eye* MIT Press.

Frenkel, K.A. (1991) 'The human genome project and informatics'. *CACM* **34**, 41–51.

Fröhlich, A. & J.C. Shepherdson (1956) 'Effective procedures in field theory'. *Phil. Trans. Roy. Soc. Ser. A* **248**, 407–432.

Gale, W.A. & K.W. Church (1990) 'Poor estimates of context are worse than none'. In *Proc. June 1990 DARPA Speech and Natural Language Workshop* Morgan Kaufmann, 283-287.

Gale, W.A., K.W. Church & D. Yarowsky (1992a) 'Estimating upper and lower bounds on the performance of word-sense disambiguation programs'. In *Proc. 30th Annual Meeting of the Association for Computational Linguistics*, 249–256.

Gale, W.A., K.W. Church & D. Yarowsky (1992b) 'One sense per discourse'. In *Proc. February 1992 DARPA Speech and Natural Language Workshop* Morgan Kaufmann, 233–237.

Garey, M.R. & D.S. Johnson (1979) *Computers and Intractability: A Guide to the Theory of NP-Completeness* Freeman.

Gathen, J. von zur (1990) 'Functional decomposition of polynomials: the tame case'. *J. Symb. Comp.* **9**, 281–299.

Gazdar, G. (1983) 'Phrase structure grammars and natural languages'.

In *Proc. 8th International Joint Conference on Artificial Intelligence*, 556–565.

Gazdar, G. (1988) 'Applicability of indexed grammars to natural languages'. In *Natural Language Parsing and Linguistic Theory*, Uwe Reyle & Christian Rohrer (eds.), Reidel, 69–94.

Gazdar, G. & G.K. Pullum (1981) 'Subcategorization, constituent order and the notion head'. In *The Scope of Lexical Rules*, M. Moortgat, H. v.d. Hulst, & T. Hoekstra (eds.), Foris Publications, 107–123. Also in *Linguistics in the Morning Calm*, Linguistic Society of Korea (ed.), Hanshin Publishing Co., 195–209.

Gazdar, G. & G.K. Pullum (1985) 'Computationally relevant properties of natural languages and their grammars'. *New Generation Computing* **3**, 273-306. Reprinted in *The Formal Complexity of Natural Language*, Walter J. Savitch, Emmon Bach, William Marsh & Gila Safran-Naveh (eds.), Reidel, 387–437 (1987).

Gelernter, D. & N. Carriero (1992) 'Coordination languages and their significance'. *CACM* **35**, 97–107.

Gianni, P., B.M. Trager & G. Zacharias (1988) 'Gröbner Bases and primary decomposition of polynomial ideals'. *J. Symb. Comp.* **6**, 149–167.

Gilb, T. (1988) *Principles of Software Engineering Management* Addison Wesley.

Goel, A.L. & K. Okumoto (1979) 'Time-dependent error-detection rate model for software and other performance measures'. *IEEE Trans. Reliability* **28**, 206–211.

Goguen, J.A. & T. Winkler (1988) *Introducing OBJ3* Technical Report SRI–CSL–88–9, SRI International Computer Science Laboratory.

Goldberg, D.E. (1989) *Genetic Algorithms in Search, Optimisation and Machine Learning* Addison Wesley.

Good, I.J. (1984) *Mechanical Proofs about Computer Programs* Technical Report 41, Institute for Computing Science, University of Texas at Austin.

Good, I.J. & R.F. Churchhouse (1968) 'The Riemann hypothesis and pseudorandom features of the Möbius sequence'. *Math. Comp.* **22**, 857–862.

Goodwin, C. (1981) *Conversational Organization: Interaction between Speakers and Hearers* Academic Press.

Gray, P.M.D. (1984) *Logic, Algebra and Databases* Ellis Horwood.

Gray, P.M.D., K.G. Kulkarni & N.W. Paton (1992) *Object-Oriented Databases: A Semantic Data Model Approach* Prentice Hall.

Gray, P.M.D. & G.J.L. Kemp (1994) 'Object-oriented systems and data independence'. In *OOIS'94 Proceedings*, D. Patel, Y. Sun & S. Patel (eds.) Springer Verlag, 3–24.

Gray, W.D., B.E. John & M.E. Atwood (1992) 'The précis of Project Ernestine or, an overview of a validation of GOMS'. In *CHI '92 Conf. Proc.* ACM SIGCHI.

Gray, W.D., B.E. John & M.E. Atwood (1993) 'Project Ernestine: validating a GOMS analysis for predicting and explaining real-world task performance'. *Human Comp. Int.* **8**, 237–309.

Greatbatch D., P. Luff, C. Heath & P. Campion (1993) 'Interpersonal communication and human–computer interaction: an examination of the use of computers in medical consultations'. *Int. J. of Interacting with Comp.* **5**, 193–216.

Greene, D.H. & D.E. Knuth (1982) *Mathematics for the Analysis of Algorithms* Birkh user.

Gries, D. (1990) 'The maximum-segment-sum problem'. In *Formal Development of Programs and Proofs*, E.W. Dijkstra (ed.) Addison Wesley, 33–36.

Gruber, T.R. (1993) 'A translation approach to portable ontology specifications'. *Knowl. Acq.* **5**, 199–220.

Guha, R.V. & Douglas B. Lenat (1994) 'Enabling agents to work together'. *CACM* **37**, 127–142.

Gunter, C.A. & D.S. Scott (1990) 'Semantic domains'. In *Handbook of Computer Science, Volume B: Formal Models and Semantics*, J. van Leeuwen (ed.) Elsevier, 633–674.

Guthrie, J.A., L. Guthrie, Y. Wilks & H. Aidinejad (1991) 'Subject-dependent co-occurrence and word sense disambiguation'. In *Proc. 29th Annual Meeting of the Association for Computational Linguistics*, 146–152.

Guy, K., L. Georghiou, P. Quintas, M. Hobday, H. Cameron and T. Ray (1991) *Evaluation of the Alvey Programme for Advanced Information Technology* HMSO.

Hardy, G.H. (1916) *The Integration of Functions of a Single Variable (2nd. edition)* Cambridge University Press.

Hardy, G.H. (1940) *A Mathematician's Apology* (with a foreword by C.P. Snow, 1967) Cambridge University Press.

Harel, D. (1987) 'Statecharts: A visual formalism for complex systems'. *Sci. Comp. Progr.* **8**, 231–274.

Harel, D., H. Lachover, A. Naamad & A. Pnueli (1990) 'Statemate: a working environment for the development of complex reactive systems'. *IEEE Trans. Soft. Eng.* , .

Haselgrove, C.B. (1953) 'Implementations of the Todd–Coxeter algorithm on EDSAC-1'. Unpublished.

Haselgrove, C.B. (1958) 'A disproof of a conjecture of Pólya'. *Mathematika* **5**, 141–145.

Heath C., M. Jirotka, P. Luff & J. Hindmarsh (1993) 'Unpacking collaboration: the interactional organisation of trading in a City dealing room'. In *Proc. 3rd European Conf. on Computer-Supported Cooperative Work P ECSCW '93* Kluwer 155–170.

Heger, A. Sharif & W.V. Koen (1991) 'KNOWBOT: an adaptive data base interface'. *Nucl. Sci. Eng.* **107**, 142–157.

Hehner, E.C.R. (1984) 'Predicative programming'. *CACM* **27**, 134–143.

Hehner, E.C.R. (1989) 'Real-time programming'. *Inform. Proc. Letters* **30**, 51–56.

Henrion, M. & B. Fischhoff (1986) 'Assessing uncertainty in physical constants'. *Am. J. Phys.* **54**, 791–798.

Hentenryck, P. van 'Constraint logic programming'. *Knowl. Eng. Rev.* **6**, 151–194.

Henzinger, T., Z. Manna & A. Pnueli (1991a) 'Timed transition systems'. In *Proc. REX Workshop – Real-Time: Theory and Practice* Springer Lecture Notes in Computer Science **600**.

Henzinger, T.A., Z. Manna, & A. Pnueli (1991b) 'Temporal proof methodologies for real-time systems'. In *Proc. 18th ACM Symposium on Principles of Programmming Languages*.

Hermann, G., (1926) 'Die Frage der Endlich vielen Schritte in der Theorie der Polynomideale'. *Math. Ann.* **95**, 736–788.

Hewitt, C. & P. de Jong (1984) 'Open systems'. In *On Conceptual Modelling*, Michael L. Brodie, John Mylopoulos & Joachim W. Schmidt (eds.) Springer Verlag, 147–164.

Heyting, A. (1956) *Intuitionism: An Introduction* (2nd edition, 1966) North Holland.

Hoare, C.A.R. (1969) 'An axiomatic basis for computer programming'. *CACM* **12**, 576–583.

Hoare, C.A.R. (1985) *Communicating Sequential Processes* Prentice Hall.

Hoare, C.A.R. & J. He (1986) 'The weakest prespecification I'. *Fund. Inform.* **9**, 51–84.

Hoare, C.A.R., He Jifeng & A. Sampaio (1993) 'Normal form approach to compiler design'. *Acta Inform.* **30**, 701–739.

Hoare, C.A.R., I.J. Hayes, He Jifeng, C.C. Morgan, A.W. Roscoe, J.W. Sanders, I.H. Sorensen, J.M. Spivey & B.A. Sufrin (1987) 'The laws of programming'. *CACM* **30**, 672–87.

Hobbs, J.R., D. Appelt, M. Tyson, J. Bear, & D. Israel (1992) 'Description of the FASTUS system used for MUC-4'. In *Proc. 4th Message Understanding Conference (*MUC-4*)*, 268–275.

Holland, J.H. (1975) *Adaptation in Natural and Artificial Systems* University of Michigan Press.

Hooman, J. (1991) *Specification and Compositional Verification of Realtime Systems* Springer Verlag, Heidelberg.

Horgan, J. (1993) 'The death of proof'. *Sci. Am.* **269**, (4) 74–82.

Huberman, B.A. (1988) *The Ecology of Computation* North Holland.

Hughes J.A., D. Randall & D.Z. Shapiro (1993) 'From ethnographic record to system design: some experiences from the field'. *J. Comp. Supported Coop. Work* **1**, 123–141.

Hunns, D.M. & N. Wainwright (1991) 'Software-based protection for Sizewell B: the regulator's perspective'. *Nucl. Eng. Intern.* September, 38–40.

Hyland, J.M.E. & C.-H.L. Ong (1994) 'Intensional full abstraction for PCF: dialogue games and innocent strategies'., Working draft.

Ince D. (1988) *Software Development: Fashioning the Baroque* Oxford University Press.

INMOS (1988a) *Transputer Reference Manual* Prentice Hall.

INMOS (1988b) *Occam 2 Reference Manual* Prentice Hall.

Ishihata, H., T. Horie, S. Inano, T. Shimizu, S. Kato & M. Ikesaka (1991) 'Third generation message passing computer AP1000'. In *International Symposium on Supercomputing*, 46–55.

Jackson, Michael (1983) *System Design* Prentice Hall.

Jackson, T.O., J.A. McDermid & I.C. Wand (1994) 'Dependability measurement of safety critical systems: feasibility study'. Commission of the European Communities Joint Research Centre, Ispra, Contract Number 5616-93-11 ED ISP GB.

Jacky, J., R. Risler, I. Kalet, P. Wootton, A. Barke, S. Brossard & R. Jackson (1991) 'Control system specification for a cyclotron and neutron therapy facility'. In *IEEE Particle Accelerator Conference, San Francisco* IEEE Press.

Jacobs, P.S., G.R. Krupka, S.W. McRoy, L.F. Rau, N.K. Sondheimer & U. Zernik (1990) 'Generic text processing: a progress report'. In *Proc. June 1990 DARPA Speech and Natural Language Workshop* Morgan Kaufmann, 359–364.

James, L. (1994) 'Practical experiences in automatic requirements elicitation: the real issues'. In *Proc. Requirements Elicitation for Software Systems, University of Keele*.

Jelinek, F. & J. Lafferty (1991) 'Computation of the probability of initial substring generation by stochastic context-free grammars'. *Comp. Ling.* **17**, 315–323.

Jelinski, Z. & P.B. Moranda (1972) 'Software reliability research'. In *Statistical Computer Performance Evaluation*, Academic Press, 465–484.

Jenks, R.D. & R.S. Sutor (1992) *AXIOM: The Scientific Computation System* Springer Verlag.

Jerrum, M.R. & A. Sinclair (1989) 'Approximate counting, uniform generation, and rapidly mixing Markov chains'. *Inform. and Control* **82**, 93–133.

Jiao, Z. & P.M.D. Gray (1991) 'Optimisation of Methods in a Navigational Query Language'. In *Deductive and object-oriented databases (Proc. DOOD 91 Munich)*, C. Delobel, M. Kifer & Y. Masunaga (eds.) Springer Verlag, 22–42.

JIMCOM (1987) *The Official Handbook of MASCOT, version 3.1* Joint IECCA MUF Committee on MASCOT.

Jirotka, M., P. Luff & C. Heath (1993) 'Requirements engineering and interactions in the workplace: a case study in City dealing rooms'. *ACM SIGOIS Bulletin* **14**, 17–23.

John, B.E. (1990) 'Extension of GOMS analyses to expert performance requiring perception of dynamic auditory and visual information'. In *CHI '90 Conf. Proc.* ACM SIGCHI.

Johnson, D., C. Aragon, L. McGeoch & C. Schevon (1989) 'Optimisation by simulated annealing'. *Operations Research* **37**, .

Jones, C.B. (1986) *Systematic Software Development using VDM* Prentice Hall.

Jordan, D.T., C.J. Locke, J.A. McDermid, C.E. Parker, B.A.P. Sharp & I. Toyn (1994) 'Literate formal development of Ada from Z for safety critical applications'. In *Proc. Safecomp '94* (to appear).

Joseph, M. & P. Pandya (1986) 'Finding response times in a real-time system'. *Comp. J.* **29**, 390-395.

Juffa, N. (1994) 'Efficiency'. Article 328c9fINN1hg@iraun1.ira.uka.de in comp.arch.arithmetic.

Jurkat, W.B. (1961) 'Eine Bemerkung zur Vermutung von Mertens'. *Nachr. Österr. Math. Ges., Vienna* , 11.

Jurkat, W.B. (1973) 'On the Mertens conjecture and related general Ω-theory'. In *Analytic Number Theory*, H. Diamond (ed.) Princeton University Press 147-158.

Kahn, G. (1974) 'The semantics of a simple language for parallel processing'. In *Information Processing '74* North Holland.

Kahn, G. & G.D. Plotkin (1993) 'Concrete Domains'. *J. Theor. Comp. Sci.* **121**, 187-278.

Karmarkar, N. (1984) 'A new polynomial time algorithm for linear programming'. *Combinatorica* **4**, 373-395.

Kemp, G.J.L., Z. Jiao, P.M.D. Gray & J.E. Fothergill (1994) 'Combining computation with database access in biomolecular computing'. In *Applications of Databases: Proc. 1st International Conference ADB-94*, W. Litwin & T. Risch (eds.), Springer Verlag, 317-335.

Kent, W. (1978) *Data and Reality* North Holland.

Khachian, L.G. (1979) 'A polynomial time algorithm in linear programming'. *Soviet Math. Dokl.* **20**, 191-194.

Kilgarriff, A. (1993) 'Inheriting verb alternations'. In *Proc. 6th Conference of the European Chapter of the Association for Computational Linguistics*, 213-221.

Kilgarriff, Adam (1995) 'Inheriting polysemy'. In *Computational Lexical Semantics*, Patrick Saint-Dizier & Evelyne Viegas (eds.), Cambridge University Press.

King, J.J. (1984) *Query Optimisation by Semantic Reasoning* UMI Research Press.

Kirkpatrick, S., S.D. Gelatt & M.P. Vecchi (1983) 'Optimization by simulated annealing'. *Science* **220**, 671–680.

Knight, J.C. & N.G. Leveson (1986) 'Experimental evaluation of the assumption of independence in multiversion software'. *IEEE Trans. Soft. Eng.* **12**, 96–109.

Knuth, D.E. (1973a) *Fundamental Algorithms (2nd edition)*, Volume 1 of *The Art of Computer Programming* Addison Wesley.

Knuth, D.E. (1973b) *Sorting and Searching*, Volume 3 of *The Art of Computer Programming* Addison Wesley.

Knuth, D.E. (1981) *Seminumerical Algorithms (2nd edition)*, Volume 2 of *The Art of Computer Programming* Addison Wesley.

Kopetz, H., A. Damm, C. Koza, M. Mulazzani, W. Schwabl, C. Senft & R. Zainlinger (1989) 'Distributed fault-tolerant real-time systems: the MARS approach'. *Op. Syst. Rev.* **23**, 141–157.

Korte, B. & L. Lovasz (1981) 'Mathematical structures underlying greedy algorithms'. In *Fundamentals of Computation Theory*, F. Gecseg (ed.), Springer Lecture Notes in Computer Science **117**, 205–209.

Koskiennemi, K. (1983) *Two-level Morphology: a General Computational Model for Word-Form Recognition and Production* University of Helsinki.

Koymans, R. (1989) *Specifying Message Passing and Time-critical Systems with Temporal Logic* PhD thesis, Technical University of Eindhoven.

Krovetz, R. (1994) 'Learning to augment a machine-readable dictionary'.. In *Proceedings of EURALEX-94,* 107–116.

Kupiec, J.M. (1992) 'Robust part of speech tagging using a hidden Markov model'. *Comp. Speech Lang.* **6**, 225–242.

Lambert, S. & S. Ropiequet (eds.) (1986) *CD ROM: the new papyrus* Microsoft Press, Redmond, WA.

Landau, E. (1930) *Grundlagen der Analysis* (4th. edition 1965 Chelsea, New York).

Lann, G. le (1990) 'Critical issues for the development of distributed real-time computing systems'. Technical Report 1274, INRIA, Rocquencourt.

Lavi, J. & M. Winokur (1992) *Embedded Computer Systems Specification and Design – the ECSAM Approach* Israeli Aircraft Industries, Technical Report.

Leech, J. (1963) 'Coset enumeration on digital computers'. *Proc. Camb. Phil. Soc.* **59**, 257–267.

Leeuwen, J. van (ed.) (1992) *Handbook of Theoretical Computer Science* Elsevier.

Lehman, M.M. & L.A. Belady (1985) *Program Evolution: Processes of Software Change* Academic Press.

Lenstra, A.K. (1993) 'Factorization of RSA-120'. News article 1993Jun11.191436.7505@walter.bellcore.com.

Lenstra, A.K. & H.W. Lenstra Jr. (eds.) (1993) *The Development of the Number Field Sieve* Springer Lecture Notes in Computer Science **1554**.

Lenstra, A.K., H.W. Lenstra Jr. & L. Lovász (1982) 'Factoring polynomials with rational coefficients'. *Math. Ann.* **261**, 515–534.

Lenstra, H.W. (1987) 'Factoring integers with elliptic curves'. *Ann. Math.* **126**, 649–673.

Leveson, N.G. & P.R. Harvey (1983) 'Analysing software safety'. *IEEE Trans. Soft. Eng.* **9**, 569–579.

Leveson, N.G., & C.S. Turner (1993) 'An investigation of the Therac-25 accidents'. *IEEE Computer* **26**, (7), 18–41.

Li, Jingke & Marina Chen (1991) 'Compiling communication efficient programs for massively parallel machines'. *IEEE Trans. Par. Distrib. Systems* **2**, 361–375.

Liouville, J. (1835) 'Mémoire sur l'intégration d'une classe de fonctions transcendantes'. *Crelle's J.* **13**, 93–118.

Littlewood, B. (1976) 'A semi-Markov model for software reliability with failure costs'. In *MRI Symp. Computer Software Engineering* Polytechnic of New York, Polytechnic Press, 281–300, .

Littlewood, B. (1979) 'Software reliability model for modular program structure'. *IEEE Trans. Reliability* **28**, 241–246.

Littlewood, B. (1981) 'Stochastic reliability growth: a model for fault removal in computer programs and hardware designs'. *IEEE Trans. Reliability* **30**, 313–320.

Littlewood, B. (1988) 'Forecasting software reliability'. In *Software Reliability Modelling and Identification* Springer Verlag, 141–209.

Littlewood, B., S. Brocklehurst, N.E. Fenton, P. Mellor, S. Page, D. Wright, J.E. Dobson, J.A. McDermid & D. Gollmann (1993) 'Towards operational measures of computer security'. *J. Comp. Security* **2**, 211–229.

Littlewood, B. & D.R. Miller (1989) 'Conceptual modelling of coincident failures in multi-version software'. *IEEE Trans. Soft. Eng.* **15**, 1596–1614.

Littlewood, B. & L. Strigini (1993) 'Assessment of ultra-high dependability for software-based systems'. *CACM* **36**, 69–80.

Littlewood, B. & J.L. Verrall (1973) 'A Bayesian reliability growth model for computer software'. *J. Roy. Statist. Soc. C* **22**, 332–346.

Liu, C.L. & J.W. Layland (1973) 'Scheduling algorithms for multiprocessing in a hard real-time environment'. *JACM* **20**, 46–61.

Liu, Z. & M. Joseph (1992) 'Transformation of programs for fault-tolerance'. *Form. Aspects Comp.* **4**, 442-469.

Liu, Z., M. Joseph & T. Janowski (1993) 'Verification of schedulability for real-time programs'. Research Report, Department of Computer Science, University of Warwick.

Loebl, E.M. (1968) *Group Theory and its Applications* Academic Press.

London Ambulance Service (1993) *Report on the Inquiry into the London Ambulance Service* SW Thames Regional Health Authority, London W2 3QR.

Macias, B. & S. Pulman (1993) 'Natural language processing for requirements specifications'. In *Safety-critical Systems*, Felix Redmill & Tom Anderson (eds.), Chapman & Hall, 67–89.

MacLean, A., V. Bellotti & S. Shum (1993) 'Developing the design space with design space analysis'. In *Computer, Communication and Usability*, J. Beyerly, P.J. Barnard & J. Mays (eds.), North Holland.

Magerman, D.M. & M.P. Marcus (1991a) 'Pearl: a probabilistic chart parser'. In *Proc. 5th Conference of the European Chapter of the Association for Computational Linguistics*, 15–20.

Magerman, D.M. & M.P. Marcus (1991b) 'Parsing the Voyager domain using Pearl'. In *Proc. February 1991 DARPA Speech and Natural Language Workshop* Morgan Kaufmann, 231–240.

Magerman, D.M. & C. Weir (1992) 'Efficiency, robustness and accuracy in Picky chart parsing'. In *Proc. 30th Annual Meeting of the Association for Computational Linguistics*, 40–47.

Maibaum, T.S.E. (1987) *Formal Requirements Specification: A Logic for Formal Requirements Specification of Real-Time Embedded Systems* Imperial College, London.

Malone, T.W., K.R. Grant, F.A. Turbak, S.A. Brobst & M.D. Cohen (1987) 'Intelligent information-sharing systems'. *CACM* **30**, 390–402.

Manber, U. (1989) *Introduction to Algorithms: A Creative Approach* Addison Wesley.

Manning, C.D. (1993) 'Automatic acquisition of a large subcategorization dictionary from corpora'. In *Proc. 31st Annual Meeting of the Association for Computational Linguistics*, 235–242.

Marcus, M.P., B. Santorini & M.A. Marcinkiewicz (1993) 'Building a large annotated corpus of English: the Penn Treebank'. *Comp. Ling.* **19**, 314–330.

Marcus, M.P., *et al.* (1990) 'Automatic acquisition of linguistic structure'. In *Proc. June 1990 DARPA Speech and Natural Language Workshop* Morgan Kaufmann, 249–295.

McDermid, J.A. (1993) 'High integrity Ada: principles and practice'. In *Ada: Towards Maturity. Proc. 1993 Ada UK Conference*, L. Collingbourne (ed.), IOS Press.

McDermid, J.A. (1994) 'Safety critical systems in aerospace'. In *Proc. IEEE Workshop on Technology Transfer, Dallas* IEEE Computer Society Press.

McDermid, J.A. & D.J. Pumfrey (1994) 'A development of hazard analysis to aid software design'. In *Proc. COMPASS'94*.

McDermid, J.A. & P. Rook (1991) 'Software development and process models'. In *Software Engineer's Reference Book*, J.A. McDermid (ed.) Butterworth Heinemann.

McDermid, J.A. & S.P. Wilson (1995) 'No more spineless safety cases: a structured method and comprehensive tool support for the production of safety cases'. In *2nd International Conference on Control and Instrumentation in Nuclear Installations, April 1995* Institution of Nuclear Engineers (to appear).

McDermott, D. (1986) *A Critique of Pure Reason* Yale University Press.

McKee, J.F. (1994) *Some Elliptic Curve Algorithms* PhD Thesis, Cambridge University.

McLuhan, M. (1962), *The Gutenberg Galaxy* Routledge and Kegan Paul.

Meertens, L. (1989) 'Constructing a calculus of programs'. In *Math-*

ematics of Program Construction, J. L. A. van de Snepscheut (ed.), Springer Verlag 66–90.

Mertens, F. (1897) 'Über eine zahlentheoretische Funktion'. *Sitzungsberichte Akad. Wiss. Wien IIa* **106**, 761–830.

Microsoft Corporation (1992) *The Windows Interface: An Application Design Guide* Microsoft Press.

Miller, D. (1989) 'The role of statistical modelling and inference in software quality assurance'. In *Software Certification* Elsevier Applied Science.

Milne, R.W. (1991) 'Why are expert systems hard to define?'. *BCS Expert Systems SIG Newsletter* **25**, 13–21.

Milner, R (1980) *A Calculus of Communicating Systems* Springer Lecture Notes in Computer Science **92**.

Milner, R. (1989) *Communication and Concurrency* Prentice Hall.

Milner, R., J. Parrow & D. Walker (1992) 'A calculus of mobile processes, Parts I and II'. *J. Inform. Comp.* **100**, 1–40; 41–77.

Mines, R., F. Richman & W. Ruitenberg (1988) *A Course in Constructive Algebra* Springer Verlag.

Mitchell, J.C. (1990) 'Type systems for programming languages'. In van Leeuwen (1992).

Moitra, A. & M. Joseph (1991) 'Determining timing properties of infinite real-time programs'. Technical Report RR172, Department of Computer Science, University of Warwick.

Mojdehbakhsh, R., W.-T. Tsai, S. Kirani & L. Elliott (1994) 'Retrofitting software safety in an implantable medical device'. *IEEE Software* **11**, 41–50.

Mok, A.K. (1983) 'Fundamental design problems of distributed systems for the hard real-time environment'. Technical Report MIT/LCS/TR-297, Massachusetts Institute of Technology.

Moller, F. & C. Toft (1989) *A Temporal Calculus of Communicating Systems* LFCS-89-104, Edinburgh University.

Morgan, C.C. (1990) *Programming from Specifications* Prentice Hall.

MPI (Message Passing Interface Forum) (1993) *Draft Document for a Standard Message-Passing Interface* Available from Oak Ridge National Laboratory, University of Tennessee.

Mullery, G.P. (1979) 'CORE – COntrolled Requirements Expression'.

In *Proc. 4th International Conference on Software Engineering* IEEE Computer Society Press.

Musa, J.D. (1975) 'A theory of software reliability and its application'. *IEEE Trans. Soft. Eng.* **1**, 312–327.

Musa, J.D. & K. Okumoto (1984) 'A logarithmic Poisson execution time model for software reliability measurement'. In *Proc. Compsac 84*, Chicago, 230–238.

Mylopoulos, J., L. Chung & B. Nixon (1992) 'Representing and using non-functional requirements: a process-oriented approach'. *IEEE Trans. Soft. Eng.* **18**, 483–497.

NCSC (1985) *Department of Defense Trusted Computer System Evaluation* DOD 5200.28.STD, National Computer Security Center, Department of Defense.

Neches, R., R. Fikes, T. Finin, T. Gruber, R. Patil, T. Senator & W.R. Swartout (1991) 'Enabling technology for knowledge sharing'. *AI Magazine* **12**, (3), 36–56.

Needham, R.M. & A. Hopper (1993) 'The view from Pandora's box'. *SERC Bulletin* **5**, 26–27.

Neubauer, C. (1963) 'Eine empirische Untersuchung zur Mertensschen Funktion'. *Numer. Math.* **5**, 1–13.

Neumann P.G. (1994) *Computer Related Risks* ACM Press.

Newell, Alan (1982) 'The knowledge level'. *Artif. Intell.* **18**, 87-127.

Newell A. & S.K. Card (1985) 'The prospects for psychological science in human–computer interaction'. *Human Comp. Inter.* **1**, 209–242.

Newman W.M. (1994) 'A preliminary analysis of the products of HCI research, based on pro forma abstracts'. In *Proc. CHI '94 Human Factors in Computing Systems* (April 24–28, Boston, MA) ACM/SIGCHI, 278–284.

Newman W.M. & M.G. Lamming (1995) *Interactive System Design* Addison Wesley.

Nielsen J. (1992) 'Finding usability problems through heuristic evaluation'. In *Proc. CHI '92 Human Factors in Computing Systems* (May 3–7, Monterey, CA) ACM/SIGCHI 373–380.

Nielsen, M., G.D. Plotkin & G. Winskel (1981) 'Petri nets, event structures and domains'. *J. Theor. Comp. Sci.* **13**, 85–108.

Norman D. A. (1986) 'Cognitive engineering'. In *User Centred System*

Design, D.A. Norman & S.W. Draper (eds.) Lawrence Erlbaum Associates 31–65.

Numerical Algorithms Group Ltd. Oxford, UK, and Numerical Algorithms Group, Inc., Downer's Grove, Il, USA.

Oakley, B., & K. Owen (1989) *Alvey: Britain's Strategic Computing Initiative* MIT Press.

Odlyzko, A.M. & H.J.J. te Riele (1985) 'Disproof of the Mertens conjecture'. *J. für Reine und Angew. Math.* **357**, 138–160.

Ostrand T. (ed.) (1994) *Proc. 1994 International Symposium on Software Testing and Analysis (ISSTA)*, published in a special issue of *ACM Software Engineering Notes*.

Ostroff, J. (1989) *Temporal Logic for Real-time Systems* Research Studies Press.

Ostroff, J. (1992) 'Design of real-time safety-critical systems'. *J. Syst. Soft.* **18**, 33–60.

Ovum (1993) 'UK firms founder in software league'. *Computing*, 19 August 1993, 7 (news article about the 1992 Ovum *Software Markets Europe Report*).

Pan, V.Ya. (1981) 'New combinations of methods for the acceleration of matrix multiplication'. *Comput. Math. Appl.* **7**, 73–125.

Park, C.Y. (1993) 'Predicting program execution times by analysing static and dynamic program paths'. *J. Real-Time Syst.* **5**, 31–62.

Parnas, D.L., A. J. van Schowan & S. P. Kwan (1990) 'Evaluation of safety-critical software'. *CACM* **33**, 636–648.

Patil, R.S., R.E. Fikes, P.F. Patel-Schneider, D. McKay, T. Finin, T.R. Gruber, & R. Neches (1992) 'The DARPA knowledge sharing effort: Progress report'. In *Proc. 3rd International Conference on Principles of Knowledge Representation and Reasoning (KR'92)*, C. Rich, B. Nebel and W. Swartout (eds.), Morgan Kaufmann.

Pavey, D.J. & L. Winsborrow (1992) 'Demonstrating the equivalence of source code and PROM contents'. In *Proc. 4th European Workshop on Dependable Computing, Prague*.

Pereira, F. (1990) 'Finite-state approximations of grammars'. In *Proc. June 1990 DARPA Speech and Natural Language Workshop* Morgan Kaufmann, 20–25.

Pereira, F. & Y. Schabes (1992) 'Inside-out reestimation from partially bracketed corpora'. In *Proc. 30th Annual Meeting of the Association for Computational Linguistics*, 128–135.

Pereira, F., N. Tishby & L. Lee (1993) 'Distributional clustering of English words'. In *Proc. 31st Annual Meeting of the Association for Computational Linguistics*, 183–190.

Petri, C.A. (1962) *Kommunikation mit Automaten*, Bonn: Institut für Instrumentelle Mathematik, Schriften des IIM No. 2. Also in English translation: Technical Report RADC-TR-65-377, **1**, Suppl. 1, Applied Data Research, Princeton, NJ, Contract AF 30 (602)-3324.

Petri, C.A. (1973) 'Concepts of net theory'. In *Mathematical Foundations of Computer Science (Proc. Symp. and Summer School, Strbske Pleso)*, 137–146.

Plotkin, G.D. (1976) 'A powerdomain construction'. *SIAM J. Comp.* **5**, 452–487.

Plotkin, G.D. (1981) *A Structural Approach to Operational Semantics* Report DAIMI–FN–19, Computer Science Department, Aarhus University.

Pnueli, A. & E. Harel (1988) 'Applications of temporal logic to the specification of real-time systems'. In *Formal Techniques in Real-time and Fault-tolerant Systems* Springer Lecture Notes in Computer Science **331**.

Polson P.G. & C.H. Lewis (1990) 'Theory-based design for easily learned interfaces'. *Human Comp. Inter.* **5**, 191–220.

Pomerance, C. (1984) 'The quadratic sieve factoring algorithm'. In *Advances in Cryptology*, T. Beth, N. Cot & I. Ingemarrson (eds.), Springer Lecture Notes in Computer Science **209** 169–182.

Pomerance, C. (1985) 'The quadratic sieve factoring algorithm'. In *Proc. EUROCRYPT '84*, T. Beth, N. Cot & I. Ingemarsson (eds.), Springer Lecture Notes in Computer Science **209** 169–182.

Pratt, V.R. (1973) 'Computing permutations with double-ended queues, parallel stacks and parallel queues'. *Proc. ACM Symp. Theory of Computing* **5**, 268–277.

Premerlani, W.J. & M.R. Blaha (1994) 'An approach to reverse engineering for relational databases'. *CACM* **37**, 42–49.

Preparata, F.P. & M.I. Shamos (1985) *Computational Geometry* Springer Verlag.

Press, W.H., S.A. Teukolsky, W.T. Vetterling & B.P. Flannery (1992)

Numerical Recipes in FORTRAN (2nd edition) Cambridge University Press.

Quinn, Michael J. (1994) *Parallel Computing: Theory and Practice* (2nd edition) McGraw Hill.

Ramamritham, K., J.A. Stankovic, & P.F. Shiah (1990) 'Efficient scheduling algorithms for real-time multiprocessor systems'. *IEEE Trans. Par. Distrib. Systems* **1**, 184–194.

Randell, B., G. Ringland & W. Wulf (1994) *Software 2000*.

Razborov, A.A. (1985) 'Lower bounds on the monotone complexity of some Boolean functions'. *Soviet Math. Dokl.* **31**, 354–357.

Reed, G.W. & A.W. Roscoe (1988) 'Metric spaces as models for real-time concurrency'. In *Proc. MFPLS87* Springer Lecture Notes in Computer Science **298**, 331–343.

Resnik, P. (1992) 'Probabilistic tree-adjoining grammar as a framework for statistical natural language processing'. In *Proc. 15th International Conference on Computational Linguistics (COLING-92)* Volume II, 418–424.

Riecken, D. (1994) 'A conversation with Marvin Minsky about agents'. *CACM* **37**, 23–29.

Risch, R.H. (1969) 'The problem of integration in finite terms'. *Trans. AMS* **139**, 167–189.

Ritchie, G.D., G.J. Russell, A.W. Black & S.G. Pulman (1992) *Computational morphology: practical mechanisms for the English lexicon* MIT Press.

Rivest, R.L., A. Shamir & L. Adleman (1978) 'A method for obtaining digital signatures and public key cryptosystems'. *CACM* **21**, 120–126.

Rogers G.F.C. (1983) *The Nature of Engineering: a Philosophy of Technology* Macmillan.

Roncken, M. & R. Gerth (1990) 'A denotational semantics for synschronous and asynchronous behavior with multiform time'. In *Proc. International BCS-FACS Workshop on Semantics for Concurrency* Springer Verlag, 21–37.

Roscoe, A.W. & C.A.R. Hoare (1986) *Laws of Occam Programming* Monograph PRG–53, Oxford University Computing Laboratory, Programming Research Group.

Rost, B., C. Sander & R. Schneider (1994) 'PHD – an automatic mail server for protein secondary structure prediction'. *CABIOS* **10**, 53–60. Also research report EMBL (Heidelberg).

Rouquet, J.C. & P.J. Traverse (1986) 'Safe and reliable computing on board the Airbus and ATR aircraft'. In *Safecomp: 5th IFAC Workshop on Safety of Computer Control Systems*, Pergamon Press.

Rouse, G.W. (1991) 'Locator – an application of knowledge engineering to ICL's customer service'. *ICL Technical Journal* **7**, 546–553.

RTCA (1992) *Software considerations in airborne systems and equipment certification* DO-178B Requirements and Technical Concepts for Aeronautics.

Rumbaugh, J., M Blaha, W. Premerlani, F. Eddy & W. Lorensen (1991) *Object-Oriented Modelling and Design* Prentice Hall.

Russell, B. (1919) *An Introduction to Mathematical Philosophy* Allen & Unwin.

Russinoff, D.M. (1985) 'An experiment with the Boyer–Moore theorem prover: A proof of Wilson's theorem'. *J. Autom. Reas.* **1**, 121–139.

Sack, J.-R., A. Knight, P. Epstein, J. May & T. Nguyen (1994) 'A workbench for computational geometry'. *Algorithmica* **11**, 404–428.

Salter, R.J. (1989) *Highway Traffic Analysis and Design* Macmillan.

Sampson, G. (1986) 'A stochastic approach to parsing'. In *Proc. 11th International Conf. on Computational Linguistics (COLING-86)*, 151–155.

Sampson, G. (1987) 'Probabilistic models of analysis'. In *The Computational Analysis of English*, R. Garside, G. Leech & G. Sampson (eds.), Longman, 16–29.

Sampson, G. (1991) 'Parallel optimization of tree structures for natural language parsing'. *J. Exp. Theor. Artif. Intel.* **3**, 69–85.

Sampson, G., R. Haigh & E. Atwell (1989) 'Natural language analysis by stochastic optimization: a progress report on Project APRIL'. *J. Exp. Theor. Artif. Intel.* **1**, 271–287.

Schabes, Y. (1992) 'Stochastic lexicalized tree-adjoining grammars'. In *Proc. 15th International Conference on Computational Linguistics (COLING-92)*, Volume II, 425–432.

Schabes, Y. & R.C. Waters (1993) 'Lexicalized context-free grammars'. In *Proc. 31st Annual Meeting of the Association for Computational Linguistics*, 121–129.

Schmidt, U. (1982) *Überprüfung des Beweises für den Vierfarbensazt* Diplomarbeit Tech. Hochschule Aachen.

Schneider, S.A. (1990) *Correctness and communication in real-time systems* Programming Research Group Monograph PRG-84, University of Oxford.

Schütze, H. (1993) 'Part-of-speech induction from scratch'. In *Proc. 31st Annual Meeting of the Association for Computational Linguistics*, 251–258.

Schwarzenberger, R.L.E. (1981) *N-dimensional Crystallography* Pitman.

Scott, D.S. & C. Strachey (1971) *Towards a Mathematical Semantics for Computer Languages* Programming Research Group Monograph PRG–6, Oxford University Computing Laboratory. Also available in *Computers and Automata*, J. Fox (ed.), Polytechnic Institute of Brooklyn Press, 19–46.

Seidenberg, A. (1974) 'Constructions in algebra'. *Trans. AMS* **197**, 273–313.

SERC (1983). 'Intelligent knowledge based systems: A programme for action in the UK'. SERC-DoI, available from the Rutherford Appleton Laboratory, Didcot, OX11 0QX.

Sha, L., R. Rajkumar & J.P. Lehoczky (1990) 'Priority inheritance protocols: an approach to real-time synchronization'. *IEEE Trans. Comp.* **39**, 1175-1185.

Shafer, G. (1976) *A Mathematical Theory of Evidence* Princeton University Press.

Sharman, R., F. Jelinek & R. Mercer (1990) 'Generating a grammar for statistical training'. In *Proc. June 1990 DARPA Speech and Natural Language Workshop* Morgan Kaufmann, 267–274.

Shaw, A.C. (1989) 'Reasoning about time in higher level language software'. *IEEE Trans. Soft. Eng.* **15**, 875–899.

Siegrist, K. (1988a) 'Reliability of systems with Markov transfers of control'. *IEEE Trans. Soft. Eng.* **14**, 1049–1053.

Siegrist, K. (1988b) 'Reliability of systems with Markov transfers of control, II'. *IEEE Trans. Soft. Eng.* **14**, 1478–1480.

Silverman, R.D. (1987) 'The multiple polynomial quadratic sieve'. *Math. Comp.* **48**, 329–339.

Simon, H.A. (1969) *The Sciences of the Artificial*; 2nd edition (1980). MIT Press.

Simpson, H.R. (1990) 'A data interaction architecture for real-time, embedded, multi-processor systems'. In *Proc. Computing Techniques in Guided Flight, Royal Aircraft Establishment.*

Singer, M.F. (1990) 'Formal solutions of differential equations'. *J. Symb. Comp.* **10**, 59–94.

Singer, M.F. & F. Ulmer (1993) 'Liouvillian and algebraic solutions of second & third order linear differential equations'. *J. Symb. Comp.* **16**, 37–74.

Sipelstein, J.M. & G.E. Blelloch (1991) 'Collection-oriented languages'. *Proc. IEEE* **79**, 504–523.

SIRT (1994) Draft 47, Systems Integration Requirements Taskgroup, ARP.

Slagle, J. (1961) *A Heuristic Program that Solves Symbolic Integration Problems in Freshman Calculus* PhD. Dissertation, Harvard University, Cambridge, MA.

Smyth, M.B. (1978) 'Power domains'. *JCSS* **16**, 23–26.

Sommerville I. (1994) *Software Engineering (4th edition)* Addison Wesley.

Sowa, John F. (1992) 'Semantic networks'. In *Encyclopedia of Artificial Intelligence, 2nd Edition, Volume 2*, Stuart C. Shapiro (ed.), Wiley, 1493–1511.

Spivey, J.M. (1989) *The Z notation: a reference manual*; 2nd edition (1992). Prentice Hall.

Steltjes, T.J. (1885) 'Lettre à Hermite de 11 Juillet 1885'. Lettre 79 in *Correspondence d'Hermite et Steltjes*, B. Baillaud & H. Bourget (eds.) Paris, 1905,, 160–164.

Sterling, L. and E. Shapiro (1986) *The Art of Prolog* MIT Press.

Stifter, S. (1993) 'Geometry theorem proving in vector spaces by means of Gröbner bases'. In *Proc. ISSAC 1993*, M. Bronstein (ed.) ACM Press 301–310.

Strassen, V. (1969) 'Gaussian elimination is not optimal'. *Numer. Math.* **13**, 354–356.

Suchman L. (1987) *Plans and Situated Actions* Cambridge University Press.

Sutherland, I.E. (1963) 'Sketchpad: a system for graphical man-machine communication'. In *Proc. 1963 Spring Joint Computer Conference* AFIPS.

Swartout, W. & R. Balzer (1982) 'On the inevitable intertwining of specification and implementation'. *CACM* **25**, 438–440.

Swartout, W.R., R. Neches & R.S. Patil (1993) 'Knowledge sharing: prospects and challenges'. In *Proc. International Conference on Building and Sharing of Very Large-Scale Knowledge Bases (Tokyo)*, K.Fuchi & T.Yokoi (eds.), IOS Press.

Swinnerton-Dyer, H.P.F. (1970) 'Letter to E.H. Berlekamp – mentioned in E.H. Berlekamp'. *Math. Comp.* **24**, 713–735.

Tapanainen. P. & Voutilainen, A. (1994) 'Tagging accurately – don't guess if you know'.. In *Proceedings of the Fourth ACL Conference on Applied Natural Language Processing, 47–52.*

Tarjan, R.E. (1972) 'Sorting using networks of queues and stacks'. *JACM* **19**, 341–346.

Tarski, A. (1955) 'A lattice-theoretical fixpoint theorem and its applications'. *Pacific J. Math.* **5**, 285–309.

Taylor, J.R. (1982) *Fault-Tree and Cause-Consequence Analysis for Software* RISO-M 2326, RISO National Laboratory.

Thompson, H.S. (1983) 'Natural language processing: a critical analysis of the structure of the field, with some implications for parsing'. In *Automatic Natural Language Parsing*, Karen Sparck Jones & Yorick A. Wilks (eds.), Ellis Horwood, 22–31.

Tindell, K.W., A. Burns & A.J. Wellings (1992) 'Allocating real-time tasks (an NP-hard problem made easy)'. *Real-Time Syst.* **4**, 145-165.

Tindell, K.W. & J. Clark (1994) 'Holistic schedulability analysis for distributed hard real-time systems'. *Euromicro Journal* Special issue on Parallel Embedded Real-Time Systems.

Tokoro, M. (1990) 'Computational field model'. In *Proc. 2nd IEEE Workshop on Future Trends in Distributed Computing Systems*.

Tokoro, M. (1993) 'The society of objects'. In *OOPSLA'93 Proceedings*.

Touretzky, David S. (1986) *The Mathematics of Inheritance Systems* Pitman/Morgan Kaufmann.

Turing, A.M. (1963) 'Computing machinery and intelligence'. In *Computers and Thought*, E.A. Feigenbaum & F. Feldman (eds.) McGraw Hill, 11–35. Reprinted from *Mind* **59**, 433–460 (October 1950).

Turski, W.M. (1988) 'Time considered irrelevant for real-time systems'. *BIT* **28**, 473–486.

van der Waerden, B.L. (1930a) *Moderne Algebra I* Springer Verlag.

van der Waerden, B.L. (1930b) 'Eine Bemerkung über die Unzerlegbarkeit von Polynomen'. *Math. Ann.* **102**, 738–739.

Vijay-Shanker, K. & David J. Weir (1991) 'Polynomial parsing of extensions of context-free grammars'. In *Current Issues in Parsing Technology*, Masaru Tomita (ed.), Kluwer, 191–206.

Vincenti, W.G. (1990) *What Engineers Know and How They Know It* Johns Hopkins University Press.

von Sternack, R.D. (1897) 'Empirische Untersuchung über den Verlauf der zahlentheoretische Funktion $\tau(n) = \sum_{x=1}^{n} \mu(x)$ im Intervalle von 0 bis 150,000'. *Sitzungsberichte Akad. Wiss. Wien IIa* **106**, 835–1024.

von Sternack, R.D. (1913) 'Neue empirische Daten über die zahlentheoretische Funktion $\sigma(n)$'. In *Proc. 5th. International Congress of Mathematicians Vol. I* Cambridge University Press, 341–343.

Wallich, P. (1994) 'Wire pirates'. *Scientific American* March, 72–80.

Walters, R.C. & E. Chikofsky (1994) 'Reverse engineering: progress along many dimensions'. *CACM* **37**, 1 (Special issue devoted to reverse engineering).

Weinberg, G.M. (1988) *Rethinking Systems Analysis and Design* Dorset House.

Weischedel, R., M. Meteer, R. Schwartz, L. Ramshaw & J. Palmucci (1993) 'Coping with ambiguity and unknown words through probabilistic models'. *Comp. Ling.* **19**, 359–382.

Wetherell, C.S. (1980) 'Probabilistic languages: a review and some open questions'. *Comp. Surveys* **12**, 361–379.

White, S.M. (1993) 'Requirements engineering in systems engineering practice'. In *Proc. RE-93* IEEE Computer Society Press.

Wiederhold, G. (1992) 'Mediators in the architecture of future information systems'. *IEEE Computer* **25**, 38–49.

Wiederhold, G., P. Wegner & S. Ceri (1992) 'Toward megaprogramming'. *CACM* **35**, 89–99.

Wilson, G. (1990) 'Getting it right when the chips are down'. *The Independent*, Monday 17 December 1990, page 14.

Winskel, G. (1993) *The Formal Semantics of Programming Languages: an Introduction* MIT Press.

Wirth, N. (1977) 'Towards a discipline of real-time programming'. *CACM* **20**, 577–583.

Xie, M. (1991) *Software Reliability Modelling* World Scientific.

Yankelovich, N., N. Meyrowitz, N. & A. van Dam (1985) 'Reading and writing the electronic book'. *IEEE Computer* **20**, 15–30.

Yarowsky, D. (1992) 'Word-sense disambiguation using statistical models of Roget's categories trained on large corpora'. In *Proc. 15th International Conf. on Computational Linguistics (COLING-92)*, Volume II, 454–460.

Zage W.M. and D.M. Zage (1993) 'Evaluating design metrics on large-scale software'. *IEEE Software* **10**, (4), 75–81.

Zelle, J.M. & R.J. Mooney (1994) 'Inducing deterministic Prolog parsers from treebanks: a machine learning approach'. In *Proc. AAAI-94*, 748–753.

Zheng Yuhua & Zhou Chaochen (1994) 'A formal proof of the deadline driven scheduler'. In *Proc. 3rd Symposium on Formal Techniques in Real-time and Fault-tolerant Systems* Springer Lecture Notes in Computer Science **863** 756–775.

Zhou Chaochen (1982) 'Weakest environment of communicating processes'. In *Proc. NCC'82*, Houston, 679–690.

Zhou Chaochen, C.A.R. Hoare & A.P. Ravn (1991) 'A calculus of durations'. *Inform. Proc. Letters* **40**, 269–276.

Zipf, G.K. (1935) *The Psycho-Biology of Language* Houghton Mifflin.

Index

abstract data types, 19, 20, 147, 149
abstract data types and algorithm
    design, 11
academic vs. industrial research, 323
action systems, 234
adaptability, 150
AI, 33, 89, 116, 125, 144, 155, 317
AI and experiment, 44
AI and mathematics, 37, 41, 43, 86
AI and statistics, 42
AI and vision, 41
AI as source of ideas, 38, 46
AI, fragmentation of, 38
AI, general purpose view, 39
AI, invisibility of, 40
AI, nature of, 36
AI, quality of, 36
AI, the future, 45
algebraic specification, 19
algorithm, 1, 2
algorithm development, 77
algorithm efficiency, 7
algorithms engineering, 4
algorithms engineering and algorithms
    science, 14
algorithms in NLP, 89
Alvey Programme, 34
analytical models, 301
architecture, limits of, 145
archiving, 31, 121, 138
asynchronous system, 192
ATM networks, 289

Bachmann diagram, 113
benchmarking, 328
Birch–Swinnerton-Dyer conjectures, 67
Boolean circuit, 18
bottom-up process, 6
bounds on algorithms, 3, 79
Buchberger's algorithm, 75, 76

calculus of design, 176
calculus of processes, 276
causal independence, 276
CD-ROM, 25
chess, 39
Chomskyan transformational rules, 96
classification, 42
client–server model, 115
cognitive science, 37
combinatorial algorithms, 12, 13
combinatorial explosion, 13
communicating system, 269
communication in parallel
    programming, 60
complete induction, 7
complexity, 79, 80, 199, 201, 249
complexity, in safety-critical systems,
    199
complexity, measures of, 199
complexity classes, 80
complexity of algorithms, 2, 18
complexity of knowledge, 112
compliance, 226, 227
computability, 141, 249
computational geometry, 13
computational linguistics, 44, 88
computational morphology, 95
computational number theory, 15, 16,
    68, 79
computational psycholinguistics, 89
computational skeletons, 58
computer algebra and calculus, 73
computer architecture, 221
computer networks, 269
computer science and algebraic
    geometry, 75
computer science and geometry, 84
computer science and mathematics, 158,
    159, 165
computer science and observation, 163

368